OXFORD HISTORIES

APARTHEID, 1948–1994

SERIES ADVISORS
Geoff Eley, University of Michigan
Lyndal Roper, University of Oxford

Saul Dubow previously taught at the University of Sussex and is now based at Queen Mary, University of London. Born and brought up in Cape Town, he has degrees from the universities of Cape Town and Oxford. He has published widely on the development of racial segregation and apartheid in all its aspects: political, ideological, and intellectual. He has special interests in the history of race, ethnicity, and national identity, as well as imperialism, colonial science, and global circuits of knowledge. He is on the editorial board of the *Journal of Southern African Studies*.

Apartheid, 1948–1994

SAUL DUBOW

UNIVERSITY PRESS

OXFORD
UNIVERSITY PRESS

Great Clarendon Street, Oxford, OX2 6DP,
United Kingdom

Oxford University Press is a department of the University of Oxford.
It furthers the University's objective of excellence in research, scholarship,
and education by publishing worldwide. Oxford is a registered trade mark of
Oxford University Press in the UK and in certain other countries

First Edition published in 2014

Published in the United States of America by Oxford University Press
198 Madison Avenue, New York, NY 10016, United States of America

British Library Cataloguing in Publication Data
Data available

Library of Congress Control Number: 2013948419

ISBN 978–0–19–955066–1 (hbk.)
     978–0–19–955067–8 (pbk.)

PREFACE

As I complete this book on a sunny winter's day in Cape Town, with Robben Island visible in the near distance, Nelson Mandela survives on life support in hospital. The world waits for the inevitable, pausing to reflect on his immortality. The presidency acts to control the political aspects of Mandela's legacy, while members of his family are involved in an unseemly spat over the site of his burial. As the shadows of Mandela's afterlife lengthen, the politics of memory and memorialization are everywhere in full display. Mandela will surely be remembered as the single most important figure in the transition to the 'new' South Africa. What of the system he dedicated his life to overthrowing and which in his own person he so magnificently transcended?

A generation after its formal abolition in 1994 apartheid recedes from immediate memory. The word retains such powerful valency that its meanings have slipped their original bonds to be universalized and applied to other contexts. Apartheid is, and will surely always remain, primarily associated with racism, exploitation, and colonialism. But these are general concepts whose precise meanings are themselves deeply contested. For all its familiarity, apartheid resists easy definition. It is difficult enough to capture the nature of the system at any one moment in time, even more elusive when attempting to comprehend it as a totality. The problem is made even more intractable by the fact that the recent past is not yet properly historical. Apartheid is significantly constituted by the slipperiness of collective memory; impulses to remember and to forget exist in tension with each other.

Whites have every reason to forget the odious system that they had actively supported for so many years. Indeed, by the time the 'new' South Africa came into being, it was already quite difficult to find anyone who admitted to having actually supported apartheid. Government supporters, including President F. W. de Klerk, were well practised in versions of denial before 1994: they claimed that apartheid was misunderstood; that it was originally well intentioned but somehow became malign; that its outrages were perpetrated by others; that the cruelties and crimes were kept from them. Even as the Truth and Reconciliation Commission confirmed some of apartheid's worst atrocities, a miasma or collective amnesia began to spread. Most ordinary white people wanted to 'move on' without remaining trapped by the past. A collective embrace of Madiba (Mandela) would expiate all sins.

For some young politicized blacks, such as those in the ANC Youth League, there remains every reason to remind audiences constantly about the evils of apartheid and the heroism of those who opposed it. Hopes of restitution and personal advancement depend on this. Yet by no means all young blacks see politics as the way of the future. Many are alienated from, or disillusioned by, the political classes. The educated and the ambitious find other options more attractive. Whereas the past continues to be a usable instrument for some, others find it an almost unspeakable burden.

By the time of Mandela's presidential inauguration there was anecdotal evidence that many black youngsters were beginning to lose touch with the system they and their parents had fought to overthrow. This is not altogether surprising. For one thing, several of the key institutions and legislative underpinnings of apartheid had begun to fall into abeyance from the mid-1980s. Students and teenagers in 1994 would have known more about the civil political strife of the transition period than the system that gave rise to it. In societies emerging from extreme forms of repression, 'born-frees' (as the post-1994 generation are sometimes referred to in South Africa) are often disinclined to dwell too deeply on the pain and indignities suffered by their elders. Parents were often concerned to protect children from the trauma and routine humiliation associated with the pass laws, segregated facilities, and other reminders of social inferiority. Who would wish to blight children's futures with such memories of the past?

Academic history may not be the only way to comprehend the past but it remains indispensable. Fortunately, there are no lack of outstanding guides for students seeking concise, interpretative histories of modern South Africa. The best of these, including those by William Beinart, Nigel Worden, and Leonard Thompson, were all conceived around the time of political transition.[1] Apartheid figures strongly in these works though their scope is chronologically and thematically broader, including the history of the country as a whole. A number of texts seek to understand apartheid more closely. Several of them have titles incorporating the phrase 'rise and fall'.[2] Each targets specific markets and has particular strengths. Worger and Clark address college students; Guelke highlights the international dimensions of apartheid; Welsh's empirically detailed and insightful account is particularly strong on the politics of apartheid's demise. While none of these histories could be said to be teleological, their titles suggest a narrative arc where the end of apartheid is coded into its origins.

This book seeks to do something slightly different. In 2007 Christopher Wheeler of Oxford University Press invited me to contribute to a new historical series designed to address subjects that would revisit major events and problems in European and world history. The working brief for contributors to the series was to reappraise 'turning points' which, for this or that circumstance, might so easily have turned other ways. Wheeler had in mind Philip Roth's whimsical parody of history, 'where everything unexpected in its own time is chronicled on the page as inevitable'.[3]

---

[1] W. Beinart, *Twentieth-Century South Africa* (Oxford, 1994); N. Worden, *The Making of South Africa: Conquest, Segregation and Apartheid* (Oxford, 1994); L. Thompson, *A History of South Africa* (New Haven, 1990); also R. Ross, *A Concise History of South Africa* (Cambridge, 1999).

[2] N. L. Clark and W. H. Worger, *South Africa: The Rise and Fall of Apartheid* (New York, 2004); A. Guelke, *Rethinking the Rise and Fall of Apartheid* (London, 2005); David Welsh, *The Rise and Fall of Apartheid* (Johannesburg, 2009); also P. Eric Louw. *The Rise, Fall, and Legacy of Apartheid* (Westport, Conn., 2004).

[3] Philip Roth, *The Plot Against America* (London, 2004), 114.

Roth's observation about historical inevitability has particular salience in the South African present because the end of apartheid, and the victory of the ANC, led by Nelson Mandela, is frequently told in terms of a narrative of resistance and redemption. This book is intended to challenge such assumptions. I neither assume that racial segregation was bound to transmute into the yet harsher version of apartheid, nor take for granted that the African National Congress, led by Nelson Mandela, would eventually overthrow white supremacy. I am sceptical of 'turning points' and alert to paths not taken.

In order to understand apartheid as a complex, protean historical phenomenon, we need to engage as well as to stand back. Serious students of the subject have to refamiliarize themselves with events, individuals, and institutions whose importance once seemed self-evident but are now apt to be forgotten or passed over without comment. At the same time we have to *defamiliarize* apartheid. This requires a deliberate process of distancing so as to render aspects that once seemed obvious and self-evident rather more unusual and curious. As a South African living in Britain, I have had to approach my teaching of apartheid as something of an outsider. While this may have some disadvantages, it also opens up fresh possibilities. I am grateful to many of the students I have taught for forcing me to see my own country in new ways. If the historical past is another country, we are all in a sense visitors and explorers.

When I first came to study in Britain as a doctoral student in the early 1980s, I was part of a group of postgraduates who were concerned to elucidate the working of segregation and apartheid in the hope that this would contribute to its demise. South African history was deeply contested and political commitments could easily be read off the page. One line of academic engagement laid emphasis on the need to break down the view of the South African state as monolithic and all-powerful. Another vital area of investigation was devoted to the study of anti-apartheid struggle and resistance, particularly as seen through the labour movement, within communities, and in political organizations. Overall, there was then a broad balance between those who were interested in the workings of power and those who were concerned with understanding the predicaments and choices of the majority of people excluded from power.

This balance has shifted in recent years. We now know a great deal more about resistance and the liberation movements than we did in the 1980s. There has been enormous growth in studies of political opposition. Synoptic multi-volume histories including those produced by the South African Democracy Education Trust, as well as the long running *From Protest to Challenge* project so ably steered by Tom Karis, Gwendolen Carter, and Gail Gerhart, have transformed the field. Memoirs by anti-apartheid figures, once known to the general public only—if at all—by name and affiliation, have thickened the historical record, adding texture and personal anecdote. Many new doctoral dissertations have been produced since the 1990s about different aspects and forms of resistance. A host of excellent edited collections have emerged out of conferences dedicated to understanding the anti-apartheid struggle. This book has benefited enormously from such prodigious scholarship.

Conversely, concerns with central state power and ideology during the apartheid era have lagged behind. True, senior scholars like Dan O'Meara and Hermann Giliomee have followed up their earlier pathbreaking work on Afrikaner nationalism with major new studies. In addition, there have been fresh overviews of South African economic history produced by scholars like Charles Feinstein and Nicoli Nattrass and Jeremy Seekings. But these are exceptions to a more general rule. In South Africa, as elsewhere, new historical studies of state ideology, power, and political economy have not kept pace with the rise of social and cultural history whose purview has expanded imaginatively into realms that once seemed marginal. What was once a corrective to master narratives has become the norm; popular history 'from below' has in many ways surpassed its staid old antagonist, 'history from above'.

These considerable gains have not come without costs, which include fragmentation of the historical experience and loss of analytical connections. This book represents an effort to reintegrate, in a broad interpretative and synoptic manner, histories of state power and of resistance in South Africa. One important question that seems to me to be insufficiently addressed is not why apartheid was defeated, but how it survived so long. This requires a close understanding of the ways in which the system of apartheid worked, its sophisticated ideology, and its capacity for adaptation and reinvention. Strategies to ensure compliance and invite effective complicity were integral to apartheid's success in sustaining itself. Of necessity, this involves close attention to structures of state power as well as the ideologies that sustained such power. Yet ideology is too easily seen as a prefabricated package, and sometimes invoked as an explanation without sufficient examination. Ideologies themselves are dependent on ideas that are often more unsettled and less instrumental than when they are seen to cohere in support of political movements. Ideas that gain traction have lives of their own—and these often cannot simply be remade or shut down. They have distorting effects and generate unintended consequences.

Along with institutions and organizations, ideas feature prominently here. One of the contentions in this book is that 'apartheid' was an idea as well as an ideology. Apartheid became politically compelling to its adherents in the 1940s because the word itself condensed a powerful set of fears and hopes; reciprocally, the fact that the system of racial discrimination and exploitation came to be conveniently expressed in a single word helped the *anti*-apartheid movement, in all its many forms, to coalesce. In 1948, when South Africa was still a full member of the British Commonwealth, the 'apartheid' label distinguished it from several other regimes in Africa based on white minority rule. The idea of apartheid was decisive in ushering the 1948 Afrikaner alliance into power. It gave power and purpose to the apartheid state, but also rendered it vulnerable through the very act of highlighting its exceptionality.

Long after the government stopped actively espousing apartheid ideology, the anti-apartheid movement kept the idea of apartheid alive as a means of focusing the energies of a highly diverse and divided opposition movement. The idea of apartheid imposed limits on its reinvention. It became inseparable from the ruling regime. Above all, the transition to a post-apartheid future entailed removing the legatees of 1948 from political office; the legacy of the apartheid state has proved more resistant to transformation.

Leon Wessels, a long-time National Party politician, has commented perceptively on the offensive word 'apartheid' which in his view helped to turn South Africa's domestic policies into an international issue, rendered the country a pariah, and gave it global significance.[4] Wessels is pictured on the front cover of this book (the young man is the figure in the middle of the trio of white equestrians seated on white police horses, part of a guard of honour attending a speech given by Prime Minister Hendrik Verwoerd to mark the 50th anniversary of the ruling National Party in 1964). Wessels's autobiography traces a personal political journey that culminated in his embrace of human rights and his public apology for apartheid in 1990.

It is unlikely that this book could have been completed without substantial research leave and I am deeply grateful for the award of an AHRC fellowship which took me out of all teaching during 2012. This grant also gave me the opportunity to consult primary material at the Mayibuye Centre at the University of the Western Cape, the Institute for Contemporary History at the University of the Orange Free State, and the Historical Papers collection at the University of the Witwatersrand. I thank the librarians and custodians of these collections, Michele Pickover especially. The African Studies department of the University of Cape Town library has always been very welcoming. I owe a special debt of gratitude to Sue Ogterop, senior librarian at Special Collections, Lesley Hart of the Manuscripts and Archives section, and their colleagues, for support, suggestions, and hospitality.

William Beinart, Jeremy Krikler, and Hilary Sapire all read the draft of this book in its entirety. Their suggestions, recommendations, and objections have been invaluable. Paul Betts, Signe Gosmann, Lindie Koorts, Ian Macqueen, Peter Vale, and Richard Wilson read sections of the manuscript. All made sharp as well as generous comments from which I have learned a great deal. The highly professional OUP editorial production team led by Cathryn Steele and Emma Slaughter, and including Jackie Pritchard and Gail Eaton, was exemplary.

---

[4] Leon Wessels, *Vereeniging: Die Onvoltooide Vrede* (Cape Town, 2010), 65. My father, Neville Dubow, discussed this iconic image by David Goldblatt in the *Vrye Weekblad*, 26 October 1990.

PREFACE

I feel honoured to be able to use images produced by four of South Africa's finest photographers who have together documented apartheid from its very beginnings to its end: Ernest Cole, David Goldblatt, Jürgen Schadeberg, and Paul Weinberg. Without their cameras, apartheid might have looked quite different.

Cape Town, July 2013

CONTENTS

LIST OF ILLUSTRATIONS

Cover Photo: The commando of National Party stalwarts which escorted prime minister and National Party leader Hendrik Verwoerd and his wife Betsie to the party's 50th anniversary celebrations at de Wildt, Transvaal. October 1964. Photograph by David Goldblatt.

ABBREVIATIONS AND GLOSSARY

AAM	Anti-Apartheid Movement
ANC	African National Congress
APLA	Azanian People's Liberation Army
ARM	African Resistance Movement
AWB	*Afrikaner Weerstandsbeweeging* (resistance movement)
AZACTU	Azanian Confederation of Trade Unions
baaskap	outright domination (boss-ship)
BC	Black Consciousness
BCP	Black Community Programmes
BPC	Black People's Convention
Charterists	supporters of the Freedom Charter
CODESA	Convention for a Democratic South Africa
COSAS	Congress of South African Students
COSATU	Congress of South African Trade Unions
CUSA	Council of Unions of South Africa
Dompas	pass-book
DRC	Dutch Reformed Church
FOSATU	Federation of South African Trade Unions
highveld	the elevated interior plateau of the country
MK	*Umkhonto we Sizwe* (Spear of the Nation)

NACTU	National Council of Trade Unions
NUM	National Union of Mineworkers
NUSAS	National Union of South African Students
OAU	Organization of African Unity
oorstrooming	engulfment
PAC	Pan-Africanist Congress
Poqo	armed wing of the Pan-Africanist Congress
SABRA	South African Bureau of Racial Affairs
SACP	South African Communist Party
SAN-ROC	South African Non-Racial Olympic Committee
SASO	South African Students' Organisation
SAYCO	South African Youth Congress
sjambok	animal hide whip
Spro-cas	Study Project on Christianity in Apartheid Society
SWAPO	South West Africa People's Organization
TRC	Truth and Reconciliation Commission
tsotsi	hoodlum
TUCSA	Trade Union Council of South Africa
UDF	United Democratic Front
UWUSA	United Workers' Union of South Africa
verkrampte	narrow-minded, hardline
verligte	enlightened or pragmatic
volk	people/nation
ZIPRA	Zimbabwe People's Revolutionary Army

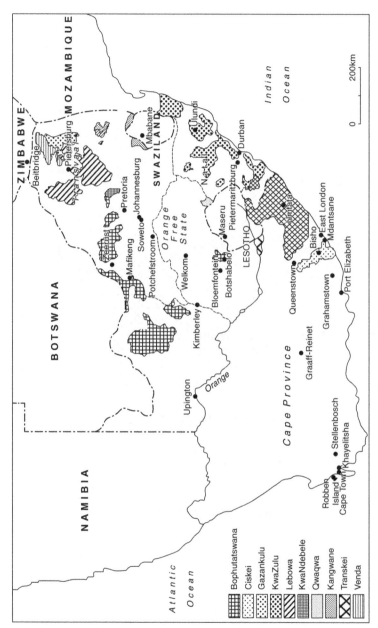

South Africa, showing black homelands, c.1980

Bophutatswana
Ciskei
Gazankulu
KwaZulu
Lebowa
KwaNdebele
Qwaqwa
Kangwane
Transkei
Venda

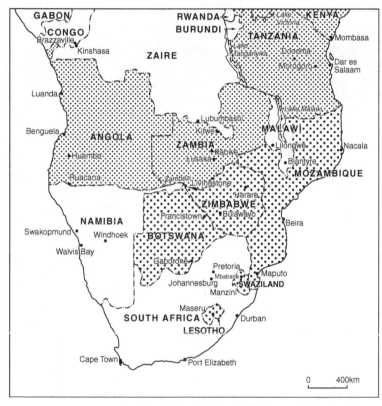

Southern African Region, c.1980

CHAPTER 1
THE APARTHEID ELECTION, 1948

An Electoral Shock?

'Apartheid' was the electoral slogan which brought radical Afrikaner nationalism to power in South Africa in May 1948. The stunning victory of the *Herenigde Nasionale Party* was almost entirely unanticipated by journalists, politicians, and the public, prompting the question whether the election was lost by the government or won by the opposition. On the eve of the election Prime Minister Jan Smuts's deputy, J. H. Hofmeyr, recorded privately that his party would maintain or even improve its position.[1] Nationalist leader D. F. Malan was almost as surprised by his victory as his old opponent, Smuts, who suffered the additional humiliation of losing his own seat in the rural heartland of Standerton. In the previous election of 1943, the governing United Party had emerged with double the number of seats of the Nationalists and in 1948 it seemed to be comfortably set to defend its overall parliamentary majority of 25.

How black South Africans viewed the impending change of government is not easy to establish. A mixture of fear and indifference would be a reasonable guess. In his memoir, Albert Luthuli, later president of the ANC, reflected that it was doubtful 'whether anybody realized how significant the election was to be'. 'For most of us Africans, bandied about on the field while the game was in progress and then kicked to one side when the game was won, the election seemed largely irrelevant.'[2] Walking to his Johannesburg lawyers' office on the day the result of the 1948 election was announced, the young ANC leader Oliver Tambo was

1

confronted by a youth who spat in his face. Tambo interpreted this hostility as a clear statement of the new racial order, noting to himself that it would help to clarify the nature of the enemy.[3]

The surprise of Malan's victory was magnified by the widespread view that Smuts, who towered over South African politics, was unassailable. Though past his political peak and visibly ageing, Smuts still bestrode the political stage. His leadership in the Second World War had proved valuable to the allies, capping a remarkable career as a statesman that stretched back to the First World War and before this to his romantic role commanding guerrilla forces in the South African War of 1899–1902. The crowning moment in Smuts's political life came in 1947 when he hosted the British royal family on their South African tour. This much publicized event was a mark of the personal esteem in which Smuts was held within the Commonwealth. The man of war was also an apostle of international peace. Smuts was the only signatory to the Charter of the new United Nations organization who had also participated in the League of Nations. He helped to draft the inspiring preamble to the United Nations Charter and was largely responsible for the inclusion there of the phrase 'human rights'.

As much as he was revered, the old Boer war hero was also reviled. Afrikaner nationalists charged Smuts with having sold out to capitalist imperialism by siding with Britain in two world wars and for supporting the mining industry against white workers in two bloody strikes. Charismatic, but remote and aloof, Smuts was out of touch with domestic politics. He had made a mistake in assuming that his own people would never turn against him. Hubris proved his undoing.

Although Malan's parliamentary lead over Smuts was just five seats in 1948, a pact secured with the splinter Afrikaner Party led by N. C. Havenga proved sufficient to form a government. In the Senate their majority was just one. The Nationalists' hold on power was tenuous and many considered their victory to be merely a temporary aberration. It was only by virtue of an electoral system favourably biased towards white rural constituencies, where Afrikaner farmers predominated, that the nationalist alliance was in a position to form a government at all: significantly fewer votes were cast for Malan and Havenga (41.2 per cent) in 1948 than for the opposition United and Labour parties (50.93 per cent).[4]

South Africa's new prime minister, Daniel François Malan, was a stalwart of Cape nationalist politics, a dogged rather than dynamic leader who steered a prudent path between the party's constitutional and authoritarian tendencies. Many Nationalist leaders were known to have been Nazi sympathizers during the war. Those who had fought Hitler's armies in North Africa and the Mediterranean dubbed them the 'Malanazis'.

Aged 74 at his accession to the premiership, Malan at first seemed fazed by his success. He had been a minister in several rural parishes of the Dutch Reformed Church in the Cape before giving this up in 1915 to pursue a political career, initially as founding editor of the Cape's Afrikaans newspaper *Die Burger*. Malan's religious outlook was orthodox and his political views were conservative rather than radical. He was relatively unaffected by the dogmatic neo-Calvinist abstractions that had taken root in centres like Potchefstroom. He disapproved of the young, rigidly ideological extremists based in the Transvaal and viewed their political leader, J. G. Strijdom, with great suspicion.

Malan saw the 1948 election as the providential outcome of a long and bitter political struggle to secure Afrikaner power and to redress the wrongs of British imperialism. Announcing victory, he is said to have proclaimed: 'Today South Africa belongs to us once more. For the first time since Union, South Africa is our own, may God grant that it will always remain our own.'[5] Here Malan was echoing the National Party's campaign 'psalm' which began with the chant: 'Love for what is your own: | Your own nation | Your own citizenship | Your own South Africa.'[6] These sentiments played on the emotional chords which had dominated Afrikaner nationalist political movement for a generation: unity of and pride in the *volk*, Christian-Nationalism, anti-imperialism, and republicanism.

Malan's victory was as much as anything a victory over his own Afrikaner nationalist constituency. It was only since the 1943 election that he had managed to establish himself as Afrikanerdom's unchallenged leader. A recent biographical study portrays Malan as an ageing, reticent politician, who was never in full control of his cabinet and who was primarily concerned to consolidate Afrikanerdom's historic victory in a rapidly changing world that he scarcely understood.[7] Steeped in the Cape's traditions of coexistence between English- and Afrikaans-speakers, Malan was disinclined to force the divisive issue of republicanism. He understood that a substantial proportion of white South Africans, Afrikaans- as well as English-speaking, continued to value the Commonwealth connection and were suspicious of ultra-nationalism.

Malan's victory exposed the lethargy of the governing United Party and showed that the wartime achievements of Smuts were less substantial than they seemed. Smuts's government could claim some credit for having engineered a successful war economy. The most vigorous economic growth was in secondary industry where the gross value of output (at constant prices) in 1948/9 was twice what it had been in 1938/9. Manufacturing now exceeded agriculture as well as mining as a percentage of GDP.[8] But economic expansion also highlighted long-term imbalances and exacerbated social tensions that the government seemed poorly equipped, even reluctant, to tackle.

Rapid economic growth had done much to erode white poverty—an issue of central importance to the Nationalists—but Smuts's government was ill positioned to profit from this. Rather than assuaging opposition voters, the relatively benign economic and political situation of the post-war era encouraged festering grievances. There was widespread resentment over the unavailability of basic commodities, adequate housing, and delays in finding employment for ex-servicemen. Price inflation stretched the household budgets of many ordinary voters. Consumers complained about the lack of availability of white bread and temporary shortages of meat.

Amongst whites, it was Afrikaners who were most acutely affected by urban poverty, a long-festering problem that the 1932 Carnegie Commission into Poor Whiteism had brought to widespread public notice. Afrikaners constituted around 29 per cent of the urban population in 1910 and 50 per cent in 1936, though they were still heavily outnumbered by English-speakers in cities like Cape Town and Johannesburg. Feelings of inferiority and insecurity pervaded the new Afrikaner arrivals in the cities. A conference organized by the Dutch Reformed Church in 1947 to consider the problems of urban life concluded that as many as three-quarters of Afrikaners in the cities were working class. A high proportion of this group was poorly educated and insecure.[9] Crucial to the National Party's victory were its electoral breakthroughs in the urban areas of the Witwatersrand. By 1948 there were for the first time as many or more Afrikaners resident in urban than in rural areas.

Ordinary working-class Afrikaners felt doubly vulnerable. On the one hand, they suffered from a deep sense of inferiority as regards English-speakers. On the other, they felt deeply alarmed by the rapidly growing urban African population. Between 1936 and 1951 the proportion of Africans living in cities grew from 17.3 per cent to 27.2 per cent, while in Johannesburg the African population grew by nearly 60 per cent between 1936 and 1946, outnumbering white residents for the first time. Perhaps 100,000 people lived in informal settlements on the city's periphery, with few amenities or services. In East London, in 1950, of 66,000 African residents, 85 per cent were recent migrants from the countryside. A striking feature of this pattern of urbanization was the rising number of African women living in towns and cities.[10] Many of the new African migrants succeeded in 'eluding capture' by the state, in Philip Bonner's striking phrase. Unclear lines of responsibility meant that the jurisdiction of municipalities overlapped uncertainly with the police, the Central Housing Board, and the departments of Justice and Social Welfare.[11] Administrative chaos heightened worries that blacks were living beyond official control.

This sense of lack of order made the authoritarian solution of apartheid highly attractive. It also fed into deep racial anxieties. Fear of the *swart gevaar* (black peril) and of *oorstrooming* (swamping) were well-rehearsed tropes, especially for those whites living a precarious existence in towns and cities. A substantial proportion of the electorate was persuaded that Smuts's deputy and heir apparent, Jan Hofmeyr, was a closet liberal whose actions posed a threat to white supremacy. The wartime government had indeed given strong indications that it would countenance a permanent African presence in the cities—unlike the National Party which insisted on turning back the tide of African urbanization.

During the war years tentative moves had been made by the Smuts government to legalize black trade unions, ease the onerous pass law system, and improve social welfare and educational provision for Africans. The Nationalists were quick to seize on these reforming measures, half-hearted and inadequate as they were, as dangerous threats to white supremacy. White farmers complained of their inability to compete for labour against the mines and secondary industry. They also resented the continued low price of maize which had been imposed by the government as a war measure.

Key to the success of the Nationalist electoral campaign was its capacity to place the United Party on the defensive. It also managed to deflect attention from the fratricidal politics that had so divided Afrikanerdom during the war years. South Africa's entry into the war in 1939 had split the government, triggering a constitutional crisis that eventuated in the resignation of General Hertzog as prime minister and his replacement by Smuts at the invitation of the Governor-General. Out of office, the Nationalists reconstituted themselves as a reunited *Volksparty* under Malan's leadership.

The pre-eminence of the remodelled National Party was challenged by a number of right-wing paramilitary organizations, the *Ossewabrandwag* in particular, which was overtly sympathetic to the Nazis, rejecting parliamentary politics in favour of a republican *volk* state. In parliament the Nationalists were sniped at by the Nazi-supporting *Nuwe Orde* which briefly existed 1940–3. Holding the ring, or attempting to do so, was the *Afrikaner Broederbond*, a self-selected secretive body composed of the Afrikaner elite. It had started as a cultural organization in 1918 but soon expanded its interests to take a lead in political and social matters too.

By the mid-1940s the *Broederbond* (now numbering around 2,800 members grouped in 180 cells) presided over a dense network of overlapping civic and cultural affiliates centred on the economically powerful northern regions of the country. The *Broederbond* proved highly influential in developing strategies and propaganda to support the achievement of a Christian-National republic under Afrikaner rule. In 1934 the *Broederbond* issued a statement proclaiming the need for Afrikaner domination under its own leadership. Its practical initiatives focused on the need for the *volk* to 'uplift itself': well-executed plans of social mobilization entailed sponsorship of business and insurance organizations, the formation of Afrikaans trade unions, and support for institutions advocating the principle of self-help. With extensive interests in culture, welfare, education, news, sports, and politics, the *Broederbond* created a large number of front organizations to secure its objectives. Elsewhere, its members were deputed to influence or establish control of organizations and societies on which they had representation.

One of the *Broederbond*'s signal successes was to broker an accord in 1942 between the warring *Ossewabrandwag* and the National Party in the form of a Draft Constitution. This document envisaged a future South Africa as a Christian-National, Afrikaner-dominated sovereign *volk* state existing outside of the British empire. Notably, this statement of shared principle made no mention of 'apartheid', though a commitment to strict racial segregation, subject to continued availability of African labour, was tacked on at the end.[12] By 1944 republicanism was no longer such a divisive factor within Afrikanerdom. With Germany's defeat, fascism was much less alluring. The *Ossewabrandwag* began to disintegrate as a mass organization and therefore diminished as a rival to the National Party. The relaxation of internecine strife allowed the *Broederbond* to turn its attention more fully to the colour question.

This shift in focus was reflected more broadly in the 1948 election campaign. The Nationalists deliberately chose to play down their core republican ambitions, reassured war veterans that they would be cared for, and desisted from attacks on Jews and English-speakers.[13] Malan's decision to downplay threats against English as an official language helped to make the National Party more electable. Its well-organized and highly motivated party machine concentrated more broadly on the need to guarantee white supremacy and Christian civilization.

The Nationalists scored heavily as they played up the dangers of black domination while attacking Smuts's temporizing equivocation and perceived weakness on the colour question. This was a tried and tested tactic: in the 1929 'black peril' election General Hertzog had secured a notable victory over Smuts, allowing him to take forward his plans for racial segregation. In the 1934 election, Malan campaigned on the issue of 'mixed marriages', asserting that ever more rigid boundaries were needed to protect the virtue and purity of working-class white Afrikaner women. Racial populism, highlighting fears of miscegenation or *bloedvermenging*, was a proven vote-winner. The slogan of 'apartheid' was a clever means of condensing such anxieties since it played both to the fears of ordinary voters and to the ambitions of opinion-forming intellectuals.

The 1948 election campaign was replete with allegations that Smuts and Hofmeyr wanted to 'plough the Afrikaner under', that blacks would take jobs from whites, perhaps even act in supervisory roles over whites.[14] Personalizing such vague threats proved highly effective. As the historian Keith Hancock observes, the Nationalists displayed considerable propaganda flair in producing 'a slogan and two bogeymen'. The first bogey was personified by Smuts's deputy, Jan Hofmeyr, who was vilified as a 'kaffirboetie' or 'friend of the native'; the other bogey embodied a more abstract fear, that of godless Communism. In response to these twin dangers the slogan of 'apartheid' was offered as a panacea.[15]

Nelson Mandela is one of many who cite the ugly electoral slogan 'The Kaffir in his place, the Coolies out the country'.[16] Oddly, no evidence of this slogan has been found in the official record or in newspapers, though it is perfectly possible such sentiments were aired on the hustings. Everyday lived traditions of racism and habits of mind remain to be analysed alongside approved official discourse. Each reinforced the other in South Africa's complex racial order, albeit in ways that require further research and conceptualization.[17] It is difficult to assess whether vernacular fears about the rising tide of colour were expressed with greater intensity or ugliness than had been the case in previous election campaigns. On the one hand, crude outbursts of racial hatred may have been relatively subdued during the election campaign because the promise of apartheid reassured supporters that a solution to the problem of race was at hand. On the other, racial fears may have been heightened at this time as a reaction against the calls for racial equality that were then being expressed externally at the United Nations and domestically by the reinvigorated African National Congress and the Natal and Transvaal Indian Congresses.

During the war years, the ANC became far more vocal in its demands for universal citizen rights for all. A major strike by African mineworkers in 1946, which was brutally put down by the police with the loss of twelve lives, served as a clear indication that blacks' industrial power and demands were increasing. In addition, over 50,000 Africans took part in strike action in the period 1940–5.

The wartime government was concerned by black industrial action and inclined to ascribe much of this to Communist agitation rather than to legitimate grievances. Most whites did not yet regard black political activity as a direct threat and were not attuned to its significance. Ordinary white voters remained far more absorbed by intra-white ethnic contestation. A parallel wave of strikes in the mines by white workers in 1946 and 1947 seemingly took place in a different moral and political universe from that of the African Mineworkers' Union. The context in which white worker militancy found expression was significantly conditioned by long-standing fears that whites' statutorily protected positions in skilled work-categories were under threat from competition by cheap black labour. Yet the industrial conflict which absorbed white mineworkers did not focus on black workers. Rather, it took the form of an internal struggle for control of the white Mineworkers' Union, which duly fell under the control of radical Afrikaner nationalists in 1948. The takeover was part of a coordinated Afrikaner nationalist effort to organize Afrikaner workers within an ethnically based class alliance. This helped to secure victory for the National Party in 1948 and to sustain it thereafter.[18]

The National Party's official election campaign offered the country a choice between 'integration and national suicide' on the one hand, and apartheid and the 'protection of the pure white race' on the other.[19] Race formed part of the sediment of daily life and was subconsciously present in the fears and anxieties of whites. But neither race nor apartheid was the only issue confronting voters in 1948. According to Giliomee, apartheid policy was a 'relatively minor' aspect of the Nationalists' electoral campaign. Afrikaans newspaper editorials may have highlighted the issue of race, but this concern was not reflected in newspaper letter columns. At least as important was the perception that Afrikaners had been discriminated against by the Smuts administration.[20] Bread-and-butter issues, government incompetence, anti-communism, and a sense that the world was turning against white South Africa, were prominent themes as well.

The use of 'apartheid' in Malan's 1948 campaign certainly proved effective as a means to discomfit the government and unite the opposition. To this extent apartheid was more tactical ploy than coherent policy. That the Nationalists were unable to define precisely what they meant by apartheid, when challenged to do so, did not detract from the utility of the word. In some ways it made the idea even more effective by allowing many different constituencies to overlook policy contradictions and unite around a vague cure-all. Most significant, as far as the government's supporters were concerned, was the fact that apartheid connoted Afrikaner strength and resolve.

This discussion of the 1948 election modifies several reigning assumptions: first, the Afrikaner nationalist view that Malan's victory marked the natural fulfilment of its political destiny; second, the opposing African nationalist view (supported by much left-wing analysis) that shifts in white politics did not matter all that much given the overall reality of white supremacy; and, third, the notion that the 1948 election was entirely about apartheid.

Apartheid

A neologism coined in a newly minted language, 'apartheid' translates as 'apartness' or 'separateness'. In addition to denoting spheres of physical and social demarcation it carries with it a sense of moral or spiritual imperative. The apartheid concept first emerged in the context of discussions by Dutch Reformed Church missionaries in the 1930s, only gaining wider political currency in the 1940s. In 1943 the authoritative Cape Afrikaner newspaper *Die Burger* referred to apartheid as 'the accepted Afrikaner viewpoint'. The following year, Malan, as leader of the opposition, deployed it for the first time in the South African parliament. Later in 1944, Malan explained that apartheid was not the same as the existing policy of segregation which denoted separation in the sense of 'fencing off'. Instead, he characterized apartheid in more positive, totalizing terms, as a policy designed to 'give the various races the opportunity of uplifting themselves on the basis of what is their own'.[21]

It was only around the 1948 election campaign that apartheid moved beyond the arcane discussion groups of the policy-making intelligentsia and came under sustained public scrutiny. At the start of the campaign the *Cape Argus* dismissed apartheid as a vote-catching device which, if implemented, would 'involve all South Africa in economic ruin'.[22] In similar vein, Harry Lawrence, a leading government minister, dismissed Malan's policy as a damp squib, predicting that at a time of full employment (for whites) voters would have no truck with apartheid's abstruse and impracticable proposals.[23] The historian Arthur Keppel-Jones opined that the substitution of apartheid for segregation was a psychological curiosity since they amounted to the same thing. It was akin to changing an old trade name for a new one in order 'to take the fancy of the consumer. Same firm, same product, new label.'[24] This, it turned out, was an underestimation.

Despite urgent calls for clarification, the new government was cautious about explaining precisely what apartheid entailed or how theory would be translated into action. It was apparent to all that apartheid would be far more systematic and stringent than the existing policy of segregation. But how, and to what extent?

Institutional racial segregation had been government policy since the creation of the Union of South Africa in 1910. Its roots went back to the mid-nineteenth century and for many historians well before that time. The landmark segregationist package of 1936 effectively ended any hopes that blacks in South Africa might gain franchise rights and removed the vote from those Africans in the Cape who had previously qualified (10,628, 2.5 per cent of the Cape electorate). The 1936 legislation restricted black landownership to specified 'native reserves' which were held in trust by the government. These were envisaged in 1936 to be expanded to around 13 per cent of the country from a little less than 8 per cent at the time of the 1913 Natives Land Act.

It has often been claimed that, as a result of colonial conquest and racial segregation, 87 per cent of South Africa's land came to be owned by whites, who only constituted around 15 per cent of the population. This 'narrative of dispossession' is misleading. In the first place, neither landownership nor demography was ever fixed in time. Secondly, the figure of land in white ownership includes urban areas as well as national parks and takes no account of unproductive agricultural areas of the country or of regional variations.[25] Nevertheless, the stark inequality of land ownership and wealth along racial lines is undeniable. At the time of the 1936 Native Trust and Land Act it was broadly accepted that

11

environmentally depleted communal reserves were already wholly inadequate to support rurally based Africans. Part of the promise of the 1936 legislation was to maintain existing land 'in trust' for Africans and, gradually, to expand it.

Another important dimension of racial segregation was to consolidate racial hierarchies in the urban areas. Prior to 1948, Africans were subject to many laws restricting their occupational rights in an effort to ensure that skilled work was restricted to whites. Blacks' spatial mobility was governed by a range of onerous pass laws, which proceeded from the assumption that Africans should not be allowed to live in 'white' towns and cities unless in paid employment. In the rural reserves, where Africans were supposed to live under 'tribal' conditions, they were ruled by proclamations issued by the Native Affairs Department. The Governor-General was deemed to be 'supreme chief' of all natives. Blacks were seriously disadvantaged in respect of social amenities, such as education, health, and welfare.

The continuities between the age of racial segregation and the age of apartheid are so clear that, in the view of many analysts, apartheid was not so much a departure as the entrenchment of an existing racial order. This view does not take into account the extent to which the segregationist compact of 1936 was under pressure a decade later. The war effort and the war economy had made all too plain that segregation was a ramshackle system, full of inconsistencies, and in many cases in retreat. Segregation was plainly unable to cope with the social needs and political demands of Africans whose presence in the cities could no longer easily be controlled.

Smuts had himself suggested in 1942 that segregation had 'fallen upon evil days', a comment that was widely interpreted to mean support for liberal reforms (but which he proved disinclined to act upon in practice). The urgent question in 1948 was whether apartheid was something wholly new or whether it was merely a new term for segregation. Did apartheid mean an attempt to remodel segregation along new, stricter lines? Did it imply an end to, or a modification of, the system of African migrant labour upon which white industry was by now wholly dependent?

Speaking in the Senate in 1948, Dr Verwoerd denied that apartheid was a policy of 'total' segregation or that it had been fraudulently sold to the electorate: apartheid was an ideal but the government accepted that it was not practicable.[26] In an open letter to an American churchman in 1954, Dr Malan reprised the views he had articulated since 1948. Apartheid, he explained, was in essence the traditional racial policy practised since the beginnings of European settlement over 300 years. It expressed 'the deep-rooted colour consciousness of the white South Africans'. This consciousness was itself the 'physical manifestation of the contrast between two irreconcilable ways of life, between barbarism and civilization, between heathenism and Christianity'. It was conditioned by the overwhelming demographic imbalance between blacks and whites.

Malan also insisted that apartheid was 'a positive and non-repressive policy' based on the Afrikaner's divine calling and his privilege to convert the heathen to Christianity without obliterating his national identity. In theory apartheid could only be achieved by dividing the country into two states with whites in one and blacks in the other. But Malan acknowledged that full implementation of the policy would take 'very many years'. It was an 'experiment which is as yet only in its initial stages'.[27]

This, then, was the way in which apartheid was publicly presented by the first Nationalist parliament: as a more rigorous, methodical, and fair application of age-old principles of racial segregation; as the most effective manner of guaranteeing the security of white, Christian civilization; and as an ideal to be worked towards with benefits accruing to blacks as well as whites. The message to ordinary white voters was clear: white supremacy and established racial boundaries would be maintained at all costs.

Beyond the public gaze much speculative work had already been done in respect of the idea of apartheid—though it was by no means clear that the opportunity would arise to put such nostrums into practice. In the decade leading up to 1948 a number of important interventions were made on the theory of apartheid. An influential series of books written by the Pretoria University sociologist Geoff Cronjé (two of which feature 'apartheid' in the title) were conceived as a comprehensive solution of South Africa's racial problems. The South African Bureau of Racial Affairs (SABRA), a dedicated study group composed mainly of Stellenbosch

University intellectuals, was formed in 1948 with the backing of the *Afrikaner Broederbond*. A year earlier, Dr Malan appointed a commission, chaired by the senior politician Paul Sauer, to formulate apartheid policies suitable for adoption by a Nationalist government.

The Sauer Commission was in part intended to forestall the Native Laws Commission on African urbanization, appointed by Smuts in 1946 and chaired by Judge Henry Fagan. These rival reports shaped the respective platforms of the government and the opposition in the ensuing election. They provide a useful way into understanding the political alternatives entertained by the two leading white political parties of the day. The Fagan Commission accepted African urbanization as a fact and recommended adapting the pass laws and migrant labour system to recognize the reality of racial interdependence in the economy (in 1948 the proportion of white employees employed in industry was 34 per cent and in decline).[28] By contrast, the Sauer Commission looked to a more comprehensive solution to the native question along the lines of 'total segregation'. For this reason, the Sauer Commission has often been viewed as a blueprint for the apartheid system.

In fact, the differences between the two Commissions were more a matter of emphasis than underlying intent. Both assumed the need to maintain white supremacy. The Fagan Commission sought to reform the existing segregationist system by making it more flexible. Sauer sought to buttress and extend segregation wherever possible in order to render racial policy more consistent and uncompromising. On the crucial issue of labour, neither report envisaged a rapid end to the system of oscillating African migrancy from the countryside: Fagan sought to reduce dependence on temporary migrants by allowing African families to settle permanently in white cities and to ease influx control; Sauer opted to maintain the migrant labour system so as to prevent this outcome, insisting that Africans could only be temporarily resident in urban areas and that their real homes should remain in the rural 'reserves'.

The Sauer Report is better seen as a reflection of many different voices and interest groups within Afrikaner nationalism than as a coherent statement. It should thus be understood as part of the process of creating an Afrikaner discourse about race and as part of a more general effort to

14

mobilize and unify the *volk* around an agreed agenda. Sauer's Report emerged through careful soliciting of Afrikaner views: 5,000 circulars were sent out to opinion-formers—academics, politicians, and knowledgeable experts—generating 500 responses. These were then distilled into policies.[29]

Deborah Posel has argued that the Sauer Report was internally contradictory and fundamentally ambiguous. It gave voice both to purists who envisaged apartheid as a form of total segregation, and to pragmatists who considered that full apartheid was not feasible, or whose direct material interests would be compromised by the loss of access to African labour.[30] This interpretation presupposes that the Sauer Report was *intended* to offer a clear and unambiguous statement. An alternative reading would see its real purpose as bringing together different ideological strands within Nationalist thinking—secular as well as religious, racist, and ethno-culturalist—into mutual dialogue. Viewed in this way, the Sauer Report was an important step towards creating an Afrikaner consensus around apartheid; it was by no means a clear or unambiguous formula intended for implementation.

Two modestly sized files in the possession of the new Minister of Native Affairs, E. G. Jansen, are perhaps a better guide to government thinking in 1948. These comprise views either solicited or selected by the incoming government. They include advice on a range of topics, including those from old administrative hands with experience of segregation such as E. N. Braadvedt, ruminating on his Natal days, and E. G. Stubbs, author of the 1924 segregationist pamphlet *Tightening Coils*.[31] There are also submissions from younger men seeking preferment like S. J. van der Walt, who boasted a doctorate on the topic of segregation, and C. M. Hulley from Ixopo.[32] In response to an official request, A. M. Lewin-Robinson of the South African Public Library recommended a number of key texts relevant to apartheid, including writings by Geoff Cronjé, A. C. Cilliers, Margaret Ballinger, and Alfred Hoernlé. The overall picture is of a department rapidly having to formulate and condense policy, albeit without much clear direction and with limited expertise.

Of greater importance, given the authors and the scope of their submissions, are the detailed memoranda from men of current influence.

Dominee J. G. Strydom of the Dutch Reformed mission church (see below) argued for a practical, Christian solution based on three or four extensive 'black provinces' in which Africans would acquire full citizenship rights. N. J. van Warmelo, the ethnologist based within the Native Affairs Department, proposed an enhanced form of self-government founded on the existing 'tribal system'. W. W. M. Eiselen, the Stellenbosch anthropology professor who was soon to become Verwoerd's key adviser as secretary of the Native Affairs Department, sent a detailed eleven-page policy document grounded in the promotion of 'Bantu culture'. As Eiselen would continue to maintain throughout his career, the overlap of intellectual abilities across racial groups meant that putative genetic capacity was not a reliable basis for constructing a policy of apartheid. The only 'sane, unbiased and honest policy' was one that aimed at separation and 'self-realisation' as the 'ultimate goal'. This entailed an urgent programme to rehabilitate the existing reserves, though it would be premature to 'seek a final formula' at this stage.[33]

The submissions by Strydom, Eiselen, and Van Warmelo are commensurate with the view that apartheid, in 1948, was being presented as an ambitious and idealistic plan, one that was based above all on Afrikaner traditions and experience. Yet, there is little hint of the detailed, doctrinaire policies that would emerge a decade later. A strong sense of caution and pragmatism is evident, not least in the short four-point internal memorandum on policies set out by D. F. Malan on 2 September 1948. Here it was argued that, given the inadequacy of the 1936 segregationist legislation as a 'solution', separation in social, residential, and political and industrial spheres was desirable. But total territorial separation was not yet judged to be practical. A small number of whites would have to remain in African areas, just as the requisite number of Africans would continue to be present in white areas.[34]

Afrikaner Nationalism

Although apartheid was a theory about how to treat blacks, it was in the first instance a theory that emerged out of discussions about the special nature and God-given tasks of Afrikaners. Its key policies were almost entirely foreshadowed by racial segregation in pre-1948 South Africa, and indeed, in much of British settler Africa. To this extent it was more than just a reworked solution to the age-old problem of how to reconcile the competing needs and desires of whites and blacks. What was novel was its presentation as the distinctive product of Afrikaner thought. By 1948 several convergent strands of thought around the apartheid idea were evident. Underpinning them was a much mythologized argument from history. According to this interpretation apartheid was the logical and inescapable outcome of 300 years of ongoing struggle in South Africa. During this time Afrikaners had constantly to defend their physical and cultural integrity in order to prevent themselves from being 'ploughed under'. Their resistance to British domination had led them to *trek* beyond the colonial boundaries of the Cape colony in the mid-nineteenth century. Heroic Afrikaner pioneers established themselves in the interior which, it was fallaciously claimed, was largely empty and devoid of indigenous inhabitants.

The very term 'Afrikaner' signalled a desire on the part of Nationalists to identify as white Africans, torchbearers of Christian civilization drawn together by a unique culture and calling. The African tribes encountered by the Boers were often hostile and it was only through feats of stubborn fortitude and by the grace of God that they overcame constant threats to their existence—as the defeat of the vastly more numerous Zulu warriors at Blood River in 1838 so vividly showed. As farmers or 'boers', they were productive workers of the land who possessed an instinctive understanding of the country's land and its peoples.

According to nationalist history, by then widely taught in Afrikaans schools and universities, the combined forces of British imperialism and capitalism in the nineteenth century subjected Boers to a range of injustices which threatened their traditional way of life and imposed foreign forms of rule. Greed and rapacity, evidenced by the desire to gain control of the country's mineral wealth, caused heightened conflict and the catastrophe of the South African War. Farm burnings laid waste the country and thousands of women and children died in military concentration camps. From the start of the twentieth century, enforced Anglicization threatened to overwhelm Afrikaners' distinct culture and language. Industrialization and urbanization were a further blight. In the alien environment of the cities, ordinary Afrikaners were mired in poverty and vulnerable to competition in the labour market from cheap African labour. In these conditions, spiritual and bodily degradation was represented as a constant threat.

This narrative of national suffering and redemptive resistance to oppression suffused Afrikaner nationalist historiography at the time. It was given new force from the start of the twentieth century as the experience of urban poverty, social fragmentation, and spiritual confusion, gave rise to a generalized sense of alienation and loss. During the depression years of the 1930s the Dutch Reformed Church became increasingly closely involved with the amelioration of Afrikaner urban and rural poverty. The landmark Carnegie Commission into Poor Whiteism, which reported in 1932, had close links to the Dutch Reformed Church.

M. E. Rothmann, organizing secretary of the ACVV (Afrikaans Christian Women's Society), contributed the section of the Carnegie Report on impoverished mothers and daughters within the family. Philanthropy and social work, often closely tied to localized church activity, provided an important avenue for women activists to help define the concept of the *volksmoeder* in public discourse.[35] As the Afrikaner nationalist movement began to mobilize politically around the issue of poverty, and sought to resolve these socio-economic problems at the level of state action, so members of the Dutch Reformed Church and organizations like the ACVV became more closely politically aligned with the broader nationalist movement.

As well as socially engaged action, the Afrikaans churches provided fertile ground for new theological ideas linked to the need to maintain racial and ethnic boundaries. Consensus was difficult to achieve. When a national policy of racial segregation was presented to the electorate in the 1920s, the Dutch Reformed Church, although temperamentally supportive of segregation in practice, was disinclined to lend unequivocal endorsement to segregation at the level of national politics. Its hesitancy was conditioned by ideological schisms between hardline clergymen who wanted to entrench segregation and moderates who favoured partial differentiation, protection, and gradual 'upliftment' of blacks.[36] Differences of opinion on the relationship between church and state were also in evidence. Unanimity was in any case difficult to achieve because the

DRC, like the National Party, was a regionally based federal organization encompassing different ideological tendencies.

An important impetus for early formulations of the apartheid idea came from the missionary wing of the Dutch Reformed Church which was directly in contact with black adherents. While pietists in the Dutch Reformed Church focused on the individual's relationship with God and tended to be conciliatory on matters of race relations, from the late 1920s missionary leaders in the Orange Free State stressed the need to develop a more communal approach, specifically linking evangelical work to education and politics. For historians like Giliomee, the core of the apartheid idea emerged out of the efforts of these missionaries to reinforce Afrikaner ethnic identity by protecting its authentic cultural and spiritual *eie* (the quality of 'own-ness'). By contrast, the policy of *gelykstelling* (equalization or levelling), supposedly endorsed by English-speaking missionaries and liberals, was decried as a cause of 'race degeneration' or 'bastardization'. The Afrikaner *volk*, it was averred, had an ingrained aversion towards racial mixture or equality. It was God's Will that their distinctive identity be protected. It was therefore possible to concede that humans were equal in the eyes of God without accepting equality in this world.[37]

In 1935 a meeting of the Federal Council of the provincial Dutch Reformed Churches adopted a common missionary policy which proved decisive in crystallizing views on the colour question. Whereas church pronouncements on segregation were equivocal in the mid-1920s, firm pronouncements were now made in respect of Afrikaners' traditional antipathy towards racial mixing. The right of every nation to be itself was affirmed. Perceptions of economic and social vulnerability made the need for policy solutions more urgent. Although segregation was justified in respect of historical experience rather than on the basis of scripture, existing segregationist theory and practice was considered no longer adequate to the task. The logic of Afrikaner nationalism strained towards the more systematic concept of 'apartheid'—a term introduced into Dutch Reformed Church discussions by J. G. (Valie) Strydom in 1938.[38]

This year also saw the triumphal re-enactment of the centenary of the Great Trek, which culminated in a national festival on a hillside overlooking Pretoria witnessed by upwards of 100,000 emotional people.

An imposing, bunker-like monument to Afrikaner history with art-deco forms (bearing a strong resemblance to the Whilhelmine *Völkerschlacht-denkmal* in Leipzig) was commissioned on the site. When the Voortrek-ker Monument was inaugurated on 16 December 1949 its architect, Gerard Moerdyk, explained its symbolism in terms of the 'great civilising deed' of the Voortrekkers and the 'settling and securing of a white civilisation in the interior of South Africa'.[39] Romanticized readings of Afrikaner historical experience, rendered in marble friezes and stone carvings of heroes in traditional dress, used the past to narrate the future.

The historic trek was given new meaning and force by the metaphor of a 'tweede' or second trek, a movement designed to establish Afri-kanerdom in the citadels of the modern cities. By now, roughly half the Afrikaner population were living in cities and towns. Yet they continued to form only a small proportion of the professional classes and had barely begun to penetrate the upper echelons of the financial and business sectors. They were a distinct minority of senior civil servants. Afrikaners were heavily represented in working-class areas and it was to this con-stituency that apartheid was directed in particular.

The iconography of the Voortrekker Monument reflected a new, sacralized version of history which cast Afrikaners themselves as God's chosen people. In the words of sociologist Dunbar Moodie, the increasingly pervasive ideology of Christian-Nationalism became a 'civil religion'. With this, a distinctive theology of apartheid, based on exegetical readings of scripture, began to emerge. An important source of such thinking derived from the conservative Dutch theologian and politician Kuyper (1837–1920), whose writings introduced a powerful tradition of neo-Calvinist thought into the Dutch Reformed Church as a whole.

Key tenets of Kuyperian theology included the notion that society was an organic whole, albeit one that was divided into separate spheres. In the case of society the principle of 'sovereignty in every sphere' should apply, ensuring separation between state, church, and social institutions. The principle of diversity or 'pluriformity' entailed that each ethnic or racial group should maintain their own separate national or spiritual identity. Kuyperian neo-Calvinism was a metaphysical philosophy with

Figure 1. Author, 'Voortrekker Monument'.

broad applications. It concerned nationalist as well as apartheid thinking which, though increasingly closely related, were not quite the same.

On the occasion of the *Broederbond*-sanctioned 1944 *Volkskongres* on Afrikaner racial policy, attended by representatives of some 200 church and cultural organizations, the leading nationalist poet Totius (J. D. du Toit) unveiled a Kuyperian-inspired biblical justification of apartheid. Here he emphasized God's role as 'Hammabdil' or 'the Great Divider': that which God wished to remain separate in nature or society should never be conjoined. For example, the lesson of the Tower of Babel was said to be that God caused those who wished to build an undifferentiated humanity to speak mutually incomprehensible languages. It surely followed that equality or intermixture between different peoples was intolerable.

In 1947, a meeting of churchmen in Pretoria responded to recent United Nations criticisms of South African race policy. The discussion revealed a clear line of division between the pragmatic, evangelical wing led by the Stellenbosch University theologian G. B. A. Gerdener, who was disdainful of neo-Calvinist apartheid dogma, and Kuyperian-influenced purists like J. H. Kritzinger who were strongly inclined to find support for apartheid by means of scriptural exegesis. It was the latter approach that gained ground and the Council of Dutch Reformed Churches was now persuaded to endorse elaborate scriptural proofs for apartheid prepared by the New Testament expert E. P. Groenewald.[40] Theologians like B. J. Marais, Ben Keet, and P. V. Pistorius would soon contest scriptural justifications of apartheid, but their objections were overridden or ignored. Instead, the Dutch Reformed Church synods proceeded to refine and sanction Groenewald's work, culminating in its acceptance by the Federal Council of Dutch Reformed Churches in 1957.

The extent to which theological ideas had been absorbed into the Nationalist movement by the 1940s is remarkable. In the first three decades of its existence the National Party, founded in 1914, concentrated on political issues like Afrikaans language tuition in schools, the constitutional connection, the British Commonwealth, and economic upliftment of Afrikaners. The need to maintain cultural distinctiveness, work towards *volk* unity, and to seek redress for humiliations past and present, were all well-rehearsed themes. These were largely secular expressions of ethno-nationalism. The elaboration of Christian-National ideology from the mid-1930s marked a new phase because it introduced an overarching theological dimension into debates that assigned Afrikaners a unique purpose. Increasingly, this distinctive mission came to be defined in the utopian language of apartheid.

North and South

Christian-Nationalism was represented most powerfully in northern university centres like Potchefstroom, Pretoria, and Bloemfontein, all of which were situated in areas that had suffered major social dislocation and white poverty since the South African War. By contrast, the oldest region of Afrikaner cultural and political influence, the agrarian western Cape, tended to be more pragmatic and cautious. Here, long traditions of parliamentarianism, a well-established rural-based Afrikaner middle class, and a growing commercial and financial sector, all acted as a restraint on political extremism.

The appeal of Christian-Nationalism was in its totalizing philosophical reach and its radical novelty. Its power was enhanced by its capacity to inspire new organizations and societies in places where Afrikaner institutions—including the National Party—were relatively weak. Not only did it speak directly to the Afrikaner sense of *eie* ('own-ness'), Christian-Nationalism also offered means to infuse political practice with the fervour of confessional belief and the lure of absolute truth.

This much was apparent in a new generation of well-connected ideological hardliners from the north, prominent amongst whom were Piet Meyer, Nico Diederichs, and Geoff Cronjé, as well as the future prime minister H. F. Verwoerd, a northerner by adoption. These intellectuals were all born in the first decade of the twentieth century, none had direct experience of the South African War or of direct British rule, and all were focused on urban industrial problems. They came of political age as students in Europe in the 1930s when they were exposed to radical-right ideas and witnessed at first hand the crises of liberalism and the challenge of Communism. Together they were responsible for introducing a potent new strain of uncompromising cultural nationalism or *volksnationalist* ideology into the mass *volksbeweging* or people's movement.

As a leading member of the militant *Ossewabrandwag* and the *Broederbond*, which he went on to head, Meyer played an important role in articulating its vision of an authoritarian Christian-National Afrikaner republic. He also assumed an important position in the growing Afrikaner trade union movement, emphasizing the dangers of class-based politics and seeking to ensure that the primary loyalties of Afrikaner workers were directed to the furtherance of a distinctive form of corporate *volk* socialism. Within the Christian-Nationalist world view, Communism, liberalism, and imperialist capitalism formed a trinity of alien (*volksvreemde*) forces. Here, as elsewhere, a convergence with European radical-right traditions is clearly apparent.

For a time, men like Meyer, Diederichs, and Cronjé were captivated by the lure of right-wing authoritarianism. But most Christian-Nationalists parted company with Nazism. The cult of individual personality was regarded as an affront to the ultimate authority of God; totalitarianism conflicted with the principle of 'sovereignty in every sphere'; and 'blood and soil' *herrenvolkism* variety was widely regarded as a foreign influence that was alien to Afrikaner traditions. From the mid-1940s, cults of violence, uniforms, and marching had increasingly limited appeal.

For the young Diederichs (who eventually was invested as state president) the idealized 'nation', defined above all by its spiritual and cultural qualities, represented the pinnacle of total human achievement. Individuals were important only insofar as they contributed to the furtherance of the nation, and thereby to the will of God. While there are distinct fascistic overtones in many of his early writings and pronouncements, Diederichs recoiled from the reductive view that biological descent was the principal criterion of nationality. And although he gave qualified endorsement to the idea of a *volk*-state, he regarded the state's principal purpose as serving the interests of the nation—not the reverse. God, as creator of the universe, remained the supreme authority.

Notwithstanding such assurances, the romantic *volksnationalist* tradition differed in emphasis and approach from scripturally based conceptions of Christian-Nationalism. In 1935 Diederichs was reproached for his idolization of the nation by theologians like H. G. Stoker based at Potchefstroom University.[41] As adumbrated by the likes of Diederichs, Meyer, or Verwoerd, the *volksnationalist* outlook was decidedly opposed to equality or 'equalization' especially where colour was concerned. Yet,

24

it is important to note that neither the *volknationalists* nor the scripturalists foregrounded race in the 1930s and early 1940s. Nation was the key operative category.

Biological Race

A notable exception to this general rule was the Pretoria University sociologist Geoff Cronjé whose jointly written 1947 book *Regverdige Apartheid* (A Just Apartheid) included E. P. Groenewald's scriptural justifications of apartheid. This indicated the wish to amalgamate Christian-National and romantic nationalist traditions with a strong emphasis on contemporary social reality. Cronjé's writings on apartheid are suffused by visceral fears of racial mixing and contamination prompted by the dangers of whites and blacks living adjacent to each other in degrading conditions of poverty. The moral purity of Afrikaner women, who could so easily produce 'bastard' children, should at all costs be protected. Anticipating later refinements in apartheid policy and thinking, Cronjé distinguished between the threat to white supremacy posed by Indians, who were characterized as aliens; coloureds, who were culturally and physiologically deracinated; and Africans, whose 'Bantu' characteristics had to be preserved by preventing them from becoming 'detribalized'— a well-rehearsed trope which has echoes throughout British colonial Africa.[42]

On account of their relative social proximity to whites, Indians and coloureds figured disproportionately in Cronjé's fears. They represented a different kind of danger from the mass of ordinary Africans. In the cleansed and ordered society that apartheid's theorists sought to construct, Indians represented a particular threat. They were relatively recent immigrants whose success as traders and businessmen presented direct competition to whites. Coloureds posed a different problem. They were visible evidence of past racial intermixture and were therefore to be shunned. They were also disparaged for lacking a pure culture of their own (most in fact spoke Afrikaans).

It was not uncommon within international eugenic and racial thinking to focus fears on those socially or racially defined groups who posed the greatest threat to imagined boundaries. This is why many eugenist criminologists were far more concerned by the 'feebleminded' (who could pass as normal and might, therefore, carry their taint into the general population) than less mentally able 'idiots' or 'imbeciles' (who could not). It also helps to explain why the capacity of Jews to assimilate to the dominant order—and achieve prominence as Communists as well as capitalists—posed such a threat to anti-Semites in South Africa (just as it did in other parts of the world). Anti-Semitism was a significant mobilizing force within the Afrikaner nationalist movement, in the 1930s and 1940s most especially.[43]

Racial eugenists were frequently more worried by perceived threats to race purity and white racial prestige than they were concerned to assert racial difference as fact; the existence of innate racial differences was taken for granted. Racial hysteria was commensurately greater when more advanced representatives of subject groups—'westernized' urban Africans for example—came into contact and competition with socially vulnerable 'poor' whites. This helps to explain why the 'detribalized' African was so much more a figure of hate and contempt than Africans conforming to what was taken to be tribal tradition: assertive urban Africans, often condemned for being 'cheeky', posed a far greater challenge to the existing social order.

Cronjé's obsessive preoccupation with blood purity and horror of mixture and contagion was given an even more overt eugenic spin by the geneticist Gerrie Eloff, who essayed a Christian-National theory of racial biology. In 1942 Eloff proposed a view of the *boerevolk* as a distinct biological type. The Afrikaner race, he reasoned, was the fortuitous result of mixture between European Nordic and Alpine races; its purity had to be protected like a 'sacred pledge' against 'poisonous infiltration'. Afrikaners' distinctive racial composition offered the key to understanding their divine national destiny.[44]

The eugenic writings of Cronjé and Eloff, as well as a sprinkling of anthropologists and psychologists, constitute a distinct sub-tradition of biological determinism in Afrikaner thinking. In itself, the ideological appeal of such prognostications was limited. Biological-based evolutionist theory sat uneasily with literal readings of scripture. Moreover, they opened up the troubling possibility that Afrikaner poverty might itself be eugenic in origin. This constrained the utility of eugenic ideas for mainstream Afrikaner nationalism. However, when linked more loosely to popular fears about racial intermixture and contamination, and when dignified by the putative historical desire to maintain racial boundaries, racial thinking carried strong emotional weight: it evoked generalized feelings of anxiety, disgust, and hatred.

Race awareness was thus a palpable aspect of South African life. It was deeply entrenched in daily life, in relations based on paternalism, and in social custom. Crude vernacular racism was endemic in political campaigning, in parliamentary debates, as well as in private discourse. Apartheid ideology depended on race awareness and did much to arouse racial consciousness though it did not create such awareness. Nor did apartheid promote active race hatred or even condone it at an official level. The oppression of blacks by the state meant that acts of private or collective violence, such as lynching, were far less common in segregationist South Africa than in the American South.[45]

What made apartheid persuasive as an ideology was the manner in which it channelled race awareness into a defensible philosophy of difference operating at multiple levels. Conspicuous care was taken by leading apartheid thinkers, especially once they achieved power, to use circumlocutory language when it came to asserting racial inferiority and superiority. In the post-war world, crude racism was a diminishing political asset. Insistence on difference based on culture was in any case more flexible and durable, and in many respects more insidious.

All the composite elements of apartheid thinking were beginning to coalesce by 1943 when the term started to be used by D. F. Malan in his political speeches. The idea, or aspiration, had been current in Afrikaner theological and intellectual and policy-making circles for a decade and more. The *Bond vir Rassestudie*, an earlier think-tank, adopted apartheid as early as 1936 in order to distinguish the Afrikaner concept of total segregation from the less rigorous notion of segregation.[46] Journals such as *Koers* and *Inspan* provided ample space for the elaboration of key ideas. The mission council of the Dutch Reformed Church, in a memorandum presented to the government in 1942, stated its support for the 'principle of race-apartheid' on the grounds of self-preservation and Christian charity. For all this, apartheid thinking was not yet indispensable to nationalist concerns in the way that anti-imperialist republicanism or poor white poverty already was.

27

Apartheid as Route to Power

The 1944 Volkskongres on the 'colour question' was a definite sign that the Nationalist movement was beginning to shift its focus from internecine struggles and intra-white ethnic competition to think about white supremacy as a whole. Conceived of as a distinctively Afrikaner method of achieving this aim, apartheid succeeded in expanding an inward-looking ethnic nationalist struggle onto the terrain of national politics as a whole. This much was evident in the Sauer Report which, for all its lack of overall coherence, showed that a substantial degree of consensus was being achieved among different sections and constituencies of the Nationalist alliance.

The Sauer Report did not show that the Afrikaner nationalist alliance *required* apartheid in order to realize its ambitions—for example, that apartheid was primarily driven by economic need. Rather, it indicated that apartheid policies offered sufficient advantages to different class and occupational constituencies—farmers, businessmen, trade unions, etc.—to make it broadly acceptable and, moreover, to promise distinct advantages. Those who maintain that apartheid was ultimately driven by economic factors have to reckon with the curious fact that the Afrikaner economic movement (represented by industrial and business bodies, trade unions, and self-help organizations) embraced apartheid only after the 1943 election.[47]

It is well to remember that, until this point, the idea of apartheid was principally the domain of intellectuals and theologians. There was no overwhelming reason to suppose that the ideological musings of professional thinkers would prevail in the context of a new party coping with the constraints of power, unless it could be shown to be compatible with, or indeed advance, the material interests of a sufficiently broad constituency. This proposition was successfully made by ideologists who aimed to weld together different constituencies into a sense of common purpose for the purpose of ethnic mobilization. Apartheid, in other words, was not either an economic or an ideological construction: it is better thought of as the formula that allowed Afrikaner nationalism to cohere as an election-winning force.

Nor can apartheid thinking be reduced to a preoccupation with racial exclusivity, though obsessions with racial purity were prominent in the pronouncements of some of apartheid's most ardent advocates. The most detailed account of nationalist politics in the war years, published in 1947 by Roberts and Trollip as 'an essay in contemporary history', focuses entirely on disunity within the nationalist movement over questions such as republicanism and constitutional democracy. There is virtually not a word on the colour question and no specific mention of apartheid.[48] The fact that a specifically Afrikaner perspective on the colour question emerged relatively late in the development of a nationalist movement is a reminder that apartheid only became synonymous with Afrikaner nationalism shortly before the 1948 election.

The interpretation sketched out above questions the widespread assumption that apartheid was the natural fulfilment of Afrikaner nationalism. It was the means to a more immediate end: political power. In a speech shortly after the 1948 election, the future prime minister, J. G. Strijdom, was reported as saying that before the Nationalist Party 'could reach its ultimate goal—a republic—it would have to solve the colour problem'.[49] This suggests that, for some powerful hardliners, apartheid was the chosen means to achieve ethno-nationalist power. Dan O'Meara in his influential book *Volkskapitalisme* (1983) argued that the Afrikaner nationalist movement was principally motivated by economic forces within the context of an ethnically based class alliance. It is more plausible to put forward a weaker case, namely, that the political success of Afrikaner ethnic mobilization was the outcome of a process whereby different sectional economic interests, farmers and white workers amongst them, were persuaded that apartheid was mutually economically advantageous.

Revisionist scholars from the 1970s were largely correct in attacking the view that apartheid was driven by unreasoning racial prejudices (though in doing so they were apt to ignore the salience of racial ideology). There were important material factors in play, too, which the nationalist alliance was adept at marshalling into a common electoral front. But these were not of themselves decisive. Ethno-nationalist ideology was also key and here anti-imperial republicanism was key. As Chapter 2 shows, Verwoerd was a republican before he made apartheid his own.

The historian of Afrikaner nationalism Hermann Giliomee comes closest to explaining the interplay of material and non-material factors that brought Afrikanerdom to power in 1948. In his estimation apartheid's 'racist outcomes was not a goal in itself; political survival was'.[50] Yet Giliomee's characterization of apartheid as a 'radical survival plan' begs the question: what exactly does 'survival' mean, particularly when there was no real physical threat to Afrikaners as a self-constituted ethnic unit or *volk*?

From the 1870s to the 1930s, Afrikaner nationalism saw ethnic survival as a means of resisting Anglicization, either through aggressive imperialism or as a consequence of the diluting influence of Anglo-Afrikaner Smutsian 'South Africanism'. When political survival came to be understood principally in terms of the need to resist African nationalism, Afrikaner ascendancy could only be maintained within the context of white supremacy as a whole. Every apartheid prime minister understood this and therefore had to square the particular needs of Afrikaner nationalism with white supremacy as a whole.

In its early phase, apartheid provided a divided and fissiparous movement with common purpose. This sense of purpose was achieved by providing the movement with a broader, external focus of activity, namely the capacity to present itself as the guarantor of white supremacy and western, Christian civilization in Africa. Apartheid thereby provided the nationalist movement with political dynamism as well as unifying philosophy. By allowing Afrikaners to project their power and ambitions on a broader scale, it drew attention away from the issues that divided them. The conviction that they had developed a unique solution to an age-old problem—specifically, the unresolved problem of colour—provided Afrikaners with heightened moral purpose, pride in belonging, and claims to political primacy. Apartheid policy therefore signified growing communal confidence, namely the capacity to think and plan in terms broader than the Afrikaner *volk* alone; in other words, to project Afrikaner nationalist thinking onto society at large and to remodel South African society in its own image. For Afrikaners who nursed feelings of inferiority and resentment towards English-speakers, one of the distinct attractions of apartheid was its intellectual coherence and even its moral vision.

The late adoption of apartheid by the Afrikaner nationalist movement goes some way to explaining why the supporters of Smuts so underestimated Malan's challenge in 1948. Years of internecine nationalist squabbling had led many supporters of Smuts to believe, rather complacently, that Afrikaner extremists were more concerned with fighting each other than in forming a united front. Smuts gravely misjudged the depth of institutional mobilization that had already been achieved. Afrikaans churches, universities, newspapers, cultural societies, lobbying circles, and professional groupings were operating at a feverish pitch by this stage.

Even if Christian-Nationalist theory was too recondite and abstruse for many ordinary Afrikaners to engage with, the fact of its existence stood as comforting proof that Afrikaners were the possessors of their own distinctive philosophy. The nationalist movement, grouped in a parallel version of civil society, was by now highly motivated and well entrenched in institutional life. The National Party, albeit federal in composition (perhaps because it *was* regionally constituted), was closely connected to its electorate and more responsive to local concerns than the government. Crucially, its campaign in 1948 was far more effective and professional than that mounted by the listless United Party.

Those liberals and opposition politicians who argued during and after the 1948 election that 'apartheid' was merely a slogan or a fantasy were disingenuous, self-deluding, or misinformed. Disingenuous, because they were reluctant to acknowledge that apartheid marked a refinement of the existing segregation system to which English-speaking and avowedly liberal thinkers had themselves contributed so fulsomely. Self-deluding, because they chose to believe that apartheid's inner contradictions and ambiguities would detract from its electoral appeal and that fantasies born of fear would be rejected because they were fallacies. Misinformed, because they failed to appreciate the growing unity of purpose within the nationalist movement after 1942. The existence of so many competing organizations and institutions, as well as the recent legacy of turbulent dissent, was misinterpreted as proof that the Afrikaner nationalist movement was terminally divided. To the contrary, it indicated its vigour, hunger, and developing maturity.

CHAPTER 2
THE CONSOLIDATION OF APARTHEID

The First Phase of Implementation

When parliament reconvened in August 1948 to debate the new government's first budget, General Smuts, now leader of the opposition, pressed Malan to explain his intentions. 'Apartheid', Smuts averred, was mere propaganda, a confused catchword 'wrapped in a mass of misrepresentations'. Following the line of the Fagan Report, he insisted that it was simply impossible to do without African labour and that white farmers would not contemplate making available extra land for those displaced to the reserves. Malan replied coolly that apartheid had been fully explained in the party's election manifesto. Rather than saying what apartheid was, he explained what it was not. It did not entail eliminating African workers from European areas and nor was it merely 'a policy of oppression'. To the contrary, apartheid had *positive* aspects insofar as it would enable Africans to develop institutions of their own and to enjoy a large measure of self-government in the reserves. Specifically, it would enable Africans 'to retain their own national character'.[1]

In September, Smuts returned to the question, charging the government with bad faith for introducing a radical shift in policies on colour, including possible changes to the constitution, without adequate explanation or respect for the 'sacred clauses' of the Act of Union in 1910. Challenged to explain the opposition's policies, Smuts was forced to admit that it had never supported 'equal rights' or 'racial mixture'. He had always been committed to 'European paramountcy'. Was this 'your apartheid?' Malan enquired. Smuts conceded that it was. The exchange highlighted Smuts's discomfort. Unable and unwilling to renounce white ascendancy, he was left with a narrow base from which to attack the government: apartheid's impracticability, its 'pinpricks' and irritations, the country's vulnerability to international criticism. To the government's new policy of Christian-Nationalism, Smuts merely countered with time-worn pronouncements of Christian 'trusteeship' and 'guardianship'. When asked whether he agreed with the recent decision to impose apartheid on railways in the Cape Peninsula, Smuts could do no more than say it would cause 'bad blood'.[2] Such pusillanimity would characterize the parliamentary opposition for many years. It merely emboldened the government to proceed further.

J. G. Strijdom, leader of the Transvaal Nationalists, who succeeded Malan as prime minister in 1954, was one of those who disdained moralizing about the finer points of trusteeship and Christian duty. He was an outright believer in *baaskap* (boss-ship)—without the intellectual trimmings. Speaking in parliament, shortly before the 1948 election, Strijdom mocked those who pretended they could not understand what the Nationalists meant by apartheid. Quite simply, it meant that he would not sit in a bus alongside a 'native'. Apartheid was essentially a matter of domination:

Either you are baas, the equal, or the inferior, one of the three. If you are not baas, you must be a man's equal ... It is so clear and logical. If you say that you do not want to dominate the Native it simply means that you stand for a policy of equality.[3]

There was no ambiguity either when Strijdom pronounced in 1955 that 'Our task in South Africa is to maintain the identity of the white man: in that task we will die fighting.'[4] Such frank assertions of white superiority played well to the base of the National Party.

Any hopes that the new government would reconsider its intentions following its unlikely win soon evaporated. What the government lacked by way of a master plan was compensated for by an eagerness to improvise on the part of government departments. Immediately after the election 'Europeans only' notices sprang up on Cape Town suburban trains enforcing racial separation in first class coaches. Post offices erected partitions at counters prior to creating segregated entrances. The new Minister of Native

Affairs, E. G. Jansen, announced his intention to control African urbanization more rigorously. The Minister of Labour announced an end to the training of African building workers. A bill drafted by the Smuts government to allow recognition of certain African trade unions was dropped. Malan stated the government's intention to segregate university education so as to avert 'friction' between 'Europeans' and 'non-Europeans'.[5] An Act of primary legislation in 1949 defined South African citizenship for the first time. This was interpreted by English-speakers as a deliberate move to disadvantage British migrants (who enjoyed rights by virtue of being British subjects) and as a step towards severing the Commonwealth connection. Blacks were not actually deprived of South African citizenship in 1949—this would only happen when the apartheid homelands gained nominal independence—but the legislation nonetheless marked a further step in the process of making citizenship race dependent.

Malan also announced that the government would move to repeal the chapter of Smuts's messy 1946 Asiatic Act which provided for token communal representation of Indians in parliament and the Natal Provincial Council. Anti-Indian sentiment featured high on the Nationalists' electoral agenda and Malan had already threatened to repeal the Indian franchise when he came to power. For the Nationalists, the announcement also had the pleasing effect of splitting the opposition, since the highly conservative English-speaking Natal caucus of the United Party, which was obsessed by Indian 'penetration' into white areas and commerce, was strongly opposed to Indian representation in its provincial legislature. Thus, when the *Natal Mercury* declared with warped logic that the province 'was in no mood to accept discriminatory legislation' it was in fact supporting Malan: it meant that Natal should not have to accept Indian provincial representation if other parts of the country were not obliged to do so![6]

Initiatives such as these were a clear indication that Malan's new cabinet was eager to act fast in order to prove the government's apartheid credentials. That two of the measures mentioned above affected provincial arrangements in Cape Town and Natal indicated that the central state was willing to impose its authority on the regions. It also signalled that the position of coloureds and Indians was coming under direct scrutiny. In September Malan announced that qualifying coloured voters in the Cape would be removed from the common voters' roll. So, too, would the continued existence of (white) 'native representatives' in parliament, a legacy of the 1936 segregationist legislation. Franchise rights had been constitutionally entrenched at the time of Union so the removal of coloured voters would probably require a two-thirds majority in both houses, which the government could not hope to secure in the short term. Only by tampering with the Union constitution could this outcome be achieved.

The government indicated that it was prepared to do so but by early 1949 no specific proposals were forthcoming. The principal reason for the delay was hesitation on the part of Malan's coalition partner, Havenga. For a variety of reasons relating to the 1936 segregationist settlement and his personal loyalty to General Hertzog, Havenga was reluctant to meddle with the existing constitutional arrangements. As a highly regarded Minister of Finance under Hertzog's premiership, Havenga's views could not easily be countermanded. His moderating influence indicated that the zealous radicals in the National Party did not yet have a free rein. They moved to increase their majority by granting South West Africa six seats in parliament, albeit without formally violating the terms of the United Nations mandate in that territory.

In the case of foreign affairs Malan exhibited caution, realizing that he needed to retain whatever influence he could abroad. Just as the retention of Havenga was calculated to steady the markets, so Malan kept the experienced D. D. Forsyth as Secretary for Foreign Affairs, a decision that his British counterparts found reassuring. Aware of the dangers of isolation at the United Nations, Malan strove to maintain good relations with Britain and the United States. South Africa's participation in the Korean War was an important signal of the government's determination to situate the country as part of the anti-communist western alliance.[7]

Another example of the cautious 'diplomacy of isolation' was Malan's visit to Israel in 1953, the first to the newly created Zionist state by a foreign prime minister. In 1930 Malan had been responsible, in his capacity as Minister for the Interior, for introducing a Quota Act targeted against Jewish immigration. Anti-Semitism, so potent a mobilizing strategy in the 1930s and early 1940s, was henceforth played down by the Nationalists and, indeed, the comparison between Afrikaners and Jews as 'chosen people', both of whom gained their national sovereignty in 1948, was a sub-theme in Christian-National narratives. As international opprobrium focused more and more on Israel and South Africa, so the strategic alliance between the two countries grew stronger. For all that the Nationalists berated Smuts's internationalism and affected indifference towards international criticism, the Nationalists were keen to maintain the country's standing overseas. Malan maintained some of Smuts's sub-imperial ambitions in his 'African Charter' which was adumbrated at various times from 1945 to 1953. This projected white leadership and Christian tutelage as a positive force for regional development. It even spoke of 'Africa for the Africans'—a formulation which meant both that South African whites were at home on the tip of Africa and that the continent had to be protected from Communist and 'Asian' (Indian) infiltration.[8]

The government moved quickly to secure its control over the civil service which was nominally non-political in line with British traditions. When Evered Poole was passed over as army chief of staff in 1948, and the head of the railways was replaced by an Afrikaner a year later, it became clear that political affiliations would henceforth determine the pattern of senior positions in the government administration. In departments like the police, justice, education, and native affairs, where English-speakers had long been strongly represented at senior levels, loyal Nationalists were rapidly promoted. Patronage was a key means of retaining and rewarding reliable National Party functionaries in the fast-growing apartheid bureaucracy. Competence was a lesser consideration. By 1959 the process of 'Afrikanerization' meant that of more than forty governmental departments and sub-departments, only six were headed by English-speakers.[9]

The Afrikaner capture of the state was consolidated through public corporations like the railways, the electricity supply commission, and the national steel industry. The 'civilized labour' policy, which had been used to secure jobs for unemployed whites on the railways in the 1920s and 1930s, was now extended to include the civil service more generally. O'Meara calculates that in the decade after 1950 total state employment increased from 480,000 to nearly 800,000. Afrikaner males were the main beneficiaries of a large-scale process of bureaucratic expansion which included the creation of many new quasi-official state organizations and institutions.[10]

If Malan's narrow parliamentary majority restricted his ability to challenge constitutionally sensitive political rights, there was plenty of scope for the government to press ahead on other issues. In 1950 an amendment to the so-called 'Immorality Act' outlawing interracial sex was passed, extending the scope of existing legislation. This prohibition was enforced with intrusive callousness through most of the apartheid era, providing a rich seam of voyeuristic outrage in newspapers as well as parliament and the pulpit. Another significant piece of legislation passed in 1950 was the Suppression of Communism Act. Its immediate political effect was to drive the Communist Party underground. The insidious measure defined Communism so broadly as to encompass any organization or individual whose views were considered to be radical. It became a favoured means of controlling dissent as well as a tactic to delegitimize opposition in the eyes of fearful white voters.

The Group Areas Act of 1950, which allowed the government to 'proclaim' residential and business areas in towns and cities for designated race groups (including Indians and coloureds), was also based on prior segregationist legislation. The 'Group' was extensively used to remove communities and individuals who found themselves living in the 'wrong' place, most notoriously in the racially mixed and politically vibrant areas of District Six (Cape Town) and Sophiatown (Johannesburg). But not everyone resisted the opportunity to gain new housing. For instance, in Durban, many working-class Indians welcomed the opportunity to establish footholds in newly laid-out townships where they now paid rent to the municipal authorities rather than private landlords.

A new departure, with no direct precedent in the segregationist era, was the Population Registration Act (1950). This ensured that every child was assigned a racial category on birth. The measure was one of the foundational mechanisms of the growing apartheid state. It gave rise to the hated 'reference book' or *dompas* which Africans were obliged to carry and to produce on demand following the passage of the Natives (Abolition of Passes and Co-ordination of Documents) Act in 1952, whose Orwellian title meant extension rather than abolition. A burgeoning government bureaucracy developed in order to record a full national racial register, with direct implications for citizenship, employment, residential, and social rights. In disputed cases—often relating to marriage—local Race Classification Boards were established to adjudicate.

The Population Registration Act introduced the principle of biological ancestry into every aspect of social existence and in so doing made apartheid the most oppressive system of racial rule in the post-war world. Yet, for all its pretensions to scientific rigour and taxonomical precision, the Act could not be made workable without making allowance for criteria like 'appearance' 'descent', and general 'social acceptance'. This was especially important in the case of 'coloureds' who were defined negatively, namely as an individual 'who is not a white person or a native'. The complexity of categorization meant that coloureds were subdivided into various sub-categories with a residual group defined as 'Other Coloureds'.

As in so many aspects of apartheid, a considerable degree of rackety administrative flexibility enabled the system to survive and adapt. Here, as elsewhere, popular racism worked alongside bureaucratic and legal formulations, each level supporting and reinforcing the other. The principles of the Population Registration Act became internalized by the vast majority of South Africans; for all the anguish that they caused, only a tiny fraction of determinations were ever contested.

The African Nationalist Response

During the Second World War the African National Congress emerged as a modern, mass campaigning organization dedicated to the inclusion of blacks as full, equal citizens, in a unitary state. South Africa's entry into the conflict highlighted Africans' indispensability in the national economy and the international fight against fascism found local echoes in demands for freedom and rights. A new generation of assertive intellectuals and activists came to the fore from the early 1940s including figures like Nelson Mandela, Govan Mbeki, Walter Sisulu, Oliver Tambo, Anton Lembede, and A. P. Mda. Grouped in the ANC Youth League, they challenged the conservatism and elitism of the established leadership. As 'Africanists', they stressed self-reliance and pride, while questioning the influence exerted on the ANC by Christian liberals on the one hand, and Communists on the other. As cosmopolitan intellectuals, they took close account of anti-colonial movements in Africa and Asia and began to think of themselves as participants in a global fight for freedom.

In 1943 the ANC published a seminal document, *Africans' Claims*, which adapted the principles set out in the Atlantic Charter for local use. The language of *Africans' Claims* marked a clear shift in ANC strategy: previous appeals to restore the privileges enjoyed by 'civilized' Africans were rephrased in terms of a democratic 'bill of rights' applicable to all adult citizens; the citation of specific grievances and injustices requiring amelioration transmuted into a much broader social vision encompassing basic economic reforms, a 'fair' redistribution of land, and the provision on an equal basis of health and educational services.

Rapid urbanization dramatically altered the context in which the ANC's struggle for rights was pursued. The growth of urban slums and informal settlements in the major conurbations of the country diminished the state's capacity for surveillance and control, thereby opening up new political space for mobilization. James 'Sofasonke' Mpanza, a flamboyant shantytown leader on the outskirts of Johannesburg, created a large personal following and used his influence both to enrich himself and to intercede with the authorities on behalf of his constituents. Industrial strikes, bus boycotts, pass law protests, and the growth of squatters' movements were all powerful manifestations of a growing urban crisis. The ANC was by no means the instigator of all these actions, but it was increasingly aware of the need to engage with popular struggles and more prepared than ever before to adopt a directly confrontational attitude to the state. This was the flip-side of white fears of *oorstrooming* which helped to propel the Nationalist victory.

In 1949 the ANC Youth League unveiled its Programme of Action, which was subsequently adopted by the ANC. The Programme defined the object of struggle as the achievement of 'national freedom'. It committed the organization to a campaign of boycotts, strikes, and civil disobedience as well as a one-day work stoppage. The Programme of Action crystallized much of the radical thinking which had developed within the ANC Youth League over the previous five years, and set the stage for the political campaigns of the 1950s. It was as much a response to segregation as it was to the inauguration of apartheid.

In his autobiography, Nelson Mandela recalls that at a meeting held with Oliver Tambo and others on election day the question of a new government was barely discussed. To Mandela's surprise, Tambo's response to the election result was, 'I like this. . . . Now we will know exactly who our enemies are and where we stand.'[11] Whether or not these exact words were said, the story highlights a recurrent dilemma faced by the ANC in its fight against white supremacy: to acknowledge the white political system, pay close attention to differences between factions and parties therein, and strategize accordingly—or, alternatively, to minimize recognition of white politics in order to concentrate on the fight against the system, maintain unity, and avoid the traps of co-optation and reactive response.

In fact, the ANC did both. The ANC was increasingly disposed to combine with other racially defined groups—coloured, Indian, and white too—with similar political outlooks in mounting a common front against apartheid. But this was not easily achieved. Apartheid legislation bore unevenly on different sectors of society. Anti-apartheid organizations were often regionally specific and shaped by the demographics of race and class. The ANC also had to decide whether its 1949 Programme of Action should remain within the law and honour Gandhian traditions of passive resistance, or whether more confrontationary tactics should be adopted. A clear decision on this issue could not be reached: in the 1940s and 1950s ANC presidents Xuma and Luthuli counselled caution, fearing a backlash from the government, whereas the increasingly influential Youth League favoured militancy and began to consider the need for direct revolutionary action.

Campaign against Unjust Laws

On 1 May 1950 a one-day work stoppage in opposition to apartheid legislation organized by the Communist Party and the Transvaal Indian Congress resulted in the deaths of eighteen Africans, killed by police using guns and batons. This galvanized the ANC into launching its

National Day of Protest on 26 June, in collaboration with the Indian Congress, the (Coloured) African People's Organization, and the now illegal Communist Party. By Mandela's own estimation the 26 June protests and stay-at-home was only a 'moderate' success. Although the public response was uneven it helped to inaugurate a tradition of civil action involving competing or fractious anti-apartheid groupings in a common front or alliance. 26 June, celebrated as 'Freedom Day', henceforth became the occasion for many more protest initiatives, including the landmark Congress of the People in 1955. In symbolic terms, Freedom Day marked the start of the ANC's efforts to challenge the government's monopoly on public commemoration.

This was graphically illustrated when the government marked the tercentenary of the 'founding' of South Africa by the Dutch East India Company by way of the 1952 Van Riebeeck Festival, named after the Dutch commander who first established a European presence at the Cape. Considerable resources were devoted to a programme of public events and pageants celebrating the development of a united white nation and the arrival of western civilization in Africa. These efforts were not wholly successful and the events were soured by a lack of common accord. It was unclear, for example, whether it was Afrikaner power or white unity that was being honoured. Underlying tensions between Cape Town, the self-proclaimed 'mother city' where van Riebeeck established his outpost, and the Transvaal, indisputably the industrial heart of the country and centre of Afrikaner nationalist republicanism, could not be contained. Van Riebeeck was himself deficient as a national icon. He was responsible for founding settlement on behalf of a Dutch mercantile company, not a nation, and he was a pragmatic sailor and settler rather than a hero.

The Festival is now best remembered because of the anti-apartheid counter-narrative that developed by way of response. The climate of animosity was especially feverish in the Cape because the period of the Festival coincided with a key legal judgement on the government's right to proceed to disenfranchise coloured voters by means of the 1951 Separate Representation of Voters Act. The non-European Unity Movement, a left-wing organization predominantly composed of coloured school teachers and intellectuals in Cape Town, organized public boycotts. Unity Movement thinkers wrote a series of public history historical texts which interpreted South African history as the constant unfolding of colonial capitalism and land dispossession. Official white history was ingeniously subverted in books and pamphlets, including Dora Taylor's *Role of the Missionaries in Conquest* and Hosea Jaffe's *Three Hundred Years*, both published in 1952.[12]

Also in this year the African National Congress launched its Campaign for the Defiance of Unjust Laws; its timing coincided with the climax of the official Van Riebeeck celebrations and therefore served as a dramatic expression of two irreconcilable competing nationalisms. Beginning with staged acts of non-compliance with apartheid regulations in Port Elizabeth and Johannesburg, and emerging out of the 1950 Day of Protest and the 1949 Programme of Action, the Defiance Campaign represented a concerted effort to join together a broad coalition of African and non-African organizations in clear rejection of six 'unjust laws'. One of the original causes, the Franchise Action Council's bid to prevent the removal of coloureds from the common voters' roll, ceased to be a focus of protest as the campaign developed.[13] Though its objectives were in some ways inchoate, and its impact uneven, the Defiance Campaign was an innovative experiment in the politics of mass civil disobedience. Like the near contemporaneous civil rights movement in the United States, it drew strongly on Gandhian roots but also unleashed more aggressive responses at a local level.

Letters of protest from ANC leaders to the government were ignored or treated with contempt. When Walter Sisulu and ANC president James Moroka wrote to the prime minister protesting that the government 'continues to insult and degrade the African people by depriving them of fundamental human rights enjoyed in all democratic communities', Malan's private secretary took issue with this point and gave voice to an explanation based on *baaskap* and biological race determinism:

I think, that it is self-contradictory to claim as an inherent right of the Bantu who differ in many ways from the Europeans that they should be regarded as not different, especially when it is borne in mind that these differences are permanent and not man-made. If this is a matter of indifference to you and if you do not value your racial characteristics,

you cannot in any case dispute the European's right, which in this case is definitely an inherent right, to take the opposite view and to adopt the necessary measures to preserve their identity as a separate community.[14]

As far as the government was concerned the ANC had no right to approach the prime minister directly; it should rather direct any grievances it had to the Native Affairs Department, now under the political leadership of the uncompromising Hendrik Verwoerd. In effect the government was declaring that the African National Congress, its affiliates and allies, were irrelevant to the country's political future.

Beginning on Freedom Day, 1952, selected ANC activists were enjoined to pledge to serve their country and its people by conspicuously defying apartheid laws. In towns and cities all over South Africa 'volunteers' (with Mandela in the role of volunteer in chief) gave the ANC's thumbs-up salute. They chanted 'Afrika!' and 'Mayibuye' as they conspicuously ignored apartheid restrictions at park benches, railway stations, post offices, and other segregated institutions. Khaki uniforms, white shirts, and lapels in the ANC colours were frequently worn. Self-discipline and peaceful collective action was the guiding moral philosophy. Confrontation was mostly avoided by advertising plans in advance and limiting the numbers of individuals involved in any one action; there were prayers expressing Christian sacrifice and martyrdom. The hope was that by inviting arrest and imposing intolerable burdens on the state's capacity to police its own regulations, the system would be rendered inoperable.

Between June and December 1952, over 8,000 resisters were arrested and jailed. The eastern Cape and Transvaal saw the bulk of activity. Participation was low in the Free State and Natal. Care was taken by the ANC leadership to manage the campaign of civil disobedience and to avoid provocation so as to avert the potential for outbreaks of violence.[15] But the ANC was not always able to maintain full control over protesting crowds. The Defiance Campaign proved a vent for deep popular frustrations that were sometimes expressed in powerfully racialized terms. When rioting broke out in Port Elizabeth, Kimberley, and East London (where a white Catholic nun was beaten and burnt to death in her car) the ANC called off the national campaign, fearing that popular anger was

Figure 2. Men being taken off to trial in lorry (raised hands in thumb-salute): Jürgen Schadeberg, 'Treason Trialists taken from a Johannesburg Prison to the Drill Hall Court for the first day of the Treason Trial—December 1955'.

getting out of hand. New research suggests that as many as 250 blacks were massacred after police opened fire on a mass meeting in East London on 9 November 1952, far more than the official death toll of nine dead and fewer than 30 wounded.[16] The police hushed up the scale of the deaths and the ANC distanced itself from the rioters and lawless youths (*tsotsis*). For the most part, the Defiance Campaign's rich imagery of peaceful and disciplined protest came to be remembered as a high point of non-violent resistance through the long years of exile.

The government easily met the policing challenge without undue difficulties. Tellingly, not one of the 'unjust' laws was repealed. Instead, parliament hurriedly passed draconian new measures to contain and punish protest. One of these, the Criminal Law Amendment Act (1953), sanctioned whipping and fines as punishment for political dissent, even passive resistance. Another provided for the imposition of a state of emergency to maintain public order. A flurry of banning orders, arrests, and trials weakened the leadership of the campaign alliance and led to Moroka's replacement as ANC president. Well before the end of 1952, the momentum of the Defiance Campaign had been halted.

The MalaNazis

Another powerful response to the Malan government was registered by ex-servicemen. Participation in the war and in educational schemes like the Army Education Service raised the hopes of many soldiers for post-war social reconstruction along more egalitarian and democratic lines. However, returning from North Africa and Europe, they were shocked to find a new government in power in 1948 composed of 'home front fascists' who had vigorously opposed South Africa's participation in the war. Their outrage was confirmed when, in 1948, Malan freed Robey Leibbrandt and other war traitors. Leibbrandt, who had represented South Africa at the 1936 Berlin Olympics as a boxer and became enamoured of Nazism, took part in an outlandish German plot (Operation Weissdorn) to assassinate Smuts and overthrow the government.

The War Veterans' Torch Commando was established in 1951 to oppose the disenfranchisement of coloured voters and the broader constitutional ramifications that would surely follow. It boasted as one of its leaders 'Sailor' Malan, an RAF fighter pilot and hero of the Battle of Britain, whose rural Afrikaner background (he was a distant relative of the prime minister) and broad South Africanism lent the movement considerable popular appeal. Other leaders of the Torch emerged out of another veterans' organization, the Springbok Legion, which was oriented towards the Communist Party. There were more conservative participants in the Torch Commando such as those who equated defence of the Constitution with Englishness (and in the case of anglophone

Natal, recognition of provincial independence). An important supporter of the Torch Commando was mining magnate and United Party politician Harry Oppenheimer who exerted a constraint on its popular radicalism.[17]

For a period, the Torch represented a potentially formidable threat to the government. At its height it claimed a membership of 250,000 and proved able to mobilize tens of thousands in evocative night-time flame-lit rallies against the government's 'rape of the constitution'. But although able to mobilize a broad coalition of anti-Nationalist opinion in support of democracy, it was a coalition rooted in a culture of wartime idealism and nostalgia that proved unable to agree on a political vision on the future. The non-racism and left-wing views of some of its members were by no means universally shared. An unpublished draft statement geared to merger with the United Party accepted 'no mixing of blood' and a firm commitment to residential segregation.[18]

Formed expressly to oppose the Separate Representation of Voters' Act and unseat the government, the Torch Commando portrayed the Nationalists as usurpers of freedom. Yet they proved unable to agree on the admission of coloured veterans as members and lacked a clear policy agenda. There was no connection with the ANC's Defiance Campaign. The Torch failed to form any effective link with the Franchise Action Council, in which coloured activists predominated. It operated within the constraints of white politics and, in Neil Roos's estimation, 'never once challenged the fundamental social hierarchy of race...'.[19]

Having flared into existence as the largest mass movement in the country's history in 1951, the Torch was extinguished by 1953 when the Malan government was re-elected on a much more secure footing. The National Party's ability to face down militant extra-parliamentary activism emanating both from the Torch Commando and the Defiance Campaign heralded its success as the unambiguous voice of a new kind of whiteness. From now on white radicalism would only ever find full legitimate expression in alliance with black organizations like the ANC.

Global Responses

South Africa's emergence as an international problem marks a key moment in the era of post-war global politics, in particular, the expanded scope of international jurisdiction in respect of race, human rights, and imperialism. The fact that apartheid was proclaimed official South African policy just as the United Nations issued its Universal Declaration of Human Rights in 1948 was a telling marker of the country's retrogressive political trajectory. This began to mark it out as an international pariah: the iniquity of apartheid was one moral and political issue that countries, large and small, aligned and non-aligned, could mostly agree on—albeit not always from the purest of motives. Whereas pre-war segregation was not so different from practices elsewhere in British colonial Africa and Asia, statutory racial discrimination was becoming indefensible in a world where decolonization and rights were gaining ground. Apartheid South Africa, followed by Israel, Rhodesia, and other African colonies, were now at the centre of debates in the General Assembly.[20]

For the so-called Afro-Asian bloc at the United Nations—the term became current around the Bandung Conference in 1955—apartheid was anathema because it exemplified the twin evils of colonialism and statutory racism. South Africa's international status was bound to have deteriorated after the Second World War. Yet it is questionable whether the country would have emerged as an international pariah had the slogan of 'apartheid' not proclaimed South Africa's exceptionality so stridently.

To be sure, the country's race policies were raised as a concern by the United Nations from the start of the organization's existence, though initially only indirectly. This was because article 2(7) of the United Nations Charter laid down that matters of domestic jurisdiction lay outside the jurisdiction of the international body. Contestation over sovereignty—national self-determination in the case of South Africa, leadership of the non-aligned movement in the case of India, and of humanity at large in the case of the United Nations—all found a focus on the issue of South Africa's racial policies.

At the very first session of the General Assembly, in 1946, South Africa was charged by India with discriminating against citizens of Indian descent in respect of the 1946 Asiatic Land Tenure and Representation Act and of violating bilateral agreements entered into between the two countries. In that year India became the first country to impose trade sanctions on South Africa. Whereas Smuts took the narrow legal view in 1946–7 that the United Nations was not competent to intervene in matters concerning a country's sovereign rights, the Indian delegation, led by Mrs Vijaya Lakshmi Pandit, adopted a broader legal and humanitarian approach. At the UN General Assembly in 1946 she insisted that South Africa's discriminatory treatment of Indians in the country constituted a denial of human rights and fundamental freedoms as laid down in the UN Charter.

South Africa was in Mrs Pandit's words a 'test case' in 'the minds of millions of people in India and other parts of Africa and Asia [who] have been moved to intense indignation at all forms of racial discrimination...'. The issue was personally awkward for Smuts since he himself had played a key role in drafting the section of the preamble to the United Nations that mentioned 'human rights'. In private, Smuts reflected ruefully on the way in which he, a spokesman for human freedom, had been exposed as a hypocrite for his views on race. 'Colour', Smuts recorded, 'queers my poor pitch everywhere'.[21]

Another angle of attack came in the form of criticism of South Africa's role in South West Africa (Namibia), whose legal status as a 'Class C' mandate under the defunct League of Nations remained an ongoing matter of international debate. In November 1946 Smuts attempted to persuade the Trusteeship Committee of the United Nations to allow South Africa to incorporate South West Africa on a formal basis. India and the Soviet Union objected and in the course of the debate South Africa's 'native policy' was subjected to vociferous criticism. The leader of the ANC, Alfred B. Xuma, used the issue of South West Africa at this time to draw attention to the treatment of blacks in South Africa.[22] The question of South West Africa's sovereignty reached the world court at The Hague and the problem was only finally resolved with Namibian independence in 1990.

In 1953, a UN commission report determined that the policies of apartheid contravened the principles and spirit of the Charter and its Preamble. It concluded that 'the doctrine of racial differentiation and

48

superiority on which the apartheid policy is based is scientifically false, extremely dangerous to internal peace and international relations . . . and contrary to "the dignity and worth of the human person" '.[23]

From the perspective of domestic electoral politics, external criticism of South Africa played into the hands of the government and greatly discomfited the parliamentary opposition. It was Smuts, after all, whose vainglorious role as international statesman had proved so counterproductive. At the 1953 general election the National Party consolidated its position, in part by portraying external criticisms of its policies as unfair and Communist-motivated. Generations of South African politicians condemned United Nations attacks as hypocritical, and sometimes affected indifference to its criticisms. Yet they also craved international acceptance. Over the entire history of apartheid, enormous energy was invested into explaining South African racial policies to the outside world in the hope of gaining a sympathetic ear.

Newly independent countries like India were able to assert their credentials as international anti-colonial powers by adopting a principled position against apartheid. The Soviet Union expressed solidarity with anti-imperialist movements by taking a lead against South Africa in the Security Council. Consensus on how to tackle the problem of apartheid took time to emerge. European colonial powers and the United States did not want to be seen as supporters of racism, yet they did not either want to concede their vital economic interests in South Africa or abandon a strategic ally.

Placed on the defensive, South African diplomats fought to disallow the General Assembly from debating 'apartheid' by presenting the domestic jurisdiction clause of the United Nations as a reason for non-interference in its affairs. This legal precept allowed a handful of countries, including Britain and France, to tone down General Assembly resolutions on South African racial policy during the 1950s. It was only after the Sharpeville Massacre in 1960—and following Verwoerd's decision to leave the Commonwealth—that Britain abandoned its abstentionist position to endorse a UN vote declaring South Africa's racial policies to be in flagrant violation of the Charter.[24] The support of the United States for the 1960 vote at the UN 'marked a dramatic change in its attitude to South Africa'.[25]

As the leader of the West, the United States' position on trade and arms sanctions was critical, not least in the Security Council. But the United States, like Britain, refused to accept that South Africa represented a threat to international security. Cold War rivalries persuaded leading western countries of the necessity to retain South Africa as a regional bulwark against Communism. South Africa's participation in the Korean War (and Malan's stated desire to join NATO) marked a significant shift from his party's commitment to neutrality during the Second World War.[26]

Under the Truman and Eisenhower administrations, the principle of white supremacy was not seriously questioned by US officialdom. The United States' attitude to South Africa at the United Nations at the United Nations was fairly consistent until Sharpeville: 'try to avoid the issue' and maintain a policy of benign neglect.[27] This was matched by a hiatus in transatlantic engagement between African-American activists and the ANC in the decade after 1948. American concern with apartheid was significantly conditioned by the rise of the civil rights movement in the late 1950s and the inauguration of the Kennedy administration in 1961. The Sharpeville massacre thus resonated strongly with American domestic politics and split public opinion.

From 1946 to 1960 the British delegation to the United Nations took the principal role in deflecting international criticisms of South Africa. As South Africa's largest trade partner and by far the greatest source of foreign investment during this period, Britain still wielded considerable influence. The Royal Navy remained the guarantor of the sea route around the Cape. London was still the most important posting for South African diplomats, ahead of Washington, Berlin, and Paris.

Britain's official position was laid out by officials who, in 1950, presented four arguments for maintaining close relations with South Africa. The considerations were (i) strategic (the shipping route round the Cape, the Simonstown naval base, uranium); (ii) economic (trade and investment, gold supplies in support of the sterling area); (iii) regional (continued British control of the 'High Commission Territories' in southern Africa); and (iv) diplomatic (maintenance of the Commonwealth connection, prestige, influence).[28] Patrick Gordon Walker, Secretary of State for Commonwealth Relations, was reported to have said to an audience in Cape Town in 1951: 'we are both great African powers.'[29] This flattered

South Africa's own self-image during the 1950s as a force for regional stability and representative of western, Christian civilization.

Through the 1950s and beyond, British governments habitually took the view that apartheid was regrettable and probably unworkable, but offset this discomfort by insisting that maintaining good relations with the country was vital. The London *Times* South African correspondent, reporting the Nationalist victory in 1948, set the tone by shedding a tear for Smuts and expressing cautious optimism in respect of Malan.[30] The right wing of the Conservative Party in Britain fought a stout rearguard defence of its African colonies in the 1950s, identifying decolonization with national loss and socialist advance. H. V. Morton, writer of travelogues like *In Search of England*, moved to South Africa in 1948. To this nostalgic conservative, not to say reactionary, South Africa 'seemed to preserve all that was best about prewar England, but with better weather and a more compliant servant class'.[31] In the decade after 1964 when South Africa's economy boomed, nearly 170,000 Britons settled in South Africa.[32]

Vocal public opinion in Britain was at variance with such quiet assent. Well before Sharpeville, solidarity groupings with roots in the anti-slavery movement like the Movement for Colonial Freedom, led by Fenner Brockway, and Canon John Collins's Christian Action, began to develop an anti-apartheid profile in Britain. The anti-apartheid cause was taken up in the 1950s by progressive Labour and Liberal politicians like Hugh Gaitskell, Barbara Castle, Michael Foot, and Jeremy Thorpe. The British Trades Union Council was actively concerned with the plight of fellow unionists in South Africa. The Communist Party of Great Britain and its Africa Committee had well-developed internation-alist tendencies; it viewed anti-colonialism and anti-imperialism as an important dimension of the struggle to build socialism within the capitalist metropole, and was ready to serve as a conduit of fraternal support to South African Communists. In the 1950s student unions at Cambridge and in Glasgow were beginning to become active in anti-apartheid solidarity campaigns, particularly in the field of education.[33]

The *Manchester Guardian* and *The Observer* under the editorship of David Astor were strongly attuned to the forces of anti-colonialism. Astor was an early backer of the *Africa Bureau*, founded in 1952 by Michael Scott, and developed as a campaigning and research organization by Colin

Legum and Mary Benson, both writers and political émigrés from South Africa with independent links to the labour movement and the ANC respectively. Expatriate students became active in the Committee of African Organizations which played a key role in the boycott movement. A Committee Against Racialism in Sport was formed in 1956. This served as a forerunner of the later sporting boycott.

Christian moralists and activists played a crucial complementary role in the ecumenical world. Prominent here were a triumvirate of 'turbulent priests': Michael Scott, Ambrose Reeves, and, especially, Trevor Huddleston, all of whom had extensive pastoral and political experience of South Africa in the 1950s.[34] The Christian message of suffering and redemption was in some respects an updated version of nineteenth-century evangelicalism, anti-slavery, and missionary-based improvement. Such ideas and sentiments had new resonance among those sections of the British public who felt a sense of guilt and responsibility in respect of Britain's colonial past.

The Treason Trial in South Africa provided an important focus for solidarity work. In 1956 British Defence and Aid was formed by Canon John Collins and others to support the plight of those on trial. Over a quarter of a century, and notwithstanding South African government attempts to subvert it, Defence and Aid (soon to become International Defence and Aid) developed innovative methods to smuggle money into South Africa to provide legal aid and material help to the families of apartheid prisoners. Trevor Huddleston's indictment of apartheid, *Naught for your Comfort* (1956), which told of his experiences in Sophiatown and other urban Johannesburg centres in the 1950s, became an instant classic. It did much to establish the moral foundations of anti-apartheid activism in Britain.

Scandinavia and Holland took a strong anti-apartheid line from the 1950s and backed this up with substantial moral and financial aid to liberation movements. In the case of the Scandinavian countries, public solidarity campaigns supported by the churches and trade unions were closely allied to official action, especially when the Social Democrats were in power. In 1959 Swedish students began to demonstrate against apartheid and in support of black students. Influential individuals formed a Fund for the Victims of Racial Oppression in South Africa.

Per Wästberg, who witnessed the Treason Trial and returned from southern Africa in 1959, wrote passionately about key figures in the liberation movement and forged strong links with the anti-apartheid movement in Britain. Wästberg was also closely associated with the campaigning Swedish South Africa Committee, formed in 1961.[35] Of the approximately £100m that was secretly sent by the International Defence and Aid Fund to support victims of apartheid oppression in the period up till 1990, it is estimated that around half derived directly from the Swedish government, and another 20 per cent came via the UN Trust Fund for Southern Africa. At least 1.7bn Swedish Kronor was donated directly by the Swedish governments to six designated liberation movements in southern Africa.[36] The willingness of Scandinavian countries to offer humanitarian assistance via the liberation movements proved crucial to the ANC in exile, which was otherwise dependent on Soviet bloc countries for military assistance. Sweden was the first industrialized country to recognize the southern African liberation movements. Its diplomatic support was highly valued by the ANC. From 1961 Oliver Tambo made regular visits to Sweden, cultivating close relationships with politicians like Olof Palme as well as activists like David Wirmark and Per Wästberg.

Strijdom and *Baaskap*

In 1954, D. F. Malan resigned as prime minister. He did his utmost to secure the succession for his presumptive heir, Finance Minister Havenga. In the event, Havenga lost out to J. G. Strijdom, the National Party's Transvaal leader. Malan's efforts to deny Strijdom were laced with personal invective, yet there was more to the conflict. Strijdom's unabashed championship of white ascendancy and his thorough commitment to republicanism differed from the more cautious and courteous approach favoured by Malan.

Strijdom's victory was also a clear signal that the power struggle within the governing party, between north and south, had tilted towards the Transvaal. Strijdom revelled in his sobriquet 'Lion of the North', a phrase that reflected both his reputation for toughness as well as the fact that he had been the sole 'purified' National Party member of parliament in the Transvaal after the realignment of politics in 1933–4. Strijdom was not successful, however, as a leader and died of heart disease while in office in 1958. A supportive insider was reported to have said that the Lion of the North had turned out to be an 'emaciated tabby cat'.[37]

The view of Strijdom as a transitional figure between the defining premierships of Malan and Verwoerd belies the reality that white supremacy continued to be entrenched remorselessly. In 1955 the constitutional barrier to the removal of coloureds from the voters' roll was circumvented by an Act that virtually doubled the size of the Senate and thus gave the government the two-thirds majority it required. Disenfranchisement via the Separate Representation of Voters Amendment Act duly took place a year later. The humiliation of coloureds was compounded when segregation was imposed on Cape Town buses and trams in 1956. Internationally, South Africa signalled its contempt for the United Nations by reducing its delegation to token representation in protest against the organization's interference in its 'essentially domestic' racial affairs. This decision was revoked later in the year, reflecting the government's fears of isolation. For all its tough talk, successive South African governments proved attentive to outside criticism.

The Strijdom administration's intention to subordinate and humiliate Africans was revealed in a host of ways. One of the most overt was the long-feared announcement that African women (whose right to live in the cities was already restricted by virtue of a 1952 amendment to the Natives (Urban Areas) Act) would be issued with 'reference books'. The response came in the form of a wave of local protests culminating in a dramatic march by as many as 20,000 women from all parts of the country on 9 August 1956 to the seat of government in Pretoria. The deputation was led by a racially representative quartet—Lilian Ngoyi, Helen Joseph, Rahima Moosa, and Sophie Williams—who presented a petition in silence. Then they chanted 'Wa thint' abafazi, wa thint' imbokodo. Strijdom uzakufa' (You touch the women, you touch the rock. Strijdom you will die). They proceeded to disperse down the elegant terraced gardens of the Union Buildings.[38] Not for the first time, women successfully exploited the structural tension between their symbolic location at the moral core of the family and their marginality from centres of power to great political effect. For all this, within five years nearly four million women carried passes.

The march to Pretoria, organized jointly by the Federation of South African Women (est. 1954) and the ANC Women's League, marked a highpoint in female militancy, which included their prominent participation in the Defiance Campaign and in transport boycotts. Albeit closely allied to the ANC, the Federation was protective of its formal independence and was constituted on a non-racial basis. Its distinctive campaigning style and message, which underlined the honour and prestige of motherhood, were clear statements that the government would be frustrated in its desire to treat blacks as a homogeneous mass. Albeit not feminist in any conventional sense, the militancy displayed by women was also a signal to African men, including leaders of the ANC, that women would not accede to traditional forms of patriarchy. Their rejection of passes as an encroachment on the moral authority of motherhood was thus also directed towards African men. Stereotypes of female weakness were inverted in order to shame pass-bearing men for their loss of masculinity: 'Give us your pants, the women will wear them!' was a popular and provocative cry.

Perhaps the clearest signal of the government's intention to subordinate Africans was the Bantu Education Act of 1953. This measure aimed to bring all educational provision under the control of the state. It effectively meant the end of the independent church and mission school system which, for a century, had successfully schooled a small elite of Africans. Many mission school graduates had gone on to become political leaders. The intention of the Act was to suffocate independent thought and crush the aspirations of the improving elite. Hendrik Verwoerd, who introduced the Act, stated its intentions baldly in the Senate in June 1954:

The Bantu must be guided to serve his own community in all respects. There is no place for him in the European community above the level of certain forms of labour. Within his own community, however, all doors are open. For that reason it is of no avail for him to receive a training which has as its aim absorption in the European community, where he cannot be absorbed. Until now he has been subjected to a school system

55

which drew him away from his own community and misled him by showing him the green pastures of European society in which he was not allowed to graze.[39]

The Bantu Education Act was especially resented by the African middle class, evoking impassioned protests on the part of teachers as well as students and parents. Verwoerd's much quoted justification contained two distinct messages. On the one hand, it suggested that blacks were to be treated as mere units of cheap labour, hence the inappropriateness of teaching academic subjects like mathematics which Africans would not be able to utilize in practice. In the memorable phrase of the Unity Movement intellectual I. B. Tabata, this was 'education for barbarism'.[40] Or, as ANC spokesman Duma Nokwe put it: 'Dr Verwoerd's ideal member of the Bantu Society will be an automaton who will grow the "green pastures" for the Europeans, but who will be blind to the wealth he is creating, insensitive to and dumb about his sufferings, deaf to anything else except the commands of the master.'[41]

On the other hand, Verwoerd's use of terms like 'own community', and 'bantu' (in preference to 'native') were keywords in the developing discourse of expanded ethno-nationalist culturalism. This sought to dignify apartheid with theoretical and moral legitimacy. Bantu education envisaged a system of enforced multi-culturalism in which Africans would be schooled in a manner appropriate to their cultural development. Verwoerd's reference to pastures and grazing thus spoke to both constituencies: it likened Africans to simple docile animals, while also evoking the idea that blacks were naturally tribal and therefore best suited to life in the rural reserves where, in principle, there would be no constraint on their ambitions. Verwoerd's plans for Bantu education were calculated to appeal to the mass of ordinary Africans who remained outside of the education system altogether. Although particular academies— like Adams College in Natal or St Peter's College in Johannesburg—were much prized, the system of schooling for blacks was very limited, acutely short of resources, and in a state of collapse. Thus, much as the provision of inferior education was resented by the relatively privileged, the creation of a mass system of schooling was regarded as a quantitative if not qualitative benefit by those who remained entirely beyond the education system. Teachers' associations were split between those committed to a total boycott and those which felt it was better to continue the struggle 'from within'. In the decade after 1955 the numbers of Africans receiving primary education more than doubled to two million within a decade (though by 1964 only 3 per cent of Africans were in secondary school). This was one reason why campaigns to boycott or subvert the new education system proved shortlived.[42]

That apartheid acted at once to constrain the African elite, while also providing limited opportunities that had not previously existed for the majority, is key to understanding its capacity to ensure compliance. The point is well illustrated in another iconic example of apartheid brutality during the Strijdom premiership: the destruction of Sophiatown and the Western Areas in 1955. Unlike most areas of black urban settlement, Sophiatown was a suburb of Johannesburg where Africans had managed to purchase land by freehold after it was laid out in 1903. By the 1940s it had developed into a culturally vibrant oasis, where ANC leaders like A. B. Xuma and Robert Resha lived alongside musicians and artists such as Hugh Masekela and Gerard Sekoto, as well as writers and journalists like Bloke Modisane and Can Themba. The sharp rhythms of *marabi* music and distinctive chords of 'township jazz' lent African inflexions to American jazz. *Drum* magazine, with its racy mix of photojournalism, glamour, and political reporting, served as Sophiatown's house journal. Informal drinking venues, known as shebeens, where home-brews like *skokiaan* were served, were the pulsating heart of this culturally rich and diverse neighbourhood. To its detractors, Sophiatown was a dangerous slum and symbol of urban disorder where *tsotsis* (hoodlums) and organized gangs like the Berliners, the Americans, and the Russians engaged in widespread criminal behaviour.

The government began a campaign to remove Sophiatown and the other parts of the 'Western Areas' in 1950, referring to these as 'black spots' and 'slums', words redolent of the language of hygiene and cleansing that typified the apartheid's state's vaunted desire for orderly governance and clear racial boundaries. In the centre of the city, blacks living on the top floors of apartments and tall buildings ('locations in the sky') were targeted. So were the 'slumyards' that developed in cramped neighbourhoods below.

The Natives Resettlement Act (1954) provided the legislative basis for the removal of Sophiatown's residents to the newly built township of Meadowlands, whose unlikely name conjured up *faux* pastoral associations. Despite concerted efforts to oppose the removal the government proved intransigent and in February 1955 a military-style operation caught resisters unprepared. Sophiatown (together with Newclare and Martindale) was destroyed by the end of the decade and a total of 60,000–70,000 Africans removed to the South Western Townships (SOWETO). An orderly white working-class suburb was built on the ruins of Sophiatown. It came to be known as *Triomf* (triumph).

The destruction of Sophiatown, like the predominantly coloured area of District Six in Cape Town, left scars that never healed. In both cases a culture of memorialization and sense of loss was all that remained. Yet, for all the protesting leaflets bearing the defiant message 'We shall not move!', the resistance to removals in Sophiatown was neither uniform nor constant. The state prised people out by driving wedges between Africans and coloureds, as well as landlords, tenants, and squatters. For the latter, the acquisition of matchbox brick houses and waterborne sewerage represented a material gain, whatever the ensuing loss of freedom and community.

Forced removals from Sophiatown and District Six, as well as from Cato Manor in Durban, are amongst the best-known instances of the application of the Group Areas Act. They took place in large metropolitan areas, aroused popular resistance, and have duly been immortalized in countless memoirs and histories. These iconic examples of urban ethnic cleansing were all the more poignant because their cosmopolitan composition was anathema to apartheid's insistence on managed social and spatial order.

It is well to remember, however, that the operation of the 'Group' took place throughout the country, in small towns as well as cities, often well beyond the purview of newspapers and political activists. In small towns like Kroonstad, as Isabella Kentridge observes, non-white areas could be more 'mixed' than larger conurbations, partly because the operation of urban segregation had previously been in the hands of town councils lacking in resources and political will. Under apartheid, however, no urban area remained immune from the operation of the

'Group' as bureaucrats set to work to fillet out coloureds, Indians, and Africans in the 'non-white' sections of town and created spatial buffer zones between them.[43]

The effects of such removals for individuals, families, and communities were profound and trans-generational in their impact. From the government's perspective, the rigorous application of spatial apartheid succeeded in its primary objective of dividing communities according to presumed racial and cultural hierarchies. The fact that there were gainers as well as losers from the process (better houses and amenities were often on offer) was frequently divisive, since relative deprivation encouraged people to focus on tangible benefits rather than the larger picture of overall racial rule. In subsequent years this made generalized resistance to apartheid domination all the more difficult to mount.

The rigorous enforcement of pass laws, imposition of Bantu Education, application of the Group Areas Act, and flagrant manipulation of the constitution, exemplify the way in which *baaskap*, bureaucracy, and doctrinal apartheid were interwoven and mutually reinforcing. This was also demonstrated by the 1956 Industrial Conciliation Act which went so far as to deny Africans the status of 'employee', a measure that dealt a major blow to trade union rights and precluded the potential for non-racial labour unity. The denial of basic rights was extended through a welter of security legislation and array of punishments reserved for use against non-compliant subjects.[44]

Verwoerd and Eiselen at Native Affairs

Prior to Verwoerd's unexpected move to Native Affairs in 1950, the Department was a political backwater with low visibility and lacking in prestige. E. G. Jansen, appointed Minister of Native Affairs in 1948 on the basis of his prior experience in the post under Prime Minister Hertzog (1929–33), carried on in much the fashion of the segregationist era: he presided over a relatively decentralized administration, the senior ranks of which were largely English-speaking, and whose officers regarded 'native administration' as something of a vocation to be practised with tact as a specialist art. In respect of labour, the Department of Native Affairs was reluctant to help farmers competing against mines and industry if this meant intervening in the market to subsidize them. Jansen was immediately perceived as ineffectual by a rising group of *Broederbond*-affiliated experts on the 'native question' who sought decisive action and an end to liberal muddling. He was duly relieved of his position and offered the governor-generalship in 1950.

From the start Verwoerd imposed a new regime in Native Administration, transforming the Department into a highly centralized bureaucracy and imparting a firm sense of direction. Scientific management and technical planning were all key aspects of his authoritarian statism. In this sense he was more the master-builder of apartheid than its architect. The top tier of English-speaking administrators was soon passed over or eased out of positions of influence. Afrikaans became the preferred language of communication.

Verwoerd's Secretary of Native Affairs, Werner Eiselen, did much of the foundational thinking. Like Verwoerd, he had worked as a professor at Stellenbosch University. Born into a Berlin missionary family based in the northern Transvaal, Eiselen trained as an academic anthropologist. The vaunting vision of 'positive' apartheid was, to a significant extent, his own. Eiselen sought to restore African culture to an idealized 'tribal' state. Separate education was the chosen instrument to achieve this. Eiselen's conception of apartheid as the fulfilment of ethnic destiny by way of separate development was often in advance of Verwoerd's. Together, Eiselen and Verwoerd used the Native Affairs Department to fashion the idea of apartheid into practical existence. In so doing, the outlying province of native administration acquired enormous powers and expanded rapidly until it became a veritable 'state within the state'. Douglas Smit, a former secretary of native affairs, was barely exaggerating when he described Verwoerd in 1953 as 'a Napoleon in Native Affairs who was trying to set up a great Black empire under his supreme dictatorship'.[45]

The Native Affairs Department had long been oriented towards the rural areas and the reserves, practising forms of indirect rule geared to the maintenance of the tribal system. From the mid-1930s schemes were introduced in the African reserves so as to improve agricultural productivity and combat environmental degradation. Under the policies of 'reclamation' or 'betterment', experts pressed the need for stock-dipping and cattle-culling as well as fencing and contour terracing. More often than not, policies were not executed. As in other parts of colonial settler Africa, conservationist ideas were often strenuously resisted by Africans as an unwelcome interference with livelihoods and ways of life. In the post-1945 period, environmental and social policies of betterment increasingly focused on the economic viability of the African reserves, including the question of labour supply to urban areas. This more comprehensive approach necessitated distinguishing between peasant cultivators and migrant wage-labourers. Concentration of human settlement implied removing access to land for some people. With the advent of apartheid, rural development in the homelands became tied ever more closely to the separate political future of these territories, as the 1955 Tomlinson Commission fully recognized.[46]

In the urban areas, the presence of the Native Affairs Department also became more conspicuous from the 1930s. Here, its narrow jurisdiction overlapped with municipal authorities and other government agencies in respect of labour, housing, and welfare and the administration of justice. The consequences of this unsystematic approach were clearly apparent by the 1940s. The main concern of the Native Affairs Department in the 1950s therefore lay in gaining control of the urban areas and in responding to the perceived threats of *oorstrooming*.

The Native Affairs Department's increasing intervention in the rural reserves reflected conceptions of the reciprocal relationship between rural development and urban planning.[47] Managing the flow of labour from rural to urban areas was key to imposing apartheid as a coherent system. If the South African economy is imagined as a traditional egg-timer with two bulbous parts at each end (the rural reserves and the urban areas), labour would have to flow through the narrow aperture connecting the two. This was precisely where the blockages in the system proved most acute. Control over the movement of labour was the weakest element in the pre-1948 system of segregation. It also proved to be the single most intractable aspect of grand apartheid, particularly as increasingly coercive mechanisms were introduced to retard or reverse the process of urbanization.

Verwoerd, the apostle of centralized planning, moved swiftly to integrate all aspects of labour and urban policy under his charge. The

Native Laws Amendment Act (1952) revised a raft of already existing legislation affecting Africans in urban areas. This umbrella Act now afforded state officials extensive powers of arrest in the case of Africans deemed to be idle or disorderly. It made provision for the creation of labour bureaux which Africans seeking employment would have to register with. Section 10(1) made it illegal for Africans to be in 'proclaimed' towns and cities for longer than 72 hours unless they were born in the area, had lived there continuously for 15 years, or had worked for the same employer for ten years. Residency rights could be lost if, during this time, an individual had fallen foul of the law. The Natives (Abolition of Passes and Coordination of Documents) Act of 1952 created the hated 'reference books' which all Africans of 16 and over had to carry and produce on demand.

These measures formed key planks in the armoury of 'influx control' measures by which the state sought to regulate the labour market and limit Africans' rights to live in cities and towns, in effect creating a division between urban 'insiders' and rural 'outsiders'. To be sure, such legislation had precursors in the segregationist era, namely the pass laws and the 1923 Urban Areas Act which promised to prevent Africans from residing in towns unless required to 'minister to the needs of the white man'. But segregationist-era legislation was unevenly enforced and had increasingly fallen into abeyance, often with the tacit approval of the Smuts government. Apartheid aimed to reverse the lackadaisical implementation of racial segregation.

What was novel in the Verwoerdian scheme was the attempt to intervene in the labour market at source so as to regulate the flow of labour from rural areas to cities. In order to accomplish this, a vast tiered network of labour bureaux was developed which forced Africans to register their availability for employment. The system was designed to perpetuate migrant labour and restrict urbanization by processing applicants in the rural areas. Labour bureaux were intended to allocate labour to various sectors of the economy, often in defiance of market forces.

From the 1950s it became illegal for any employer to engage an African worker who was not officially registered at an official labour bureau office. By these means it was hoped that systematic planning, overseen by an omniscient bureaucracy, would control urbanization in a rational and orderly fashion. The notion of a labour contract as something freely entered into by two parties was thereby fundamentally altered. In all, these innovations amounted to a degree of demographic dirigisme that had never before been attempted. Yet by the end of the decade it was becoming apparent that the labour bureaux system was failing to achieve its objectives. 'Employers and work seekers alike simply flouted the rules and made their own arrangements.'[48]

The key to Verwoerd's effort to integrate urban and rural initiatives, and to exercise unprecedented powers over the individual person, was a 'reference book', known colloquially by Africans as the *dompas* (idiot book). This would link data concerning an individual's birth, race, residency, tribe, tax status, and employment status. The 1950 Population Registration Act made this theoretically possible. By the mid-1960s a universal archive of some 10m fingerprint records and photographs was maintained in the Central Reference Bureau or *Bewysburo* (Bureau of Proof).

This ambitious device constituted the heart of Verwoerd's ambitious 'biometric state', which was perhaps unequalled in scope by any country in the world at this time.[49] Large-scale computerization began in 1966. The major constraint to the successful issuing of reference books was not so much political resistance by Africans to registration as the near impossibility of marshalling the bureaucracy and managing the technology to complete the process in the eighteen months allowed for by Verwoerd. By 1960, when pass-burning protests by Africans eventuated in the Sharpeville Massacre, the hopelessly clogged machinery of the Central Reference Bureau was probably less able to issue useful intelligence about its subjects than the earlier systems it replaced.[50]

Self-Governing Bantu Homelands

Within nationalist policy-making and political circles there was from the start a view that apartheid had to be presented as a morally defensible system which would be of advantage to all. This could only be sustained by insisting that the losses incurred by Africans in white urban areas would be made up by greater opportunities in the reserves. Christian-National theory, *volks* nationalism, and cultural relativist ideas drawn from anthropological theory, all provided justification for the idea that cultures were unique systems that merited special treatment or protection. It followed that ethnic and national units should be accorded their own separate channels of expression and, perhaps, even a measure of political recognition.

This was the premise of the 1951 Bantu Authorities Act which provided for the creation of 'tribal authorities' in rural African reserves. It gave the government extensive powers to proclaim chiefs and councillors, regardless of whether they enjoyed popular legitimacy. Elements of direct and indirect rule were thereby built into a system of governance which, although centralized in Pretoria, was devolved to rural authorities at a local level. Although not apparent at the time, the Act laid the basis of the future Bantustans, notionally self-governing 'tribal' states whose emergence represented the apogee of the apartheid fantasy. The 1951 Act was bitterly opposed by Africans who rejected government-sponsored 'retribalization', viewing this as a further erosion of their residual citizenship rights. Yet, in dispensing power and patronage to favoured proxies, the legislation had the potential to attract some degree of support.

Some of this had been foreshadowed by Verwoerd in his major 1948 speech to the senate on the meaning of 'apartheid'. Here, Verwoerd's assertion that South Africa was a 'white man's country and that he must remain master here' was offset by the vague assurance that in the reserves 'we are prepared to allow the Natives to be the masters'.[51] This concession contained not even a hint of eventual independence for the Bantustans; it was introduced merely as a defence against accusations that apartheid was solely about oppression. Total segregation might be fine in principle but it was not practicable. At this point, Verwoerd's main contribution to the explication of apartheid lay in his ability to present existing government pronouncements in a manner that suggested overall coherence.

We should not be surprised by the absence of original ideas in Verwoerd's inaugural speech on apartheid. His intervention into public affairs in the mid-1930s was on the poor white question, a matter in which the Stellenbosch university professor of sociology and psychology could claim some expertise. As editor of *Die Transvaler*, the leading source of nationalist opinion in the north, Verwoerd was preoccupied by the campaign for republican independence. This commitment he shared with his close political ally in the Transvaal, J. G. Strijdom, who saw the solution of the colour problem as a precondition for the attainment of a republic. It was only as Minister of Native Affairs that Verwoerd began to make apartheid his own. Apartheid was thus in no sense Verwoerd's invention, however much it was his creation. The logic of planning and the ideology of apartheid became mutually reinforcing under his dominant style of leadership.

A less contentious but highly significant dimension of the 1951 Bantu Authorities Act was the abolition of the Natives Representative Council, established under the segregationist legislation of 1936. The demise of the Representative Council was mostly unlamented—it was famously denounced in 1946 by councillor Paul Mosaka as a 'toy telephone'. Nevertheless, to do away with the Council was more than a confirmation of its obsolescence. In his final message to the Council, Verwoerd stated baldly that it was useless for the Bantu people to become engaged in 'general principles of higher politics'.[52] Henceforth, Africans would have to express their political ambitions through the tribal or ethnic devices envisaged by the Bantu Authorities legislation. The Transkei *Bunga*, a long-established forum which allowed for some political engagement between rural notables and government authorities, voted itself out of existence in 1955. It was replaced by the more compliant tribally based Transkei Territorial Authority.

To the intellectuals grouped in the South African Bureau of Racial Affairs (SABRA), the Stellenbosch University based think-tank inspired by the *Broederbond*, apartheid could only be made to work as a coherent and just system if Africans could be able to live full lives in the native reserves, the deep countryside allocated for communal African use. This entailed dispensing altogether with black labour in white areas and developing the economic capacity of those rural areas set aside for Africans. Partial segregation, the purist SABRA intellectuals insisted, was morally fraudulent and politically short-sighted because it would inevitably lead to integration.

Over the first decade of apartheid, SABRA worked energetically to promote the idea of 'vertical' rather than 'horizontal' apartheid: the former envisaged total separation but erected no barriers to advancement within racially (or culturally) defined polities; the latter was characteristic of old-style segregation in that it set racially defined limits to social advancement in a society that was effectively mixed. For SABRA idealists, like Nic Olivier, it was essential to increase expenditure on the reserves so as to make them economically self-sufficient. Considerable sacrifices would have to be made by whites, for only by extending the area of the reserves and dispensing with black labour could apartheid be made workable.

Many SABRA intellectuals welcomed the Bantu Authorities Act as a step in the direction of positive apartheid. But the government proved loath to purchase the land required to extend the reserves under the terms of the 1936 segregationist legislation, fearing a backlash from white farmers who neither wanted their land expropriated nor wished to live alongside African farmers without access to their labour. Verwoerd moved to damp down the SABRA vision of total segregation, making clear in 1955 that it was not the government's intention in the foreseeable future to remove Africans from white areas or to dispense with their labour. His urban housing programme was precisely intended to satisfy the economic demands of industry and suggested that an African presence in the cities was permanent.

In 1955 the findings of the Tomlinson Commission, established to investigate the rehabilitation of the reserves, became public. This large-scale investigation, which had been formed in 1950 with the active support of SABRA, concluded that £105m of government money would be required to create a fully diversified economy in the reserves. The ambitious scheme entailed separating farmers from non-farmers and promoting industrialization.[53] Verwoerd rejected the Tomlinson recommendations and set about whittling them down. Likewise, Eiselen cautioned that the tempo of development envisaged by Tomlinson was too rapid. There were rising tensions between SABRA idealists on the one hand and National Party pragmatists, as well as outright supremacists, on the other. Conflict was exacerbated when some SABRA members openly rejected the removal of coloureds from the common voters' roll, arguing that coloureds were integrally part of white—and indeed Afrikaner—society. Disagreement between SABRA intellectuals and the National Party intensified and reached breaking point by the end of the decade. Verwoerd resigned his membership of SABRA and in 1961 a SABRA faction loyal to him was able to purge the organization of its outspoken moral idealists, some of whom later emerged as liberal critics of the government.

This episode has correctly been interpreted as a corrective to the once common view that Verwoerd was the author of the apartheid masterplan—he is indeed better seen as its chief architect or engineer. It also serves as a reminder that the competing and conflicting views evident at the time of the Sauer Report had not been resolved a decade later. The key question as to whether white South Africa ought to dispense with black labour and institute total apartheid remained. Supporters of outright white domination were wholly disinclined to pump resources into the reserves, whereas ideological purists believed that apartheid could be developed as a morally legitimate political solution to the problem of colour, adding that this was ultimately the best guarantee of white survival.

Verwoerd himself proved inconsistent. He ruled Tomlinson out on the grounds of expense in the mid-1950s—rejecting in particular the £30m envisaged for industrial development—but was nevertheless prepared to pour considerable resources into the creation of Bantustans as proto-states from the early 1960s through mechanisms such as the Bantu Investment Corporation. The policy of industrial decentralization, which encouraged firms to locate on the white side of the borders adjoining the homelands, was an expensive and wasteful policy that was largely driven by political and ideological concerns.

While Verwoerd revelled in his role as apartheid's major ideologue, his approach was often characterized by political calculation and expedience. This is not necessarily contradictory: successful conviction politicians invariably have to show flexibility and pragmatism in order to achieve their ends. The fact that Verwoerd's ideological fervour was balanced by pragmatism is not therefore so remarkable. What does stand out in Verwoerd's character is his total belief in his own rectitude, his implacable need to retain absolute control over his party, and his refusal to brook any challenges to his growing authority.

An important dimension of Verwoerd's charismatic leadership was the manner in which he used the force of intellectual logic, rather than emotion, to outwit opponents and, in the process, demonstrate that Afrikaners were fully the equal of English-speakers. This was amply shown in his confrontation with Macmillan over the 'Wind of Change' address in 1960.[54] Achieving parity with white English-speakers in social and political terms was what initially brought Verwoerd into politics, which is why republicanism was so vital to his ambitions; the apartheid mantra was initially conceived as a means to achieve such Afrikaner parity (or mastery), though it increasingly became identified with white supremacy as a whole. The more grandiose aspects of apartheid had much to do with Verwoerd's personal ambition and the way in which he used his position in the Native Affairs Department to carve out a personal political empire. To this extent, apartheid was as much the making of Verwoerd as it was his personal making.

Congress of the People, 1955

Whereas Afrikaner nationalism was founded in opposition to British imperialism, it came of political age as the defender of white supremacy against African nationalism. Yet apartheid's ideologues found it difficult to recognize modern African nationalism at all because to do so was to admit Africans' existence as self-motivated political citizens. It was far easier to portray African nationalism as a cipher for other malign forces conspiring within and outside the country's borders; above all, liberalism and Communism. The mirror image of this fear of the alien philosophies of liberalism and Communism can be seen in the pattern of anti-apartheid resistance where the presence of non-Africans in nationalist politics frequently proved divisive. Whereas Africanists within the ANC Youth League like Mandela, Sisulu, and Tambo came to value cooperation with non-Africans through the struggles of the early 1950s, others like A. P. Mda, Potlako Leballo, and Josias Madzunya remained deeply suspicious of white and Indian interference. They were able to tap into a deep well of popular thinking that viewed freedom as synonymous with African leadership.

The highpoint of multi-racial opposition to apartheid came in 1955 when the African National Congress and its partners, the Indian Congress, Coloured People's Organization, and the Congress of Democrats (largely composed of white members of the outlawed Communist Party), met at Kliptown outside Johannesburg to agree the Freedom Charter. Nearly 3,000 delegates attended the event, overcoming police harassment and logistical obstacles in an exuberant show of unity. The ANC was effectively confirmed as first among equals within a movement structured as an alliance of interest groups (trade unionists and women) and peoples (African, coloured, Indian, and white). Strikingly, every constituent organization bore the name 'South African' in its title, thereby reinforcing the idea that the Congress movement's goal was a unitary state in which 'national' and 'cultural' differences would be accorded recognition so long as this did not jeopardize the achievement of a common or supra-South African nationality. Africanists resented the formal inclusion of whites, coloureds, and Indians. Some left-wing critics of the Congress objected that the structured multi-racialism of the Congress of the People mirrored the official racial categories of the apartheid state.

The culminating moment of the Congress of the People was the adoption of the Freedom Charter. This replaced the ANC's *Africans' Claims* and its 'Bill of Rights' as a founding manifesto of democratic aspiration. It continued to serve as such for forty years until it was formalized and superseded by the post-1994 constitution. Amongst the liberal-democratic principles proclaimed by the Freedom Charter were the right of the people to govern; freedoms regardless of race, colour, or sex; equality before the law; and equal access to education, housing, and medical care.

More controversial were two studiedly ambiguous provisions: the opening statement which declared that 'South Africa belongs to all who live in it, black and white', and the provision to transfer into common ownership the country's mineral wealth, banks, and monopoly industries. The Africanist element within the ANC strongly resented the implication that Africans did not have prior if not superior rights to the country; on the issue of economic nationalization, liberals and anti-communists wondered whether the nationalization clause, inserted at the last minute by Congress of Democrats' representative Ben Turok, amounted to a covert manifesto for Communism. Although the Freedom Charter was said to have been produced by 'the people' in a democratic process of soundings and submissions, critics alleged that its formulation was controlled and manipulated by a group of white left-wingers in the Congress of Democrats. It is now generally accepted that Springbok Legion and Communist Party intellectual Lionel 'Rusty' Bernstein was the guiding hand in the formulation of the Freedom Charter.[55]

Treason Trial

The state was sufficiently alarmed by the revolutionary potential of the Freedom Charter to institute a coordinated crackdown on extra-parliamentary organizations. In 1956, 156 leading activists representing nearly fifty bodies broadly associated with the Congress of the People were arrested in dawn raids and charged with 'high treason'. As defence lawyer George Bizos has drily observed, 'South Africa has had more than its fair share of treason trials.'[56] (Only thirteen years before, Nazi sympathizer Robey Liebbrandt had been convicted for conspiring to overthrow the wartime Smuts government, and there were more treason trials to come in the 1980s.) This feature of its legal culture is both an indication of the country's fundamentally divided character as well as its peculiar reliance on law and the judiciary.

In this, the most high-profile treason trial to date, the state alleged a countrywide conspiracy to use violence to overthrow the government and replace it with a Communist state. The accused included ANC president Albert Luthuli, Nelson Mandela and Walter Sisulu, Indian Congress leaders Yusuf Dadoo and Ahmed Kathrada, Helen Joseph and Lilian Ngoyi of the Federation of South African Women, and Communists Joe Slovo, Ruth First, and 'Rusty' Bernstein. It was a racially mixed and ideologically diverse convocation. In bringing so many leaders from different organizations together from all over the country in a single venue (and allowing them to be released on bail) the state unwittingly provided an occasion for the Congress Alliance to confer and cement relationships. Luthuli, whose moral authority and statesmanship shone through during the trial, remarked wryly: 'I doubt whether we could have devised so effective a method of ensuring cohesion in resistance and of enlarging its embrace, as did the government when it set the Trial in motion. We of the Congresses did not waste the opportunity given.'[57] This was the moment when the nationalist struggle became genuinely national.

The Treason Trial dragged on until 1961 and eventually resulted in the acquittal of all defendants (most of whom had had their cases dismissed by this time). Under close questioning the state's leading witness, a supposed expert academic on Communism, was forced to admit that the Freedom Charter was a response to white supremacy rather than a revolutionary document. No act of violence was alleged to have been committed. At issue were the ideas and hopes embodied in the Freedom Charter and the intentions of the individuals involved to put these into practice. Justice Rumpff eventually ruled that the prosecution had failed to prove that the ANC advocated violence or that it had become a Communist organization.

This was not a 'show trial' with a preordained outcome and scripted confessions. Sufficient legal protections remained within the judiciary to ensure due process. Defendants did not complain of torture or abuse. The defence brilliantly exposed contradictions in the overly complex prosecution case and argued that the Freedom Charter represented a vision of the future rather than an incitement to overthrow the state (such motivation was crucial to the definition of 'treason'). In the context of apartheid South Africa, the defence insisted, serious disaffection was to be expected. The liberation movement was able to use the trial to advantage by propounding its own ideals. Defendants skilfully used the courtroom to publicize the anti-apartheid message in South Africa and abroad, and the world took notice.

Several eminent international legal figures observed the proceedings and the overseas press gave extensive publicity to the trial. By charging the defendants with 'treason' the prosecution was effectively claiming that the apartheid government was identical with the state; supporters of the accused argued to the contrary that the apartheid government was merely a political regime and that the only real opposition in the country was now extra-parliamentary.

Although the state lost its case, the Congress Alliance could not claim victory. The drawn-out proceedings disrupted the momentum of popular struggle, creating a serious power vacuum within the ANC. Public shows of unity were dispelled by allegations of financial irregularities, dissent, and criticisms in respect of an absence of internal democracy. Africanists within the ANC used the interregnum to reassert the radical nationalist agenda set out by Anton Lembede and A. P. Mda in the 1940s, arguing that the ANC's 1949 Programme of Action had been subverted by multi-racialism.[58] These schisms could not be contained, and in 1959 a group led by Robert Sobukwe and Potlako Leballo split away from the ANC to form the Pan-Africanist Congress.

The popular energy released by the Congress of the People dissipated as the Treason Trial dragged on. On 21 March 1960, while Albert Luthuli was in the witness box adumbrating the ANC's commitment to non-violence, news filtered in of a massacre at Sharpeville. A state of emergency was declared and many of the Treason Trialists were arrested in police swoops. By the conclusion of the Trial the ANC and PAC were already outlawed. As the ANC secretary-general Duma Nokwe drily remarked to co-accused Helen Joseph, 'This trial is out of date.'[59]

The era of the Treason Trial marked the end of legitimate mass resistance in South Africa and with it a particular style of politics based on mass action and non-violent civil disobedience—in many aspects more like the contemporaneous civil rights movement in the United States than anti-colonial struggles in other parts of Africa. The government concluded that its draconian security legislation was inadequate and that the formal legal process was an encumbrance to its grip on power; many of those opposed to apartheid were reluctantly coming to the realization that peaceful protest and popular mobilization alone could not overthrow apartheid.

Crucially, the Treason Trial helped to dramatize apartheid to the outside world and so helped to prime the international community to appreciate the enormity of Sharpeville. The International Commission of Jurists objected to the way in which the charges had been drawn up.[60] Scandinavian countries showed concern. Louis Blom-Cooper, who attended the Treason Trial as one of two British observers, wrote in 1959 that 'Not since the burning of the Reichstag in Berlin in 1933—with the notable exception of the special trials at Nuremberg—has a trial attracted such international attention as the Treason Trial in the Union of South Africa.'[61] The Dean of the Harvard Law School, reviewing the trial, concluded with the statement: 'The free world cannot be unconcerned when there is a land where eighty per cent of the people are unfree.'[62]

As well as marking the closure of open mass resistance to apartheid, the Treason Trial brought a new generation of political figures to national and international attention. These were the men and women who came to prominence through the Defiance Campaign, the 1956 march to Pretoria, and the Congress of the People. This was a remarkable achievement in a country where politics was largely understood as white politics and parliament was still regarded as the arbiter of public debate.

In the *Handbook of Race Relations*, published by the Institute of Race Relations just after the 1948 Nationalist victory, a chapter on 'Politics' begins with the assertion that the 'non-European' people of South Africa 'play a very minor role in the political life of the country' and that no single organization had yet emerged entitling it to speak for blacks as a whole.[63] A decade later such a statement would be repudiated by many observers. The ANC and the Congress Alliance had clearly succeeded in establishing a major presence in South African politics—which the challenge represented by the PAC from 1959 to primacy in the liberation movement did nothing to weaken. ANC membership, perhaps 5,000 in 1948, grew rapidly to more than 100,000 by the end of the 1950s. Even pro-apartheid intellectuals in SABRA found their way to private discussions with ANC leaders like Luthuli, notwithstanding Verwoerd's explicit disapproval.[64] It took another quarter of a century for Afrikaner intellectuals with links to the government to repeat this exercise with the ANC.

CHAPTER 3
SHARPEVILLE AND ITS AFTERMATH

Sharpeville and Langa

The year 1960 was one of seismic upheaval in South Africa. It began with the death of 437 men (all but six of them black) in a pit collapse at Coalbrook colliery south of Johannesburg, on 21 January, brought about by flagrant disregard of engineering safety in pursuit of profit. On 21 March, police fired more than 1,000 rounds of ammunition at a crowd in the black township of Sharpeville which had gathered round a low wire fence at the local police station to protest against the pass laws. Sixty-nine people were killed, many of whom were shot while running away, and approximately 180 casualties were recorded.

Nothing links these two events other than their close geographical and temporal proximity—and a sense that both were to a significant extent structurally created accidents, products of systemic failure in a society that placed little value on ordinary human life. The Coalbrook disaster has long been forgotten; by contrast, the Sharpeville Massacre, which soon eclipsed interest in the Coalbrook catastrophe, continues to resonate in historic memory as an iconic symbol of apartheid intransigence and cruelty—and of popular resistance to oppression.[1]

On 3 February, Harold Macmillan, the British prime minister, delivered a much heralded speech to both houses of the South African parliament in which he momentarily shocked white South Africa by warning that a 'wind of change is blowing through the continent'. A new African national consciousness, he explained, was evident in many different places and this political consciousness had to be accepted as

74

'a political fact'. The impact of the speech on white South Africa was rather less momentous than many British historians choose to remember. Macmillan made no direct reference to apartheid and his deputation did not make contact with the ANC or other opposition movements. Nor did he want to risk profitable ties or security links with white South Africa. His chief message was that Britain would no longer stand behind white minority regimes in Africa or impede decolonization. A visibly angry Verwoerd responded that white South Africans, while describing themselves as 'Europeans', were rooted in the continent and had 'nowhere else to go'. They were responsible for bringing civilization to Africa and they remained the link between Africa and the West. In an allusion to the policy of separate development, Verwoerd assured Macmillan that blacks would be given rights in those parts of the country which their forefathers had settled, adding that it was 'the white man who has made all this possible'.[2] The South African prime minister's spontaneous and articulate response to Macmillan's polished address made for a moment of political theatre; even Verwoerd's critics acknowledged that it was a performance of formidable power.[3]

While the reverberations of the Macmillan–Verwoerd dialogue were still being felt in white political circles, Sharpeville erupted. The immediate cause was a call by the newly created Pan Africanist Congress for a nationwide campaign against the pass laws in conjunction with a stayaway from work. The campaign, which had been timed to pre-empt a similar campaign on the part of the ANC, was poorly planned. In trying to seize the political initiative the breakaway movement sought to demonstrate its readiness for action and its preparedness to confront the apartheid state directly.

Whereas the ANC's Defiance Campaign had been carefully orchestrated to avoid violence and stressed discipline and restraint, the PAC was inclined to allow popular anger to be vented. Its strategy was to march to police stations across the country without passes and demand arrest in the hope that the state's penal system would be overwhelmed. Passes affected all Africans living in urban areas and epitomized white supremacy and racial domination in the starkest manner. They were resented no less by the ANC, which was already planning its own campaign. Yet there was an added edge of direct confrontation in the

PAC's adoption of the uncompromising slogan 'No Bail! No Defence! No Fine!' Outright resistance to passes was especially conducive to mass mobilization on the part of Africanist militants who dared to believe they could sweep the apartheid system away. The PAC's leader, Robert Sobukwe, counselled caution and reiterated the principles of 'absolute non-violence'. But the PAC's 'task teams' had little compunction about stirring up the crowd and mobilizing young urban thugs or *tsotsis*.

Despite evidence of rising tensions in the days leading up to the event, there was no suggestion that Sharpeville was on the verge of an explosion. Sharpeville was a relatively small, typically bleak 'model' black township, built in the 1940s to house Africans who had been relocated from the neighbouring 'white' city of Vereeniging. It was known more for football and jazz than politics. Although the PAC established a relatively strong presence in Sharpeville there were probably no more than 300 paid-up members just before the slaughter. Violence might just as easily have met anti-pass protestors in nearby Evaton or in Orlando (Soweto) where the PAC had its stronghold. There is no reason to believe that the police intended to shoot at the crowd of around 5,000 and much more to suggest that officers panicked. No order to shoot was ever issued.

There is probably more to be learned about the psychopathology of race by studying the consequences of the shootings than by attempting to account for its origins. As well as failing to administer adequate medical treatment to the wounded, there is evidence that police officers treated the dead and the dying with a contempt born of fear, prejudice, and hatred. This was expressed with particular ferocity towards women who had earlier taunted the police by lifting their dresses and jeering. Some of the policemen may have regarded shooting as an exemplary act of collective punishment. African policemen were alleged to have prodded or killed the wounded with assegais, knobkerries, and rods of sharpened steel. Tensions heightened by a convergence of animosity along lines of race and sex were part of the intimate politics of killing. Dehumanization, abetted by assumptions of racial superiority, created a disembodied sense of distance that allowed ordinary men to take aim against fellow human beings.

In many standard accounts of modern South African history, the fact that black policemen made up nearly half of the force of 294 deployed at

Sharpeville is apt to be overlooked. Their presence in such strength (black police constituted roughly half of the national force by 1955) serves as an important reminder that the apartheid state sought actively to divide communities against themselves and always depended on the recruitment and collusion of collaborators. Most insidious were the black agents or 'askaris' who were recruited to infiltrate the liberation movements.[4]

Even as the shock waves of Sharpeville spread through South Africa and round the world, Langa and Nyanga townships in Cape Town erupted. In the western Cape, Africans constituted only a small proportion of the 'non-white' population. The government's desire to preserve this region as a coloured 'labour preference' area meant that Africans already resident there were all the more determined to resist the pass laws. The PAC established itself amongst migrant workers in the townships of Cape Town under the leadership of a young student from the Transvaal, Philip Kgosana, and with the active assistance of members of the Liberal Party who shared the Africanists' hostility to Communism (and were inclined to overlook their racialism). Speaking in Cape Town in February 1960, Robert Sobukwe assured his audience that 'in the new Africa we are going to, there will be no Indians and no Europeans, but we will all be Africans'. Amongst ordinary migrant workers the tone of agitation was more racially polarized, assertive, and militant.[5]

The demonstrations that began in Langa and Nyanga on 21 April gathered momentum as news of the slaughter at Sharpeville filtered through. Anger was vented by stone-throwers along with threats to 'kill the white men'. Several unarmed protesters were shot dead in Langa that night. Ten days of unrest and strikes could not be contained by the police. PAC Task Force teams operated as paramilitary gangs and clashed with police. The pass laws were temporarily suspended. Buoyed by this unprecedented concession, and infuriated by further police raids in Langa, 30,000 silent protesters, largely unorganized, marched peacefully and in silence to the centre of the city on 31 March. They gathered on the historic Grand Parade opposite the police station—a more prudent move than the original plan of marching on parliament. Liberal politician Helen Suzman reflected on the confusion and panic in government circles at this time. 'I don't see how they will ever reinstate the old order.'[6]

77

The police offered Kgosana a meeting with the Minister of Justice on the understanding that the young leader would disperse the demonstrators. There were rumours (never verified) that Kgosana was betrayed by Liberal advisers who persuaded him to agree to this plan. Whatever the truth, Kgosana accepted the compromise in order to avoid the likelihood of lives being lost—and thereby lost the initiative.[7] After dispersing the crowds in central Cape Town, Kgosana returned for his promised meeting with the minister. But he never saw the Justice Minister and, instead, was arrested. A police and military cordon was thrown around the townships of Langa and Nyanga. Large-scale arrests were made and considerable violence was meted out on strikers and detainees. Newspaper reports spoke of indiscriminate brutal beatings by police wielding *sjambok* whips. By 11 April the three-week disturbance was over and active resistance in the urban areas decisively quelled.

Rural Revolts

Events in the rural areas provide a counterpoint to the Sharpeville/Langa conflagration. In pockets of the African countryside simmering discontent continued, just as it had done through much of the 1950s. Throughout the decade, the state's efforts to impose apartheid governance in the rural areas gave rise to a series of fierce localized struggles. The Bantu Authorities system (sarcastically referred to as 'uzifozonke'—'cure all ills') was a particular focus of resentment, especially when this entailed the replacement of chiefs who enjoyed popular legitimacy by pliant government nominees. The extension of rural taxation, a key aspect of the system, was another major burden. Also unpopular were government efforts to promote land 'reclamation' or 'rehabilitation' in an attempt to promote soil conservation and agricultural productivity. Such measures involved schemes like cattle-culling, compulsory dipping, and fencing, interventions which vulnerable farmers regarded with deep suspicion, fearing that their already marginal status would be further undermined.

In 1950, a rebellion broke out in the heavily overcrowded Witzieshoek reserve in the Orange Free State. This was directed by migrant workers (some of whom had imbibed radical nationalist and socialist ideas) against a paramount chief accused of imposing cattle-culling measures on behalf of the state. In the western Transvaal town of Zeerust, in 1957, women resisting the imposition of pass laws helped to foment a revolt against a tribal chief, Albert Gopane, who was reviled as a government collaborator. In Sekhukuneland, a bastion of resistance to colonial rule in the nineteenth century, a movement of migrant workers with ANC and Communist Party sympathies known as *Sebatakgomo* rose in revolt after the deportation of a popular chief in 1958 and an incident in which police opened fire on a village crowd.[8] Following riots in the Durban township of Cato Manor, where several policemen lost their lives after women stormed the local beer hall in protest at the municipal monopoly, there were sporadic disturbances in rural Natal and Zululand against agricultural 'betterment'. These included the destruction of dipping tanks, crop-burnings, and militant protests by stick-wielding women. The ANC neither expected nor fully understood the anger of women, whose primary motivation was defence of their livelihoods.[9]

The most extensive, sustained, and well-organized rural revolt took place in Pondoland and neighbouring Tembuland in the eastern Cape between 1960 and 1963. Here, too, resistance to agricultural betterment policies featured strongly. The crisis was prompted by the leadership of Botha Sigcau, a non-hereditary chief appointed to head the Transkei Territorial Authority, who was widely regarded as collaborating with the government. Despised for having publicly sworn loyalty to Verwoerd, Sigcau was said to have kept life-size portraits of the prime minister and Minister of Bantu Administration on the mantelpiece of his chambers (with a much smaller signed photograph of the British royal family placed in the background).[10]

In June 1960 opponents of the Bantu Authorities system met on Ngquasa Hill between Bizana and Lusikisiki. Armoured police supported by helicopters threw tear gas and opened fire, killing 11 Mpondo and wounding 60 more. A committee demanded the removal of Chief Botha Sigcau, withdrawal of the Bantu Authorities and Bantu Education Acts, an end to passes, and called for African representation in parliament. In neighbouring Tembuland, resistance centred on the role played by Chief Kaizer Matanzima who had been controversially invested in 1958 as a paramount chief. Simmering resentment led to widespread hut burnings from 1960, coupled with agitation against agricultural rehabilitation projects. Matanzima's supporters launched reprisals. The state weighed in with imprisonment and banishments, often imposed by unpopular chiefs, who now acquired additional powers under the much hated Proclamation 400.[11]

The wave of rural disturbances and killings of pro-government chiefs and headmen in the late 1950s signalled the potential for a broadening of political resistance. In the case of Pondoland, unrest peaked after the Sharpeville crisis. The Communist ANC leader Govan Mbeki argued that 'a struggle based on the reserves had a much greater capacity to absorb the shocks of government repression and was therefore capable of being sustained for a much longer time than a struggle based on the urban locations'. According to Mbeki, peasant struggles might in the long run prove more of a challenge to the government than urban resistance, and 'a proper blending' of peasant and worker struggles should be a priority.[12] The countryside risings in the 1950s offered evidence of extensive rural–urban networks, often sustained by the migrant labour system, which served as a natural transmission belt for ideas and propaganda.

Although many ANC leaders had roots in the countryside, the organization's modernizing ideology was strongly oriented to organizing the urban masses. The ANC seldom offered more than rhetorical support for peasant resistance. It did little to build a presence in rural areas, largely failing to capture the powerful but inchoate strands of Africanist resistance that gravitated more naturally to the Pan Africanist Congress or the All African Convention based in the eastern Cape. Here, Murphy argues, African nationalist organizers 'became increasingly removed from popular politics at the very time that popular political consciousness had become radicalised'.[13]

The ANC's ambivalent relationship to the countryside is partly explicable as a reaction by modernizing progressive cosmopolitans to the government's insistence that Africans were naturally 'tribal'. Rural revolts were, in any case, isolated, mostly defensive, and generally oriented to local rather than national objectives. In some ways they were conservative, for example, in seeking to protect the institution of chieftainship and 'tradition' against intrusive government manipulation. Peasant uprisings lacked a broad encompassing ideological vision and were seldom articulated in the universalizing language of freedom favoured by Marxist theorists of proletarian-led revolution.

Senior ANC figures like Govan Mbeki were thus never able to persuade their peers of the political potential represented by the hard-pressed peasantry. Differences within the Communist Party over whether to favour rural- or urban-based resistance mapped onto entrenched theoretical divisions over the relative importance of national and class struggle. Thus, left-wing and liberal intellectuals like Jack Halpern and Charles Hooper, who wrote about the Sekhukuneland and Zeerust uprisings, were exceptional voices.[14] Had the official voices of liberation been more receptive to the rural areas, which featured so prominently in nationalist struggles elsewhere in Africa, it is possible that the capacity of the state to contain resistance in 1960 would have been far more stretched than proved to be the case.

A State of Emergency

For a brief moment Sharpeville and Langa rocked the government. Huge quantities of foreign capital were repatriated overseas, the gold price and the stock market fell sharply, and the Finance Ministry was forced to take strong measures to protect against a deterioration in the government's reserves and its balance of payments. Stayaways momentarily paralysed commercial and industrial activity in the major urban centres. The prospect of serious economic decline and the certainty of international isolation prompted alarm bordering on panic throughout white South Africa. A state of emergency was declared in all the country's major urban areas as well as many rural districts, giving the police sweeping powers of arrest and detention. Parliament voted in favour of banning of the ANC and PAC, citing their allegedly revolutionary objectives. By the middle of May some 2,000 political leaders and activists, including Luthuli and Sobukwe, were taken into custody under the emergency regulations.

In this febrile environment some radicals ventured to hope that the government might collapse. Other leaders, like Oliver Tambo, prudently left the country in order to establish an exile presence for the ANC. Some figures with the ear of the government pressed for a permanent relaxation of the pass laws and a process of cautious reform aimed at stabilizing the urban black population. One of these was the businessman Anton Rupert, who had met Philip Kgosana at a dinner party just before the Langa uprising. Another was the influential editor of *Die Burger*, Piet Cillié. Immediately after Sharpeville he pronounced that 'the word "apartheid" has hopelessly failed' and argued that the future of white South Africa would depend on improvements in the position of urban blacks. Three cabinet ministers, including Eben Dönges (Verwoerd's main competitor as Strijdom's replacement), attempted without success to persuade the prime minister to abolish the reference book system.[15]

Expressions of moral confusion within Afrikanerdom were abundantly evident when eleven leading theologians of the three Dutch Reformed Churches contributed to a volume entitled *Delayed Action* (1960) which cast serious doubt on apartheid's theological foundations and called for a new outlook on racial attitudes. One contributor, Albert Geyser, was sacked from his professorial position at Pretoria University and convicted of heresy. A Dutch Reformed minister in Krugersdorp told his congregation after Sharpeville and Langa 'that bullets and imprisonment could not solve the Native problem'. He was pressured to resign. At the end of 1960 the World Council of Churches convened the Cottesloe Consultations in Johannesburg, a landmark ecumenical gathering born of the anguish of Sharpeville, which united in 'rejecting unjust discrimination'—though not necessarily apartheid as a whole.[16] Verwoerd took these criticisms seriously and in his 1961 new year address to the nation he warned dissident churchmen that they were speaking without the authority of their synods and congregants.

The international response to Sharpeville and Langa was immediate and remarkable in its unanimity. Opinion-forming newspapers like the *New York Times* gave unprecedented attention to the crisis. In Washington an unusually forthright State Department statement deplored violence 'in all its forms'. At Westminster a strong motion against apartheid was tabled on 22 March. Spontaneous demonstrations at South Africa House in London were described by *The Times* as 'Something new in public protests'.[17] The Indian parliament prepared to discuss a motion condemning the 'mass killings' while in Lagos a 'committee of Nigerian patriots' was formed to lead mass demonstrations.[18]

On 1 April 1960, the UN Security Council passed a historic resolution (134) condemning the Sharpeville killings and called upon the South African government to abandon its policy of apartheid and racial discrimination. Britain and France abstained. The following month the General Assembly declared South African policies to be a flagrant violation of the UN Charter. In a significant shift Britain supported this position, dropping its previous stance, which was that South Africa's racial policies were essentially a 'domestic concern'. The United States' support of the Security Council resolution marked a similar change in attitude. In both cases a groundswell of popular anger helped to shift official attitudes. The United Nations Secretary-General Dag Hammarskjöld prepared to visit South Africa, charged with upholding its Charter. He did so in 1961 and might have returned had he not died in a plane crash later that year.

Consolidation

Verwoerd remained coolly recalcitrant and elected to tough it out. Reporting the events at Sharpeville to parliament on the day after the killings, he noted blithely that disturbances were not new to South Africa nor confined to it. Unrest, he reasoned, was a periodic phenomenon and 'came in cycles as a result of incitement in regard to some or other matter of law'. Admittedly, a large number of people had been killed but this was only because blacks were becoming more bold—or cheeky—('manhaftig').[19] Minister of Bantu Administration de Wet Nel opined that race relations had never been better. An official in his department issued an edict forbidding handshakes between blacks and whites (since this was not consonant with 'Bantu tradition');[20] urban administrators were ordered to address township residents as 'man' rather than 'mister' or 'sir'. Blithe condescension and overweening paternalism were hallmarks of the Verwoerdian style. In keeping with the pretence of normality and business as usual, an official commission of inquiry into the Sharpeville disturbances was announced. Notwithstanding the doubts of more far-sighted government supporters, the National Party as a whole retained full confidence in the power of the state to put down insurrection. For its part, the United Party opposition proved supine in the face of government insistence that agitators were responsible for the disturbances; it too subscribed to the view that white supremacy had to be defended at all costs.

On 9 April, the day after the outlawing of the ANC and PAC, Verwoerd's composure was further tested when he delivered a speech at the annual Rand Easter Show in Johannesburg culminating in the peroration: 'We shall fight for our existence, and we shall survive.' At this point, a wealthy English farmer with a long history of mental disturbance, said to be possessed by 'a violent urge to shoot apartheid' but with no clear political affiliations, mounted the platform and fired two bullets into the prime minister's face at point blank range.[21] Extraordinarily, Verwoerd survived and he was back in active politics less than two months later.

While Verwoerd was incapacitated, the acting prime minister and representative of 'Cape' nationalism, Paul Sauer, caused serious ructions in the party by calling for a 'new approach' and suggesting that the events at Sharpeville had closed the 'old book of South African history'. The air was thick with rumours of a coalition government. But Verwoerd ended all speculation when he announced from his hospital bed that he would not change course. For the prime minister, the disturbances only underlined the necessity to complete the process of separate development.[22] If anything, the attack on his life strengthened Verwoerd's resolve and extended his mesmeric authority over the National Party. Once back in active politics he moved quickly to repress the reformist impulses evident in opinion-forming circles like SABRA and the Dutch Reformed Churches. The state of emergency was lifted. At the end of a tumultuous year Verwoerd announced that the government's colour policies would have to be defended 'like walls of granite'.[23]

Far from deflecting the government from the republican cause, which had been an article of faith for Verwoerd well before he took up the cause of racial separation, Sharpeville brought this prospect closer. At the start of 1960 Verwoerd made the unexpected announcement that a referendum would decide the vexed question of whether South Africa should become a republic. His move was interpreted by some as an effort to shift attention away from his increasingly unpopular apartheid policies. There was even doubt whether Afrikaners were sufficiently united behind the idea to win the vote. The referendum was duly held, as scheduled in

October, further indicating that the government would not be deflected from its course.

During the referendum campaign Verwoerd made concerted over-tures to the English-speaking electorate and used the political crisis—as well as the bloody civil war which broke out in the newly independent Congo—to underline the imperative of unity in defending white supremacy. The pro-republican campaign slogan, 'To Unite and Keep South Africa White', amply reflected fears of black domination and lessened long established ethnic rivalries. Sufficient English-speakers were convinced of this argument to endorse the republican proposal with a 'yes' vote of 52 per cent.

The narrow margin of victory indicates that by no means all Afrikaans-speakers, who constituted more than 55 per cent of the white electorate, voted with the government. Some must have opposed the republic, per-haps because of fears of international economic isolation or out of residual loyalty to the British monarch and existing constitutional arrangements. But English-speakers were shifting their allegiances. At the 1961 general election (which was called two years early) the National Party significantly strengthened its position and won a majority of votes for the first time. One of the factors in this victory was the support for the government of English-speakers, responding to the call for 'national unity'.[24]

The republican campaign did indeed reveal that English-speaking South Africans were far less wedded to Britain and the multi-racial Commonwealth than they had been a generation or more before. It also demonstrated the government's willingness to expand insular Afrikaner nationalism into a greater defiant white nationalism. A symbol of this shift was the token inclusion in 1961 of two conservative English-speakers in the cabinet. More significant was the decision to abandon efforts to restrict white immigration (which some Afrikaner nationalists feared would dilute their power).[25] At first Verwoerd was prepared to retain South Africa's membership of the Commonwealth. But, under pressure from member states who insisted on a declaration of principles that included criticism of apartheid, Verwoerd withdrew South Africa's membership application.

On his return to South Africa from the Commonwealth heads of government meeting on 20 March 1961, Verwoerd was welcomed by tens of thousands of adulating supporters as the leader of 'the white man in Africa'. Air force jets roared overhead. Verwoerd declared that his withdrawal from the Commonwealth was a victory, not a defeat. For many of his supporters this was indeed Verwoerd's finest hour. He had turned the long divisive issue of republicanism into a unifying position of apparent strength and thereby realized the twin-pronged aim of the 1948 apartheid manifesto: white supremacy *and* Afrikaner dominance.[26] From this moment on until his assassination in 1966, Verwoerd enjoyed more complete control over cabinet and country than any South African leader before or after.

A Revolutionary Moment?

Just as Verwoerd used the Sharpeville crisis to entrench his control, so key leaders of the Congress alliance used the opportunity to press for more radical responses. The banning of the ANC and PAC meant that armed resistance, hitherto canvassed only as a possibility by a select group of ANC and Communist Party cadres, became a central priority. One of the foremost advocates of guerrilla action was Nelson Mandela, whose influence in the ANC was now in the ascendant.

Mandela's own account, supported by most ANC historiography, represents the formation of MK as unavoidable if not inevitable. This interpretation has since come into question. It is true that Mandela met Luthuli in June 1961 to get the ANC leader's assent for the formation of MK, but there is strong circumstantial evidence to suggest that Luthuli was never wholly persuaded of the decision to abandon the principle of non-violence, nor fully appraised of preparatory talks about the potential for insurrection.

In pressing the case for armed resistance, the dynamic and impetuous Mandela began to surpass Luthuli, who enjoyed high personal and moral standing within the movement, as well as having the capacity to reach beyond it as a natural statesman (rather like Mandela thirty years later).[27] Luthuli addressed enthusiastic racially mixed crowds in Cape Town, Durban, and Johannesburg during 1960 and was awarded the Nobel Peace Prize in 1961, the first South African to achieve this honour.

Luthuli was by no means the only figure within the ANC alliance to oppose the turn to violence. Influential members of the Indian Congress such as Maulvi and Yusuf Cachalia, both steeped in the ethos of passive resistance, spoke against, as did Ahmed Kathrada and Monty Naicker. Luthuli's trusted adviser, Moses Kotane, who was general secretary of the SACP as well as a senior member of the ANC executive, opposed armed struggle at a key meeting in June 1961, fearing a crushing backlash from the South African state. He informed Mandela that there was still a place for 'the old methods if we are imaginative and determined enough'. Kotane nonetheless agreed to take the proposal to the ANC national executive. The resulting compromise led to the creation of an independent military organization, Umkhonto we Sizwe (MK), commanded by Mandela and Joe Slovo of the Communist Party. The ANC remained formally committed to peaceful methods of opposition.[28]

The decision to embrace the armed struggle was thus far more contentious than standard ANC historiography allows. In the context of a severe government crackdown open debate was not possible, yet secret deliberations did take place in which influential figures expressed doubts about the political wisdom or viability of resorting to violence.[29] Luthuli's reluctance to embrace armed struggle was based in his Christian morality but it was also a political assessment which questioned the view that Sharpeville constituted a 'turning point' requiring a major strategic change in direction.[30]

Since the end of the Defiance Campaign secret discussions had been taking place between senior liberation movement leaders, including Mandela and Sisulu, about the limits of principled pacifism and the necessity to resort to armed resistance. Indeed, some trace the formation of the underground organization back to 1953 when the M-Plan, a hierarchical cellular form of street mobilization suited to clandestine work, was devised. The principal architect of the (as yet unactivated) contingency plan was Mandela, but the theoretical and organizational influence of the Communist Party, which was quietly reconstituted at this time, is also evident.[31]

Towards the end of 1960, senior ANC and Communist Party militants sought support from China and Russia. In Beijing, the South African mission was met by Mao Tse Tung and Deng Xiaoping. It is not known whether China or the USSR endorsed a military campaign at this time. Mandela and other ANC leaders toured parts of Africa in

1961–2, including Algeria and Ethiopia, to explore the possibilities for guerrilla war. The South African Communist Party decided to create sabotage units in late 1960 or early 1961.[32] This, in turn, acted as a spur to the ANC.

The decision to endorse the armed struggle remains a subject of animated debate. In the first place, it leads us to ask how the shift affected the subsequent political and organizational development of the ANC and, specifically, whether the decision hastened or delayed the eventual defeat of white supremacy. If those in favour of armed struggle had known that it would take another thirty years for the ANC to reconstitute itself legally within South Africa, might this have affected their decision? It is also worth asking whether the opportunities for mass opposition were indeed exhausted in 1960 and, if so, was this temporary and might prospects have revived more quickly if the liberation movements had remained underground and at home?

Assuming Verwoerd had died at the hands of David Pratt in April 1960 it is not altogether inconceivable that some form of meaningful political process—along the lines of the much talked about 'national convention'—could have been inaugurated between Luthuli and a more flexible successor to Verwoerd (e.g. Dönges or Sauer). The overwhelming political crisis and palpable sense of fluidity might just have made this possible, and there were overseas mediators like Dag Hammarskjöld who were primed to intervene. But Verwoerd did not die and, in any case, it remains unlikely that whites were ready to countenance any real loss of power.

Secondly, the decision to endorse armed struggle raises questions about the relationship between the Communist Party and the ANC. New evidence that Mandela was briefly a member of the Communist Party around the time of Sharpeville—notwithstanding his earlier strong ideological opposition to the Party in the 1940s—proves little in itself. If Mandela did join (or align himself with) the Party, as now seems likely, it is almost certain that this was for pragmatic rather than doctrinal reasons.[33] Based on his experience of working closely with Communists from the Defiance Campaign, Mandela had probably come round to the view that membership of the Party was strategically advantageous to the ANC.

Paul Landau attributes the pressure for the turn to armed struggle to the 'Sophiatown group', headed by Mandela, Sisulu, and Nokwe. Their antagonists included 'Africanists' in the Transvaal ANC as well as sceptical members of the Communist Party such as Moses Kotane and Rowley Arenstein, some of whom felt that the Party would do better to work with trade unionists.[34] This complicates the view that the turn to violence amounted to a Communist Party 'takeover' and suggests that it has to be seen more as a tactical alliance between Mandela's youthful faction and the Johannesburg wing of the Communist Party. Personal ambition surely played a role, for Mandela's ascendancy to a position of leadership after 1960 was inseparable from his role as MK's commander in chief. This position was achieved with the active support of the Communist Party, which realized that clandestine organization was not only necessary in the new political circumstances, but also advantageous to its enhanced role in the vanguard of the struggle.

With an active membership numbering no more than 500 at this time, the Communist Party was tiny, but its membership was a highly dedicated and self-selecting elite that exercised disproportionate influence on the ANC. It does not, however, necessarily follow that Mandela was being 'used' by the Communists to amplify their own influence. This claim can just as easily be reversed, namely, to argue that Mandela was willing to use Communist Party resources and organizational capacity in order to advance the cause of orthodox African nationalism. If this was a relationship of convenience or a tactical alliance, no one could predict who would get the better of the deal.

Much depended on contemporary assessments of South Africa's readiness for revolutionary change at this time. In the pages of the radical journal *Africa South*, an instructive debate on the country's revolutionary potential began in the period leading up to Sharpeville. In 1958, Julius Lewin (drawing on the Harvard historian Crane Brinton) concluded that South Africa did not manifest the 'classic' conditions favourable to revolution: a rising but frustrated middle class—rather than poor people suffering from outright oppression—and an inefficient state machine with uncertain control over its armed forces. Lewin concluded that the resistance campaigns and industrial strikes of the 1950s had not threatened the security of the state in any fundamental regard.[35]

This intervention promoted a series of responses by theorists associated with the ANC and the Communist Party, some revealing the influence of the theory of 'colonialism of a special type' which was to become the central doctrine of the Communist Party. Jack Simons detected greater fluidity than was outwardly apparent, observing that 'South Africans are no more aware of the dangers than are people living on the volcano's edge.' Michael Harmel took issue with the typology of classic revolutions (Britain, America, France, and Russia) and looked to Asia and Africa for inspiration. Democracy and self-government, he averred, were not 'slegs vir blankes' (for whites only). Nor did revolution necessarily entail violence. The certainty of revolutionary change in South Africa lay in the fact that no minority government could endure once the majority took the path of 'resolute resistance and organization against it'—and there were plenty of examples to indicate that this was indeed happening.[36] Independent-minded Marxist intellectual biologist Eddie Roux argued similarly that much depended on what one meant by revolution: modern colonial revolutions were a new phenomenon in that they combined social, economic, national, and racial factors—the last of which was of the greatest significance. Unlike Harmel, Roux concluded that the majority of blacks in South Africa 'still accept their second-grade status as inevitable'. As long as this illusion remained, the government was invulnerable.[37]

Sharpeville and Langa do not provide conclusive evidence for either side of the argument about South Africa's readiness for revolution. Nor does it vindicate what would soon become liberation movement orthodoxy: the view that 1960 was a turning point that ended the possibilities of open, peaceful opposition. R. W. Johnson has suggested that, like Russia in 1905, events caught revolutionaries by surprise and were therefore not fully exploited. In the rush to defend the urban centres of South Africa during 1960, his argument goes, the towns and countryside were denuded of police, but there was no concerted move to exploit the vacuum and overwhelm the state.[38]

Sabotage and Insurrection

On 16 December 1961, ten small explosives were detonated in Johannesburg and Port Elizabeth by Umkhonto we Sizwe, the newly formed armed wing of the ANC. Government installations were targeted (the only person who died was himself a saboteur). The date was highly symbolic since it occurred on an official public holiday dedicated to celebrating the Voortrekkers' defeat of the Zulu army at Blood River in 1838. So, too, was the timing of the explosions, which took place just a day after Albert Luthuli's return to South Africa with the Nobel Peace Prize.

MK's actions occluded Luthuli's message more effectively than the government had managed to do. Pamphlets announcing the birth of MK stressed the liberation movement's disinclination towards violence, adding, 'We hope that we will bring the government and its supporters to their senses before it is too late...'[39] This hesitant pronouncement left unclear whether the intention was to sound a warning in the form of 'armed propaganda' or else lay the foundations for guerrilla war. Few revolutions could have been launched on such tentative—and tenuous—foundations. The explosions were nonetheless an eloquent statement of a major change in ANC strategy and a clear indication of Mandela's growing influence.

Sharpeville was not the reason for the turn to armed struggle so much as the catalyst. The decision had been brewing since the mid-1950s. The rural revolts in Zeerust, Pondoland, and Sekhukuneland raised the possibility of more sustained insurrection. In Africa, Cuba, and Asia, revolution was in the air. The decision, though controversial, was not arrived at in a hasty manner, nor did it mark a total break with the ANC's past. Notably, the oaths taken by MK cadres to 'put my life at the service of my people' bore a resemblance to those taken by volunteers during the Defiance Campaign. In both cases considerable care was taken by the leadership to maintain discipline and avoid indiscriminate violence.

The decision to launch MK's sabotage campaign was also prompted by the need to stay ahead of other groupings that were gravitating towards violent methods of opposition.

On 29 September 1961 an offshoot of the Liberal Party, the so-called National Committee of Liberation (later the African Resistance Movement), attempted unsuccessfully to torch the Johannesburg Bantu Administration Tax Office. The individuals drawn to this tiny movement were brought together by their abhorrence of apartheid, a common belief in non-racism, and the experience of being imprisoned during the state of emergency. Organized in small regional cells, their numbers included several handfuls of young radicalized liberals and democratic socialists, Trotskyists, ex-Communists, and anti-Communists, as well as a few dissident members of the Transvaal ANC who were frustrated by lack of direction and administrative chaos within the ANC. A couple were ex-servicemen with experience of working with dynamite. Their main qualifications were daring, resourcefulness, and a degree of recklessness.

The NCL/ARM mounted around twenty successful sabotage operations, bringing down electricity pylons and radio masts with stolen explosives.[40] Its campaign came to an abrupt end in 1964 when a police raid on the home of one of the leading members yielded detailed written evidence in defiance of accepted protocol. In July a petrol bomb placed in the concourse of Johannesburg railway station killed one person and injured twenty-three more after a telephone warning failed to be acted upon. The already divided group collapsed in rancour.

Other than their divergent political tendencies and the huge disparity between the political constituencies they could claim to represent, the operations mounted by the NCL/ARM and MK had much in common. Their scale of operations and choice of targets were comparable. Both were racially integrated outfits which sought to avoid loss of human life, both were forced to improvise, and both lacked training, experience, and adequate security precautions—leading to widespread accusations of amateurism.

Although there were some discussions between the two embryonic resistance organizations cooperation was not forthcoming. MK distanced itself from the NCL/ARM while the latter insisted that no single group bore sole responsibility for fighting for freedom. Had they managed to combine they might have achieved more. The fact that they did not is indicative of the fact that the ANC, although the leading liberation organization, was by no means pre-eminent. Nor was it seen by many militants as providing effective leadership.[41]

The greatest challenge to the ANC was the PAC which also turned to violence after Sharpeville. In December 1961 Poqo—meaning 'pure' 'independent', or 'alone'—announced itself, promising in a pamphlet circulated in Cape Town, 'We die once. Africa will be free on 1 January.

The Whites will suffer—the African people will rule.'[42] Poqo's insurrectionary style was simple and direct: unlike the ANC, it had no compunction about attacking whites or using terror. Nor was it constrained, like the ANC, by the coded language of multi-racialism. In place of theorizing and planning, the PAC professed millenarian redemption, trusting that exemplary militant action would arouse a spontaneous wave of popular resistance. Traditional medicine and purificatory rituals were used to strengthen the bodies of combatants. The unvarnished language of race war circulated freely, if covertly, amongst many of its ordinary adherents.

Some in the ANC dismissed Poqo's racial nihilism as 'primitive', suggesting that its revolutionary strategy was deficient, while also revealing an attitude of condescension towards the rural migrants who were so prominent in its ranks. In the period up 1960–3, when Poqo was eventually contained, there were killings of informers and collaborators (including headmen and chiefs) as well as attacks on police stations in various parts of the country. The largest act of insurrection was in the rural centre of Paarl, outside Cape Town; around 250 men armed with home-made weapons and knives attacked the police station in 1962.[43] With the arrests of more than 3,000 Cape-based PAC members in 1963, its capacity to mount further attacks from within South Africa was nullified.

The Rivonia Arrests and Crackdown

In the case of MK, operations were brought to an abrupt halt in July 1963. A police raid on Lilliesleaf farm in Rivonia, north of Johannesburg, yielded virtually the entire underground leadership drawn from the ANC, Communist Party, and Congress of Democrats: Walter Sisulu, Govan Mbeki, Raymond Mhlaba, Ahmed Kathrada, Lionel Bernstein, Denis Goldberg, and Bob Hepple among them. Many incriminating documents relating to the manufacture of explosives and Communism were captured as well as a copy of Operation Mayibuye ('let it return'), a detailed—but fanciful—revolutionary plan involving landings on the east coast of South Africa by sea and air and 7,000 guerrillas based in four locations. Further arrests, including Arthur Goldreich and Harold Wolpe, ensued.

Mandela was already in prison, having been detained the previous year after an audacious period on the run, during which he played the role of heroic outlaw to the full. He left South Africa illegally to train briefly as a revolutionary in Morocco and Ethiopia and then returned, making dramatic entries at meetings (thereby earning himself the sobriquet 'the black pimpernel' in the press) until he was apprehended in August 1962. At the Rivonia trial, which concluded in July 1964, Mandela, Sisulu, and six other defendants were convicted of various charges relating to sabotage and attempted revolution and sentenced to life imprisonment. They only narrowly escaped hanging.

The Rivonia trialists were defended by Bram Fischer, a principled and courageous lawyer, scion of a prominent Orange Free State Afrikaner family, who was at the time a secret leader of the Communist Party.[44] Fischer was himself sentenced to life in 1966 after a desperate period trying fruitlessly to hold the underground Communist resistance network together. In the view of the government, Fischer was a traitor to Afrikanerdom. Many anti-apartheid activists regarded him as the epitome of self-sacrifice to the liberation movement and of commitment to the principles of non-racialism.

The period 1961–4 thus saw the last outright resistance to apartheid within South Africa for more than a decade. Revolutionary hopes, born out of frustration at the government's intransigence and elation at its apparent vulnerability, dissipated. By the end of this period the liberation movements were immeasurably weakened whereas the power of the apartheid state was commensurably entrenched. Historians continue to debate the achievements of the insurrectionary moment, the manner in which it was pursued, and its effects on the pattern of repression.

The majority view in the liberation movement remains that there was simply no alternative to armed struggle, all avenues of legitimate protest having been exhausted; others maintain that the move to armed struggle was premature, poorly executed, and self-defeating, not least because it foreclosed on areas of open mass resistance and mobilization (like industrial action) that had not been fully explored. The choice in 1960–1 was not only between 'passive' resistance and 'insurrection'; lying low, rebuilding organizational structures, and waiting for more propitious times, must also have been an option.

These retrospective judgements need also to take account of the prevailing mood. Few government opponents genuinely believed in the early 1960s that the government could be overthrown, but some idealistic activists and revolutionaries did consider (or hope) that the apartheid state, having been rocked by Sharpeville, might be quickly toppled. The rapid process of decolonization in Africa and Asia, together with examples of successful insurrection in Cuba and Algeria, was a live and sometimes infectious source of hope that freedom was there to be grasped. But the relative ease with which the largely self-taught and part-time soldiers of MK and the NCL/ARM were disrupted showed that they had badly underestimated the professionalism of the security police.

In the case of the PAC, the decision to embrace violence had been relatively straightforward. For the ANC it was problematic, for political, moral, and strategic reasons. Traditions of non-violence, exemplified by Luthuli and shared by Mandela, ran very deep in an organization that remained powerfully influenced by gradualism, mission Christianity, and Gandhian principles of non-violence. The standard ANC/MK vindication of the armed struggle greatly oversimplifies the political and moral uncertainties of the time. It also underplays the fact that the decision to move the struggle underground increased the ANC's reliance on the Communist Party, whose influence on African nationalism became more profound in the context of underground struggle. The growing dependence of the ANC on Communists—organizationally, materially, and ideologically—also provided convenient cover for the government's blanket crackdown and delegitimization of African nationalism.

The view that Communist-inspired revolution was the underlying cause of subversion and disorder became an article of faith for the government. It persisted with the myth that most Africans were amenable to apartheid—and that the minority who were not were victims of propaganda and agitation. B. J. Vorster, who became Justice Minister in 1961, assured Verwoerd that Communism could not be fought by adherence to the 'Queensberry rules'.[45] He duly set about rebuilding the police force 'special branch' into a powerful unit under the direction of J. H. ('Lang Hendrik') van den Bergh, a fellow *Ossewabrandwag* member with whom Vorster had been interned during the war as a

Nazi sympathizer. In memoirs of the period many veterans of the struggle attest to the significant shift in the scale of police and government repression after 1960. In the 1950s, when opposition was open, political activists could generally rely on a relatively independent criminal justice system and, for whites at least, a measure of fair play on the part of the police. By the 1960s new techniques, including solitary confinement, detention without trial, and physical intimidation, were becoming routine.

The 1963 General Laws Amendment Act authorized the police to detain political suspects for up to ninety days without access to visitors or lawyers. It also enabled the detention, for an indefinite period after the expiration of their sentence, of anyone found guilty of sabotage. This marked a serious ratcheting up of the state's already formidable repressive machinery. Van den Bergh worked to establish a secret intelligence-gathering operation which, by the end of the decade, morphed into the much feared Bureau of State Security (BOSS). Whereas many of the Treason Trialists attested to the police's adherence to procedure at the time of their arrest (none was tortured), by the time of Rivonia, apartheid South Africa was well on the way to becoming a police state (albeit a thinly resourced one) with torture and abuse featuring as established practice. The Rivonia arrests marked a personal success for van den Bergh.

Mandela's Speech from the Dock

Unlike the Treason Trial, which secured no convictions, there could be no doubt that most if not all of the Rivonia defendants were guilty, as charged, of involvement in sabotage. The only question was whether those found guilty would be hanged. Prosecutor Percy Yutar pushed hard for death sentences. An orthodox Jew, evidently seeking to impress the authorities with his loyalty, Yutar was personally antagonistic towards the Jewish-born Communist 'traitors' who comprised a high proportion of those involved in the Rivonia plot. Mandela decided to turn the courtroom into a trial of the apartheid state itself, arguing that his actions were guided by his conscience. He made use of a legal convention that allowed him to address the court from the dock, rather than entering the witness stand. This allowed him to speak to the world, not just the courtroom, and to do so from a position of strength and without cross-examination. The presence of many foreign journalists and the active interest of the United Nations gave Mandela a unique opportunity to immortalize, even sacralize, a struggle whose future was, to say the least, uncertain.

In the course of a brilliantly crafted address, widely considered to be one of the great speeches of the twentieth century, Mandela reviewed the history of the ANC and his own political development. He anticipated possible martyrdom with extraordinary dignity and gravity. Addressing an international as well as local audience, Mandela began by disavowing the state's charge that the struggle was being manipulated by foreigners or Communists: 'I have done whatever I did, both as an individual and as a leader of my people, because of my experience in South Africa, and my own proudly felt African background, and not because of what any outsider may have said.' Mandela paid tribute to the Communists as the only political group who were prepared to treat Africans as human beings and as equals, but he denied that he was himself a Communist. Instead, he defined himself as an 'African patriot' and he affirmed his commitment to democracy.

Concluding, and now speaking without notes, Mandela reiterated that he had fought throughout his life against white domination just as he had fought against black domination. 'I have cherished the ideal of a democratic and free society in which all persons live together in harmony and with equal opportunities.' Turning to Judge Quartus de Wet, Mandela declared that this was the ideal which he hoped to live for and to achieve. Against the advice of lawyers, who greatly feared a death sentence, Mandela added a final coda: 'But if needs be, it is an ideal for which I am prepared to die.'

A great silence followed these words, followed by the sound of suppressed sobs in the public gallery.[46]

Mandela's speech was reported in full by the *Rand Daily Mail* and it was afforded extensive coverage overseas. When the guilty verdicts were handed down on 12 June 1964, *The Times* in London opined that 'the verdict of history will be that the ultimate guilty party is the government in power—and that already is the verdict of world opinion.'[47] Life imprisonment was the sentence. Whether the judge was dissuaded from imposing capital punishment on Mandela and his co-accused because of the quality of the legal arguments, the independence of the judiciary, a disinclination to create martyrs, or fear of the growing tide of international anti-apartheid opinion, cannot be known for certain. All indications are that the state meant what it said when it called for the death sentence and that white public opinion would have approved.[48] What is undeniable is that Judge Quartus de Wet's prudent decision profoundly influenced the subsequent history of South Africa.

On the day that Mandela delivered his statement from the dock a United Nations-appointed Group of Experts chaired by the Swedish internationalist Mrs Alva Myrdal called for a fully representative National Convention (a demand which ANC leaders like Luthuli as well as a host of liberals had pressed since the mid-1950s) to seek a constitutional solution to South Africa's problems as well as an amnesty for all political prisoners.[49]

The involvement of these overseas experts was dismissed with contempt by the South African government and by Verwoerd in particular. If the prime minister bothered to read Myrdal's report, he might have been heartened, for although the Group warned of impending disaster in South Africa, it also acknowledged that South Africa was experiencing a 'wave of prosperity', indicated by fresh overseas investment and growing white immigration. Campaigns for international sanctions, as advocated by the UN Group of Experts, were losing momentum.[50] For South Africa's rulers the immediate post-Sharpeville economic and political crisis was manifestly over. A counter-revolution was in full swing.

CHAPTER 4
APARTHEID REGNANT

Economic Prosperity

The decade of the 1960s was the era of high apartheid. It was also a time of rapid economic expansion and rising employment, during which most whites experienced unprecedented growth in their material well-being. Measures taken to address the crisis of capital outflow in 1960–1 were so successful that banks became inundated with liquidity by 1963. Local investors snapped up equities and share prices soared from 1962. Substantial sections of the white middle class with no previous direct involvement in the stock market now became speculators.[1] Rapid returns did much to banish white anxieties. Afrikaners shared fully in the new economic prosperity as a new ethos of consumerism flourished. By the end of the decade whites, numbering less than one-fifth of the total population, commanded close to three-quarters of the country's share of income.[2]

The 1950s mantra of saving 'for stability' was replaced by exhortations to 'spend for success'.[3] Ranch-style homes with swimming pools and tennis courts came to epitomize the ambitions of a burgeoning suburban middle class which was domesticating the great outdoors, American-style. Middle-class Johannesburg was said to have the greatest concentration of swimming pools anywhere in the world aside from Beverley Hills.[4] Even lower-middle-class whites would expect to employ at least one live-in female 'maid'. Dressed in regulation cap and apron, she would typically work very long hours, carry the madam's infants on her back, and live in small servant's quarters at the back of the house.

Wealthier households might employ gardeners or 'house-boys'. The intimacy of personal relationships between servants and employers was carefully coded: many madams would never know the full names of their employees who, despite being responsible for nearly all the cooking and cleaning (including bringing early morning tea to the master bedroom), would have to eat their own food from special enamel plates and serve cheap cuts of 'boys meat' to the gardener.

On the dams of the highveld and the waterways of the Cape and Natal, new leisure pursuits like powerboating and waterskiing served as conspicuous evidence of white prosperity. Golf and tennis were taken up along with the more demotic and hypermasculine team sport of rugby. Cabinet ministers were equipped with Cadillacs. Farmers preferred Mercedes Benz. Car ownership rates amongst whites in the 1960s ranked with some of the most motorized countries in the world. The lifestyle aspirations of most ordinary white South Africans was well expressed in an iconic advertising jingle of the early 1970s: 'braaivleis, rugby, sunny skies and Chevrolet'. Further down the white social scale, contentment might be derived, in the words of one wit, from one-litre brandy, two-litres of Coke, and a three-litre Ford.[5]

This growth in prosperity was underpinned by an economy whose real GDP increased by an average of 5.8 per cent each year until 1970, an era of almost uninterrupted growth (though in international comparative terms not as spectacular as was widely assumed). By the end of the decade South Africa's foreign reserves quadrupled from a low of some $240m in 1960. Over the same period American trade with South Africa grew by 79 per cent, British trade by 88 per cent, and Japanese trade by 379 per cent. Reflecting on these boom conditions, the economist Hobart Houghton noted that few would have predicted that 1961 would be 'the prelude to one of the greatest waves of economic expansion that this country has ever experienced'.[6] His observation brings to mind C. W. de Kiewiet's old adage that 'South Africa has advanced politically by disasters and economically by windfalls'.[7]

In mining, a mainstay of the South African economy, the value of gold sales increased some 85 per cent during the 1960s; profitability soared as a result of increased labour productivity and static real wages. In addition to increased gold production, uranium production generated highly profitable exports. The De Beers mining house maintained tight control over the international sale of this abundant commodity and succeeded in creating new consumer demand in the US market with its highly successful 'a diamond is forever' campaign.

Manufacturing, which experienced substantial growth from the 1930s and through the war, underwent spectacular expansion and modernization in the post-war era. Late adoption of new technologies allowed industrialists to take advantage of relative 'backwardness' while investors were attracted by the availability of cheap capital and labour. In 1962 the chairman of the Board of Trade and Industries proudly declared that no country in the world had experienced such a thorough transformation of its industry as had South Africa over the past twenty-five years; industry's share of GDP increased from 23 per cent in 1948 to 31 per cent in 1970.[8] Yet, despite rising per capita income, the gap between white and black workers increased. During the Second World War wages paid to Africans increased more rapidly than for whites, yet between 1948 and 1955 the wage share of African, coloured, and Indian workers declined relative to whites. Simply put, white capitalists and workers benefited at the expense of black workers.[9] Notwithstanding demographic growth in favour of blacks, Africans' share of total personal income *shrank* from 22.2 per cent in 1946–7 to 19.3 per cent in 1970. Furthermore, the ratio of per capita incomes of whites to blacks increased from more than 10:1 in 1946–7 to 15:1 in 1970. Over the same period Afrikaners' share of whites' income rose from 27.9 per cent to 32.4 per cent.[10]

In agriculture, where low wages and poor capitalization meant that farmers were forever 'crying out for labour', the 1960s signalled important changes which had a direct bearing on the development of apartheid. Dams and large irrigation schemes made it possible to grow commercial crops in areas where pastoralism had been the only viable form of production. Maize and wheat began to be cultivated on an industrial scale in areas of the Free State and Transvaal. The government devoted more and more resources to subsidizing commercial agriculture. By 1967 the total amount spent on supporting white farmers was almost double that devoted to African education, a revealing index of the state's developmental priorities.[11]

The commercialization of agriculture (which included bananas in Natal and mangoes, avocados, and citrus in the Transvaal) fundamentally altered the terms upon which labourers were recruited and utilized. In the early apartheid years, the government resorted to the use of prisoners—often pass law offenders—in order to satisfy the labour demands of white farmers. The abject conditions endured by agricultural labourers in the Transvaal neighbourhood of Bethal became the basis of a major ANC and trade union-led campaign—the so called potato boycott—when the journalist Henry Nxumalo and photographer Jürgen Schadeberg exposed the exploitation of farm workers in *Drum* magazine in 1952.

From the 1960s persistent labour shortages in the agricultural sector became surpluses, perhaps for the first time in the country's history. The exponential increase in the availability of tractors had a fundamental effect on patterns of labour demand and rural demography. As well as mechanization, the expanding size of farms entailed efficiency gains though economies of scale. This allowed farmers to dispense with many permanent African farmworking families (as well as seasonal migrants). Families and individuals who had long lived on white-owned farms now faced forced repatriation to the newly created ethnic Bantustans. Whereas 2.58m Africans lived on white-owned farms in 1951, this figure fell to 1.95m in 1996 (during which time the African population as a whole increased from 9.6m to 30.9m).[12]

Among the agriculturalists who benefited disproportionately from the availability of state-funded credit and subsidies in the 1950s and 1960s was a new class of affluent Afrikaner 'cheque-book' farmers. In her 1974 novel *The Conservationist*, Nadine Gordimer captured the arrogant presumption of Mehring, urbane industrialist and part-time farmer, who expresses his connection to the land through his nostalgia for nature. More recently, in *Agaat*, Marlene van Niekerk brilliantly evokes the swaggering masculine figure of Jak de Wet, the smooth, well-connected master of 'Grootmoedersdrift' who 'dreamed of a completely mechanised farm that would require only one or two pairs of hands'—and whose callous materialism underlies his alienation from both family and farm community.

The losers were African sharecroppers and labour tenants who were relentlessly squeezed off white-owned farms though a combination of the growing forces of agrarian capitalism and the tightening grip of the apartheid state. Charles van Onselen's epic account of the life of Kas

Maine and his family, on the South African highveld, is an epic of survival and resourcefulness. But gritty perseverance was not enough to arrest the slow but sure process of economic strangulation. In 1948, Kas Maine managed to harvest more than 1,500 bags of maize, sorghum, and sunflower seed after settling with Walter Moormeister, owner of the land upon which he worked. The following year, he and his family were compelled to move to another farm. Kas Maine's rural skills as a share-cropper allowed him to survive and, at moments, he managed to revive his family's fortunes. Nevertheless, for all his resilience and adaptability, Kas ended up impoverished in a shack close to the gaudy Bantustan casino of Sun City, where he died in 1985 at the age of 91.[13]

Modernization

The Afrikaner entrepreneurs, who earlier developed their business skills on behalf of the *volk* (in ventures like insurance, banking, and publishing), were now free to become fully-fledged capitalists on their own behalf: in 1954, Jan S. Marais struck out on his own after building a career in the Afrikaner economic movement to become the founding director of Trust Bank. With its modern steel and glass buildings, obliging mini-skirted tellers, and eagerness to attract non-Afrikaner custom, Trust Bank enjoyed rapid growth and redefined the austere image of consumer banking. Marais, an admirer of most things American, was named 'businessman of the year' in 1964 by the *Financial Mail*.

Anton Rupert, the business tycoon who founded the international Rembrandt conglomerate, started off in the 1940s with a tiny tobacco company (supported by a substantial loan from the nationalist start-up investment company Federale Volksbeleggings), and a strong ideological commitment to Afrikaners' rightful place in the world of business.[14] Albert Wessels also tapped the Afrikaner economic movement, in his case by managing a clothing manufacturing company, Volkshemde-en Klerefabriek (Veka). He subsequently acquired the franchise for Toyota South Africa in 1961. The new company flourished by selling rugged and economical pickup trucks (bakkies) through a well-dispersed network of dealers.[15] Industrialists and businessmen like these symbolized Afrikanerdom's dynamic aspirations, though their material success also proved troubling to traditionalists who feared the corrosive effect of acquisitive consumerism on the unity of the *volk*.[16]

Active state involvement in economic development and modernization was a conspicuous feature of the apartheid era. The Industrial Development Corporation, established by Smuts as part of the war effort, gained a new lease of life as the apartheid state poured money into heavily subsidized manufacturing developments in 'border areas' around the black homelands. Verwoerd would not countenance white entrepreneurs investing capital in the homelands on the grounds that this would entail 'economic imperialism'.[17]

A raft of parastatals were promoted by the IDC as part of South Africa's growing military-industrial complex, including Foskor (phosphates), Safmarine (shipping), and Alusaf (aluminium). Another of these ventures, Sasol, was created in 1950 to produce oil from coal using a locally adapted version of German and American processes. It helped to stimulate a large new petro-chemical industry ranging from fertilizer to paints. Above all, the availability of Sasol-produced petrol to motorists stood as a national symbol of technical prowess and energy self-sufficiency. Other huge government parastatals were involved in the production of steel (ISCOR), fertilizer, and munitions (Armscor). By the mid-1960s direct and indirect state involvement in the economy accounted for over 40 per cent of domestic investment. Some referred to this form of corporatist development as 'state capitalism'.[18]

Immediately after Sharpeville, the government authorized a vast irrigation project along the Orange River. Its centrepiece was the hydro-electric Verwoerd Dam. Construction began in 1966. The scheme incorporated a large-bore concrete tunnel, 82km in length and 5m in diameter, which sent water to the Fish River in the eastern Cape. Strategic and ideological considerations were powerfully to the fore in the commissioning of these prestige projects. As a contributor to a symposium organized by the Afrikaans Academy for Arts and Science proclaimed in 1960: 'The power of a nation (*volk*) has always depended on the level of technological progress in its military, agricultural, and industrial spheres.'[19]

Modern Afrikaner power was also celebrated in the built environment. Monuments to great nationalist historical achievements—the Voortrekkers, the Afrikaans language, and assorted heroes—were constructed in reinforced concrete and liberally dispersed around the country. Large-scale government offices were erected in Pretoria and other major centres. Imposing new tertiary institutions like the Rand Afrikaans University in Johannesburg, or the University of South Africa in Pretoria, were designed to dominate rather than to fit in with the landscape. Commercial modernist architecture, conspicuous in banks and insurance houses, served as visible sculptural proof of the *volk*'s growing corporate strength. In rural towns as well as in cities, new churches were erected in face-brick and concrete. Their flat angular planes and soaring wings made the point that Christian-National theology, despite its strict conservatism, was fully equipped to provide spiritual succour in the present and future.[20]

Bantustans

The most hubristic aspect of 'high' apartheid concerned policies towards Africans. At the level of official policy apartheid ideology evolved from the pronouncement of white domination—*baaskap*—to an elaborate and obfuscatory ideology of 'multi-national' development. Verwoerd himself signalled the shift to 'positive' apartheid by insisting that 'separate development' should replace the otiose term 'apartheid'. In practical terms crude repression remained ubiquitous, not least because the scale of social engineering needed to achieve separate development could not be achieved without compulsion and force. For those caught up in the criminal justice system by not carrying their pass books, for Africans removed from white farms and white urban areas, or for servants contravening the orders of their masters and mistresses, bureaucratic compulsion remained an everyday reality.

Separate development was not so much the antithesis to *baaskap* as its ideological antidote. It was touted by Verwoerd as a way to reduce everyday racial friction by normalizing separation and providing an outlet for African political ambitions. The 1959 Promotion of Bantu Self-Government Act, which made provision for African self-determination in separate homelands or 'Bantustans', signalled a momentous change: it dispensed with the old assumption that 'bantu' were a single 'homogeneous people' and instead envisaged the creation of self-governing African territories, supposedly based on historically determined ethnic or 'tribal' grounds.

Just prior to the announcement of 'self government' for those living in Bantu homelands, secretary of the Bantu Administration department Werner Eiselen presented what he called 'Harmonious Multi-Community Development' as a local adaptation of the British Commonwealth model with white South Africa playing the part of the 'mother country'. The issue of eventual political independence was treated cautiously after this possibility appeared on the legislative agenda.[21] The bold new plan, which was neither presented to cabinet nor discussed beforehand by the National Party caucus, held out the promise of sovereign independence for the homelands. This radical revision of policy was prompted by the hope that white South Africa could wrong-foot its external critics by mimicking decolonization elsewhere in Africa. Initially, eight such 'national units' were proposed, though their number eventually proliferated to ten. The first Bantustan to be accorded notional 'independence' was the Transkei in 1976. Three others followed.

Minister of Bantu Administration de Wet Nel introduced the new measure to parliament in terms of God's divine will and the desire of every *volk* to realize its own cultural destiny. Secular doubters and the outside world alike were assured that the future homelands were analogous to the new African states that were gaining independence elsewhere in Africa. Throughout the apartheid era, the government insisted that the homelands would satisfy the political—which is to say tribal or ethnic—ambitions of Africans. In a bid to legitimize their sovereignty (the homelands were never recognized internationally) the South African government indulged the homelands with grandiose schemes and symbols designed to underline their nationhood as well as to flatter the apartheid fantasy. The minimum specifications for homeland independence included a flag, football stadium, airport, parliament, and army, in addition to an authorized tribal lineage. Optional add-ons might include a casino for daily cross-border visitors from white South Africa.

A further bespoke marker of Bantustan identity came in the form of FM radio. From 1960 the official broadcasting corporation expanded its long-standing provision of services in English and Afrikaans with new short-range FM services tailored to different African language groups, beginning with isiXhosa, isiZulu, and isiSotho and thereafter extending to other language communities. For rural as well as urban listeners,

'Radio Bantu' offered easy and relatively cheap, anodyne entertainment. By 1970, when almost the entire population had access to FM radio, around 3m Africans were reportedly tuning in to these 'tribal' stations. They had the added advantage, from the government's perspective, of dissuading blacks from tuning into potentially subversive AM and short-wave broadcasts emanating from neighbouring states. In this manner apartheid ideology penetrated the realms of leisure and domestic life.

Broadcasting a message is, of course, not quite the same as receiving and processing it. As Jacob Dlamini reminds us, instead of narrowing expectations, radio may well have opened up the imagination by exposing listeners to a wider world than broadcast controllers intended. In addition, black announcers seem to have been able, on occasion, to subvert official surveillance by exploiting subtleties of language and meaning. It is unlikely, however, that these exceptions negated the broader propagandist effect of Radio Bantu, which sought to promote a calming paternalist picture of happy and harmonious, rural-based, separate development.[22]

In its quest to stimulate tribal awareness and legitimize the homeland system, Radio Bantu can be seen as one more example of the prescriptive cultural relativism that was so central to apartheid ideology. In the sphere of consumer culture too, newspapers catered separately to Afrikaans, English, and African consumers. Universities enrolled different ethnic and racial groups. Publicly funded theatre attracted separate English and Afrikaans audiences. Such cultural choices ensured that the experience of apartheid was segmented by ethnicity and class as well as race.

The Dutch theory of 'pillarization' (*verzuiling*), which entailed the vertical separation of social, religious, and public institutions, was one historic source of this institutional division and its precepts were encapsulated in Christian-National ideology. From mid-century it was given new secular social-scientific backing through the anthropological discipline of *volkekunde* ('bantu-ology'). Supported by Afrikaans universities, *volkekunde* was expressly designed to invest the new ethnic homelands with scientifically approved national traditions and to train officials in principles of governance.[23] Notwithstanding their common training a generation before, by the 1960s English- and Afrikaans-speaking anthropologists operated in entirely separate professional and institutional spheres. Much the same goes for history and for other disciplines in the social sciences.

Verwoerd's rejection of the Tomlinson proposals, which envisaged a programme of land rehabilitation and industrial development within African reserves, was a clear statement that the government was not prepared to dispense with black labour in white areas. Nor was there ever any genuine prospect that the homelands might become economically self-sustaining. Few of the planned states were internally contiguous. Bophuthatswana, for example, was comprised of seven landlocked enclaves (reduced from a dozen) situated conveniently close to South Africa's industrial heartland in the Transvaal (now Gauteng) so as to facilitate supplies of labour. Bizarrely, one of these islands, Thaba Nchu, was situated hundreds of kilometres away in the Orange Free State to the east of Bloemfontein. Where the borders of Bantustans adjoined industrial centres, daily black commuters endured many long hours travelling to work from their 'own' countries. Their grinding ordeal

Figure 3. Marabastad-Waterval bus: 8:45 p.m., 45 minutes to the terminal, Kwa Ndebele. 1983. Photograph by David Goldblatt.

was memorably recorded in David Goldblatt's photographs of exhausted workers travelling from KwaNdebele to Pretoria.[24]

Impoverished and maladministered as they were, the homelands were not merely labour reservoirs, though this was certainly one of their prime functions. Nor were they simply a means of franchising the task of apartheid repression to authorized 'puppet rulers'. They were complex political and social entities with significant variations between them. For one thing, there were significant differences in scale between tiny homelands like Qwaqwa and much larger territories like Kwa-Zulu or Transkei. Some followed Pretoria's edicts slavishly, others operated in a more autonomous manner. Pretoria's grip on the homeland governments was not always entirely secure. Some homeland politicians skilfully exploited the fact that South Africa was dependent on their cooperation in order to legitimize apartheid; this meant that they could exact more advantageous terms for their cooperation. The differing way in which the homeland government system fragmented in the 1980s (see Chapter 8) is evidence of their differential incorporation into the apartheid state.

As William Beinart points out, the homelands have to be seen in longer historical perspective than the temporal moment of apartheid. During the colonial era, the rural areas that became homelands were neither fully absorbed into, nor perfectly configured to serve the interests of, white-dominated society. The institution of chieftaincy often retained popular appeal and tribal leaders, even those authorized by Pretoria, were not always subject to easy control. Nor were the homelands cheap to run: for all that they were a source of cheap, exploited labour, they absorbed significant state resources. Beinart judges that, by the 1970s, Pretoria expended more money on the administration of the homelands than was recouped by employers through cheap labour.[25]

Influx Control and 'Surplus People'

Verwoerd's overweening belief in the developmental capacity of the technocratic state—and in his own rectitude—led him to think that he could control African urbanization by introducing systematic residential segregation and by fine-controlling the 'influx' and 'efflux' of African labour. Measures like the Group Areas Act, the pass laws, and the labour bureaux equipped the Native Affairs Department and the police to act with a unity of purpose that seemed impossible (and not necessarily desirable) in the segregationist era. From the 1950s, Verwoerd focused on the problem of housing. Sweeping new planning powers allowed the Native Affairs Department to build labour dormitories or 'locations' for Africans with legal rights to reside in urban areas. Ideally, these were to be sited well away from city centres, accessible by highway, and ringed by perimeters which could easily be policed.

Within large black townships in major cities like Johannesburg, concerted efforts were made to contain migrant labour hostels in particular zones or to demarcate areas for different 'tribal' groups. This not only conformed to Christian-National preconceptions of ethnic 'ownness', it also facilitated the overall process of divide and rule. In many townships, the mechanisms of control changed from an older, makeshift, welfare paternalism to a harsher style of bureaucratic governance which Bozzoli refers to as urban 'racial modernism'. Typically, this involved 'loss of citizenship, class, status, cultural security, authority and power' on the part of urban communities; with this erosion of layers of social buffering came a greater propensity for political instability.[26]

A great deal of thought was given to the construction of houses and the racialization of space. In some cases, 'site and service' schemes were created which gave residents a tiny plot, a toilet, access to water, and scope to build their own shacks out of corrugated iron and wood. More commonly, matchbox brick houses were erected in great numbers during the 1950s and 1960s with careful consideration to expense and design. Specialist professional expertise was canvassed from the National Building and Research Institute, set up in 1946 as one of the core agencies of the recently created Council for Scientific and Industrial Research. Architects from Wits University who had absorbed the ideas of Le Corbusier, Ebenezer Howard, and Lewis Mumford brought modernist ideas and garden city ideals to bear in the execution of 'Native Housing Policy'.

Such schemes had been worked out in the expansive liberal environment of the 1930s and 1940s, but it was Verwoerd who gave the professional planners and architects the opportunity to build low-cost housing with scientifically approved 'minimum standards' on a vast scale. If experts like D. M. Calderwood and J. E. Jennings disapproved of apartheid, their misgivings were tempered by professional excitement, a sense of mission, and the comforting claim that home-building was a social good. It turned out that green belts or 'park strips' in beautifully drawn architectural plans could easily become military buffer zones surrounding bleak featureless fields of barrack-like housing. In order to reduce expenditure, detailed technical research and experimentation was conducted so as to cut radically the costs of materials and maximize labour efficiency.

Concessions in the job reservation system were made to allow Africans to be used as skilled builders in black townships. Most important, building programmes were funded wherever possible out of direct and indirect African taxation, a precedent that had already been established in the field of education. Revenue from municipal beer halls proved an especially profitable source of income. Large-scale employers were also tapped for funds. From 1950 to 1970 around 400,000 housing units were built, substantially solving the housing problem which the Smuts government had proved unable to cope with. By any standards, this was an enormous achievement for the apartheid state.[27]

The number of houses built was far more a response to the needs of whites than the demands of blacks. Verwoerd forecast with spurious precision—and quite erroneously—that the urban African population would start to decline in 1978. This required reversing the flow of urbanization by removing all Africans surplus to the requirements of whites to the tribal homelands or Bantustans. Advocates of apartheid, like segregationists before them, understood that the key to retaining white control over cities depended on reinvigorating the African rural reserves. Yet the creation of self-governing homelands or Bantustans configured on the basis of assumed ethnicity was barely conceived—or indeed conceivable—until the end of the 1950s. Historians who ignore this wrongly assume that the era of 'high' apartheid in the 1960s flowed naturally from the policy pronouncements of the late 1940s. To do so is to impute a degree of continuity and singular ideological purpose that has little basis in fact.

The government's hope that the omniscient *Bewysburo* or 'bureau of proof' would manage to assemble a comprehensive archive on every black person, and that this information could be tied through the tax and pass systems to the labour bureaux, was a still-born fantasy by the mid-1950s. But Verwoerd did not give up on his belief that, through systematic planning and elaborate controls, the state could tame the vagaries of the labour market and manage urbanization. The inability of the state to achieve these ends through bureaucratic methods meant that coercion was the only reliable alternative. In this sense, the higher ideals of apartheid required an intensification of *baaskap*.

A parallel judicial system, centred on native commissioners' courts in the urban areas, developed to process the huge volume of pass law offenders whose 'crimes' would otherwise paralyse the conventional criminal justice system.[28] Policemen, black as well as white, served as the frontline enforcers—a feature notably different from that pertaining in the racial regime in the American South. In 1960, when the pass laws were briefly relaxed in the aftermath of Sharpeville, there were 370,000 convictions for transgressors. By 1970, official figures record that 631,000 persons were prosecuted for infringements of the pass laws. Such cases constituted more than a quarter of all prosecutions in the criminal justice system, affecting 3–4 per cent of the African population.[29]

Between 1960 and 1982 as many as 3.5 million people from all over South Africa—more than 10 per cent of the total population—were compulsorily relocated 'in the name of apartheid'.[30] Verwoerd never managed to achieve his object of turning round the flow of Africans to the cities. Nevertheless, urbanization was significantly slowed for a period of twenty years from 1955, while the population of the homelands more than doubled from 1951 to 1970 and doubled again by 1996.[31] Colin Murray memorably characterized the creation of concentrated population settlements (formally situated within the Bantustans and conveniently adjacent to metropolitan labour markets) as a process of 'displaced urbanisation'.[32]

The scale of population removals does not compare with the tens of millions of Europeans who were subject to forced population transfer or repatriation immediately after the Second World War. Ethnic cleansing had been employed for military purposes in the Balkan Wars of 1912–13—and indeed, the Bantustans were often criticized as a form of 'balkanization'.[33] The massive wave of population transfers and deportations that followed the Balkan wars were undertaken in the name of ethnic homogeneity and the protection of minority rights.[34] These European precedents were forged as strategy in the context of war or in the immediate aftermath of conflict. The same might be said of the expulsion of Palestinians from the newly created state of Israel in 1948 and after. What made the large-scale manipulation of population politics in South Africa distinctive was that it was conducted in peacetime and, even more strikingly, that it was intended not so much to protect minorities as to create them: in political terms, the development of a string of ethnically homogeneous black statelets was designed to deprive blacks of their South African citizenship and to transform whites from a political minority into a sovereign majority. Through the Bantustan policy apartheid took to a new level 'colonially inscribed communal land tenure as the main system under which black people could own land'.[35]

Verwoerd's feat of social, demographic, and spatial engineering was achieved at enormous human cost. The Bantustans were freely used as resettlement and dumping grounds for Africans who were (i) deemed to have no rights to be in urban areas, (ii) forced to move from existing urban areas to townships in neighbouring Bantustans—from which they were expected to commute to their existing places of work, (iii) labour tenants and squatters no longer required on white farms, or (iv) Africans inhabiting so-called 'black spots' (zones in proclaimed white areas such as mission stations, many of whose residents possessed deeds of owner-ship that were in their family's name for generations). A further category of displaced people concerned those who were victims of 'homeland consolidation', namely, Africans whose ethnicity was deemed to be at odds with the particular tribal designation of a Bantustan—regardless of how long they had lived there.[36]

The magnitude of the aggregated figure for resettlement was disguised by the fragmented nature of the dispersals, typically a few thousand persons relocated from 'black spots' in areas designated 'white' to remote farms or townships in the countryside. Secrecy and restrictions on permits to visit affected areas made it very difficult to monitor the scale of removals, let alone to comprehend the total picture, until the Surplus People Project began to piece together the process in the early 1980s. The reality for those affected was inescapable: families or individuals were often transported at short notice on white government trucks known as the 'GG' (these letters on the vehicles' number-plates signalled that they came from the Government Garage) and dumped in the open veld. Only the most rudimentary facilities were provided, such as tents or tin huts and pit latrines. Clean water and firewood were scarce, schools and clinics a rarity.

The extent of human suffering, poverty, and starvation that this policy entailed was concealed by the fact that resettlement camps were sited in remote rural areas. They were also hidden by the anonymizing effects of endemic rural poverty. The first systematic exposé of resettlement took the form of a remarkable travelogue conducted by a young Catholic priest, Cosmas Desmond, who journeyed more than 24,000 miles over a period of six months in 1969 in order to document the removals. In *The Discarded People* (1971) Desmond charted conditions in many of the country's bleak hidden resettlement camps in order to attest to the incalculable human costs of apartheid involved in apartheid social engineering. According to Desmond, population removals were the essence of apartheid. They were neither a 'sadistic aberration' nor a product of blind racism: 'It is being done because it *has* to be done if apartheid is to survive.'[37]

This is a moot point, depending in part whether we place the emphasis on economics or politics in our conceptualization of apartheid as a 'system'. Marxists argued that the population removals were designed to entrench the migrant labour system and to complete the process of full proletarianization on white-owned farms. Those dumped in the reserves were said to constitute the 'reserve army of the unemployed' whose existence exerted downward pressure on wages. It was correctly noted that the largest single category of removals were from white farms, typically labour tenants, whose services were no longer required as monopoly capital or agri-business gained control of the countryside. Yet, unless we accept that large-scale redistribution of land to African smallholders was a genuine possibility under a future socialist government (other than at the level of rhetoric) it was inevitable that the continued mechanization of white farms would result in large-scale evictions of black labour tenants, most of whom would have ended up in cities.

One of the key factors behind the resettlement programme was to prevent just this scenario, that is, to reverse or at least retard further black urbanization. Here, the preservation of white power was a powerful

Figure 4. Author, 'Resettlement area, Gazankulu, 1981'.

motivating factor. One of the government's fundamental objectives was to protect white political dominance and, in particular, to ensure that urban areas were clearly demarcated, ordered economic zones, devoid of a potentially troublesome black lumpenproletariat. Political, ideological, and bureaucratic objectives provide the most convincing explanation for relocations pursued in the name of homeland consolidation, 'black spot' removal, and the application of the Group Areas legislation in cities and towns.[38] Such forms of ethnic or racial cleansing are not explicable in economic terms alone.

Research from the 1980s has shown that rural resettlement, like its urban counterpart, was not only achieved through direct coercion. For many Africans, whose position on white farms was becoming increasingly precarious and intolerable, relocation to the Bantustans offered a chance to re-establish households as well as a base from which work-seekers might gain employment as migrant labourers. As Laura Evans demonstrates, resettlement impacted differentially on households, with women often deprived of income and forced to become more dependent on men with jobs. Where remittances were not forthcoming, households faced further impoverishment. Yet even these losses could be offset by the formation of new associational networks and the possibility of different kinds of employment as resettlement camps grew into townships.[39]

In the case of tiny Qwaqwa, whose population grew from around 24,000 in 1970 to some 300,000 in 1980, largely as a result of evictions from white farms in the Orange Free State or from neighbouring towns, relationships to local chiefs and the capacity to exploit patronage networks was a vital factor conditioning the ways in which resettled people reconstructed their lives. Marked social differentiation in households was the result.[40] It is hard to think of any apartheid policy that was more disruptive and socially destructive than the population removals of the 1960s and 1970s. Nevertheless, human ingenuity and resilience meant that the negative effects of resettlement could, over time, be mitigated.

No community's experience of removal was quite like another, for dispossession and relocation was not a unitary process. Thus, examples of resettlement with evocative names like Limehill, Stinkwater, Rooigrond, and Klipfontein have to stand as symbols of the process as a whole. The sheer human misery wreaked by the resettlement policies was graphically illustrated by 'Last Grave at Dimbaza', a film secretly made in 1974 by Nana Mahomo, a Johannesburg-born exile affiliated to the Pan-Africanist Congress. Dimbaza was a squalid resettlement camp in the Ciskei Bantustan. It had earlier came to public attention when David Russell, an Anglican priest, subsisted there for six months on the average African old age pension of 5 rands per month, suffering the effects of cold and lethargy.

Mahomo's film neatly contrasted white suburban privilege and prosperity with poverty, malnutrition, disease, and high mortality rates in the Bantustans. It closed with images of infant graves marked with plastic feeding bottles in Dimbaza. Here, according to the Black Sash women's organization, 115 children (9 per thousand of the total population) died in 1971–2, mainly of gastroenteritis. In one sequence of the film a pregnant black servant is seen feeding a suburban white child; the viewer is informed that her own son has died of malnutrition while her daughter is being cared for hundreds of miles away in a Bantustan. Her husband is meanwhile compelled to live separately in an all-male barracks in Soweto.[41]

Mahomo's target audience was international. In showing the consequences of the 'twin apartheid policies of resettlement and migrant labour', he pointed to the involvement of major foreign-owned corporations reaping profits from South Africa by paying their workers poverty wages. When the film was screened on public television in the United States in 1975, it was followed by a debate featuring the South African ambassador 'Pik' Botha, and the *New York Times* columnist Anthony Lewis. Mahomo was not able to participate in the discussion because WNET's president, Jay Iselin, accepted that the South African government could not allow its ambassador to appear with a black representative from South Africa. The film was viewed in South Africa by senior state officials and parliamentarians and the government responded with a series of propaganda films of its own, designed to counter 'Last Grave at Dimbaza's' significant international impact and samizdat circulation on South African university campuses.

Influx controls, population resettlement, and Bantustan creation involved a heady mix of self-deluding ideological vision and cynical calculation. The homelands were at one level an expensive folly aimed at achieving an unrealizable apartheid fantasy; at another level the use of ethnicity proved successful as a means of dividing opposition and manipulating demography and space, while facilitating the continued flow of migrant labour on highly unequal terms to the cities. It remains an open question—and probably an unanswerable one—whether the economic waste and profligacy involved in the creation of the Bantustans was offset by the political stability that allowed white South Africa to exploit black labour effectively and attract inward investment in the post-Sharpeville decade. What is clear is that short-term gains for white supremacy were illusory and bought at enormous human cost.

As we have seen, Verwoerd believed that systematic planning, overseen by an omniscient bureaucracy, would tame the vagaries of the market and control urbanization in a 'rational' and 'orderly' fashion. The labour bureaux, which were grafted onto the existing taxation and pass law system from the 1950s, used the voluminous data created by the Population Registration Act. Extensive and highly expensive techniques—fingerprints, photographs, statistical enumeration, and computing power—were deployed by the *Bewysburo* or 'Bureau of Proof' to organize information in a massive and unmanageable archive. This data was distilled into the 'reference' or 'pass book' which Africans were compelled to produce on demand at pain of instant arrest.

The domains of information-gathering and labour allocation were kept formally separate, though both fell under the burgeoning Department of

Bantu Administration, whose ever expanding size and authority (it was often dubbed a 'state within a state') was not matched by increased functional capacity: staff shortages were evident from the mid-1950s and skills were often lacking. Forgeries and corruption became endemic. The bureaucratic methods of labour allocation, which treated each individual only as a 'unit', relied on an oppressive apparatus to maintain order and efficiency.

Over time the sheer number of arrests under the pass laws, and the process of 'endorsing out' those caught illegally in the cities, became virtually impossible to manage. The bureaucrats' reflex was to refine legislation, reduce people to statistics, and always to insist on control. Often this was fictive. One of apartheid's defining features was the contrast between the maintenance of a high degree of 'law and order' in areas denominated as 'white', and the situation in many black townships where misrule and disorder were tolerated by the state.[42] The writ of government authority and control was in key respects an illusion, but it remained an illusion that most white voters continued to subscribe to, if only to allay their fears that any relaxation of power would end up in chaos.

The manifest contradictions between policy and practice were typically smoothed by euphemism and collective denial. In 1963 a delegation of women from the Black Sash met the Minister of Bantu Administration and Development and officials to discuss their concerns about the impact of the Bantu Laws Amendment Bill on family life and to highlight the cruel consequences for individuals. The Department was impervious to criticisms of the cruelty, inefficiency, and inconsistencies associated with the operation of influx control. Officials merely restated, politely and patiently, the need for control; in doing so they resorted to a practised technical vocabulary that characterized people as 'idle' and 'undesirable', 'surplus' labour, 'endorsed outs', 'missing women', and, in their tortuous logic, 'prescribed Africans who are exempt'.[43]

Education

Bantu education was one of the most despised of the apartheid measures because of the way in which it set a clear limit on African aspirations by subjecting students to a strictly regulated and elementary educational curriculum. From the perspective of Verwoerdian ideology, the Act made logical sense: the state centralized education within the Native Affairs Department, provided sufficient training to equip labourers with the most basic functional skills, and reinforced the notion that Africans should achieve their full cultural potential and political ambitions only in the Bantustans. This objective was clearly stated by Werner Eiselen, a key influence on the conception as well as the implementation of apartheid education, who argued that 'black education should be aimed at developing a higher Bantu culture and not at producing black Europeans'.[44]

Although the effects of Bantu education were disastrous on many levels (including skills shortages), in the short term it met pent-up demand by providing a rudimentary mass-based education to many primary and secondary students who previously had no schooling at all. It also inculcated a sense of inferiority and lowered expectations for a generation and more. Until 1972 the state refused to allow the private sector to be involved in black education and actively discouraged black technical training in urban areas. To this extent, Bantu education helped to secure white supremacy, though, as will become clear, its determination to subject all aspects of black education to official diktat became the proximate cause of the Soweto uprisings of 1976–7.

The principles of Bantu education were extended to the tertiary sphere with the so-called Extension of University Education Act of 1959. This initiative provided for the creation of special 'ethnic' universities for Africans, as well as one each for Indians and coloureds; moreover, it determined that the so-called 'open' universities (Cape Town and Wits) would in future be able to enrol non-white students only with special government permission.[45] Given the tiny numbers of African university applicants at this time, it was hardly a response to need (in 1956 only two in a thousand Africans were at university).[46] Situating all the African universities in remote rural areas was a perverse but very deliberate decision. Intended to redirect black ambitions and energies back into the homelands, it often had the effect of undermining them from within.

The Extension of Universities Act was passed in the face of strong parliamentary opposition, including a substantial body of dissident

119

Afrikaner opinion. It was seen at the time as one of high apartheid's great follies, a testament to the ideologically driven search for purity as well as the condescending arrogance of Verwoerd who, in 1958, informed a journalist, 'I do not have the nagging doubt of ever wondering whether, perhaps, I am wrong.'[47] The extent to which the government was prepared to take its ideological approach to education to extremes was shown again in 1962 when the cabinet decided that 'non-Europeans' would not be allowed to participate in racially mixed scientific and professional organizations. Leaders of such organizations saw this as a potentially crippling blow to their international credentials; they also observed that the injunction would have very limited practical effect in view of the fact that so few blacks were members of scientific institutions.

Unlike the new Afrikaans universities, which were lavishly supported, and designed to serve as visible proof of Afrikaner cultural and scientific accomplishment, the new 'bush' or 'tribal' colleges (as they were dismissively referred to) were third-rate institutions—not least because they were wholly controlled and largely staffed by *Broederbond*-approved graduates of the Afrikaans universities. By so doing, the government placed approved white, largely Afrikaner graduates, in a position of direct oversight over African, coloured, and Indian students. In the early 1970s, it was from within these most unloved apartheid institutions that fundamental new challenges to white hegemony would emerge.[48]

Opposition from Within

Even at the height of its power the autocratic apartheid state was not totalitarian; dissent and criticism was accepted, within certain limits. Some of this came from within otherwise loyal Afrikaner circles. Piet Cillié, editor of the Cape newspaper *Die Burger*, gave voice to the pragmatic ideas of Stellenbosch University intellectuals, often in coruscating fashion. In 1964 he warned, 'We can not and should not become the last bastion of a wrong order when the Afrikaners as a people had been forged in resisting a similar order.'[49] More forthright still was Schalk Pienaar, Cillé's former deputy editor, who assumed the editorship of the newly formed Sunday newspaper *Beeld* in 1965 and took an independent line from the National Party. Pienaar saw Verwoerd's dogmatism as inimical to the future of Afrikanerdom. He became an outspoken proponent of reform, while retaining a belief in apartheid as an ideal.

In common with many socially liberal Cape Afrikaners, Pienaar was strongly opposed to the 'northern' view that 'coloureds' should be treated as a distinct racial group, preferring to see them as *bruin* (brown) Afrikaners who deserved a measure of direct political representation. He expressed outrage at irksome examples of *klein* or 'petty' apartheid such as the spectacle of Indian golfer 'Papwa' Segolum, winner of the 1963 Natal Open, being handed his trophy in the rain because the Group Areas Act precluded him from entering the clubhouse. Pienaar was sceptical of the view that the homelands were a panacea or that black nationalism could be headed off indefinitely.[50]

These *verligte* critics were not yet opponents of apartheid. Rather, they grew out of a long tradition of 'lojale verset' (loyal opposition) and 'voortbestaan in geregtigheid' (survival/continued existence in justice). These concepts were closely associated with the renowned poet N. P. van Wyk Louw, who sought to elaborate a morally defensible version of apartheid and Afrikaner nationalism during the 1940s which was capacious enough to allow the speaking of truth to power. In the case of van Wyk Louw, the inclination to moral honesty and debate did not lead to a critique of the fundamentals of apartheid; instead, it became a sophisticated form of apologetics that served to revalidate Afrikaner nationalism and the ethical basis of separate development.

In 1963 a new Afrikaans literary journal, *Sestiger*, was founded. The term soon came to denote an emerging group of bohemian Afrikaans writers and intellectuals, collectively known as *Sestigers* (generation of the 1960s), who sought to challenge Afrikaner nationalism from a more socially radical perspective. Impatient with apartheid's constrictions— on themselves as individuals as much as on others—writers like Bartho Smit, Etienne Leroux, André Brink, Jan Rabie, Uys Krige, and Ingrid Jonker turned to European existentialism and surrealism in order to break with the parochial literary conventions of pastoral realism as typified by the *plaasroman* (farm novel). One of those who developed a new aesthetic of rebellion and resistance was Ingrid Jonker, a talented and troubled young poet—sometimes compared to Sylvia Plath—who drowned herself in 1965. Her friend and lover, André Brink, was the author of *Kennis van die Aand* (1973), the first novel in Afrikaans to fall foul of the censor's law. It was banned for blasphemy, pornography, and endangering the security of the state.[51]

The *Sestigers* were by no means entirely disowned by the Afrikaner nationalist establishment, who alternated between chastising the young rebels from pulpits and awarding them literary prizes from podiums. Within the Calvinist family, minor acts of rebellion by misguided children were tolerated so long as the authority or respect of the father figure was not wholly impugned. Ingrid Jonker publicly campaigned against the very censorship laws that her estranged father, Abraham, championed in parliament.[52] In 1969 André Brink wrote to Prime Minister Vorster, drawing a parallel between De Gaulle's suppression of students on the streets of Paris and the violence meted out to protesting students by police on the steps of St George's Cathedral in Cape Town. Brink expressed the facetious wish that the prime minister should sleep peacefully. In reply, Vorster replied that he did not take advice from 'pink liberals' and expressed the hope that Brink would sleep well 'in spite of the curlers in your hair'.[53]

Intense struggles between censors and artists were one arena in which the battle to define the boundaries of what was politically permissible or morally permissive was played out. In Brink's case, the experience of being 'banned' by the government's Publications Control Board, coupled with harassment by the police Special Branch, impelled him to become fully committed to an anti-apartheid position. Open defiance was also expressed by the leading poet and *enfant terrible* of Afrikaner letters, Breyten Breytenbach, who scandalized white South Africa when he married his Vietnamese partner in contravention of the Immorality Act.

Breytenbach lived in exile in Paris until he returned secretly to South Africa in 1975 on behalf of a small resistance group, Okhela, which was loosely linked to the ANC. Arrested and jailed for treason, Breytenbach later wrote a searing account of his imprisonment as *The True Confessions of an Albino Terrorist* (1985). This inward meditation on power and dissidence repudiates Afrikanerdom and Afrikaans, but nonetheless seeks to reposition the language as a hybrid or creole African tongue so as to invoke a greater sense of South African-ness.[54]

The state showed no mercy to Breytenbach, despite the fact that his poetry continued to be prescribed for study in schools. In a personal letter to Breyten's father, who had petitioned the government for his son's early release, an unforgiving Prime Minister Vorster consoled him with the thought that Breyten's betrayal was compensated for by another son, Jan, a legendary 'counter-terrorist' leader in the military. The tight-knit, sometimes intimate circles within which Afrikaner dissent often occurred aroused much bitterness and controversy. But it could also be seen as a self-referential, interior conversation that amounted to a form of intellectual 'complicity'.[55] The net effect may have been to strengthen, rather than diminish, Afrikaner hegemony in the 1960s and 1970s, not least by encouraging the perception that apartheid could only be reformed 'from within'.

Liberal Voices and Institutions

By the 1960s the majority of English-speakers had accommodated themselves to government policy, albeit without necessarily actually voting for the government. Many grumbled about the more authoritarian and puritanical aspects of government, as well as the absurdities of apartheid policy, while taking comfort in their marginalized, minority status. Jokes about Afrikaner stupidity—encapsulated by the stock figure of 'Van der Merwe'—abounded. Disengagement from politics seemingly excused English-speakers from complicity in the more odious aspects of apartheid. Notably, they were the only group in the category-obsessed apartheid state who generally avoided being defined in ethnic or national terms. They saw themselves as normal, non-ideological, voices of reason, squeezed uncomfortably between the unpalatable extremes of Afrikaner and African nationalisms.

Newspaper cartoons and satire were licensed forms of dissent that were mostly allowed by the state. The best of the cartoonists—David Marais, Abe Berry, Bob Conolly, John Jackson, among them—were technically able, sharply satirical, and alert to the more ridiculous aspects of apartheid. But they posed no real threat and were easily tolerated.[56] Tom Sharpe, the English-born and -educated comic writer, wrote farcical novels such as *Riotous Assembly* (1971) or *Indecent Exposure* (1973) which caricatured the stupidity of apartheid functionaries like the police.

Counter-culturalism in the 1960s found expression in the music of folk and pop singers like Colin Shamley and Four Jacks and a Jill who could be implicitly subversive, albeit without representing any challenge to the state.[57] Jeremy Taylor wrote satirical songs, the best known of which, 'Ag Pleez Deddy' (1961), gently mocked a white suburban child's entreaties to see a movie at the drive-in and eat an 'Eskimo Pie' ice-cream. Sixto Rodriguez's iconic anti-establishment record *Cold Fact* circulated widely amongst white hippies and left-wingers in the 1970s. Several songs from this lyrical album became anthems of wistful youth rebellion.[58]

Perhaps the greatest impact of these kinds of tolerable dissidence was to flatter English-speakers by reassuring them that they remained in touch with a wider international world and that they were therefore not responsible for apartheid, let alone part of an elite that benefited directly from the economic exploitation of blacks. This represented no real threat to the state, notwithstanding the screeching voices of criticism denouncing decadent, hippy culture. But even as indirectly critical voices, the white counter-culture helped to maintain a subversive space that was to be expanded by more radical new left ideas from the end of the 1960s. Such ideas gained currency amongst the minority of English-speakers who remained intractably opposed to the government.

Above all it was through literature that some of the most articulate anti-apartheid voices were heard. Alan Paton's *Cry the Beloved Country* (1948) was a landmark in liberal protest writing. This iconic novel enjoyed a sensational response in South Africa and abroad, especially in the United States where it was made into a film by Zoltan Korda in 1952 and re-released over and again for book clubs and schools. Rather like *Uncle Tom's Cabin* a century earlier, Paton's text was widely criticized for its moralizing liberal paternalism and for propagating a genre of writing centring on Africans' problematic encounter with modern urban life ('Jim Comes to Joburg').[59]

In the post-Sharpeville period new writers came to the fore who consciously departed from Paton's sentimentalizing Christian human-ism. Nadine Gordimer first came to attention in South Africa in the 1940s. She gained international notice with her first published novel, *The Lying Days* (1953), which was praised by the *New York Times* for offering insight into 'the whole panorama of this explosive continent's most explosive corner'.[60] Gordimer's short story collection *Friday's Footprint* was awarded the W. H. Smith Commonwealth Literary prize in 1961 and listed by the *New York Times* as one of the 200 best works of fiction in the world.[61] Many accolades followed, culminating in her receipt of the Nobel Prize for Literature in 1991. Gordimer's long career as a novelist encompasses the entire apartheid (and post-apartheid) era and cumulatively explores the psychological ambiguities and moral choices of life under South Africa's evolving racial system. Her acute awareness of history, coupled with her facility as a critical essayist, have made her one of the country's great interpreters: South Africa's 'archivist and lighthouse-keeper'.[62]

The dramatist Athol Fugard, whose literary career mirrors Gordimer's in some respects, staged his first play, *No-Good Friday*, with a racially mixed cast at the Bantu Men's Social Centre in Johannesburg in 1958. Fugard came to international attention with *Bloodknot* (1961), a play exploring the relationship between two unlikely brothers, one black, the other coloured. First staged in London in 1963, with Ian Bannen and Zakes Mokae, *Bloodknot* was hailed as a major 'piece of Resistance literature'. In New York it was critically acclaimed as the 'most original and penetrating play' of the 1964 season.

Fugard's trademark is his ability to tell a finely textured story through closely observed attention to relationships between marginalized, but at the same time ordinary, representative characters. His method of bearing witness homes in on specific everyday details so as to illuminate larger themes about human existence, and this combination lends his anti-apartheid message universal appeal.[63] As well as touring worldwide, Fugard's plays were performed in South African theatres that refused to obey segregationist strictures like The African Theatre Workshop in Sophiatown, The Space in Cape Town, and the Market Theatre in downtown Johannesburg. These venues became the fora for experimental 'protest' and 'township' theatre and did much to broker a spirited exchange of radical, counter-cultural ideas for non-racial audiences and performers alike.[64]

As white writers, both Gordimer and Fugard have attracted criticism over the years. In 1963 *Blood Knot* was dismissed by the English theatre critic Kenneth Tynan for merely reflecting white guilt.[65] Yet the inescapable fact remains that most anti-apartheid protest in the 1960s was dominated by white, liberal voices, with the capacity to disturb the consciences of other white liberal voices in the West. This collective moral conscience did much to universalize the evils of apartheid. It is seldom mentioned in histories of the anti-apartheid movement.

To ignore the importance of international voices like Fugard and Gordimer in the 1960s is also to underestimate the extent to which the efflorescent domestic expressions of black cultural and political life in the 1950s were crushed after Sharpeville. The 1950s was quintessentially the generation of *Drum*, a magazine catering to aspirational black urban sophisticates, which gave voice to muscular journalists and short story writers like Nat Nakasa, Can Themba, Lewis Nkosi, Bloke Modisane, and Todd Matshikiza. By the mid-1960s, this generation of writers, who wrote so powerfully about the experience of apartheid, were subject to censorship and banning or were driven into lonely, rueful, exile.

A special *Government Gazette*, published on 1 April 1966, 'banned' no less than forty-six authors, which effectively meant that their work was erased from public view.[66] Black poets like Denis Brutus, Arthur Nortje, James Matthews, and Oswald Mtshali continued to write from within South Africa or abroad. A few novels were published, including Richard Rive's *Emergency* (1964), Bessie Head's *When Rain Clouds Gather* (1969), and Alex La Guma's *A Walk in the Night* (1962). There were also autobiographical works and memoirs focusing on the experience of apartheid, such as Es'kia Mphalele's *Down Second Avenue*, Noni Jabavu's *Drawn in Colour* (1963), Todd Matshikiza's *Chocolates for my Wife* (1961), and Bloke Modisane's *Blame Me on History* (1964). Yet, taken altogether, the literary output of black South Africans was relatively thin during the 1960s, and the work of most black authors that did emerge was characterized by isolation, loss, despair, and nostalgia.

Political opposition to the apartheid government during the 1960s was silenced but not entirely eviscerated. Following the banning of the Communists, the Liberal Party was the only non-racial political organization left intact. It chose to disband after the Prohibition of Improper Interference Act (1968) outlawed racially mixed political activity. The official opposition United Party barely offered any resistance to the government and, in 1959, a number of reformers split away to create the Progressive Party.

From 1961 to 1974 only one Progressive remained in parliament, the redoubtable Helen Suzman, a consistent defender of civil liberties and courageous inquisitor of power in the legislature. Suzman also used her position to defend women's rights and attend to the welfare of black political prisoners. On economic issues, she was an orthodox supporter of the free market, a stance that disappointed many on the left. The Progressive Party was heavily dependent on the support of English-speaking big business and it eschewed the universal franchise (until 1978), holding to the view that educational and property qualifications had first to be satisfied in order to gain the vote.

Outside of parliament the Black Sash, established in 1955 by white women to defend the constitution, mixed respectability and high moral purpose with practical social awareness. It has strong claims to be the first modern human rights campaigning organization in the country. The Sash's network of 'advice centres' gave invaluable legal help to people who fell foul of the pass laws and the migrant labour system.

The Christian Institute (1963–77) and the South African Council of Churches were key repositories of ecumenical conscience, with a breadth of constituency that few other institutions could match. As will be shown in Chapter 6, the commitment and organizational capacity of the churches was a crucial resource, not least in the emergence of Black Consciousness thinking from the late 1960s. Yet, from the perspective of young black religious leaders like Allan Boesak, there were limits to what 'concerned white Christians' in organizations like the Christian Institute and the Black Sash could achieve: 'Everything was done for us, on our behalf.'[67]

The Christian Institute and South African Council of Churches were responsible for establishing The Study Project on Christianity in an Apartheid Society (1969–73) which brought together a diverse range of religious and secular opinion to deliberate on the country's underlying problems. In the process, it helped to nurture a new generation of radical thinkers. The South African Institute of Race Relations' centrist orientation led it to desist from direct political engagement. But it published authoritative facts and statistics in its annual reports and provided research which proved valuable to activists in community organizations, trade unions, and universities. It too acted as an important network for the spread of critical ideas and information.

Public interest lawyers like George Bizos, Sydney Kentridge, Issie Maisels, and Arthur Chaskalson managed at times to win notable victories in the courts and thereby helped to expand the realms of political dissent. They were supported by academic lawyers like Ben Beinart at the University of Cape Town. The pro-business but anti-government English liberal press managed to be both conformist and critical. Its most outstanding example was the *Rand Daily Mail* which, under the general editorship of Laurie Gandar (1957–69), remained a vital source of information, supporting intrepid investigative journalism into prison conditions, the operation of the pass laws, and general misuse of power.

Liberal universities, such as the large civics (the University of Cape Town and Wits) as well as regional institutions (Rhodes in Grahamstown and the University of Natal), were also significant brokerages and repositories of anti-apartheid thought.[68] Such universities provided relatively protected spaces where liberal and radical ideas could be essayed. Yet their overall record as 'anti-apartheid' institutions was rather ambiguous: although the liberal universities resisted the 1959 Separate Universities Act as a matter of principle, they conformed to apartheid strictures in practice, finding that their elite status could cushion them from the needs of society as well as the wishes of government.

The contradictions and complacencies of the liberal university were exemplified in 1968 when 300 students at the University of Cape Town occupied the central administration building for ten days to protest against the university council's timidity in rescinding its appointment to a lectureship of Archie Mafeje, a black anthropologist, following direct pressure by the government. Cape Town University's abject handling of the Mafeje appointment highlighted some of the tensions and dilemmas of liberal institutions under apartheid. The argument was conducted over the head of Mafeje himself, who seems to have been the object rather than the subject of protest. But for the participants themselves the experience was a moment of radical epiphany.[69]

The student occupation, with its protest songs and 'teach-ins' (much inspired by student leader Rick Turner), spread to Wits University in

Johannesburg too, and was the nearest South Africa came to the European and North American events of 1968. It also served to highlight ambiguities in the National Union of South African Students (NUSAS), a national federal body comprising more than 20,000 mostly white English-speaking students with a history going back to the mid-1920s.

Having lost the affiliation of Afrikaans campuses in the 1930s, NUSAS nevertheless maintained links with Africans at Fort Hare, Turfloop, and a few other 'tribal' black tertiary educational institutions. Its leadership was generally more radical-inclined than its comfortable, anglophone base, and its leaders periodically outraged conservative opinion by declaring war on the South African 'way of life'—for example, by inviting Martin Luther King to open its 1966 congress (Robert Kennedy came instead in June, and was met by enthusiastic crowds in Soweto and elsewhere).[70] Justice Minister John Vorster referred to NUSAS in 1963 as 'a cancer in the life of South Africa that must be cut out'.[71] But he did not succeed in carrying out his threat. By the end of the 1960s, new left and neo-Marxist ideas were freely circulating within the organization and NUSAS, challenged by criticisms from the Black Consciousness movement, was forced to reassess its role as a liberal voice.

Liberalism in 1960s South Africa may not have run deep, but its institutional reach was broad, and its history long. It was a 'thin' universalist creed, but resilient for all its fragility. Despite its limitations, ambiguities, and self-regarding complacency, liberalism could also be idealistic and courageous. In practice, the liberal tradition had to deal with two major issues which it found difficult to acknowledge let alone to grapple with: first, the effective complicity of anglophone corporations in the apartheid 'system' and, second, widespread questioning of the assumption that liberal precepts were generally applicable and that the fight against apartheid racialism could just as well be led by whites as blacks.

Increasingly, liberals found themselves assailed from all political directions. During the sit-in over the Mafeje affair at the University of Cape Town in 1968, students from the leading Afrikaner University of Stellenbosch travelled to Cape Town and stormed the UCT administration buildings with the intention of ending the sit-in themselves. When protesting students from Wits University sent a delegation to see

Prime Minister Vorster in January 1969, they were intercepted by Afrikaans students from Pretoria University who forcibly shaved off the long hair of the 'hippies'. This was the contra- counter-culture. Far more challenging to white liberals were the black students from the newly constituted South African Students Organization; two months later, they greeted visiting NUSAS students with sarcastic cries of 'Hello Baas, Hello Missus'.[72]

CHAPTER 5
THE OPPOSITION DESTROYED

Into Exile

By 1965 the liberation movements in South Africa had been smashed and eviscerated. Bram Fischer bravely sought to keep the Communist Party alive within the country—at great personal cost—but with his arrest its cellular structure effectively collapsed. Hopes that apartheid could be defeated within a relatively short time were sometimes expressed: the PAC announced that liberation would occur in 1963, while the more cautious ANC tended to speak of 'five years' (but who knew when to start counting?). It was not only the analysis of the liberation movements that proved mistaken. The incoming US ambassador to South Africa was reportedly advised by the State Department in 1960 to prepare for black majority rule within 18 months to 5 years.[1]

For the ANC and the PAC the new reality was that they were both engaged in a fight for organizational survival and legitimacy away from home. Operating in the alienating and corrosive environment of exile, jealousies, rivalries, and fears about enemy infiltration were ubiquitous.

The bleak situation within South Africa is captured in the first stanza of 'This Kid is No Goat' by Oswald Mtshali:

> Where have
> All the angry young men gone?
> Gone to the Island of Lament for Sharpeville.
> Gone overseas on scholarship,
> Gone up North to milk and honeyed Uhuru.
> Gone to the dogs with the drink of despair.[2]

Recent efforts to chart continuities in the underground movement and to question the impression of political 'quiescence' from the mid-1960s are not very convincing. The evidence provided—deep underground cells, occasional pamphleteering, secret support networks, and efforts to spirit cadres out of the country—only serves to reinforce ANC historian Francis Meli's admission that, 'After Rivonia, the underground machinery of the liberation movement was almost completely destroyed, with the ANC and other political leaders in jail, exiled, banned or under one form of restriction or another.'[3]

The scale of this defeat appears even more devastating when one considers that it occurred at just the time that other settler societies in Africa (Algeria, Kenya, Mozambique and Angola, Rhodesia) were rapidly losing ground to African nationalist movements—or about to capitulate to them. Ellis and Sechaba's remark that 'All that was left of the nationalist opposition . . . was a few sad exiles out of touch with home'[4] is a harsh judgement, but not so wide of the mark.

Liberation Movements in Africa

Rebuilding the liberation movement in exile posed enormous challenges. The first objective was to establish an overseas presence. Hopes that newly independent African countries would prove receptive to the liberation movements were often unfulfilled. While several countries hosted refugees, promises of material assistance were rarely met. The Organization of African Unity provided rhetorical support but little by the way of material aid. The ANC's distinctive multi-racial alliance forged in the 1950s did not translate easily into the decolonizing world of the African continent. Here, the ethos of pan-Africanism and the distinctiveness of the 'African personality' predominated. Translating the open style of politics of that decade into a more secretive and security-conscious form of organization entailed a very different oppositional culture.

In Tanzania, where the African headquarters of the ANC external mission was based, the involvement of non-Africans and Communists was frowned upon.[5] After 1960, the direct influence of the South African Communist Party on the ANC became significantly stronger, especially through the agency of the MK High Command, which was composed of select members of the Party's central committee and the ANC. Revolutionary action, backed by theory, suited the Party's view of itself as an elite vanguard and created intimate bonds between the leadership of both organizations. But this convergence heightened fears that the Communists were exercising undue influence. It was not unusual for Communists to work together with nationalists elsewhere in the world. Nevertheless, the closeness of the relationship was exceptional on the African continent. Whites working for the ANC in Africa were often presumed to be Communists.[6]

Leaders of new independent states like Kwame Nkrumah of Ghana, the 'black star of Africa', were intuitively attuned to the PAC. It spoke the language of Africanism and appeared to represent a more militant and direct threat to apartheid. Nkrumah was regarded as a hero by PAC militants in South Africa. Some Poqo cadres looked to the Mau Mau insurrection in Kenya for inspiration. When Mandela travelled in Africa in 1962 to gain support for the ANC he was taken aback by the weight of support for the PAC.[7]

In an effort to overcome divisions and to demonstrate African unity, a number of African states persuaded the ANC to join a South African United Front in 1960. This included the PAC as well as liberation movements from South West Africa (Namibia).[8] The Front was a reluctant merger of unequals which, coming just a year after the PAC split, testified more to the weakness of the exile movements and their dependence on outside patronage than it did to their willingness to combine forces. Despite hopes for its future, and some propaganda successes, the Unity Front collapsed within two years amid lack of trust and insuperable rivalries. The ANC responded by presenting an 'African image' to the world in an effort to prove itself the vanguard of the liberation movement and to dispel accusations that it was insufficiently black.[9]

The PAC established itself in Basutoland in 1962, birthplace of Potlako Leballo, its acting president. A small mountain kingdom entirely encircled by South Africa, the country's existence as an independent nation (it became Lesotho in 1966) was testimony both to African resistance to colonial conquest and an accident of imperial history. Infiltration by spies and the growing hostility of the host administration eventuated in Leballo's expulsion in 1964. Thereafter, the PAC moved its principal operations to Tanzania.

Attempts to infiltrate Poqo guerrillas in 1963–4 so as to deliver a decisive 'blow' to white South Africa proved fruitless. A mission to send guerrillas into South Africa via Mozambique in 1968 was also ineffective. While retaining demonstrable ideological appeal in the deep rural areas of the eastern Cape and in urban areas where migrants were based, the PAC failed to establish a sound organizational profile. Its years in exile were characterized by turbulent factional splits, shortage of funds, and chronic maladministration.[10] Leballo's highly personalized, not to say idiosyncratic, form of leadership proved destabilizing.

In exile, survival rested to a considerable extent on the extent to which organizations could project themselves as legitimate representatives of the oppressed. External recognition by the Organization of African Unity and the United Nations gave the PAC formal equivalence to the ANC. But this recognition masked the extent to which the PAC leadership in exile was losing touch with its membership. Notwithstanding these setbacks, the PAC proved tenacious. Its insistence that South Africa was an indivisible part of 'Afrika' had appeal, and the term it customarily used to describe South Africa—Azania—gained currency amongst Africanist groupings well into the 1980s.[11]

By 1965 the ANC was beginning to erode the PAC's claims to primacy in Tanzania. However, the success of the ANC's authentic 'African image' was double-edged: the policy strained the politics of democratic 'multi-racialism' and brought to the surface ongoing divisions relating to the role of non-Africans in the ANC which festered throughout the 1960s.[12] Smaller partner organizations within the Congress Alliance (such as the Coloured People's Congress) feared that they were being eclipsed. In 1966 the Coloured People's Congress dissolved itself and joined the PAC, having in its own words failed to persuade the ANC to 'open its doors for all the oppressed groups'.[13]

In London, where the ANC's external mission in Europe was centred, the ANC's African image also proved problematic. As a hub for anti-colonial organizations, and a traditional place of gathering for émigrés and exiles, London was well suited to serve as a diplomatic and organizational centre for the ANC. Several leading members of the

Communist Party, whose secretariat was largely white and Indian, settled in Britain. Its tight-knit cellular structures offered a home, a family, as well as clear political direction. London was also a natural destination for liberal and radical fellow-travellers who were sympathetic to the liberation movement but not necessarily formally part of Congress Alliance structures. In effect, this meant that the political—and racial—complexion of the ANC in London was quite different from its composition in post-colonial Africa.

White, coloured, and Indian activists were often well educated and equipped to pursue professional careers alongside their political commitments. They were able to work in solidarity organizations associated with the developing anti-apartheid movement. As the split away of the Coloured People's Congress showed, it was not possible to reproduce in exile the same structured multi-racialism that characterized the Congress Alliance of the 1950s. The so-called 'London Debates' of the mid-1960s marked an attempt to redefine the terms upon which non-Africans might participate in the Congress movement. A special committee, chaired by Yusuf Dadoo, was established in London in an effort to reconfigure the Congress Alliance, and to consider the balance between armed activity and other forms of political and solidarity work.[14] A settled consensus proved elusive.

In Africa the question of race was more pressing. Leading non-African Communist Party members like Yusuf Dadoo, Joe Slovo, and Ruth First were banned from Tanzania. Others were made to feel unwelcome and henceforth based themselves in London.[15] Meanwhile, influential ANC figures like Robert Resha and Tennyson Makiwane, both Communists and former members of the Youth League, were coming under the influence of Africanist currents of thought, thus exacerbating internal tensions with and within the Party. Tennyson Makiwane used the refrain: 'Africa is ours. Others must stay in Britain.'[16] In 1969, Ben Turok, a member of MK based in Tanzania, wrote a letter of complaint to the ANC National Executive in which he urged that the 'cancer of colour be not allowed to play the part it is now playing within our movement'.[17] In exile during the 1960s, old divisions of race and ideology within the Congress Alliance, now exacerbated by distance and displacement, were resurfacing.

Broadly speaking, the configuration of support for the ANC/MK was formed on a triple-legged structure: military training and financial backing was received from states in the Soviet bloc; political and ideological support for the anti-apartheid movement was forthcoming from civil society organizations in western Europe (the Swedish government provided a stream of funds) and the United States; Tanzania and the 'frontline' African states provided military bases and places of refuge. The liberation movement relied on support from all three at different times and with differing levels of enthusiasm—with the United Nations (and to a lesser extent the Commonwealth and Non-Aligned Movement) serving as points of brokerage and gateways to diplomatic recognition. Widespread international revulsion towards apartheid made it possible for the liberation movements to seek support from the Soviet Union, China, and the West at varying times. This tested the political and diplomatic skills of the ANC's leadership in Lusaka and London, but over the long run gave it a breadth of experience and contacts which could be turned to advantage.

Financial and organizational pressures posed constant problems. Lack of resources and a chronic tendency to factionalism greatly reduced the PAC's effectiveness by the end of the 1960s. The ANC proved better able to adapt to exile with its ability to command support from many different sources. Nevertheless, it suffered as a campaigning organization as a result of being increasingly distant from its 'people'.

The aura that surrounds Nelson Mandela has tended to eclipse the singular role played by Oliver Tambo, often known as 'O.R.', in the long years of exile. Tambo's official designation as the ANC's 'deputy' president indicated weakness to some, yet this ultimately proved to be a strength since it underlined the idea of collective leadership—in contrast to many other nationalist struggles in Africa which became overly identified with a single individual.

Tambo's consummate diplomatic and negotiating skills, logical lawyer's mind, and careful cultivation of a consensual style of collective leadership, were assets that sustained the ANC over thirty difficult years of displacement.[18] Tambo was also sufficiently confident to vest moral and political authority with those left behind: Albert Luthuli, living under conditions of banishment in Natal, and those imprisoned on

Robben Island, foremost among them his friend and trusted compatriot Nelson Mandela. Without Tambo's cautious diplomacy and aversion to egotism, it is quite possible that the ANC in exile might have fragmented around factions or imploded.

Tambo's Christian background and beliefs, as well as his mild-mannered approach, helped him to cultivate relationships with a relatively broad-based moral community of liberal-minded anti-apartheid activists in Britain and Europe. An early diplomatic triumph was the link he forged with sympathetic Swedish politicians like Olof Palme and David Wirmark. A Swedish branch of Christian Action was set up in 1959. Per Wästberg's books about his experiences in southern Africa were published in 1960 and sold 160,000 copies.[19] Scandinavian solidarity was to prove an important neutral source of financial support in the bi-polar politics of the Cold War.

The personal bonds of trust that Tambo enjoyed with Moses Kotane, long-term secretary-general of the Communist Party as well a member of the ANC National Executive Committee, also proved crucial in maintaining a working relationship between the two organizations. Kotane was a fine analytical thinker who remained very closely attuned to nationalist currents of thought as well. Like Tambo, he 'displayed an impressive virtuosity in straddling the different arms of the movement'.[20] Tambo memorably described Kotane as 100 per cent Communist and 100 per cent ANC.

International Anti-Apartheid

London provided a natural base for a network of organizations, solidarity groups, and individuals who were willing and able to give material and political support to the liberation movements. Here, exiles could operate within a dense network of campaigning groups, political parties, trade unions, churches, student organizations, and universities. The primacy, or at least the special place, of the ANC was generally accepted. But the ANC was only the most senior partner in a broadly based network of anti-apartheid and Africa-wide organizations comprising what Håkan Thörn refers to as a developing 'global civil society'. The fight against apartheid was indeed the most globalized of all anti-colonial struggles.

The Anti-Apartheid Movement (AAM) was formed in London directly after Sharpeville. It emerged out of efforts, spearheaded by the Committee of African Organizations, to inaugurate a boycott of South African goods. The methods of the boycott committee drew on long-established South African traditions of non-compliance, carefully tailored to suit British circumstances. Its inaugural meeting, in June 1959, featured speeches by a carefully selected mix of leading African nationalists (Julius Nyerere and Kanyama Chiume), Christian activists (Scott and Huddleston), as well as spokesmen from the ANC (Tennyson Makiwane) and South African Indian Congress (Vella Pillay). Patrick van Rensburg, an Afrikaner dissident with links to the Liberal Party in South Africa, helped to expand further the base of the boycott movement.

While the boycott committee recognized the centrality of the ANC in the liberation movement, it was never merely a front for the ANC. A new wave of post-Sharpeville exiles brought fresh vitality and experience to the Anti-Apartheid Movement, yet there was a concern on the part of some that it should remain British-run rather than serve as a political base for South African expatriates; accusations that the Anti-Apartheid Movement, like the ANC, was run by non-Africans and Communists were not uncommon.[21] Many black British activists felt estranged from the Anti-Apartheid Movement on account of its racially mixed constituency. They were often more sympathetic to the cause of pan-Africanism.[22]

Along with the consumer boycotts of South African goods, there were moves to isolate South Africa in the area of sport and culture. The South African Non-Racial Olympic Committee (SAN-ROC) established a presence in Britain and the United States after its founder, Denis Brutus, was hounded into exile. The International Football Federation suspended South Africa's membership in 1961. The suspension was lifted in 1963 (following a stage-managed visit led by right-wing British football administrator Stanley Rous) and reimposed a year later. South Africa did not take part in the 1964 Tokyo Olympics and was expelled from the Olympic movement in 1970—the first country to suffer this indignity.

Cricket and rugby were by far the most important sports to white South Africa, having emerged as symbols of colonial pride and potency in the context of competitive 'test' series against the British home nations and white dominions at the start of the twentieth century. In 1965 Verwoerd refused entry to a New Zealand rugby team because it included Maori players. He explained his decision to a gathering of Afrikaner youth in September that year.[23] Here Verwoerd reiterated his view that racial mixing on the sports field, as in any other social sphere, posed a grave threat to whites and white Christian civilization.

From the late 1960s, moves to exclude the 'Springboks' from international cricket and rugby aroused enormous publicity in Britain, New Zealand, and elsewhere. No longer was it deemed sufficient to isolate South Africa by placing pressure on remote and unaccountable international sporting organizations. There were now active attempts to disrupt public sporting events featuring South African players. Student activists in Britain took the initiative with pitch invasions and protests, as in the landmark 1970 'Stop the Tour' campaign, led by Young Liberal activist Peter Hain.[24]

In the early 1960s, declarations were passed by playwrights in England and Ireland that their work should not be performed before segregated audiences. In 1965 the British actors' union, Equity, invited individual actors to pledge not to work in South Africa. The American Committee on Africa persuaded sixty cultural figures to 'say no to apartheid'. As has been argued in the previous chapter, international awareness of the horrors of apartheid and its underlying immorality were greatly stimulated by books and plays performed in London and New York.

Music, art, and photography were also evocative mediums of protest. In 1957, a young schoolboy, Ernest Cole, decided to give up on his 'third class' Bantu Education in order to train as a photographer. He worked on the magazine *Drum*, as well as the *Rand Daily Mail* and *The World.* Cole posed as 'coloured' so that he could evade the pass laws (he even managed to persuade a sceptical examiner at the Race Classification Board to re-register him as such) while continuing to live as an African. This mobility allowed Cole to record 'the truth about life in black South Africa' in a unique series of documentary photographs depicting the lives of miners, arrests under the pass laws, township removals, drinking in shebeens, religious meetings, and so on. Cole left South Africa for New York in 1967, where he met the journalist Joseph Leyleveld, who wrote the introduction to Cole's remarkable photographic testament, *House of*

Figure 5. Pass law arrest (view of man from above): Ernest Cole, 'Pass raid. Sometimes check broadens into search of a man's person and belongings', from Ernest Cole, *House of Bondage* (London, 1968), 47. © Ernest Cole Family Trust.

Bondage (1967). As for so many exiles, displacement meant 'the surrender of his creative obsession'; though formally free, Cole 'was also stranded'. He died before his 50th birthday, destitute and homeless, a week after Mandela's release in 1990, barely remembered within South Africa and neglected outside.[25]

Many black South African writers suffered similar neglect and alienation in exile. Musicians like Abdullah Ibrahim, Bea Benjamin, Hugh Masekela, Miriam Makeba, and Louis Moholo-Moholo flourished: their distinctive renditions of South African urban jazz reached new heights of artistic expression under the influence of international exponents of jazz like Duke Ellington, Harry Belafonte, Thelonious Monk, and John Coltrane. But other fine jazz musicians, like Dudu Pukwana, Mongezi Feza, and Johnny Dyani (all of 'The Blue Notes'), found life in exile much tougher, and died young. Within South Africa, some of the stars from the 1950s, like Kippie Moeketsi and Dolly Rathebe, continued to play, though their careers were blighted by apartheid strictures. The cumulative toll on black cultural expression was severe. This helps to explain why Black Consciousness made poetry, writing, and drama such a priority in the 1970s.

Military Aid

Even before the formal setting up on an ANC External Mission, the ANC and Communist Party began to cement links with the socialist and the non-aligned world. ANC leaders Walter Sisulu and Duma Nokwe travelled widely in eastern Europe and the Soviet Union in 1953, seeking to develop solidarity links with the Communist world. Two years later, Moses Kotane and Maulvi Cachalia represented the Congress Alliance at the Bandung Conference, using the occasion to journey widely in Asia— including India and China—as well as Poland and Egypt.[26] In 1960 an ANC/SACP delegation led by Yusuf Dadoo met with Mao Tse Tung and Deng Xiaoping in Beijing, who showed interest but remained uncommitted on the subject of the armed struggle. A small number of ANC cadres received military training in Nanjing, where the emphasis was on non-conventional rural guerrilla techniques such as making explosives from cow dung.[27]

After the Sino-Soviet split relations between the ANC and the Soviet Union became much closer. The PAC was left to cultivate relations with China; it modelled its Azanian People's Liberation Army (successor to Poqo) on the People's Liberation Army. Tambo visited Moscow in 1963 and again in 1965, where the small ANC/SACP delegation was met by senior Soviet leaders at Party headquarters. A significant outcome of these visits was a grant of $300,000 in 1963 and a further $560,000 for 1965/6, on top of $112,000 for the Communist Party of South Africa. In the estimation of the well-placed Russian historian Vladimir Shubin, these disbursements amounted to nearly 85 per cent of the ANC's total income at the time.[28] In addition to material support, the Soviets began to train MK guerrilla commanders in Odessa, on the Black Sea, from 1963. Prominent amongst the early military recruits (totalling around 500 cadres in 1965) were Joe Modise, Moses Mabhida, and Ronnie Kasrils.[29]

Military and security training was also undertaken in East Germany, Czechoslovakia, and Bulgaria. For Communist Party/MK activists like

Mac Maharaj, who trained in the GDR, acceptance of Communism and of the infallibility of the Soviet Union was unconditional.[30] Techniques acquired from organizations like the East German Stasi would later be seen in the harsh enforcement of discipline and treatment of enemy 'spies' in ANC guerrilla camps in Angola.[31] Hardline ideological Stalinism was also evident in Communist circles in London, though here such tendencies were tempered by the influence of social democratic, constitutional, and other liberal ideas.

There had been hopes in the early 1960s that African countries would offer military assistance. Mandela received brief instruction with the Algerian FLN in Morocco before returning to South Africa. For the most part, however, promises of training and support from African countries were not fulfilled. The major exception was Tanzania where the ANC established four guerrilla training camps after 1963. By the end of the decade these facilities housed perhaps 2,000 Umkhonto cadres. Many accounts speak of the hardships in such camps. Situated in remote areas, badly administered, inadequately resourced, and plagued by intrigue and conspiracy, cadres experienced poor morale. There were repeated instances of desertions and small-scale mutinies. Isaac Maphoto, who was based at Kongwa, Tanzania, remembers it as a prison:

The ANC didn't have money and we were in a place far away from civilisation. You could hardly see a person with a suit and most of the women we had access to were prostitutes. We relied a lot in those days on East Germany. I remember one time we had no salt; we had to wait for salt, which came from East Germany. We waited two/three months. They brought us tinned food left by Hitler in the 1930s. We ate that and people would vomit.[32]

The Islanders

For the ANC and PAC prisoners on Robben Island conditions were even harder. There, the South African authorities provided rations on the basis of racial categories: mealie meal (maize porridge) formed the bulk of everyone's diet, but even here racial strictures came into play. 'Coloureds' and 'Asiatics' were allocated bread and jam; 'Bantus' had to do without. They also received less sugar.[33] In the first few years African prisoners were issued with sandals and short khaki trousers as if they were servant 'boys', an indignity that Mandela found especially irksome. Until the 1970s, when conditions improved considerably, prisoners slept on sisal mats, with only thin blankets for warmth. Cold showers, sometimes using seawater, were the only means of washing. During the day, prisoners were forced to break rocks at the lime quarry. Brutal assaults by prison guards, hard labour, lack of access to newspapers, and only intermittent contact with families, were designed to remind political prisoners of their powerlessness.

In a concerted effort to maintain their personal and collective dignity, political prisoners combined to challenge guards. Hunger strikes and refusal to work in the quarry led to negotiations with the authorities. Political prisoners developed innovative methods of education and self-improvement. Internal divisions proved problematic. Disputes between ANC and PAC prisoners were often sharp and ill-tempered, though Mandela and Robert Sobukwe (who lived under special conditions of isolation until 1969) retained a high mutual regard. A handful of Trotskyites, led by the intellectual educationist Neville Alexander, challenged the ANC on issues like non-racism and the 'national question'.

Amongst the ANC prisoners, theoretical disputes between Marxists and nationalists encouraged the formation of cliques. Debates about the implications of the Freedom Charter were invariably divisive. Doctrinal differences with Govan Mbeki and Harry Gwala, both hardline Marxist-Leninists, put them seriously at odds with the more flexible leadership of Mandela, Sisulu, Mac Maharaj, and Ahmed Kathrada. There were serious ideological differences bearing on the potential for mobilizing in the Bantustans and, also, the question of whether the Robben Island leadership could or should be in charge of the revolution.[34]

The creation of a secret 'High Organ', headed by Mandela and composed of senior leaders who had previously served on the ANC National Executive, provided direction and political purpose. Self-belief and political conviction were key to survival but these qualities were tested to the limit in conditions of geographical and emotional isolation. Censorship of letters was designed to demoralize prisoners as much as to maintain security.[35] Those who were serving life sentences were aware that life meant life in the South African criminal justice system. In a letter from the Island, written in 1968, Kathrada ruminated on the indefinite terms of confinement:

How many more years of imprisonment, no one can tell. There is no fixed period for a life sentence. Besides, there is no remission for political prisoners. So I am under no illusion as to the time I still have to serve.[36]

Umkhonto we Sizwe and the Region

Until the mid-1970s, apartheid's iron grip on dissent was significantly enhanced by the cordon sanitaire provided by neighbouring states. Namibia, Rhodesia, and Mozambique and Angola were all subject to forms of settler control. Newly independent Zambia and Botswana were sympathetic to liberation movements, but neither could risk offering more than ancillary support, mostly by hosting refugees.

In the guerrilla camps of Tanzania there was growing frustration about the lack of meaningful military action. Despite the availability of around 500 trained fighters by the mid-1960s, the leadership was hesitant to act because of the lack of suitable terrain for guerrillas along South Africa's northern borders, the presence of vigilant white farming communities, and the absence of an independent African peasantry which might provide shelter and cover. The destruction of the ANC and Communist Party underground network after Sharpeville and Rivonia meant that incoming guerrillas lacked sanctuary in urban areas. Umkhonto fighters, desperate to prove themselves in battle and to 'return home', were unimpressed by what they saw as an ineffective, internally divided, and self-serving MK command structure.

Small-scale attempts were made to send fighters through Botswana in 1966. The insurgents were quickly apprehended by the local police. A more organized effort to infiltrate into South Africa began in July 1967, when a group of around 50 Umkhonto fighters crossed the Zambezi River (together with ZIPRA guerrillas fighting the Smith regime in Rhodesia) into the Hwange game park.[37] They were named the Luthuli

Detachment in honour of the recently deceased ANC president. We are left to wonder whether Luthuli would have welcomed this honour.

Rhodesian troops quickly intercepted the insurgents, who had meanwhile split into two units. Clashes with the Rhodesian security forces ensued for a month. A contingent of South African 'police' were sent to Rhodesia to help defeat the 'terrorists' who, in the grim words of Prime Minister Vorster, had been sent to 'kill our children without warning in the night'.[38]

By the end of the campaign, in mid-September, around 30 MK fighters had been killed, and 20 captured or escaped back to Zambia. In December, and again in February 1968, further groups of MK/ZIPRA guerrillas crossed the Zambezi further to the east. The Sipolilo campaign, as this offensive was termed, proceeded according to a similar pattern: the guerrillas were soon tracked down, and for several months firefights ensued with the Rhodesian security forces. The numbers of deaths on each side cannot be known for certain but the ANC listed 23 of their own killed in the second phase of the campaign.[39]

The Wankie/Sipolilo campaigns provided the ANC with new heroes (Chris Hani, Charles Ngwenya) as well as martyrs (Paul Petersen and Patrick Molaoa). The domestic South African media paid little attention and preferred to see the raids as remote acts of terrorism primarily of concern to Ian Smith's rogue regime. As far as the South African government was concerned there was no credible security threat. It was far more concerned with the activities of SWAPO guerrillas in South West Africa and in June 1967 passed the so-called 'Terrorism Act'.[40] This far-reaching measure defined terrorism as any act committed with the intention of endangering law and order or inciting others to commit such an act; it allowed for indefinite detention of suspects on the authority of a senior police officer.

Although MK operatives acquitted themselves courageously, their effectiveness was compromised by logistical shortcomings, poor familiarity with the terrain, and the suspicious attitudes of the local peasantry. Hani's hope of establishing a 'Ho Chi Minh trail' to South Africa had no prospect of success. Even if the insurgents had managed to cross into South Africa as envisaged, it is unclear what they could have achieved in the absence of robust internal networks. The ANC historian Francis Meli welcomed the battles in Zimbabwe as the first time since the nineteenth century that the oppressed had clashed with white rulers 'in the region', yet the MK leadership was acutely aware that it had not yet managed to fire a shot within South Africa.[41]

In the recriminations that followed, the ANC High Command was accused of sending cadres off on a suicide mission; it is more likely that they were allowed to go in an effort to energize the liberation movement and alleviate torpor in the squalid base camps. Seven MK fighters, including Chris Hani, were suspended by the ANC for criticizing the exile leadership and threatened with incarceration. They were eventually reprieved by Tambo. The so-called 'Hani memorandum' made allegations of 'rot' within the organization. This included lack of political focus and wide disparity in the lifestyles of ordinary cadres and officials who were accused of helping themselves and their favourites to the perks of office. The ANC was charged with having 'lost control' of MK which, run by powerful individuals like Joe Modise and Duma Nokwe, was routinely using secret trials and harsh discipline to enforce internal control on cadres.[42]

The Morogoro Consultative Conference, 1969

Charges of malaise, absence of accountability, and lack of political direction demanded a response. It came in the form of a decision to hold a consultative conference at Morogoro, Tanzania. More than seventy delegates, representing different strands of the Congress Alliance, gathered at the end of April 1969 to address the shortcomings of the liberation movement in exile. Agenda item no. 1 struck a defiant note: 'Our objective is the overthrow of the White racialist, fascist regime together with its imperialist forces in South Africa, and to establish a democratic society on the basis of the FREEDOM CHARTER.' Item 2 stated, 'Our major weapon is the intensification of the armed struggle. Other forms of struggle are also important.' This much could be agreed upon. But it was item 3 that pointed to the underlying sense of unease: 'To what extent have we succeeded and failed in this regard, and what must be done to ensure further success?' The rest of the agenda raised specific difficulties.[43] Amid stormy scenes and recriminations, Tambo briefly resigned as deputy president together with the entire National Executive.[44] His reinstatement significantly enhanced his authority as the ANC's *de facto* leader.

The decisions taken at Morogoro addressed three interrelated issues which had come to the fore during the decade of exile: the relationship between Africans and non-Africans; the roles of the ANC and the Communist Party; and the balance between the armed and the political struggle. Simmering ethnic tensions, highlighted by the fact that all the signatories to the Hani memorandum were Xhosa-speaking, were a further source of tension. After extensive debate, the conference resolved that the ANC in exile would henceforth be open to non-Africans. However, Africans alone would be eligible for election to the ANC's National Executive Committee, which was now streamlined to improve its effectiveness.

A new Revolutionary Council, chaired by Tambo, included non-African members of the Communist Party and MK: Yusuf Dadoo, Reg September, and Joe Slovo (Indian, coloured, and white, respectively).[45] This innovation, coupled with the opening of the exiled ANC to members of any racial group, marked a significant departure from the cumbersome multi-racialism based on an alliance of racially defined auxiliary organizations. Over time, the organizational changes did much to ensure that the ANC in exile could 'move away from solidarity to [become] an effective liberation movement'.[46]

The emancipatory objectives of the ANC were given fresh theoretical expression at Morogoro through the adoption of the 'Strategy and Tactics' document. Its title conveyed a sense of purposeful direction while its Marxisant, boiler-plate prose was fully in keeping with the prevailing revolutionary ethos of 1960s anti-colonial struggles and, in particular, the Soviet-inspired concept of the national democratic revolution. 'Strategy and Tactics' helped to refine and reinterpret the Freedom Charter for the revolutionary underground, set the struggle in historical and international context, and plotted out a 'scientific revolutionary' path towards certain victory.[47]

Importantly, 'Strategy and Tactics' sought to rethink the connection between the military and political aspects of 'revolutionary armed struggle'. Emphasis was nominally given to the role of 'the African masses' (the black working class most especially) in achieving national and economic emancipation. In theory, the primacy of political organization over the armed struggle was asserted. But in practice, the ANC continued to foreground the armed struggle during the 1970s. There was relatively little attention paid to the new forms of political leadership that were in gestation within South Africa itself, beyond a recognition at the very end of the document that closer research and analysis of the 'conditions of the different strata of our people' should take place.[48] 'Strategy and Tactics' reads very much like a 'to do' list for an isolated organization mired in internal crisis.

Morogoro helped to realign the relationship between the ANC and the Communist Party in a more structured manner. The ANC, always the senior partner of the Alliance in terms of legitimacy and weight of support, was reaffirmed as principal leader of the national struggle. The Communist Party, a conduit for vital material resources (finance and military training) as well as the source of theoretical and strategic wisdom, was effectively incorporated into the highest decision-making and executive body, the Revolutionary Council. This body, comprised of all talents, imparted much needed professionalism and cohesive discipline to the underground movement. Cross-cutting membership of the ANC, Communist Party, and MK reinforced the Revolutionary Council's status at the apex of decision-making in the exile movement.

Stephen Ellis maintains that the new structures were a triumph for the Communist Party which now 'had its hands on the real levers of power while remaining formally subject to an exclusively black body'.[49] Overlapping membership did indeed fudge the question of which organization was the leading agent of the struggle. It also lent disproportionate influence to individuals who were members of two or more of these bodies, leading to persistent allegations that the Communist Party was effectively in control of the ANC.[50] The fact that membership of the Communist Party was secret added to its mystique, and may have allowed the Party to act more effectively as a pressure group by selectively recruiting amongst the most promising cadres. But this did not necessarily increase its muscle. The Communist Party was very small compared to the ANC and it was continually forced to modify its positions in order to retain influence.

The symbiotic relationship between the ANC and the Communist Party is best understood as one of fluctuating, mutual dependence rather than in conspiratorial terms. The view that the Communist Party extended its influence over the ANC at Morogoro, and continued to manipulate the nationalist organization thereafter, is simplistic. For it is equally possible to construct the converse argument, namely, that African nationalists manipulated the Party to their own advantage. Mandela himself has suggested this as a possibility. Although slow-moving and bumbling, the ANC was a big beast which proved able at key moments in its long history to adapt to new conditions (Morogoro being a prime example). The capacity to absorb different ideological tendencies, while retaining a strong sense of unity and a measure of collective self-discipline, certainly rendered the ANC more resilient than the faction-ridden PAC.

It is erroneous to presume that membership of the Communist Party and the ANC necessarily entailed strict adherence to scientific socialism (though in the case of some cadres it most certainly did). The decisive influence of Marxism-Leninism on the ANC was probably stronger and more durable in regard to revolutionary *means* than *ends*: that is to say, its impact on the organizational style and culture of the ANC (democratic centralism, Leninist vanguardism) was powerful and persistent, whereas its stated objectives (socialism, the national democratic revolution) were unrealistic and had always to be squared with the diffuse nationalism that suffused the ANC. Ironically, the revolutionary elite's vanguardism tended to make it suspicious of the very masses it claimed to lead.

Communism in South Africa was a composite ideology overlaid by doctrinal differences, organizational ruptures, and deep internal conflicts. Its adherents included hardline Stalinists, socialists, and social democratic fellow-travellers. Over time, the ideological position of individuals were apt to change. Crucially, the dedication of individual Communist Party members like Yusuf Dadoo or Joe Slovo exemplified the importance of practical non-racial cooperation, a feature unique in African liberation struggles. Not only did this allow the ANC to benefit from the widest possible source of support, it also permitted it to claim the moral high ground as an organization committed to the liberation of all South African citizens. Communist claims that its revolutionary theory was based on objective scientific analysis remained an article of faith for many, convincing adherents that freedom was inevitable. This assurance helped to sustain the liberation movement in its darkest days of exile. At least as important as the Communist Manifesto was the sense of manifest destiny contained in the dialectical teachings of historical materialism.

Morogoro proved to be a cathartic moment for the ANC. Yet the view of those, including Oliver Tambo, who thought that Morogoro was a turning point in the fortunes of the ANC, overstates the fact: the reality was that the fortunes of the liberation movement remained at a low ebb—and were about to weaken further.

One portent of this weakening position was the Lusaka Manifesto signed by fourteen African states just prior to the Morogoro conference. The Lusaka Manifesto called for the full liberation of southern Africa from apartheid, and proclaimed equal rights and human dignity for all. It also endorsed negotiations with South Africa in preference to armed struggle. This message ran directly against the wishes of the ANC. The Manifesto was ratified by the OAU and the UN and it was greeted by western governments, most notably the United States, as a positive step.[51] Just after the Morogoro conference, the Tanzanian government liquidated the ANC camps at short notice. With no other frontline state willing to act as host, MK fighters were relocated to the Soviet Union.[52] MK military activities in Lusaka were also constrained after threats of expulsion, and cadres were henceforth removed to a camp outside the capital. The effect was to make the fighting capacity of the ANC more dependent than ever on the support of the Soviet Union. Without the USSR's support at this juncture, MK might have disintegrated.

Morogoro allowed the exiled ANC to reflect and regroup with a sense of common purpose, based on the view that it was the leading force of liberation and not merely an international solidarity organization. But the discernible move to the left, and the enhanced role of non-African Communists in the organization after Morogoro, did not put an end to simmering tensions. These boiled over in 1975 when a prominent group of Africanist dissidents led by Tennyson Makiwane referred contemptuously to Morogoro as a 'multi-racial affair'. The 'Gang of Eight' was duly expelled from the ANC. Five years later Makiwane was killed by an MK unit.[53]

Political Change within South Africa

One reason why Morogoro came to be seen as a watershed in the history of the ANC is that the apartheid state and the politics of the region were beginning to change in important ways. John Vorster, who succeeded

Verwoerd as prime minister in 1966, initially insisted that he would maintain his predecessor's policies, pledging in his acceptance speech to 'walk further along the road set by Hendrik Verwoerd'. Vorster was rather more flexible than his predecessor. Although fully determined to maintain the essence of political apartheid—Afrikaner-led white domination with tribal homelands for blacks—he was aware of the need to make adjustments, particularly in respect of urban black labour. At his first cabinet meeting Vorster clearly signalled a different approach: 'Verwoerd was an intellectual giant. He thought for each of us. I am not capable of being a second Verwoerd.'[54] Many Nationalists were relieved and Verwoerd's overwhelming presence soon receded.

As well as being less dogmatic than Verwoerd, Vorster proved more willing to delegate authority to his ministerial colleagues. His threatening demeanour was duly modified by a more avuncular persona. Jean Sinclair, president of the Black Sash, observed that Vorster managed to alter his personal image from 'strong-armed Minister of Justice' to a 'benevolent, approachable, golf-loving, fatherly Prime Minister who is the essence of reasonableness and good will'.[55] Vorster appreciated that international condemnation of apartheid was growing and would have to be assuaged. He showed some preparedness to make minor concessions in respect of *klein* (small) or 'petty' apartheid, namely, segregated public facilities. Symbolic gestures aimed at relaxing apartheid strictures included desegregation of some municipal libraries and park benches, admission of black guests to certain luxury hotels, and high-profile integrated sporting events. One example was the boxing match staged in Johannesburg between Pierre Fourie and the visiting African-American light-heavyweight Bob Foster in 1973 (Foster's victory thrilled black South Africans).

Sports policy became a key test for the reformist *verligtes* in their factional battle with obdurate Verwoerdian *verkramptes*. In 1967 Vorster announced that the government would no longer interfere in the composition of visiting international sports teams (the New Zealand All Black rugby tour of that year was cancelled after Verwoerd had made it clear that they would not be welcome if they fielded Maori players). But the following year Vorster reversed this decision, personally intervening to prevent the English test cricket team from picking Basil D'Oliviera, a coloured batsman-bowler born in Cape Town, to play for his adopted country (England) in the land of his birth. The tour was cancelled.

The 'D'Oliviera affair' catalysed anti-apartheid opposition. It prompted the ruin of the 1969–70 Springbok rugby tour of Britain, which was overwhelmed by pitch invasions and anti-apartheid protests. There were further twists and contortions as Vorster's government attempted to reconcile apartheid policy with South African whites' desperate wish to play international rugby, the sport that exemplified white national pride and masculine prowess. The 1970 touring New Zealand team included a Maori player, 'Super Sid' Going, and Samoan-born Bryan Williams. They were given 'honorary white' status while in the country. So, too, was the dashing Roger Bougarel, a black member of the visiting 1971 French rugby team, whose presence was greeted with bemused fascination by South African newspapers. Concessions to visiting black sports stars were only ever intended to assuage external criticisms; there was no preparedness whatsoever to allow genuinely mixed sport within South Africa.

Verwoerd had been unwilling to engage with any African leaders (other than those he was responsible for picking himself). By contrast, Vorster inaugurated a cautious 'outward' policy with a number of African countries based on the principles of *realpolitik*. Since all neighbouring states were heavily dependent on the South African economy and its transport infrastructure, he was able to engage from a position of strength. In an address to the South Africa Club in London, journalist Piet Cillié extolled the 'thrilling and limitless adventure in African co-operation' that Vorster was embarking upon, comparing his African policy to that of Rhodes: 'South Africa can pack a lot of economic, technological and cultural power behind a good-neighbour policy.'[56]

In 1966–7 Vorster met with the prime ministers of Lesotho, Botswana, and Malawi. Diplomatic relations were established with the Malawian government in 1968, which responded by sending a (white) chargé d'affaires to Cape Town. This move caused consternation among right-wing Nationalist politicians who feared it was the thin edge of the wedge. To an extent it was. In 1972 Malawian President Banda visited South Africa, arousing further controversy within the ruling party. *Time* magazine took a different tack and commented on surprising cracks in the apartheid façade within government diplomatic circles: 'Pretoria's hostesses now consider it a social must to have at least one black man at a party; as a result, the only resident black ambassador, Malawi's sherry-sipping, highly professional Joe Kachingwe, is being run ragged.'[57]

Vorster's policy of 'détente' culminated in a carefully orchestrated meeting on the Victoria Falls railway bridge in 1975 with President Kaunda of Zambia, as part of a (failed) effort to broker a political deal in neighbouring Rhodesia.[58] This diplomatic initiative, hailed by some as a 'courageous' and 'statesmanlike' departure from the politics of the 'laager', was reversed a year later when, following the collapse of the Portuguese colonial empire, South Africa embarked upon a highly risky military invasion of Angola.

Vorster evidently took account of new demographic data revealing that the population projections upon which the Verwoerdian policy was based were erroneous. The 1970 census revealed that Africans constituted 70.2 per cent of the total population, with whites making up 17.2 per cent, coloureds 9.7 per cent, and Asians 2.9 per cent.[59]

In 1974 the Stellenbosch demographer J. L. Sadie predicted that the African population would grow to 37m by the end of the century. By contrast, whites would probably number fewer than 7m in 2000 and go on to decline to around 11 per cent of the total population by 2020.[60] Such projections caused alarm in senior government circles and became a staple of apocalyptic journalism.[61] It was already evident that more blacks lived outside the homelands than inside them. Having initially slowed the expansion of the homelands policy, Vorster's response was now to rapidly accelerate the policy of Bantustan independence, increase the government's programme of forced removals and ethnic cleansing, and propose stripping all blacks of their South African citizenship.

One area in which Vorster remained resolute was his brutal approach to policing and law and order. He extended the already far-reaching carapace of security legislation to suppress 'communism' and was responsible for creating the Bureau of State Security (BOSS) in 1969, headed by the notorious police chief H. J. van den Bergh. Operating beyond parliamentary scrutiny and with a special budget, this secretive and fearsome body accrued wide powers to act against anyone deemed to be a traitor, Communist, or terrorist. During Vorster's tenure, the country's military capability was significantly enhanced, a response to the upsurge in guerrilla activity in South West Africa/Namibia as well as the United Nations arms embargo. Conscription for all white men began to be introduced in 1967. The local development of a ground-to-air missile was announced in 1969. In 1970 Vorster declared that the country was about to embark on a programme of uranium enrichment using a 'unique' process developed by its own scientists.

Vorster's tough approach on security was not enough to allay the fears of right-wing Verwoerdian nationalists. They were deeply alarmed by his apparent lack of resolve in respect of 'multi-national' (mixed) sport, his willingness to talk with black leaders as apparent equals, and the growing divergence in racial demography. In 1967 the Potchefstroom academic W. A. de Klerk coined the terms *verlig* (enlightened, pragmatic) and *verkramp* (conservative, bigoted) to distinguish between distinct strands of Afrikaner nationalist politics. The distinction came to apply not only to race policy but also to social norms and Calvinist religious doctrine. The *Sunday Times* journalist Joel Mervis observed wryly that there were few countries in the modern world where it could be considered an insult to be called 'enlightened'.[62]

By now the *verlig/verkramp* struggle for dominance was being conducted openly and in deadly earnest. A new hard-right party, the Herstigte Nasionale Party, was formed by Albert Hertzog and other nationalist dissidents bent on maintaining Verwoerdian principles. At the 1970 election the Herstigtes failed to win any seats but the need to see them off forced Vorster to move to the right. (A telling example was the government's refusal of a visa to the African-American tennis star Arthur Ashe.[63]) The government lost nine seats to the opposition United Party in 1970 and its majority was reduced for the first time since coming to power.

Some analysts concluded that politics were opening up and that fissures were at last appearing in the edifice of Afrikanerdom. But few envisaged any significant alteration in the overall structure of white domination at the end of the 1960s. Most white South Africans, and many overseas commentators, took the view that political change could only come from within the ranks of Afrikanerdom. The only other way of forcing change was through violence. A more subtle view was voiced by the Canadian sociologist Heribert Adam in *Modernizing Racial Domination*

(1971). Far from being 'an outdated relic of a dying colonialism' unable to adapt, Adam considered that apartheid represented 'one of the most advanced and effective patterns of rational, oligarchic domination'.[64] The capacity for the system to reform and renew itself, he concluded, was considerable.

CHAPTER 6
CRACKS WITHIN THE SYSTEM

From the perspective of Pretoria, there were good reasons for the government to be optimistic at the beginning of the 1970s. The economy was buoyant, the liberation movements had been routed and internal opposition contained. Jim Hoagland of *The Washington Post*, recipient of a 1971 Pulitzer prize for his coverage of the struggle against apartheid, concluded that 'white nationalism has entrenched itself more firmly than ever at the southern corner of the continent.... The chances for a successful black revolt seem to have grown more distant with each passing year since the threat of an internal explosion was overcome in 1960.'[1]

White settler power in the region also appeared secure. The international sports boycott, the denial of African overflying rights (which forced South African Airways to fly round the 'bulge' of Africa to European destinations), and persistent criticisms emanating from the United Nations, were all reminders of the country's isolation. But none of these irritants posed insuperable threats to white supremacy.[2] Although minority rule in South Africa was ultimately sustained by force and fear, it was also naturalized through habit, caution, and compliance.

The conventional wisdom at the time was that change would either come through eventual 'revolution'—a remote prospect—or, more likely, as a result of splits within Afrikanerdom. Neither the government nor the liberation movement anticipated, or even recognized, that a fundamentally new challenge to white supremacy was already quietly gestating in the form of Black Consciousness ideology.

Black Consciousness: Ecumenical Origins

Black Consciousness' great innovation was to work on the minds of the oppressed rather than the might of the oppressor. Above all, it stressed the necessity for blacks to become the principal agents of their own psychological liberation. Initially, this meant creating new bonds of solidarity between Africans, Indians, and coloureds—principally by showing that they all shared a common identity as a consequence of their oppression. Black Consciousness began to subvert the basic onto-logical building blocks of apartheid and its 'divide and rule' mindset. It posed fundamental questions to all the prevalent anti-apartheid ideolo-gies, be this the multi-culturalism of the ANC, pan-Africanism, liberal universalism, or Marxism.

Black Consciousness was born, like the proverbial cuckoo in the nest, within the very tertiary educational institutions that the state believed should underwrite separate development. The movement began to incu-bate within the multi-racial and ecumenical University Christian Move-ment, which was founded in 1967 in Grahamstown. Its first leaders were Basil Moore, an inspiring Methodist chaplain at Rhodes University, and Colin Collins,[3] a Catholic student chaplain. Avant-garde in its thinking and practices, the UCM sought to achieve social justice by developing a contextually based theology of liberation.[4] Within just two years the UCM established thirty branches comprising 3,000 members. As the organization gravitated towards its growing black constituency—prompting many of its white student adherents to withdraw—'black theology' became an important influence.[5] The UCM's faith-based prophetic radicalism was a formative influence on the South African Students' Organization (SASO) that became the driving political force behind Black Consciousness.

During the era of high apartheid, it was often remarked that the Dutch Reformed Church was the National Party at prayer. Yet, in line with the Christian-National philosophy of 'separation of spheres', the DRC never aimed to become the established religion of the apartheid state; 'other' religions and dominations were mostly tolerated by the government.

To a surprising extent, the churches remained multi-racial national institutions under apartheid. Both the Catholic and Protestant churches had very large black memberships. Even Verwoerd proved unable to bar 'mixed' worship'.[6] To be sure, congregations mostly worshipped separately and whites typically occupied the most senior positions in church structures. But in exceptional cases black clergymen, like Desmond Tutu, could ascend to high ranks in the church hierarchy. Moreover, confessional differences never mapped directly onto racial, ethnic, or political divisions: even the Dutch Reformed Church had black members based in its 'mission' or 'daughter' affiliates. Allan Boesak, who was to become an important political figurehead in the 1980s, came to prominence from within the DRC mission church.[7]

Much of the early spread of Black Consciousness ideas was conducted through the interdenominational network of seminaries responsible for training priests. Young seminarians who were sensitive to institutional racism in church hierarchies proved intellectually receptive to contextual theology.[8] The fact that Black Consciousness thinking was initially so closely embedded in religious circles afforded it a substantial measure of protection. Until around 1972, the government was perplexed as to how to react to Black Consciousness, preferring to believe that it was an organic expression of the 'tribal' consciousness it was working so assiduously to cultivate. Black Consciousness activists skilfully used this hiatus to establish a presence that was not obviously exposed to repression.

Another religious body that proved adept in opening up new political space was the largely white Christian Institute, formed in 1963. This organization emerged from within the heart of the Dutch Reformed Church movement in the aftermath of the Cottesloe Declaration's criticisms of apartheid. Mindful of the anti-Nazi confessing movement of the 1930s, the Christian Institute skilfully used the legitimacy afforded by trans-national religious bodies to propound a clear anti-apartheid message. The 'apartheid bible' amounted to a contextual reading of the scriptures geared towards the acquisition of Afrikaner power. Apartheid's theologians proved slow to realize that alternative contextual readings could generate a quite different liberatory ideology, one that was consistent with African nationalism. It was precisely this insight that the UCM and the Christian Institute came to appreciate.

Black/Consciousness/Movement

Central to Black Consciousness thinking was the recognition that fundamental change could only come by countering the insidious influence of apartheid ideology on black people themselves. Black Consciousness theorists understood that part of apartheid's power lay in its insidious capacity to humiliate, emasculate, and dehumanize the 'black man' (gendered language of this sort was ubiquitous).[9] Overcoming fear, expurgating feelings of powerlessness, and restoring human dignity was therefore paramount. This meant that it was imperative to develop a new understanding of what it was to *be* black in South Africa prior to taking on the might of the apartheid state.

Many analysts of Black Consciousness of the time were apt to misread its significance and intent by seeking to fit it into known political categories. Black Consciousness was sometimes portrayed as a transitional 'stage' in resistance to apartheid, or as an interlude in the long narrative of the ANC-led struggle. Such views failed to comprehend that Black Consciousness did not see itself as a conventional political party or constitute itself as an alternative liberation organization. Only by considering it in its own terms can we appreciate its meaning and potential. One recent scholar who takes this approach demonstrates the utility of disaggregating each of the words that make up the compound formulation, 'Black Consciousness Movement'.[10]

The adoption of the term 'black' was noteworthy in virtue of its positive embrace of *all* oppressed victims of apartheid: African, coloured, and Indian. This usage was more inclusive than the particularist use of 'African' by organizations like the PAC. 'Black' amounted to a firm rejection of the government's favoured generic word for Africans, namely, 'Bantu'. In a striking linguistic inversion, Black Consciousness thinkers referred to government collaborators or 'puppets' (for example Bantustan leaders) as 'non-whites'. SASO increasingly used the phrase 'Black Consciousness' in its propaganda and by 1972, after strenuous insistence, 'black' began to displace 'non-white' in the English-speaking press. Not long after, Afrikaans-language newspapers (and even the government) began to replace 'bantu' by 'black'. This marked a significant milestone in SASO's discursive battle 'to reshape popular perceptions'.[11]

The term 'consciousness' suggests the movement's orientation as a philosophy of liberation, albeit one that began as a meditation on blackness and on 'being black' in the world. Existentialist and religious influences were widely evident in its early phases. So, too, was the idea of 'black power' as adumbrated by American civil rights activist and Black Panther leader Stokeley Carmichael. The choice of 'consciousness' in preference to 'power' was significant—and prudent—since it implied an 'attitude of mind' rather than a direct challenge to the state. It was only around 1972 that the (capitalized) term 'Black Consciousness' displaced alternative descriptions such as 'negritude', 'personality', or 'African existentialism'.[12]

As a 'movement' Black Consciousness signalled its difference from a conventional political party with defined goals and a manifesto. Although charismatic individuals soon emerged from its ranks, Black Consciousness did not adopt a formal leadership structure, preferring to spread its influence and philosophy through affiliate organizations sharing common aims. The stress was on challenging the apartheid mindset through active 'conscientization'[13] rather than direct confrontation with the apartheid state. Herewith lies another difference with the PAC, which considered that latent Africanist energy could be catalysed by the right sort of spark. To the contrary, Black Consciousness intellectuals appreciated that active work was required in order to arouse and sustain political awareness.

The South African Students' Organization (SASO)

Within a short period after its formation in 1969, the South African Students' Organization, SASO, established a palpable presence on black campuses like the University of the North (Turfloop), Fort Hare, Durban-Westville, and (a little later) the Western Cape. SASO's first president was Steve Biko, a Durban medical student who had received his secondary school education at the Catholic mission school, Marianhill, and at Lovedale. Other leading SASO activists included Barney Pityana, Aubrey Mokoape, Sathasivian 'Saths' Cooper, and Strini Moodley.

Interestingly, SASO's first major political initiative took the form of a challenge to white, liberal-dominated NUSAS. This was less risky than targeting the state. It also implied that assertions of 'blackness' required the norm of 'whiteness' to be destabilized. In 1968, Biko wrote to NUSAS president Duncan Innes, expressing dissatisfaction with the organization's capacity to translate into action the 'lip service to principles paid to so many of our celebrated student leaders at all occasions where we meet'. He warned that there was a move amongst black students to disaffiliate.[14] Biko denied that the new organization was seeking to supplant NUSAS as the national students' union.[15] But in 1970, SASO dramatically withdrew from NUSAS, thereby withdrawing recognition of the oldest student body in the country.

In doing so, SASO firmly rejected what it saw as the patronizing attitudes of white sympathizers and intermediaries, whose theoretical support for integration did not necessarily amount to an understanding of emancipation. From SASO's perspective, liberals were suspect precisely because of their inherited social and educational advantages. As Biko explained: ' . . . no matter what a white man does, the colour of his skin—his passport to privilege—will always put him miles ahead of the black man. Thus in the ultimate analysis no white person can escape being part of the oppressor camp.'[16]

SASO's rejection of NUSAS aroused raw emotions. However, reading between the lines, it is not difficult to detect a strong sense of mutual fascination and even empathy between the leadership of the two organizations. NUSAS leaders appreciated the import of Biko's reasoning and were conciliated by his reasonableness, even if the majority of the NUSAS student body was profoundly disturbed by Black Consciousness' repudiation of a colour-blind approach to politics.[17] The shock was even more palpable within the liberal establishment and the Progressive Party, which was accused of political irrelevance if not actual complicity in apartheid repression. Deeply affronted veteran liberal leaders, Alan Paton amongst them, countered with charges of reverse racism.

Predictably, reactionaries delighted in such liberal discomfort. Some Afrikaner nationalist opinion-makers ventured that SASO's emergence was the harbinger of a new Bantu spirit compatible with the government's theory of separate development.[18] Both traditional liberal and reactionary views misconceived the message of Black Consciousness and thoroughly underestimated its potential to unleash new radical energies.

A Composite Philosophy

Black Consciousness ideology was an eclectic mixture of theological, philosophical, and new left political ideas. While predominantly an indigenous creation, it drew widely on what we would now refer to as post-colonial theory. The teachings of Fanon and Cabral, as well as the pedagogy of Paulo Freire and theology of Dietrich Bonhoeffer, popularized by John Robinson's *Honest to God* (1963), were in broad circulation. African-American theologian James Cone, who made a major contribution to black power ideology, was widely read. Also influential were the language, style, and gestures of black power in America, including raised fists and Afro-haircuts. Black Consciousness marked a departure from Pan-Africanism by virtue of its expanded definition of blackness, though Africanist strands of thought ranging from francophone negritude (Césaire and Senghor) to John Mbiti's study of African religion were eagerly absorbed. Also inspiring were new radical histories of South Africa that foregrounded hitherto neglected millennial movements such as Ethiopian Christianity and the Industrial and Commercial Workers' Union.

In some respects Black Consciousness may be seen as a local emanation of the 'global 1968', alongside the anti-establishment radical hippydom on English-speaking university campuses and, in its questioning of authority and receptiveness to Parisian intellectual currents, the Afrikaner *Sestiger* movement. Whilst Black Consciousness did not adopt the counter-cultural individualism of 1968, it did signal a profound generational reaction against conservatism and compliance with 'the system'. It was undoubtedly the most powerful expression of South Africa's racially segmented '1968'. Striking new slogans and mottoes abounded, among them 'Black Man, you are on your own!', 'The most potent weapon in the hands of the oppressor is the mind of the oppressed', 'Go it alone', 'Buy Black', and 'black is beautiful'. Terms like 'Africanization', 'relevance', and 'conscientization' rapidly entered radical political parlance.

Unlike the established liberation movements, which tended to treat 'culture' as a secondary form of political awareness, Black Consciousness was highly receptive to artistic expression and keen to position this at the heart of the liberation experience. Emphasis on creativity and on 'conscientizing' gave rise to a burgeoning of black theatre, poetry, and music.

Like religion, cultural politics offered space for forms of popular resistance that were at once coded and powerfully resonant.

The publication of Oswald Mtsahli's volume of poetry *Sounds of a Cowhide Drum* (1971) opened the way for major new black poets such as Sipho Sepamla, James Matthews, Mafika Gwala, and Mongane Wally Serote. Publishing initiatives like Ravan Press (1971), *S'ketsh* (1972), and the iconic multi-media magazine *Staffrider* (1977) offered platforms for a vibrant new generation of Black Consciousness writers. The editorial policy of these publications was radical, populist, and determinedly unconstrained by the elite 'standards' of the academy. Contributors typically used a pared down English, mixed with local township idioms, in order to explore notions of 'blackness' and to challenge the conditions of political servitude. To the annoyance of some established intellectuals, this incipient post-colonial critique extended to the dominance of 'western' literary forms and values.[19]

In the world of drama, an effusion of new 'alternative' and community-based experimental theatre and cultural groups emerged from the early 1970s. Notable initiatives included the black-run Theatre Council of Natal (1969) and the South African Black Theatre Union (1972). From the mid-1970s, the Federated Union of Black Arts in Johannesburg and the Community Arts Project in Cape Town offered alternative centres for a diversity of cultural activities. Black dramatists gained exposure in racially mixed venues like the Market Theatre in central Johannesburg and The Space in Cape Town. Here the boundaries between 'township', 'struggle', or 'people's' drama on the one hand, and 'protest' theatre emanating from more established institutions on the other, were often blurred to great effect.[20]

Especially in its early years Black Consciousness ideology was the province of the young intelligentsia. It was always a composite amalgam of ideas rather than a honed philosophical position. Steve Biko's writings reveal a remarkable eclecticism, as well as a capacity to distil the essence of what liberation meant in theory and in daily life. Biko is said to have compiled his own personal reading list by procuring the very texts which were listed as prohibited by the official *Government Gazette*.[21]

Not surprisingly, there were many internal tensions—and sometimes glaring contradictions—within Black Consciousness thought and practice.

Was it possible to attack non-racialism, for example, without incurring the charge of being racialist? Was its communitarian approach implicitly socialist and, if so, what evidence was there that it would find appeal amongst the mass of black workers? Was national liberation coextensive with women's emancipation and, if so, was it possible to reconcile these broader aims with the ingrained sexism and patently masculinist tone of so much Black Consciousness rhetoric? As Ian Macqueen shows, the rhetoric of reclaiming black 'manhood' was not inconsistent with growing female assertiveness, both politically and in respect of dress and behaviour. Individual women within the Black Consciousness movement like Mamphele Ramphele, Vuyelwa Mashalaba, Daphne Masekela, Winnie Kgware, Deborah Matshoba, and Thenjiwe Mthintso achieved early prominence as leaders in their own right, though not necessarily in pursuit of a feminist agenda.[22]

The Black People's Convention

These conundrums were played out as Black Consciousness became more overtly political. An important development was the formation, in 1972, of the Black People's Convention which aimed to serve as a national umbrella organization for sympathetic social, cultural, and political organizations. More than 1,400 delegates representing 145 groups attended its inaugural conference. The BPC's wish to attract a more mature constituency helps to explain the election of Winnie Kgware, a senior teacher and SASO sympathizer based at the University of the North, as its first national president.[23] Whether or not she was a figurehead, this set a new precedent: no black woman had ever before served as leader of a comparable national organization.

The Black People's Convention helped to bring together a burgeoning network of grass-roots community organizations seeking to give expression to the idea of self-reliance. Here, Julius Nyerere's *ujamaa* philosophy in Tanzania was a source of inspiration. A range of health, educational, and literacy projects were undertaken under the auspices of Black Community Programmes. This was established in 1972 under the direction of social worker Bennie Khoapa with Steve Biko responsible for youth activities.[24] The intention was to give practical effect to Black Consciousness and to broaden as well as deepen its support base by locating it in (predominantly) rural communities. Significant funding was made available to the BCP from ecumenical Christian organizations like the Christian Institute and foreign churches. BCP also benefited from disbursements from the Anglo-American Chairman's Fund which evidently approved of the concept of self-reliance and social upliftment.[25]

Somewhat belatedly, the state came to the realization that Black Consciousness represented a threat rather than a vindication of separate development. On the occasion of the 1972 graduation ceremony at the University of the North (Turfloop), student leader Onkgopotse Abram Tiro publicly condemned the principles of Bantu education. He assailed homeland leaders for being part of 'the same machine which is crushing us as a nation' and called on fellow graduates to 'bear greater responsibilities in the liberation of our people'.[26] This was an extraordinary brave challenge. Just two years earlier, the all-white university Council had appointed Werner Eiselen, architect of apartheid education, as Turfloop's chancellor. At Eiselen's investiture it was stated that Turfloop should play a full role in training manpower to support the homeland system. Tiro's criticisms crossed an important symbolic threshold; his attack was an intolerable affront to the assembled dignitaries, black as well as white. He refused to issue a humble apology and was duly expelled.

Student unrest brought the police onto the Turfloop campus which resulted in the expulsion of the entire student body. Those seeking readmission had to sign pledges of good behaviour. The wave of protest soon spread to other black campuses, including Durban-Westville (Indian) and Western Cape (coloured) with calls to boycott these apartheid universities on a nationwide basis. The so-called Alice Declaration of May 1972, passed at a SASO 'formation school', condemned the 'oppressive atmosphere' at Black Institutions of Higher Learning and thereby helped to promote a sense of supra-black unity within hitherto divided and isolated 'bush' universities. Up to this point, campus protests had been relatively easily dealt with through hardline action on the part of the university authorities, often in combination with the police.

Conditions were very different at the white liberal universities where the principle of university autonomy offered some protection. In June 1972, a group of University of Cape Town students mounted a protest in support of academic freedom, prompted in part by the repressive conditions on black campuses. They gathered on the steps of St George's Cathedral near parliament where they sang the American civil rights anthem 'We Shall Overcome'. Police baton-charged the protestors and pursued them into the sanctuary of the cathedral. Similar scenes were played out in Johannesburg. Here, Wits students marching to St Mary's Cathedral were tear-gassed by police. Many were charged with contravening the Riotous Assemblies Act.

Whereas the violent assault on civic freedoms in the urban centres of Cape Town and Johannesburg occasioned a great deal of press comment, the protests on remote black campuses were barely reported. Black students still did not 'occupy a central role in South Africa's political field'.[27] Paris and Berkeley, 1968, loomed larger in liberal and radical consciousness than Turfloop did in 1972. In parliament, the Minister of Police implied that NUSAS was somehow responsible for the unrest on black campuses. The impudence of long-haired white youth and women with 'dirty long dresses' attracted far more public attention than the protest and disruption on black university campuses.[28]

Crackdown

Reverting to his reputation as a strongman, Prime Minister Vorster strongly defended the police actions and declared that he would take vigorous action to curtail errant white students. He had NUSAS firmly in his sights when he appointed the Schlebusch Commission in 1972 to investigate 'certain organizations', including the University Christian Movement, the Christian Institute, and the determinedly moderate Institute of Race Relations. As a result of its preliminary findings eight NUSAS leaders received banning orders in February 1973 under the terms of the Suppression of Communism Act, among them Neville Curtis and Paul Pretorius. A few days later, eight SASO and BPC leaders, including Biko, Barney Pityana, and Saths Cooper, were banned. Yet, beyond the government's assumption that sinister, outside 'communistic' forces were widely at work, there was still little to connect the parallel worlds of white and black student activism.

The standard claim that 'agitators' were destabilizing otherwise peaceful race relations was reflected in a new law, passed in 1974, under which bodies such as NUSAS and the Christian Institute were declared to be 'affected organizations', thereby cutting them off from foreign funding and severely restricting their activities. Beyers Naudé, head of the Christian Institute, refused on principle to testify before the Schlebusch Commission. This brought Naudé, formerly a highly respected minister of the Dutch Reformed Church and a member of the elite Afrikaner *Broederbond*, into direct conflict with the government over the principle of justice and rule of law. At his ensuing public trial for refusing to testify on oath to the Schlebush Commission—on the grounds that God was the 'highest authority'—Naudé became a Christian martyr who, in the eyes of his supporters, was guilty only of speaking truth to power; conversely, the Afrikaner establishment reviled him as a dangerous renegade.[29]

Well-established links between the Christian Institute, the University Christian Movement, and the South African Council of Churches helped to foster understanding of Black Consciousness within the radical ecumenical movement. Through experience and active engagement with African independent churches, Christian Institute leaders like Beyers Naudé and Theo Kotze—both from distinguished Afrikaans backgrounds—began to adapt to the reality that they were operating in a predominantly black society. NUSAS' leadership had come to a similar realization, accepting that white students would have to shift from seeing themselves 'as an instrument of change' to seeing themselves 'as being instrumental to change generated from elsewhere'.[30]

Study Project on Christianity in Apartheid Society (Spro-cas)

The Christian Institute, backed by the South African Council of Churches, jointly launched the Study Project on Christianity in Apartheid Society (Spro-cas). This public policy think-tank represented a bold attempt to envision a future non-apartheid society. It operated with a substantial budget under the directorship of Peter Randall, a teacher and writer as well as Assistant Director of the South African Institute of Race Relations.[31] Over a period of nearly five years from 1969, Spro-cas established six major commissions involving more than 130 'leading

South Africans of all racial and cultural groups'. Their reports and publications were designed to present practical and ethically acceptable alternatives to apartheid.[32]

The novelty of Spro-cas was its open-ended, exploratory mode and its willingness to move from the realm of religion to the secular worlds of sociology, politics, education, and economics. Through the counsels of Spro-cas, an older generation of liberals was put directly in touch with a rising new generation. White, English-speaking participants predominated, but a good sprinkling of black and Afrikaner leaders were also represented.[33] A second phase was inaugurated in 1972 when Spro-cas 2 became more action-oriented and committed to the idea of black leadership. It now sponsored the Black Community Programmes community development initiative, with substantial funding arranged from overseas church organizations. A parallel Youth Programme, geared at 'white consciousness', aimed at preparing whites to reconsider their privileges and prepare for 'meaningful change'. This initiative was led by Horst Kleinschmidt and Neville Curtis.[34]

Spro-cas' guiding ethos was Christian and liberal. Yet, with Randall's quiet encouragement, the boundaries began to be tested. In many instances, Spro-cas' guiding empirical methodology and its view of South Africa as a 'plural society' was challenged by more radical approaches, reflecting the rise of materialist thinking on the part of innovative historians and sociologists. Spro-cas' formal recommendations were less significant than its role as a catalyst for new ideas about a future society, based on a shared assumption that South African society had to undergo fundamental economic and political change, and that such changes would be initiated by blacks. No less important was the practical financial help that Spro-cas and the ecumenical church movement directed to initiatives like the Black Community Programmes and Ravan Press.[35]

For some critics, Steve Biko amongst them, Spro-cas was constrained by its desire to find 'an "alternative" acceptable to the white man'.[36] The reports which Spro-cas routinely sent to government ministers were invariably ignored, though perhaps not by all Afrikaner opinion-makers. For example, the political correspondent of the newspaper *Hoofstad* was alarmed to find Spro-cas publications being 'devoured by young Bantus and white intellectuals' in a Cape Town bookshop. He warned: 'If the

Afrikaners do not quickly wake up and fight the integrationists, even with their own weapons, separate development may lose the battle in the last ditch, the cities.'[37]

In addition to bringing university intellectuals and politicians into urgent conversation, the Spro-cas process thickened institutional and personal links between the South African Council of Churches, the Christian Institute, NUSAS, and Black Consciousness groupings. It was able to disburse funds to individuals and organizations involved in anti-apartheid activities. Given its diverse membership, it is unsurprising that Spro-cas could not agree on what apartheid was, let alone create consensus about how to end it; its significance lay in its role in bringing religious and secular voices from different traditions into conversation. At the core of the Spro-cas dilemma was the problem as to whether apartheid could be reformed from within, or whether it constituted a system of racialized exploitation necessitating the total reordering of society.[38]

Steve Biko and Rick Turner

The voices of radicalism that were increasingly heard within Spro-cas broadly divided on the growing issue of race and class. For Richard 'Rick' Turner, the radical young philosopher and politics lecturer who wrote his doctorate on existentialism at the Sorbonne and participated in the 1968 UCT sit-in, a combination of Marxist analysis and practical engagement with black workers was key. Turner exerted a profound 'new left' influence on radical white students. His powerful analysis of South Africa, *The Eye of the Needle* (1972), was published by Spro-cas.[39]

Newly appointed to a lectureship at the University of Natal, Turner developed a friendship with Steve Biko, who was then studying medicine in the university's 'Non-European' section. Turner and Biko were both developing trenchant criticisms of liberalism and they shared an interest in existentialist philosophy. Turner argued that 'in an important sense both whites and blacks are oppressed' by 'a social system which perpetuates itself by creating white lords and black slaves, and no full human beings'.[40] He maintained that Black Consciousness attacks on liberals were too sweeping; the solution lay in the development of a common radicalism capable of transforming society.

In the course of animated discussions with Turner, Biko insisted that class analysis was inclined to ignore the fundamentally racist nature of capitalist exploitation in South Africa. As much as it revealed, class analysis was obfuscatory because it allowed white radicals to overlook their privileged racial status. In a favourite jibe that invoked the stereo-typical figure of a stock Afrikaner, Biko advised whites 'who tell us that the situation is a class struggle rather than a racial one' to 'go to van Tonder in the Free State and tell them this'.[41]

As non-doctrinaire intellectuals with a shared interest in dialectical thought, Biko and Turner would probably have agreed that, in an ideal future society, race and indeed class could be transcended. But in real situations matters went awry (as when Turner led a group of white activists to assist squatters at New Farm, near Mahatma Gandhi's Phoenix settlement, where SASO students were already engaged in development work).[42] In time, the dialectical political analysis shared by Turner and Biko might have converged in the 'true humanity' of a race-less and class-less society envisioned by Biko.[43] But this remains a matter for speculation because both were killed for opposing apartheid: Biko, in police custody in 1977, and Turner at the hands of secret assassins the following January.

New Mobilizing Strategies

In the short term, the trajectories laid out by Turner and Biko diverged markedly even though dialogue between these two leading protagonists continued. SASO's attacks on NUSAS persuaded radical white students to explore new forms of activism. Instead of attempting to 'conscientize' whites, as Steve Biko had urged, NUSAS students like David Hemson and Halton Cheadle followed Turner's lead and began to establish Wages Commissions on NUSAS campuses. The first was formed at the University of Natal in 1971. The object of the Wages Commissions was to produce statistical evidence about the employment conditions, wage rates, and living conditions of black labourers. Where possible, statutory bodies were used to press for improvements. Dedicated Advice

Centres were formed, and these helped to regenerate or transform trade union structures in the Durban, Johannesburg, and Cape Town regions.

By contrast, the Black Consciousness Movement sought to broaden its profile in order to inaugurate a new, more politically active, phase of opposition. This, more confrontational, phase was entered into despite the crackdown on SASO and the Black People's Convention. An important gain was made when coloured students at the University of Western Cape, with support from the philosophy lecturer and writer Adam Small, came out in support of SASO in June 1973. A mass meeting in Athlone cheered Durban academic Fatima Meer's call for 'Power to our brothers way beyond Table Mountain'.[44] Her invocation of supra-black unity signalled a new direction in Cape Town radical coloured political activism, which was still immersed in the purist politics of 'boycottism'.

A further BCM strategy was to reconnect with the liberation movements in neighbouring countries. A number of key SASO leaders, Harry Ranwedzi Nengwekhulu and Bokwe Mafuna amongst them, succeeded in making exploratory contact with the ANC in Botswana. The perilous danger in pursuing this route rapidly became clear when Abram Tiro was killed by a parcel bomb near Gaborone in February 1974. Commemorative services for Tiro treated him as a martyr. Black Consciousness leaders called for his death to be 'redeemed by the blood of 30 million blacks'.[45]

Durban, 1973–4

The pursuit of divergent strategies by white and black student radicals (non-racial 'workerism' in the case of the former, Black Consciousness-oriented community organization in the latter) was clearly evident in the difference in approaches signalled by Biko and Turner. In January 1973, 2,000 workers at a Durban brick factory came out on strike. The workers marched to a football stadium behind a red flag (apparently intended as a traffic warning rather than a signal of their political affiliations) chanting 'Filumunti ufilusadikiza' (man is dead but his spirit still lives).[46] Over the course of the next two months, around 160 strikes took place in the Durban area, involving municipal workers, the textile industry, engineering works, and many small factories. In the majority of cases, the workers were successful in improving their weekly wages by a remarkable 10–20 per cent.

The Durban strikes were spontaneous and almost entirely unanticipated, though there had been earlier intimations of labour unrest amongst stevedores in Cape Town and Durban. In Namibia, Ovambo migrant workers mounted a successful strike in December 1971. The immediate cause of the 1973 strikes cannot be attributed directly to any single political cause or organization. While some commentators immediately laid the blame on 'agitators', the predominant view amongst newspaper commentators (and even the government) was that economic need rather than political objectives provided the cause. It is almost impossible to separate political from economic motivations. There is a strong likelihood that the emphasis laid by strikers on the right to be paid a living wage was conditioned by student involvement and the activities of the University of Natal Wages Commission.[47]

Industrial action also spread to East London and the Johannesburg region. In the course of 1973, as many as 100,000 South African workers participated in strike action. This was the largest instance of sustained worker militancy since the 1946 mineworkers' strike. The consequences proved momentous. The fact that it was illegal for Africans to withhold their labour necessitated innovative organizational tactics. New trade union structures began to emerge on a national basis with a particular emphasis on workplace rights. It was out of this nascent movement that the Federation of South African Trade Unions (FOSATU) was created in 1980.

In September 1974, SASO and the BPC raised the political temperature by mounting a public rally in Durban to mark the Frelimo liberation movement's victory over Portuguese rule in Mozambique. This decision, coming in the wake of the recent bannings of Black Consciousness leaders, marked a new willingness amongst younger leaders to confront the state (probably against the advice of Biko). In identifying with the demise of settler colonialism in Mozambique and invoking the prospect of violence in publicity flyers, SASO activists like Muntu Myeza were deliberately heightening expectations and testing legal as well as political limits. They persisted, notwithstanding the fear of government reprisals and threats that thousands of whites in Durban were mobilizing to stop them.

Amidst rising tension and revolutionary rhetoric (slogans like 'Viva' and reference to 'Azania' now began to enter political discourse) a crowd numbering around 1,500 assembled near Curries Fountain in central Durban. The rally went ahead but was forcibly dispersed by police. Earlier, students at the University of the North clashed with police on campus. Although violence was limited, these gatherings revealed a clear escalation in political conflict: Black Consciousness activists were no longer willing to avoid confrontation; the government was determined to repress the movement once and for all.[48]

The SASO-BPC Trial

In the course of a major criminal trial during 1975–6, SASO and the BPC were accused of conspiring to bring about revolutionary change through violent means. The case was thin, but the ramifications were broad. As an observer noted, ' the whole concept of Black Consciousness is on trial'.[49] Just as the Treason and Rivonia trials had helped to define the ANC's objectives a decade earlier, so the defendants in the long-running 'SASO Nine' trial used the theatre afforded by the courtroom to expound their beliefs. However, whereas the ANC trialists of the 1950s and 1960s obeyed courtroom protocol, the Black Consciousness defenders and supporters punctuated proceedings with defiant shouts of 'POWER'—AMANDLA'. All were found guilty under the Terrorism Act and imprisoned on Robben Island.[50]

Biko's case was conducted in a different register. The exchanges between him and Judge Boshoff proceeded in a spirit of wide-ranging debate and enquiry—remarkable given the seriousness of the charges. Skilful questioning by Biko's counsel, David Soggot, provided Biko with a political platform. He used this to elaborate at length on Black Consciousness' aims in a manner that was at once uncompromising and yet reasonable. In a much quoted exchange Boshoff asked the defendant: 'But now why do you refer to you people as blacks? . . . I mean you people are more brown than black.' To which Biko responded: 'In the same way as I think white people are more pink and yellow and pale than white.' This lampooning rebuff was revealing in two respects: it explained the slogan 'black is beautiful' (which had prompted the question) while ridiculing the question and the questioner.[51] Biko thereby achieved a deft moral victory that resonated through the townships of South Africa. Just a month after giving this testimony, the Soweto uprising broke out.

A Changing External Environment

The early 1970s were a crucial transition moment between apartheid's Verwoerdian high point and the re-emergence of concerted domestic opposition. A new politics of radicalism, cautious at first but increasingly insistent, was evident amongst black as well as white students, and amongst black workers too. The geopolitics of the southern African region were also becoming more fluid. Prime Minister Vorster's exercise in détente with biddable neighbouring African states held out the promise of his playing a constructive role in resolving the problems of Rhodesia and South West Africa/Namibia, while helping to hold Communism at bay. In October 1974, Vorster addressed the world and tantalizingly asked critics to 'give us six months'—without specifying quite what he meant. His vague promise proceeded from the confident assumption that South Africa's military and economic strength would allow it to dictate terms in the region.

While the demonstrable successes of Vorster's outward policy were distinctly limited, the initiative played well with the United States government which viewed close relations with the South Africa government as vital to its own economic and security interests. In 1969, the Nixon administration inaugurated a 'tilt' towards southern Africa. Operating from the assumption that 'whites are here to stay', the Nixon administration adopted dialogue as a strategy and continued to moderate criticism of South Africa at the United Nations.

The US government was mindful of the fact that more than 300 American companies (including a dozen of its biggest corporations) were active in South Africa. Together, this amounted to highly profitable investments of well over $1bn in 1970 prices, several times greater than had been the case in 1960. Carefully calibrated *realpolitik* coexisted with insensitivity to, or incomprehension of, African nationalist aspirations. One revealing instance was the decision by US ambassador John Gavin Hurd to accept an invitation to hunt guinea fowl with cabinet minister Ben Schoeman on Robben Island; political prisoners were said to have been drafted in as 'beaters'![52]

US confidence about the future of white minority regimes in Africa was badly misplaced. In 1974, a military coup swept the Caetano government from power in Portugal, thereby ending nearly fifty years of dictatorial government. The leader of the takeover, Antonio Spinola, insisted that it was no longer viable to repress the nationalist resistance movement in Africa. Overnight, the vast Portuguese colonies of Angola and Mozambique, so vital to South Africa's *cordon sanitaire*, were in the hands of black nationalists many of whom were espousing support for Marxism. Frelimo's victory in Mozambique proved an inspiration to South Africans. In Rhodesia, white minority rule was threatened by a full-scale guerrilla war. And in South West Africa/Namibia, unlawfully treated by South Africa as a fifth province, the SWAPO liberation movement was involved in a low-intensity war with the South African military. The outbreak of civil war in Angola in 1975 highlighted the instability of the region and drew in the United States, the Soviet Union, and Cuba, as well as South Africa.

New instability in southern Africa made it clear that white minority rule in southern Africa was anything but permanent. The rapid departure of the Portuguese in Angola led to civil war and the vast region soon became an intensely hot flashpoint in the misleadingly named Cold War. When Henry Kissinger toured southern Africa in 1976 he stated that American policy towards South Africa was premised on a 'clear evolution towards equality of opportunity and basic rights' within a 'reasonable' period of time.[53] The carefully modulated speech did not mention political rights, though it did hint that social reforms were desirable. At the United Nations, the United States (along with Britain and France) maintained its policy of vetoing or abstaining from substantive resolutions hostile to South African interests—including economic sanctions.

In August 1975 Vorster dispatched a secret military force into Angola as part of an effort to tip the balance in the civil war and prevent the Marxist MPLA—one of three liberation movements seeking to fill the vacuum left by the Portuguese—from consolidating control of the capital, Luanda. The incursion was initially explained as a means of defending the Calueque dam in southern Angola. It soon escalated into a full-scale invasion. South Africa's Operation Savannah lacked clear military objectives. It was embarked upon without either public backing or the knowledge of the cabinet: the government flatly denied its troops were in Angola and suffered the humiliation of having four captured South African prisoners put on public display by the MPLA at a Luanda press conference at the end of the year.

The 'little mistake', as the intervention was referred to with sarcastic understatement by a leading Afrikaans journalist,[54] was premised on a belief that the United States would provide support for the South African troops so as to forestall the Cuban-backed MPLA—the assumption being that the US government would repay the debt by ensuring continued American diplomatic and military support. South Africa's secret service, BOSS, encouraged this view. The CIA played a key covert role, with the strong backing of Henry Kissinger who, bruised by recent failures in Vietnam, was determined to resist any expansion of Soviet influence.[55] But American military backing was not forthcoming and new legislation in Senate put a stop to covert assistance. By the end of 1975 the South African military advance came to a halt some 200 kilometres from Luanda, after which it beat a hasty retreat. Although not actually defeated on the battlefield, white South Africa's belief in the invincibility of its defence force was significantly shaken—stirring faith within the liberation movements about freedom in Namibia and South Africa.

Far from ending Communist influence in the region, the Angolan civil war drew thousands of Cuban combat troops into the region. Substantial military support was provided by the Soviet Union (and China too). The conflagration, one of the largest and most protracted of the 'hot' Cold War, dragged on for over a decade during which South African forces, operating from Namibia, repeatedly invaded the country, culminating in a major set-piece military stalemate at Cuito Cuanavale in 1987–8. Here, thousands of high-calibre Cuban reinforcements proved decisive in repelling the South African military's attacks. Russian weaponry, including MiG fighters and helicopters, challenged South Africa's previously uncontested superiority in the air, undermining its army's capability on the ground.

For South Africa this largely secret war was an expensive and strategically unnecessary imbroglio that drained the country, economically and politically. Having begun as an attempt to defeat SWAPO guerrillas in the northern parts of Namibia, South Africa's growing regional involvement became increasingly intractable. Crucially, it encouraged an escalating role for the military in domestic politics as well. South Africa's annual budget for defence increased by 36 per cent in 1975 and continued to rise broadly in line with real GDP until 1989, absorbing a hefty 15–20 per cent of total government expenditure.[56] This expense, albeit fiscally sustainable, was incurred in the context of a steadily deteriorating economic and domestic political environment.

A Failing Economy

The performance of the South African economy broadly falls into two halves during the apartheid period: rapid growth (annual 2.2 per cent real GDP per capita) from 1948 to 1973, followed by stagnation or decline through the 1980s and until 1994. In the final decade of National Party rule, real GDP per capita declined by 15 per cent. Industrial expansion was especially impressive from the 1950s, overhauling mining and agriculture to reach nearly 30 per cent of GDP by the mid-1960s. Yet persistent structural weaknesses—in particular, poor efficiency, high production costs, and a limited domestic market—checked further growth from the 1970s. The average real growth rate of manufacturing was 7.4 per cent from 1947–74 but then declined to 1.3 per cent from 1975–92.

A resource-led mini-boom in the late 1970s petered out from 1980, triggering a serious long-term contraction in formal employment. The international price of gold, for so long the mainstay of the South African economy, fell sharply during 1975–6, putting pressure on government tax receipts and forcing the government to seek expensive short-term foreign loans. The surge in the price of oil in 1973, and again at the close of the decade, considerably increased inflationary pressures. Ongoing political turmoil eroded investor confidence, leading to massive capital flight and serious depreciation in the value of the rand against the dollar.[57]

For a country dependent on imports of capital goods and with wage inflation exacerbating a severe skills shortage, the prospects were worrying. The 1973 strikes indicated the depth of discontent amongst black labour as well as severe structural inequalities in the labour market. In drawing attention to the 'sheer extent of the migrant labour system', in the mines as well as in agriculture and in every major industrial centre, economist Francis Wilson concluded that most whites were oblivious to the social injustice associated with migrancy. Those responsible for the system's administration doubted that it could continue without modification. Wilson was overwhelmed by the 'sense of hurt rage of black South Africans at what is being done to them'.[58] He also found that the real wages of black mineworkers had probably fallen in the period 1889–1970, while those of white workers had improved by around two-thirds.[59] The relative fall in black wages was in large measure attributable to long-standing collusion between capitalists and the state: an overlapping matrix of controls involving the pass laws, strictly regulated mine compounds, and restrictions on trade unionism, worked together to depress the costs of migrant labour.

From 1970, the labour market began to undergo rapid change. By 1984, real wages paid to black mineworkers more than quadrupled whereas white mineworkers' wages remained more or less constant. Over this period the wage ratio of whites to blacks in mining declined from 20:1 to 5.4:1. In the manufacturing sector, blacks' average real wages increased by nearly 40 per cent between 1970 and 1976. White workers in manufacturing industry continued to earn far more than blacks, though the multiple narrowed to 4.8 in 1975 and decreased further over the next decade.[60] Nevertheless, the huge disparities in wealth and in wages paid to whites and blacks remained. In 1970, African per capita personal income was only 6.8 per cent that of whites, with coloureds earning 17.3 per cent and Asians 20.2 per cent of per capita white incomes.[61] Pressures to narrow this gap in incomes only made the differences more visible.

This inequality in wealth attracted the attention of anti-apartheid activists in Britain and the United States who began to target the exploitative practices of foreign corporations in paying 'starvation wages'.[62] Startling revelations were made by British-based journalists and activists in *The South African Connection* (1973) about overseas investment in apartheid. Britain, it was claimed, was responsible for nearly 60 per cent of all foreign investment in South Africa in 1970. Average annual returns on this investment at 10–12 per cent were 'spectacular', exceeded only by Malaysia. Rates of return on American investments were even higher at 18.6 per cent. These enormous profits, the authors asserted, were generated at the expense of impoverished black labourers.[63] Even Milton Friedman, apostle of free market economics and adviser of right-wing governments, was disquieted by the 'great discrepancy between the average income of the Whites and the Blacks in South Africa'. On a visit to Johannesburg in March 1976, he warned that the gap, whether just or not, was 'at the root of your fundamental political difficulties with the rest of the world'.[64]

External pressures were important in drawing attention to the dismal wages of black workers. Yet the relative improvement in black earnings was far more the outcome of growing assertiveness on the part of black workers themselves and, in particular, the growth of trade unionism. The 1972/3 Durban strikes proved to be a key moment in the awakening of organized black labour. Trade union demands focused attention on the appalling conditions under which blacks worked. The government held employers partly responsible for the labour unrest and preferred to see the causes as economic (which helps to explain why the strikes, though illegal, were policed with restraint).

Prime Minister Vorster advised employers to treat their workers not merely as 'labour units' but as 'as human beings with souls'.[65] In effect, he was reminding the electorate that the state would not underwrite abysmal wages paid by English-speaking capitalists in a part of the country not generally sympathetic to Afrikaners. Vorster's remarks also underlined a willingness to introduce limited concessions, so long as these did not involve granting blacks political rights outside of the Bantustans. The underlying problem for the government was that rising labour demands and growing political expectations were occurring just as the economy was moving from an era of sustained growth to one of protracted stagnation.

The Soweto Rising, 1976–7

In 1976, Vorster appointed Andries Treurnicht, conservative theologian and standard-bearer of the Verwoerdian *verkramptes*, to the post of

Deputy Minister of Bantu Administration and Education. The decision, designed to placate the prime minister's voluble right-wing critics, had explosive consequences. Treurnicht insisted on implementing a long-standing but conveniently overlooked policy ensuring that Afrikaans be used as the medium of instruction in half of all subjects not taught in the African vernacular. It was a provocative and arrogant ruling designed to satisfy Afrikaner cultural pride and one that took no account of the fact that Afrikaans was widely seen as the language of administrative oppression.

Students in Soweto, the largest black township in the Johannesburg area, were incensed. Here the ruling affected maths, a subject that Verwoerd had notoriously identified as being unnecessary for most African children. The edict added to the affront of hopelessly over-crowded classrooms, underqualified teachers, and chaotic processes of reorganization. The South African Students' Movement (SASM), a high school organization loosely affiliated to SASO, decided to make the imposition of Afrikaans-medium instruction a campaigning issue. It endorsed a boycott of classes.

On 16 June 1976, a mass demonstration of 15,000–20,000 school children, led by a charismatic young student, Tsietsi Mashinini, began marching towards Orlando Stadium. Placards wielded by students bore slogans such as 'Afrikaans stinks' and 'Away with Oppressive Afrikaans'. The marchers were intercepted by a poorly prepared contingent of police—black as well as white—who fired tear gas into the column and followed this up with live bullets. Zolile Hector Pieterson was one of the first children to be killed.[66] Journalist Sam Nzima's photograph of the dying boy, borne by Mbuyisa Makhubu with Hector's panicked sister Antoinette alongside, appeared in newspapers around the world, instantly turning Pieterson into an icon of the anti-apartheid struggle.

The insurrection that began in Soweto spread like a veld fire as townships throughout the gold producing Rand exploded into violence. The police used extreme force, sanctioned by the cabinet, in an attempt to quell the disorder. In most cases this only fuelled the fires of rebellion. 'What was remarkable', observed *Sunday Times* photographer Alf Khumalo, 'was the attitude of the children. They were so incensed with anger that many seemed oblivious from danger.'[67] According to a government statement, 176 people were killed and 1,139 injured during the first week alone. The real toll was probably far greater.[68]

Townships in major cities including Johannesburg, Pretoria, East London, and Cape Town joined the protests which spread to more than a hundred urban centres and many smaller rural towns. Only Durban and Natal remained relatively quiet. The insurrection continued with oscillating intensity for more than a year, taking the form of rioting, burning barricades, stoning of cars, and the destruction of government buildings and official beer halls. Inadequately trained police fired live rounds ('bird shot') and tear gas without restraint, often from armoured trucks, known as hippos. Helicopters surveyed the battlefield from above. The cycle of violence was sustained as funerals became public political events, resulting in further police action and shootings. Far from subduing the anger, mass arrests and detentions merely encouraged new tiers of activists to come to the fore.

Schools remained at the centre of the revolt—they were subject to attack by police and students alike. Worker stay-at-homes and consumer boycotts were enforced through a mixture of cajoling and threats. Goods presumed to have been purchased in white-owned shops, alcohol especially, were confiscated. Enforcement was aided by opportunist young thugs, *tsotsis*, who introduced a new element of instability and whose principal objectives—looting and larceny—had little in common with the students' political aims.[69] Workers participated in large-scale stay-aways in mid-September 1976. Upwards of half a million workers withheld their labour on the Witwatersrand, joined by some 200,000 workers in Cape Town.

Notwithstanding this support from workers, the ties between the student movement and organized labour were neither close nor fully elaborated: at no point was there any prospect of a general industrial strike or worker-led revolution as some theorists imagined possible. The rebellion continued, with oscillating periods of intensity, until the close of 1977. As of February 1977 the official death toll stood at 575: 496 Africans, 75 coloureds, 2 Indians, and just 2 whites.[70] One of those whites, a liberal welfare official and sociologist, was beaten to death on the first day of the violence. By strange irony, he had published research warning of the anger of Soweto's youth.[71]

Whose Responsibility?

In an attempt to sustain the comforting illusion that ordinary blacks were content with their lot, the government's instinctive response was to blame 'agitators' and foreign ideologies like 'black power' for the violence.[72] But officials could find neither conspirators nor conspiracies. Arrogance and complacency had led many government officials to ignore indications of rising tensions in townships like Soweto, where the education crisis was already acute. Two days before the uprising, a moderate community leader, Leonard Mosala, predicted that another Sharpeville would occur unless the language issue in schools was addressed.[73]

Most whites in South Africa's major urban centres had never entered a black township and scarcely knew anything about the places where their daily workers came from. They were not minded to heed warnings by prescient leaders such as Desmond Tutu, Anglican Dean of Johannesburg, who wrote an open letter to Prime Minister Vorster in May 1976 warning of a 'growing nightmarish fear that unless something drastic is done very soon then bloodshed and violence are going to happen in South Africa almost inevitably. A people can take only so much and no more.' Tutu specifically instanced black children in Soweto who refused to have Afrikaans 'rammed down their throats'. Vorster bluntly refused to meet Tutu.[74]

The perils of prediction were borne out by Jerome Caminada, former foreign editor of the London *Times*, who concluded on the very eve of the uprising that 'two elements indispensable in any popular uprising are both missing in South Africa. One is a deep fury of resentment and the other is freedom to strike at the governing system.'[75]

The violence was neither planned nor coordinated. Indeed, it was the very looseness of organization that helped to sustain rebellion. Nozipho Diseko has shown that some SASM branches were developing links with underground ANC structures in the period leading up to 1976.[76] Nevertheless, the ANC as a whole was taken by surprise and not at any stage in control of events. MK was unable to capitalize on the situation, though it did manage to infiltrate some members into the country. Mac Maharaj, a stalwart of MK and the Communist Party, conceded that 'work among the masses had been neglected inside the country. There was no political underground.' For all the talk of an 'all-round' struggle, the *de facto* position at the time of Soweto was that the armed struggle was the only way forward.[77]

The political wing of the ANC was undoubtedly buoyed by the revolt, yet also fearful that its leadership of the liberation struggle was being usurped. Only towards mid-1977 was the ANC's London-based house journal, *Sechaba*, ready to incorporate the insurrection into its own narrative of resistance, carefully reiterating the organization's role at the vanguard of the liberation movement.[78] The *African Communist*, mouthpiece of the Communist Party, gave scant attention to Black Consciousness before 1977, regarding it as something of a 'blind alley' and a deviation from the real source of revolution, the working class. It was only gradually and grudgingly that the *African Communist* came to accept that Black Consciousness organizations 'must be regarded as important tributaries to the Great River of the liberation movement headed by the ANC'.[79] As late as 1979, Thabo Mbeki reportedly bemoaned the 'arrogance' of Black Consciousness for 'thinking that the issue of liberation starts with their time'.[80]

In interviews well after the 1976 rebellion some student leaders acknowledged clandestine links to the ANC, others pronounced themselves unaware of the organization, and there were those who knew of its banned leadership or figureheads. But, even where its direct influence was not palpable, the ANC retained a distinctive presence in public and private memory. Its reputation as the oldest and best established arm of the liberation movement was sustained by a capacity to broadcast into the country on its shortwave station, *Radio Freedom*, to explode pamphlet bombs, and to sustain small clandestine cells with links to the students. An important link between the ANC and the students was the indomitable Winnie Mandela, then resident in Soweto.

The PAC's presence was vestigial in 1976–7, notwithstanding claims that its leader Zeph Mothopeng, a Soweto teacher, guided the uprising.[81] Nor were Black Consciousness organizations 'behind' the rebellion, though its slogans and ideas were undoubtedly inspirational. If any single organization was responsible for orchestrating events, this was the Soweto Students' Representative Council whose first president, Tsietsi Mashinini, had been inducted into Black Consciousness by Abram Tiro, his high school teacher. In exile, in early 1977, Mashinini insisted that the uprisings had been 'purely spontaneous'; he caused a storm in New York and London with his attacks on the ANC for its inactivity and corrupt behaviour.[82]

The issue of Afrikaans language instruction was more a detonator than an underlying cause.[83] Yet in the larger sense education was key, since it distilled the essence of Verwoerdian ideology and affected those who had most to hope for in the future and least to lose immediately: youth. One of the key contradictions of Bantu education was that it extended education far more broadly than the selective mission schools had been able to do, while constantly reminding pupils of their inferiority. Black school enrolment in secondary schools increased massively in the two decades after the introduction of Bantu education, from 46,000 in 1960 to just under 320,000 in 1975. In the decade leading up to 1976 there was nearly a fivefold increase in Africans in secondary schools.[84] This engendered rising expectations as well as growing frustrations amongst high school students, precisely the social demographic sector that was best placed to register discontent. Their anger was greatly exacerbated during the sharp economic downturn of the mid-1970s: more and more ill-educated students were now entering a contracting job market, which placed a premium on skills that entrants were unable to satisfy.

The Soweto revolt revealed a growing generational divide in urban black society. Nearly two-thirds of Soweto's residents were under the age of 30 and had grown up under conditions of ever increasing daily repression.[85] Student militants were highly disparaging of their parents for colluding in apartheid. They were resentful of teachers who administered corporal punishment with impunity. In targeting beer halls and shebeens, young blacks were not being puritanical (though there was an element of this in the Soweto students' proclamations) so much as demonstrating their anger at the effects of habitual drunkenness that dulled political awareness and put severe strains on family cohesion and resources. A common adult complaint was that their authority was being flouted by their children.[86] Nimrod Mkele, of the Institute of Black Studies, observed with a sense of bemused admiration:

No teacher or principal dares order the students around any more. One principal started telling the kids off. They heard him out and then told him: 'You know, we've always known you were a sell-out.' They beat him up and kicked him around and then put him in his car and told him he must not come back.[87]

The Soweto newspaper editor Aggrey Klaaste spoke on behalf of many parents when he declared frankly: 'We are cowards.'[88] The formation of a Black Parents' Association marked an effort to win back the respect of the students and broaden their political base. Members of this organization included figures with political and professional stature like Nthato Motlana, Winnie Mandela, and Aubrey Mokoena. The Parents' Association interceded with the authorities on practical issues including legal matters and welfare.[89] It managed to win the confidence of the students without displacing the students' centrality. The reconfigured generational relationship was seen in the case of all-important funerals which the Parents' Association helped to pay for. Whereas children's funerals would customarily have been family occasions led by senior women mourners and religious figures, they now became iconic political events led by student activists who chanted political slogans with raised clenched fists.

The 'System'

As opposed to the Defiance Campaign of the early 1950s, which was specifically targeted at unjust apartheid laws, the unplanned and often inchoate rebellion of 1976–7 was projected more widely at 'the system'. Left-wing activist and scholar Baruch Hirson argued at the time that the students' social base was far too narrow to pose a serious revolutionary threat to the state: 'They seemed to respond with the heart rather than with the mind. They were able to reflect the black anger of the townships—but were unable to offer a viable political strategy.'[90]

There is some truth in this observation, yet it relies on a narrow view of revolutionary strategy that owes more to Russia, 1917, than the populist, emotion-fuelled uprisings evident in eastern Europe after 1989, or those in the contemporary Middle East, where shows of public outrage and the politics of the street have caused regimes to fragment. The demands registered by the students were not especially radical, nor was their thinking steeped in deep political analysis. Nevertheless, the depth of their raw outrage was unmistakable, their resourcefulness remarkable, and their spirit of insurrection irrepressible.

Untutored in revolutionary theory they may have been, yet students were nevertheless exponents of an intuitive sociology born of experience and shaped by loosely configured ideas that were in fluid circulation on the streets and in schools.

In opposing 'the system', students were associating racial with class oppression. By the mid-1970s, Black Consciousness ideology had moved beyond its religious foundations and become thoroughly secularized. It was increasingly receptive to the view that economic exploitation was a crucial dimension of apartheid. The focus now extended to 'the overall impact of capitalism and imperialism on the cultural, social, and material conditions of black people'.[91] This implied that true liberation entailed overthrowing or at least significantly transforming capitalism. Resistance to Afrikaans was a metonym for Bantu education and this was in turn viewed as a prime incarnation of apartheid's racial injustice and structural inequities. Consumer boycotts and stay-at-homes were geared to highlighting the role of business in apartheid exploitation. Black functionaries in the townships, including policemen and officially sanctioned spokesmen in the widely reviled 'puppet' Urban Councils, were marginalized and attacked as 'sell-outs'.

The rapid spread of unrest to the Bantustans, where government buildings were attacked or burnt down, was another indication of awareness that cooperation with apartheid structures was intolerable. Anti-collaborationism also struck a deep chord in the western Cape. Here the Unity Movement, dominated by coloured teachers and intellectuals, retained influence. But, whereas Unity Movement politics tended to be abstract (discouraging action more often than prompting it), Black Consciousness thinking was now all about action. The convergence of protesting black and coloured students in Cape Town city centre in September 1976, where they were subjected to tear gas and baton charges, was an unprecedented statement of militancy and unity. The University of the Western Cape, previously shunned by many coloured intellectuals as a 'bush' university, emerged as an important centre of intellectual activism, founded on an understanding of apartheid oppression which linked the analysis of race to class.

Growing awareness of class-based oppression did not imply an acceptance of Marxism, much less endorsement of non-racial 'scientific' socialism. But it did signal a deepening conviction that genuine liberation and race equality could only occur by dissolving existing capitalist relations. It also contributed to a growing recognition that black society was internally divided on class lines and that not all beneficiaries of apartheid were white: hence the sometimes indiscriminate attacks by radicalized youth on perceived collaborators and informers.

Such attacks also provided the police with the means to exploit class (and ethnic) divisions by inciting vigilante groups in an attempt to foment counter-revolution. The violence that emerged between students and migrant labourers in Soweto's 'bachelor' hostels, and later in the Cape, was a reminder that apartheid did not affect everyone in the same way: with even fewer rights than urban 'insiders', unskilled migrant labourers with families in the rural areas often refused to risk their livelihoods for abstract causes, much less to accept the orders of upstart city children.

The Killing of Biko

In 1976–7 the state was not able to quash the insurrection decisively or decapitate its leadership, as had been the case after Sharpeville. Nevertheless, violence was largely contained within black areas. For most whites, secure in their suburban homes, life continued more or less undisturbed. In his first significant public comment on the uprising, more than two months after the outbreak of unrest, Vorster blithely denied that the country was in a state of crisis.[92] This assertion neglected the serious problem of legitimacy that the government faced, though there was some superficial truth to the claim that a state of 'normality' prevailed. By the anniversary of the revolt, which occasioned further riots and shootings, the state had managed to subdue the fury. A combination of mass arrests and detentions, as well as the departure of several thousand students to neighbouring countries, exhausted the rebellion by the end of 1977.

The student revolt persuaded Biko that the time was right for the BCM to unify the resistance and effect a rapprochement between the ANC and PAC. In a newspaper interview he reflected on the changed context of the struggle since the mid-1960s. The major achievement was that 'we have diminished the element of fear in the minds of black people'. Moreover, there was now 'far more condemnation of the system from average black people'. The task was now to 'form one liberation movement'. In pursuit of 'a completely non-racial egalitarian society', Biko considered that it was necessary to achieve 'a more equitable distribution of wealth' by means of a 'judicious blending' of private and state enterprise.[93]

Steve Biko was arrested at a roadblock in Grahamstown on his way back from a clandestine trip to Cape Town where he planned, unsuccessfully, to meet with the intellectual and educationist Neville Alexander. Detained in Port Elizabeth (with fellow activist Peter Jones) Biko was brutally interrogated, chained to a grille, and assaulted. He died, aged 30, of brain injuries four weeks later, on 12 September, after being transported for 1,200km, comatose and manacled, in the back of a police Land Rover.

Justice Minister Jimmy Kruger, who had been responsible for some of the most crudely belligerent government statements during the Soweto uprising, claimed that Biko had died as a result of a hunger strike and, subsequently, that his head injuries were self-inflicted. He went on to state at a National Party congress that Biko's death 'leaves me cold'. A smirking supporter applauded Kruger for allowing detainees 'the democratic right' to starve themselves to death.[94]

Biko's murder was not extraordinary—there were twenty-four deaths in police detention in 1976–7 alone.[95] Nevertheless, as Biko's close colleague and friend Barney Pityana observes, the fact that 'he touched the lives of many people of his generation, black and white', marked him out as special in the eyes of the world and turned him into a sacrificial hero in death.[96] The government soon comprehended the impact of his death and hastened to crack down on all remnants of Black Consciousness. In October, it banned eighteen anti-apartheid organizations including SASO, the Soweto Students' Representative Council, Black People's Convention, the Christian Institute, and the Black Parents' Association. Two leading black newspapers, *The World* and *The Weekend World*, edited by Percy Qoboza, were shut down.

Biko's funeral at a sports stadium in King Williamstown was attended by a crowd of more than 10,000, as well as diplomats representing a dozen western countries, including the United States. Bishop Tutu conducted the ceremony. The mourners raised clenched fists and shouted 'Amandla'. Unusually, there was no police presence, despite outbreaks of violence at memorial services elsewhere in the country. Whites in the neighbourhood focused their attention on a rugby match.[97] Such attempts to ignore the enormity of the events were in vain. The lengthy judicial inquest that followed kept Biko's name constantly in the public eye and helped to mobilize sustained criticism of the government within the country and abroad.

News of Biko's death occasioned an unprecedented international outcry. There were tributes in the United States Congress and at the United Nations by, amongst others, Secretary-General Waldheim.[98] There were countless musical tributes including Jonny Dyani's *Song for Biko* (1987) and Peter Gabriel's 1980 protest song 'Biko'. In 1984 a televised drama-documentary directed by Albert Finney, *The Biko Inquest*, based entirely on transcripts from the actual inquest, was shown in Britain. Three years later, in the midst of a new popular insurrection, Richard Attenborough's imaginative film about Biko's relationship with Donald Woods, *Cry Freedom*, was released to great acclaim.

In the years leading up to Soweto, news media in Britain and the United States had displayed only sporadic interest in South Africa. The crises in Angola, Rhodesia, and Soweto transformed the country's newsworthiness. Overseas correspondents and agencies scrambled to set up bureaux in Johannesburg. Biko's martyrdom, together with that of Hector Pietersen, framed overseas reaction to 'Soweto', which now occupied a firm place in the national and global imagination. Whereas Sharpeville was remembered as a massacre, Soweto was narrated as a revolt. For journalists the 'significant representational message' was that 'Passivity is gone'.[99]

In October 1976, Oliver Tambo addressed the United Nations General Assembly. He observed that this was the first time that 'a representative of the majority of the people of South Africa' had been invited to share a rostrum with 'the distinguished representatives of the sovereign nations and peoples of the world'. Tambo used the occasion to project the ANC as the principal leader of opposition to apartheid oppression and to elevate its moral standing more widely: 'We fight to restore power to the hands of the people. In doing so we shall also liberate the oppressor.'[100]

Up until 1976, countries sympathetic to South Africa, the United States and Britain most notably, had been able to use diplomatic pressure in order to avert international diplomatic and economic sanctions. South Africa remained a loyal ally of the West and its firm anti-communism received considerable international support, backed by conservative media commentary. But western support of—or association with—South Africa was becoming more costly. The Royal Navy's withdrawal from Simonstown in 1975 was an important symbolic statement of the declining strategic importance of the Cape sea route. The British government's support of the Gleneagles Declaration in 1977, which pledged to limit Commonwealth sporting links with South Africa, was another psychological blow. Credible reports that South Africa was about to test a nuclear device in the Kalahari Desert towards the end of 1977 led to formal statements of concern by the United States and France—as well as an unconvincing denial from Vorster.

The United States was also beginning to reassess its relations with Pretoria. A week after the outbreak of the Soweto violence, Vorster met US Secretary of State Henry Kissinger in Germany to discuss regional issues, notably the Rhodesian crisis.[101] For the Pretoria government this high-level meeting was an important confirmation of its international status. But the German government was concerned that the Soweto uprising, not Rhodesia, was now the story and hastily shifted the venue from Hamburg to a forest in Bavaria.

The focus of concern at the 'mini-summit' and in subsequent shuttle-diplomacy was overshadowed by the domestic political crisis in South Africa. In September 1976, on the eve of a further round of meetings with Vorster, Kissinger declared that apartheid was 'incompatible with any concept of human dignity'. This uncharacteristically bold pronouncement aroused fury in Pretoria.[102] It amounted to a growing recognition by the United States, supported by Britain, that majority rule was inevitable in southern Africa—and that South Africa's exceptional status could no longer be countenanced. In the period leading up to the Soweto uprising there was growing international pressure on the plan to grant sovereign 'independence' to the Transkei homeland.

Addressing the United Nations in October 1976, Tambo condemned 'the idea of Bantustan independence' as an 'outrage in Africa'.[103]

South Africa's military intervention in Angola gave further ammunition to apartheid's critics, nullifying claims that the country's ambitions in the region were constructive or peaceful. It also contributed to deteriorating relations with the United States, whose new president, Jimmy Carter, made human rights a cardinal aspect of foreign policy and took a personal interest in ending apartheid. During the course of extensive talks in Vienna, in May 1977, Vice President Mondale bluntly rejected Vorster's claim that South Africa was a 'multi-national' rather than a 'multi-racial' country. He made it clear that there could be no compromise on the principle of equal voting rights for all citizens.[104] Vorster retaliated by warning that America's African policy would result in 'chaos and anarchy in South Africa'. While Carter's actions fell short of his intentions, it was evident that the shift away from Nixon-era *realpolitik* would limit the South African government's scope to conduct domestic policy as it saw fit.[105]

Blustering protests by Vorster and Foreign Minister 'Pik' Botha to the effect that the United States had become an unwitting ally of Communism merely revealed that events were moving beyond their ability to manage them. In November 1977, the United Nations Security Council unanimously resolved to impose a comprehensive mandatory arms embargo on South Africa on account of the danger posed by the country to 'international peace and security'—a venerable UN formulation with fresh relevance as Moscow and Washington became aware that South Africa was on the verge of producing nuclear weapons.[106] This was the first time in its history that a member of the United Nations was the subject of such sanctions; it marked a significant escalation in the incremental process of curing South Africa's diplomatic isolation.

Vorster suffered further loss of authority at the beginning of 1978 with the revelations that government officials had spent some R85m in unauthorized efforts to buy political influence in the United States and Europe.[107] The audacious campaign, which numbered almost 180 secret projects, concentrated on acquisitions (not always successful) of newspapers at home and abroad. A number of overseas front organizations were provided with lavish funds to represent South African interests in a sympathetic light and to expose international 'double standards'. The abiding ethos of this 'war of representation' was that when national interests were at stake no rules need apply.[108] By the standards of later corrupt practices, the 'Information scandal' or 'Infogate' seems relatively tame, but the continuing revelations of intrigue, unaudited spending, foreign exchange violations, and overseas junkets contributed to a sense amongst voters that the government could not be trusted on anything; it punctured a prevailing white myth which held that even if the government made political mistakes, its leadership was steeped in conservative principles of Calvinist probity.

The drip-feed of scandal was widely discussed in the Afrikaans as well as English-language press, exacerbating political ructions within the governing party. Vorster was now unable to contain the ongoing battles between *verligtes* and *verkramptes* in his government. At the 1977 general election the National Party captured more electoral seats than ever (134 out of 165) but this result flattered to deceive: it was largely gained at the expense of the moribund United Party, leading to the business-friendly but anti-apartheid Progressive Party becoming the new official opposition. The magnitude of the government's victory did nothing to solve its internal ideological battles, and Vorster was left personally weakened.

South Africa's 'Infogate' came on top of the debacle in Angola, the mishandling of the Soweto uprising, and a detailed 1978 exposé by journalists about the secretive role of the Afrikaner *Broederbond*. It culminated in the resignation of Prime Minister Vorster and his heir-apparent, 'Connie' Mulder, who had been at the centre of the information scandal. Another prominent casualty was Hendrik van den Bergh, Vorster's long-term ally and head of the Bureau of State Security (BOSS). Eschel Rhoodie, the Department of Information's principal spin-doctor—who personified the scandal with his louche, huckster demeanour, taste for fine hotels, and penchant for two-tone shoes—fled to Ecuador.[109] In September 1978, Vorster was succeeded in office by Defence Minister P. W. Botha.

The political organization that gained most from the Soweto uprising was the ANC. As thousands of student activists slipped over the borders to find refuge in neighbouring countries, they discovered that it was the ANC rather than the PAC that was equipped to offer support and training. Practical realities on the ground, rather than ideological affinity, proved decisive. The ANC was able to capitalize on a wave of new recruits who brought with them the energy and street political sense that the exiled organization lacked. Most of the Soweto generation ended up in MK camps or schools, some were sent abroad for further education. MK's capacity was notably enhanced by the formation of the 16 June Detachment. But there remained formidable challenges to the effective absorption of Soweto's youth: the new guerrilla recruits were desperate to be deployed in South Africa to fight the 'Boers', yet most languished in camps in Angola and suffered a sense of displacement that 'seared the soul and sucked out spirit'.[110]

The process of integrating this young generation was not smooth and the ANC's absorptive capacity had distinct limits. Many young refugee recruits considered that their political passions and personal sacrifices were not fully appreciated by senior ANC figures in exile who stood accused of being dilatory and self-serving. Nevertheless, the ANC benefited enormously from the 1976 generation. By the end of the decade it had succeeded in enhancing its international ties as social democratic governments, led by the Nordic countries, came to accept the ANC was best placed to lead the forces of liberation. The ANC remained anxious that the Black Consciousness Movement might establish its own presence in exile. Only in 1985 did Oliver Tambo feel sufficiently confident to reflect publicly on how unprepared and organizationally weak the ANC had been in 1976.[111]

On Robben Island, where many of the most prominent Black Consciousness activists were imprisoned, the incoming complement of unruly, defiant *klipgooiers* (stone throwers) significantly altered the composition of the prisoner population. The arrival of the Soweto cohort disturbed the prison regimen since many refused to obey routine orders. Nelson Mandela describes his surprise at the way in which a teenage veteran of 1976 flatly refused to remove his cap when ordered to do so by a senior prison official by asking the 'revolutionary' rhetorical question: 'What for?'[112]

It was not clear whether the new generation of radicals on Robben Island would gravitate towards the ANC or the PAC or seek to maintain their independence. Tensions were renewed as the older organizations rallied to recruit the new intake, some of whom wanted to retain their Black Consciousness identity.[113] Violence between prisoners—endemic in all prisons—was not unknown. Mandela stood personally aloof, demonstrating authority as an elder statesman, and preferring the young radicals to find him. They were eventually persuaded that 'the authorities should be dealt with in a controlled, rational manner' and that this was not the same as selling out. ANC veterans like Govan Mbeki and Walter Sisulu devised a comprehensive programme of political education in order to provide deeper analytical perspective on political history and revolutionary strategy.[114]

To a significant extent this strategy worked: the ageing ANC cohort was infused with fresh energy and new ideas, while the Soweto generation, who sometimes dismissed study 'as a waste of time', had their political skills honed in ongoing debates. By around 1980 tensions on the Island largely abated and the ANC managed to re-establish its ideological and institutional dominance.[115] Key Black Consciousness thinkers started to take class more seriously and shifted their allegiances to those following the ANC alliance and the Freedom Charter. In Britain, and then in South Africa, high-profile political campaigns were mounted from 1978 to release Mandela. He soon became the world's most recognized and widely admired political prisoner (along with Soviet human rights campaigner Andrei Sakharov and Polish trade unionist Lech Walesa). In so doing, a living veteran of the struggle for freedom in South Africa began to eclipse Biko's martyrdom in the public imagination.

CHAPTER 7
THE LIMITS AND DANGERS
OF REFORM

Hiatus

For the first half decade from 1977, the South African government was afforded a respite. It used this interlude to stabilize the political situation and embark on a range of reforms. Not for the first time in the country's history, a resource-led boom lifted the country out of recession. From 1979 to 1980 South Africa benefited from an enormous spike in the gold price to over $800 per ounce. This gave a decided boost to economic activity and yielded a substantial budget surplus for the treasury. There were tax cuts for whites and rising social benefits for blacks. After recording a decline in GDP in 1978, annual GDP grew vigorously in 1979–81, before entering negative territory again in 1983.[1] In its 1981 end-of-year review, the Johannesburg *Star* reflected on relatively healthy economic growth, some positive indications of reform, and 'no great violence (we were more peaceful than Europe)'.[2]

The external political environment also shifted in Pretoria's favour as a troika of conservatives came to power in Europe and America: Margaret Thatcher (1979), Ronald Reagan (1981), and Helmut Kohl (1982). Ongoing pressure for mandatory economic sanctions made policy-makers and businessmen in the United States, Britain, and Germany all the more aware of their substantial investments in the still highly profitable South African economy, and of the importance of South Africa as a source of strategic minerals like uranium. The advent of self-proclaimed Marxist governments in Mozambique and Angola persuaded the ideologically driven British and American administrations of the necessity to keep South Africa firmly anti-communist—which, in their terms, meant hostility to ANC-liberation.[3]

From the government's perspective this relatively benign environment provided significant opportunities to attempt a systematic programme of reform from a position of strength, as well as to put in place a wide-ranging array of counter-revolutionary measures. The hiatus in domestic anti-government activity after the bannings and detentions of 1977 allowed the political initiative to pass to the state. Its proposed reforms, albeit rejected by forces on the right as well as the left, were vastly more ambitious than the tinkering countenanced by Vorster.

P. W. Botha, who replaced the disgraced Vorster as prime minister in 1978, broke the mould of national politics. His accession to power was largely due to the vacuum created by the information scandal which tainted the reputation of the leading right-wing contender, Connie Mulder, and split the powerful Transvaal caucus. P. W. Botha was a veteran of Cape politics with a reputation as a belligerent machine politician. Although reform-minded he fitted neither into the *verlig* nor the *verkramp* factions that had caused the Transvaal caucus to implode. As Minister of Defence, he was hawkish, technocratic, and authoritarian; as the dominant nationalist figure in the Cape, he was attuned to the thinking of sophisticated corporate interests. Botha was focused far more on the imperative to maintain white power than the defence of political doctrine. His grim, no-nonsense pragmatism was duly expressed in his graphic warning to whites that they would have to 'adapt or die'.

In 1979 Botha became the first prime minister to visit Soweto. The awkward occasion was of more than symbolic significance. Government and business interests had alike come to the view that economic prosperity and political stability depended on actively encouraging the emergence of a black middle class as a buffer against insurrection. Soweto was now the centrepiece of a substantial effort by government, supported by business interests, to improve services and amenities such as education, housing, and electricity supply.

The Urban Foundation, founded at the height of the Soweto revolt and fronted by two titans of the business world, Harry Oppenheimer and Anton Rupert, poured money into development projects and lobbied government in an effort to ameliorate the most pernicious effects of apartheid on blacks resident in urban areas. This included the promotion of 99-year leasehold schemes which would allow effective ownership of houses in townships without requiring the government to abandon the apartheid *idée fixe* that blacks should not be permitted to own property outside of the Bantustans. Advertising agencies promoted middle-class 'western' lifestyles for upwardly mobile black consumers, thereby helping to spread the message that 'free enterprise' was beneficial for all.

Such advertising was underpinned by visible changes in the racial composition of the workforce. From 1977 to 1989, the proportion of whites in semi-professional occupations (e.g. nurses, teachers, school principals, technicians) declined from around 65 per cent of the workforce to around 50 per cent; African, coloured and Indian semi-professionals filled the gap, with Africans making the greatest gains. As the traditional colour bar was breached—or 'floated' upwards—over this period, so Africans registered significant gains in semi-skilled and white-collar occupations.[4] There was some rebalancing in income distribution. Africans' share of income rose from a low of less than 20 per cent in 1970 to 30 per cent in 1991, as against a decline in income share for whites from 71 per cent to 60 per cent over the same period in 1991.[5]

Botha's Social Reforms

The crisis of education in black schools prompted a major review led by Professor J. P. de Lange, an educationist attached to the Human Sciences Research Council, which enjoyed close connections with government. De Lange's 1981 Report sought at once to improve the country's skills base and to decontaminate the legacy of Verwoerdian ideology on education: it was the first major investigation of this nature since the highly influential Eiselen Report thirty years before. In attempting to reconcile an inclusive view of education founded on equal opportunities and a single department of education, with a Christian-National pedagogy based on the assumed cultural needs of different population groups, de Lange adopted an avowedly scientific, modernizing technical discourse. His ideological fudge satisfied no one, but there was substantial consensus around the view that a massive increase in resourcing was needed.

Investment in black education did increase significantly. In the five years from 1977 to 1982 real government spending on African education increased by 200 per cent and grew by a further 75 per cent to 1987, whereas real spending on whites remained constant over the decade to 1987.[6] The enrolment of Africans in secondary school trebled in the period 1975–85 to over a million, while university enrolment increased 5 times to around 36,000. There was substantial investment, often with private involvement, in technical education. Although the gap between spending on white and African school children narrowed significantly, it remained of the order of 10:1 in 1980 with staff/student ratios stuck around 1:50 in African primary schools. Ongoing political crisis makes it doubtful, however, that very much education was actually provided.[7]

In the aftermath of the Soweto uprising there was a concerted effort by government to stabilize and stratify the black urban population. In 1979, the Riekert Commission into the utilization of 'manpower' recommended drawing a clearer distinction between 'settled' urban 'insiders' (those with section 10 residence rights in cities) and 'outsiders' ('temporary' or 'illegal' African migrants). Its recognition of the permanence and mobility of black workers in notionally 'white' urban areas amounted to tacit recognition that black urbanization could not be reversed. In other respects Riekert's logic remained true to traditional apartheid thinking. It reinforced the role of the Bantustans as repositories for unwanted labour, reiterated that urban residence rights conveyed no political rights, and envisaged a significant tightening up of influx control measures in respect of 'outsiders'. The raw demographic facts show the scale of the problem. In 1970 there were around 4.5m Africans living in urban areas, over 7m in the homelands, and 3.7m on farms. Riekert proposed to keep Bantustan residents as 'outsiders' in perpetuity.

The year 1979 also saw the release of the Wiehahn Commission report into labour legislation, one of whose major findings was the need to abolish statutory job reservation on racial lines. In a sharp break from the past, Wiehahn advocated official recognition of black trade unions and the legalization of collective bargaining, hoping that this would allow industrial conflict to be managed more effectively. The burgeoning trade union movement now found itself divided on whether or not to register officially, balancing the advantages of statutory protection against the dangers of institutional co-optation.

FOSATU, a newly established non-racial trade union federation, saw advantages in registration (and, as will be seen in Chapter 8, greatly expanded its presence as well as its collective bargaining power from the early 1980s). CUSA, which was aligned to the Black Consciousness Movement, likewise opted in favour of registration. But other vocal 'independent' or 'community' unions refused to participate in official structures on the grounds that this would compromise their political effectiveness. The South African Allied Workers' Union (SAAWU) refused to register. It suffered brutal repression, in particular within the Ciskei where Thozamile Gqwetha and Sisa Njikelana were detained, beaten, and tortured.

Anti-apartheid organizations were often confused and divided in their reaction to the Botha reforms. It was relatively easy to dismiss as irrelevant the abandonment of so-called 'petty apartheid' measures. The repeal of highly offensive legislation, like the 'immorality' and 'mixed' marriages Acts (1985) or the deracialization of sport, was denounced by the political right. On the left, critics mostly dismissed such changes as 'cosmetic'. There were also major structural changes involving labour laws, residential rights, the restoration of citizenship (1986), and the scrapping of the pass laws (1986). These could not be dismissed out of hand. They were part of a clearly articulated plan to forestall revolution. While the motivations for reform were clearly apparent, their consequences— intended as well as unintended—were by no means predictable.[8]

For anti-apartheid activists, the key issue was whether 'the system' could be reformed and, if not, what its overthrow or transformation might entail. The state was similarly engaged in distinguishing the core components of white power from those elements which it chose to refer to as 'unnecessary' or 'hurtful' discrimination. P. W. Botha calculated that the best chance of securing white domination lay in modernizing the methods by which it was sustained. So long as the government remained in control of reforms its power base was relatively secure; the danger lay in loss of control over the pace and scope of change.

Total Strategy, Total Onslaught

Control, order, power. From its reformist outset to its intransigent end, these were the constant watchwords of the Botha administration. At the start of his tenure, Botha saw power in creative terms. Heavily influenced by the military thinkers who provided his political education and with whom he felt most comfortable, Botha adopted the idea that South Africa was faced by a Communist-led 'total onslaught'. In this new, more confrontationary phase of what some have called the 'second' Cold War, such ideas found fertile ground. Fear of Communism, verging on paranoia, was deliberately stoked by politicians, state television, as well as popular magazines. Schools mounted 'youth preparedness' programmes. Anti-Communism was rooted in the anxiety that Moscow, in a desperate desire to gain hold of South Africa's resources, was using all means to stir up unrest within South Africa and the region. Ronald Reagan's characterization of the Soviet Union as the 'evil empire' in 1983 was a gift to Pretoria. From the latter's vantage point, the United Nations and the anti-apartheid movement in Europe and the United States were undermining the one country in Africa capable of maintaining civilized standards. Internal resistance was said to be orchestrated by Communist agitators who wielded undue influence within the ANC and its 'front' organizations.

The Manichean logic of such analysis suggested that the 'total onslaught' required the adoption of a 'total strategy'. This meant a centralized, managerial state capable of mobilizing all resources in order to guarantee the country's survival. The concept of a 'total national strategy', first articulated in a 1977 white paper on defence, was elaborated by Botha two years later in his 'Twelve Point Plan'. This envisaged close coordination of the economy, state administration, security services, the media, and every other public sphere.

Total Strategy drew considerably on the writings of General André Beaufre, a veteran of French colonial wars in Indo-China and Algeria, who had defined the term as 'the manner in which all—political, economic, diplomatic, and military—should be woven together'.[9] Its premise was that a successful counter-revolutionary campaign should encompass all realms of society, politics, economics, and policy, so as to engage the enemy at every level, direct and indirect. Success, in Beaufre's analysis, was ultimately a dialectical battle of opposing psychological wills; in order to win this battle, the state had to ensure that it could maintain the initiative at all times. Beaufre's ideas about counter-revolution were widely featured in South African military academies. In its local, South African distillation, 'total strategy' amounted to an attitude of mind rather than a closely worked or coherent theory.[10]

This way of thinking clearly suited the military establishment which occupied a position at the centre of power unprecedented since the Second World War. The doctrine was attractive to the military since it allowed it to claim an ever greater share of national spending to prosecute the war in Angola and combat Communist-inspired 'terrorism'. It also suited the managerial-minded Botha who, frustrated by inward-looking ideological debates about the essence of apartheid, was attracted by the forward-looking pragmatism displayed by Cape Afrikaner business leaders.

A case in point was the reception given to A. D. Wassenaar's *Assault on Private Enterprise: The Freeway to Communism* (1977), written by a leader of the insurance giant SANLAM, an icon of Afrikaner corporate success. Wassenaar's tract roundly condemned bureaucratic state interference in the economy and caused a minor furore. It earned a sharp rebuke from Vorster but was greatly welcomed by English-speaking business leaders who applauded the author's call to incorporate 'top men from the private sector' in order to solve the country's problems.[11] Botha was highly receptive. He convened a meeting of leading white businessmen at Johannesburg's Carlton Hotel, in 1979, at which a new 'reciprocal' partnership between public and private sectors was mooted.[12] It was a clear statement on the part of government that economic growth, rooted in the free enterprise system, was as an essential component in the fight against Communism.

Botha's shift in emphasis from the interests of the Afrikaner *volk* to white survival rooted in an all-embracing defence of free enterprise sent out a clear message to the right wing of the National Party, now grouped around Andries Treurnicht: there was no future for exclusivist backward-looking Afrikaner nationalism or for old-style apartheid. Nor, indeed, could the contending National Party caucuses, presided over by regional political barons, continue to dominate politics. Botha favoured a technocratic form of government with a reduced role for the cabinet and vastly increased powers for himself: this was already gestating in sweeping new constitutional proposals which were supposed to circumvent the inefficiencies of the traditional 'Westminster' system, a hangover from the days of British imperialism.

For Botha, the military reverses in Angola and the corruption of Vorster's government indicated systemic institutional failure. To combat these failings, he proposed far-reaching bureaucratic rationalization which ushered in the imperial presidency that entrenched him in power. The prime minister revived a partly defunct cabinet committee, the State Security Council, and began to build a new shadow instrument of government around it. This became the National Security Management System. From 1979 it began to oversee all aspects of government, from local municipality level to the highest echelons of state: in military terms it meant a shortened chain of command.[13]

Botha presided over the State Security Council, whose statutory membership included the head of the army as well as officials and ministers responsible for policing, intelligence, and civil order. Towards the upper end of this organizational chart sat Regional Joint Management Centres (which happened to be geographically contiguous with the Area Commands of the military). The cabinet, though in theory able to block decisions by the State Security Council, was thereby reduced to secondary status. Some commentators spoke of this centralization of power as a 'silent' military coup.[14] This view was exaggerated but it was undeniable that the 'securocrats'—a term which came into vogue from 1987—were increasingly influential.[15]

In the government's view, the logic of survival required a new form of national unity. By defining the enemy as godless Communism it was hoped that the state would be able to reach out to constituencies that had previously been excluded. Recourse to experts and a willingness to face hard facts were central to the technocratic discourse that was intended to replace old-style apartheid ideology. The 'free market' was proffered as the most rational means to allocate resources. Prosperity, more widely shared, would be the best defence against Communism. That these claims for market-led growth coincided with an increasingly centralized managerial state was only one of many confusions and anomalies—not least of which was the fact that a new system of values was being imposed upon the ruins of an old one, and all in the name of dispensing with 'ideology'.

Neo-apartheid

By the end of the 1970s, apartheid ideology was transmuting into what Deborah Posel has called a 'new language of legitimation'.[16] This de-politicized discourse was seemingly capable of incorporating a range of interests and ethnicities in a united front against an insidious enemy. In promoting national survival over Afrikaner ascendancy, hitherto core elements of the *volk* were pushed to the margins: the white working class, large parts of the rural *platteland*, as well as Verwoerdian true-believers. This shift in the demographic patterns of power eventuated in a right-wing split in 1982 when the mild-mannered and articulate but altogether intractable ideologist, Andries Treurnicht, led a break-away from the National Party to form the Conservative Party.

The loss of the right posed more than an electoral threat. It was also an existential danger that 'permeated the whole Afrikaner establishment'.[17] For Botha, the split had the compensating advantage of allowing the government to position itself at the centre of the white political spectrum. The problem was that Botha, and indeed most of his party, remained unable or unwilling to think himself out of the apartheid mindset. A bewildering vocabulary, in which trusty old formulations were mangled together with neologisms, was rapidly cobbled together in pursuit of a neo-apartheid political solution. This begged the question as to whether the government intended to reform apartheid or merely reformulate it.

The ontological centrality of population 'groups' (apparently shorn of their racial connotations) remained fundamental to neo-apartheid. 'Minorities' were presented as the essential building blocks of a 'multi-cultural' or 'plural society' that would be subject to as yet unspecified forms of 'power-sharing'. The Christian-National conception of *eie* (which connoted deep emotional attachment to the soul of the *volk*) was Anglicized into 'own affairs', denoting constitutionally protected spheres (like education and culture) which would continue to be subject to the jurisdiction of defined 'groups'.[18]

Neo-apartheid's theorists were ever keen to lend respectability to their ideas by referring to international political science. The concept of consociationalism, adumbrated by the Dutch-born American political scientist Arend Lijphart, was widely studied amongst conservative reformers. Lijphart repaid the compliment by writing a book, *Power-Sharing in South Africa* (1985), which laid out suggestions as to how a consensual form of democracy could be constructed with constitutional and institutional provisions for minority ethnic groups. It was criticized both for its acceptance of ethnic differences as a matter of 'unalterable fact' and also on account of its spuriously scientific approach.[19]

Efforts to change the discourse of apartheid frequently bore only a tangential correspondence with reality. Piet Koornhof, the reform-minded Minister of Cooperation and Development, bombastically announced to the Washington Press Association in 1979: 'apartheid as you know it ... is dying'. He went on to pledge: 'We will not rest until racial discrimination has disappeared from our statute books and every-day life in South Africa.'[20] For a brief period the powerful ministry responsible for the administration of blacks over which Koornhof pre-sided came to be known as the 'Department of Plural Relations and Development'. It was left to the *Sunday Times* to clarify the absurdity: 'It's official. A Bantu is not a Plural—even though he may have some plural relations.'[21] Christopher Hope, a wry observer of the debasement of language under authoritarian regimes, notes that South Africa is 'a land where euphemism has long been, like war, an extension of policy by other means'.[22]

Koornhof's tantalizing promises were received sceptically and caused uproar amongst die-hard right-wingers. In 1982 a package of legislation was introduced after an extended process of drafting and redrafting. Far from helping in the process of 'normalising race relations',[23] as they were supposedly intended to do, the proposed measures imposed unrepresen-tative 'community councils' on blacks in urban areas and outlined draconian measures designed to tighten up influx control, thereby enforcing the distinction between black 'insiders' and 'outsiders'. The proposals added more complexity to an already bewildering administra-tive regime, drew attention to the continued role of the Bantustans as repositories for unwanted labour, and confirmed that these territories were the only places in which Africans could exercise political rights. Anti-apartheid activists termed these measures the 'Koornhof Bills', and the name stuck. The Black Sash organization warned that, if passed in its existing form, 'it will be the most efficient form of influx control this country has ever experienced'.[24]

P. W. Botha's long-awaited constitutional proposals entailed replacing the 'Westminster' system of government with a 'tricameral' parliament featuring separate chambers for whites, coloureds, and Indians. A President's Council drawn from the three chambers would advise the executive State President. The constitutional proposals were eventually passed by a large majority in a whites-only referendum in 1983. This marked a short-term personal victory for Botha, but the cost was that opposition on both ends of the political spectrum was mobilized.

It was the vexed matter of 'power-sharing' that finally provoked Treurnicht's long-expected right-wing split away from the National Party. Of even greater significance was the effect of the new constitution on the vast majority of the population. In attempting to entice coloureds and Indians into the political process (with only very limited success),[25] the meretricious constitutional arrangements highlighted the exclusion of Africans from South African citizenship. Limited political incorporation for some was no substitute for the loss of full political rights for South Africa's majority; concessions merely drew attention to what was being withheld. The ever more complex array of legal exemptions and exceptions associated with the implementation of the Black Local Authorities and Orderly Movement and Settlement of Black Persons Bill revealed the capriciousness of rulers and bureaucrats in their pursuit of ever more complex and unworkable policies of divide and rule.

Botha's constitutional changes and reforms precipitated a full-scale crisis of governmental legitimacy. Machiavelli was familiar to thinkers with an ear to the president but the more obvious parallel was De Tocqueville's reflections on Louis XVI and the French Revolution: 'experience teaches that the most critical moment for bad governments is the one which witnesses their first steps towards reform ... Never had the feudal system seemed so hateful to the French as at the moment of its proximate destruction.'[26] In the case of South Africa's popular masses, the common rallying call was wholesale abolition of apartheid, not merely its reform.

The National Forum and the United Democratic Front

For the first time in its modern history, the focus of South African politics began to move permanently, rather than episodically, beyond the confines of the white legislature. This was signalled by the emergence of two broad political groupings in opposition to the Koornhof Bills and the new constitution: the Black Consciousness-aligned National Forum (June 1983)[27] and the United Democratic Front (August 1983) which was oriented towards the Charterist tradition originating in the ANC-led alliance politics of the 1950s. The *Rand Daily Mail* observed that 'Phoenix-like, anti-apartheid black organizations are rising up again'.[28] It was not at all clear which organization was likely to attract most support, much less how the government would react.

At its inception the National Forum embraced some 200 affiliate groups. The single most important was the Azanian People's Organization (AZAPO), which had been formed in 1978 to further the principles of Black Consciousness.[29] In the intervening years there was a move to the left in these circles. One sign was the characterization of South Africa as a system of 'racial capitalism', a formulation that sounded superficially similar to the Charterist view that racism emerged out of relations of class exploitation. The subtle, but crucial, difference lay in the Forum's continued emphasis on race, as against the Marxist view that race consciousness was a function of class relations. One delegate to the National Forum's founding conference asked the pertinent question: was this a national struggle against racial oppression or a workers' struggle against class oppression?

In his keynote address to the National Forum, Bishop Desmond Tutu questioned whether there ought to be a difference between adherents of Black Consciousness and of Charterism: the 'struggle itself is for liberation' of all people, black and white.[30] Tutu's inclusive view was not, however, compatible with the strains of black exclusivism that overrode talk of socialism. How to square the circle?

A key influence on the National Forum was the ex-Robben Islander and left-wing Unity Movement intellectual Neville Alexander, who promoted 'antiracism' in place of the 'non-racial' or 'multi-racial' tradition of the Charterists. In theory 'antiracism' was a purer form of non-racism in that it did not even recognize the existence of race; in practice, organizations subscribing to the non-racial principles of the Freedom Charter were notable by their absence. Towards the end of the 1980s it became increasingly clear that the National Forum was held together more by antagonism to the Charterists than by any clear vision of the future. For Charterists, adept at holding together different left-wing constituencies, political strategy tended to prevail over ideology.[31]

The United Democratic Front was constituted along similar lines to the National Forum with youth, civic organizations, and trade unions prominent in its composition. The impetus for its formation was based in widespread opposition to the state's neo-apartheid reform agenda, but the UDF's conception of the national struggle was broader and more inclusive than in the case of the National Forum. Above all, the UDF took the Freedom Charter of the 1950s as its inspiration. The UDF's stress on all-embracing national unity was prefigured by the prominence of non-African organizations and ethnicities in its formation. Indeed, an important catalyst in its formation was the revival of the Transvaal Indian Congress. The decision to launch the UDF in Cape Town signalled a willingness to embrace 'progressives' of every hue and ideological colouring. Mosiuoa 'Terror' Lekota, who served as publicity secretary of the UDF from 1983, explained, 'You cannot just declare non-racialism; you must build it.'[32] These words were born of hard experience. Lekota had been imprisoned on Robben Island in 1974 for his role in SASO and was one of the first high-profile Black Consciousness leaders on the island to embrace non-racism and announce his allegiance to the ANC, thereby prompting several of his compatriots to follow the same political path.[33]

The launch of the UDF in Cape Town was a huge event with hundreds of organizations represented and some 10,000 people in attendance. A number of 'patrons' and three venerable honorary presidents—Albertina Sisulu, Oscar Mpetha, and Archie Gumede—served as a visible reminder of ANC traditions and African primacy. Their selection was also conditioned by the need to represent different regions of the country. The UDF executive was racially mixed and selected with care: coloured, Indian, and (one) white representatives constituted just over half the total complement. Most of the older members of the national executive had been associated with the Congress Alliance of the 1950s and early 1960s; several younger members had moved to support the ANC through Black Consciousness activism in the 1970s.

The liberation movement had not enjoyed such public exposure since the Treason Trial and the many tributes to the Freedom Charter, coupled with the carnival-like atmosphere of the public launch, were reminiscent of the open campaigning of the Congress of the People era. Reverend Allan Boesak, who delivered the keynote address, deliberately evoked Martin Luther King's oratory by placing democratic 'rights' and inclusive non-racism at the centre of his call for an overwhelming challenge to the legitimacy of the tricameral constitution: 'We want all of our rights, and we want them here, and we want them now!'[34]

Born into a coloured community in the rural northern Cape and ordained into the Dutch Reformed *Sendingkerk* (mission wing), Boesak had been largely responsible for persuading the World Alliance of Reformed Churches to declare apartheid sinful and heretical. It was Boesak who had helped to bring the UDF into existence with his unscripted call for a united front against apartheid in a speech delivered in January 1983. This idea resonated with discussions that were already taking place within the ANC and other groups sympathetic to the Charterist tradition. Boesak was selected as the ideal person to take the initiative forward. He was an inspiring man of the cloth possessing strong leadership qualities, but he did not have any strong political following which might prove a threat to existing political groupings.

Boesak was not directly part of the ANC tradition. The most significant influence on his political outlook was radical Black Consciousness theology. In his own words, this

de-emphasised the negative connotations racial classification brought and instead emphasised the solidarity of the oppressed. It absolutely stood upon the equality of humankind. [It] ... relieved us from the perpetual burden apartheid's race-based thinking had foisted on us: the worry that being of mixed descent somehow made us 'less'.[35]

Boesak's charismatic personality and hybrid identity highlighted the potential for a new form of politics capable of transcending divisions between Black Consciousness and Charterism and, to an extent, regional differences. His politics of refusal (a reflex of left-wing Unity Movement thinking) was lightened by a spirit of inclusivity that rejected apartheid racial categories: all who identified with the struggle and refused to collaborate in oppressive structures could find a home in the UDF.[36]

In 1983 it was impossible to guess that the formation of the UDF would transform South African politics, yet it was immediately apparent that its formation was a highly significant political development. But what exactly *was* the UDF? It was a composite body representing a diverse range of groupings, from sports clubs to civic associations, religious organizations, and trade unions, many of which did not see themselves as mere extensions of the ANC. Workers, professionals, students, and business people were all part of its multi-class formation. As a regionally based federal body it was also geographically devolved. Even within regions it was highly localized. Although inaugurated as a national campaigning organization, from the end of 1984 UDF structures became increasingly township-based. While no township had precisely the same political configuration, most could identify with resistance to rent, transport, and service charges, as well as to illegitimate community councils and their 'puppet' leaders. The UDF proved highly successful in rooting itself in street-level or area-wide civic structures.

The UDF was organizationally flexible and had a remarkable capacity to evolve rapidly according to circumstance. As a coalition of anti-apartheid groups, it championed a democratic non-racial society in a unitary nation state. Ideologically, it encompassed the full ideological spectrum from social democracy to hardline Communism. The UDF was thus never just a 'front' for the ANC and the Communist Party, as hostile critics alleged, though it was undoubtedly a legatee of the Charterist tradition and it received approbation from the ANC. The ANC in exile did not initiate the UDF, nor did it have control over its day-to-day decisions—even if it wished to. The ambiguity concerning the ANC's relationship to the UDF was strategically important for both sides. Many UDF leaders looked towards the ANC for guidance and inspiration. The ANC was happy to act as a senior adviser, monitoring and advising different factions of the UDF without necessarily taking sides. In a climate of severe repression, internal arguments could be settled by knowing reference to secret ANC instructions. Yet these still had to be reconciled with the political culture of above-ground organizations in the country.

Membership of the UDF worked through affiliation and association. It was not obligatory to be 'paid up', as was the case in many trade unions. A culture of participatory democracy and consensus prevailed over a formal constitution. Under conditions of serious repression, this loose-weave texture provided tactical advantages. It also allowed factions to 'caucus' secretly in advance before 'seeking a mandate' so as to prove democratic 'accountability'. There were suspicions that the UDF was dominated by a 'cabal' associated with the Transvaal and Natal Indian Congresses. This was said to work against the principle of African leadership. There was also a left-wing socialist tendency associated with whites in NUSAS and the 'workerist' trade unions (who were themselves internally divided).[37]

Throughout the turbulent 1980s, the UDF bore the brunt of attacks by the state in the form of detentions, harassment, bannings, and, on occasion, targeted killings by shadowy elements in the security forces. Yet the umbrella body could not be suppressed, and the number of organizations that either affiliated to, or identified with, the multi-headed hydra continued to grow.[38] Trevor Manuel, who became acting general secretary in 1984, after Popo Molefe's detention, referred to the UDF as 'the organised voice of our people'. He rejected as 'spurious' the charge that it was fomenting violence in the townships and dismissed accusations that it was a front for the ANC, maintaining instead that the UDF was defined by its commitment to 'the achievement of a non-racial democracy by peaceful means'.[39]

The 1984 Vaal Uprising and State of Emergency

Initially, the UDF's sole rationale was to reject, categorically, the government's constitutional reforms. It was unclear how it would, or could, develop a common agenda beyond support for the Freedom Charter. The question as to how to advance to the next phase of political development was answered by events. On 3 September 1984, black townships in the heavily industrialized Vaal Triangle south of Johannesburg exploded into violence. The proximate causes of protests were increases in rents and service charges which squeezed already deteriorating living standards. The financial demands were imposed by unpopular bodies and at a time of rising unemployment.

Although the revolt was touched off by grievances specific to particular townships, the overarching contributory factor was government reform policies in the shape of the Koornhof Bills and the new constitution (whether by coincidence or not the Vaal uprising began on the same day that the new constitution was formally adopted). Government allegations that the UDF orchestrated the uprising are difficult to sustain, but there can be no doubt that the UDF played a major role in sustaining the revolt and that the uprising in turn gave the UDF new importance. By the end of 1985 the founding slogan 'UDF unites apartheid divides' was beginning to be replaced with a more specific objective: 'people's power'.

The urban revolt of 1984–6 was the most sustained and widespread period of resistance against white rule in South African history. In the view of Robert Price, this was more like an insurrection than a rebellion. The insurrection not only sought to destroy the form of state domination but also gave birth to new, transformational structures of popular authority.[40] To a much greater extent than 1976–7, the insurrection was geographically dispersed. It was also far more inclusive, involving action by unionized workers and community organizations as well as students and the unemployed. This unprecedented show of unity was apparent in November 1984 when as many as 800,000 workers in the Transvaal, together with around 400,000 students, took part in a two-day stayaway in support of UDF demands.[41] The following year townships around Port Elizabeth and East London in the Eastern Cape engaged in stayaways and school boycotts which also exploded into violence. The turmoil reached a peak in Langa township outside Uitenhage where twenty people were killed when police opened fire on a procession of mourners on their way to bury activists killed the previous weekend; that the Langa massacre took place on the 25th anniversary of the Sharpeville killings added poignancy to the tragedy.

The government's reaction was to declare a 'state of emergency' in thirty-six magisterial districts around Johannesburg and Port Elizabeth on 20 July 1985 (which was subsequently extended to the Cape Town area); this was the first time that the state had resorted to such extreme measures since 1960. Two days later Oliver Tambo responded on behalf of the ANC with a radio broadcast to 'the Nation' in which he called for a popular uprising: 'We have to make apartheid unworkable and our country ungovernable.' Tambo's intervention, delivered in measured tones, carried considerable weight, but it is more accurately understood as an endorsement of what was already taking place on the ground than as an instruction.[42]

In the ten months that elapsed between the outbreak of violence and the imposition of a state of emergency, some 500 people, mostly residents of townships, were killed in political violence. In the first 100 days of the emergency more than 5,000 people were detained and over 300 people were killed (according to official figures).[43] The UDF leadership was decimated through a mixture of 'preventive' detentions and treason charges. Yet it continued to operate. Stayaways and school boycotts brought communities and workers together in combined action. Attacks against 'collaborators'—black police, township councillors, and alleged informers—led to reprisals and these in turn escalated levels of violence.

The state's response was to mobilize all possible forces in line with 'total strategy'. In June 1985 eastern Cape UDF leaders Matthew Goniwe, Fort Calata, and two others were abducted and killed in a targeted assassination. Subsequent evidence revealed that the local Joint Management Centre and the State Security Council were responsible for ordering that they be 'permanently removed from society'.[44] The funeral of the Cradock Four, as they came to be known, attracted an angry crowd of well over 50,000, many of whom had travelled long distances to be there. The colours of the ANC and the Communist Party were raised in defiance, accompanied by songs praising Umkhonto we Sizwe. All this in a small, rural town with an estimated population of around 10,000–15,000 where the main economic activity was sheep-farming.

Goniwe's killing, justified within senior reaches of government as a necessary response to the 'total onslaught', pointed to growing militarization within the state. This was signalled by the decision to deploy the army to repress township revolt (hitherto the police had performed this function). In October 1984 a contingent of 7,000 troops were deployed to occupy Sebokeng, Sharpeville, and Boipatong townships in the Vaal

Triangle. Rather than subduing the simmering revolt, their presence intensified the conflict. Sebokeng was a 'model' township where the Urban Foundation had spent large amounts of money on 'upgrading' projects. Neither this largesse nor the spectacle of troops handing out badges with tag lines like 'I am your friend, trust me' did anything to lessen resentment.[45]

The spectre of troops in the townships meant that white conscripts, many of whom were confused and traumatized, were duty-bound to fire birdshot, rubber bullets, and tear gas on black youth the same age as them. International and local media saw in this escalation of state violence elements of a civil war. The End Conscription Campaign, based on liberal university campuses, responded with a 'Troops out of the Townships' rally in 1985 that attracted more than 4,000 students. This was an important signal of disaffection towards the military emanating from within white society. In the five years of its existence, which ended with its banning in 1988, the End Conscription Campaign grew from a fringe anti-war grouping to become an organization with a national presence. It mobilized large numbers of white activists and contributed significantly to the growing culture of non-racism within the anti-apartheid movement.[46]

Militarization of the Conflict

The South African military was not only involved in suppressing internal 'subversion'. It was also engaged in the active destabilization of neighbouring countries, thus blurring further the lines between the enemy within and without. A key aspect of the Botha reforms of the late 1970s was a regional strategy capable of bringing together compliant neighbouring countries and the independent Bantustans in a 'Constellation of States'. This hope was facilitated by a renewed 'tilt' to South Africa on the part of the Reagan administration, whose Africa expert, Chester Crocker, favoured 'constructive engagement' with Pretoria in order to achieve Namibian independence and resolve ongoing conflict in Angola.

Crocker's policy presumed that the South African government would act responsibly as a source of regional stability. In fact, it was increasingly behaving in an erratic fashion with the military fully engaged within and beyond its borders. Umkhonto we Sizwe, newly invigorated after the Soweto uprising, posed a fresh challenge. After an extended period of dormancy MK began to 'come back inside' South Africa. It succeeded in dispatching small numbers of cadres over the border to attack carefully selected targets, typically government buildings and police installations. These exploratory hit-and-run incidents numbered around eighty in the period 1977–80.[47] Infrastructural damage was limited and the survival rate of cadres was poor. In several instances guerrillas were killed, either when bombs went off prematurely or, in the case of the 1977 Goch Street shoot-out in central Johannesburg, when police intercepted the infiltrators. One of these, Solomon Mahlangu, who had left South Africa in 1976, was tried, hanged, and instantly immortalized as a martyr. The message left by Mahlangu—'My blood will nourish the tree that will bear the fruits of freedom'—resounded through the townships. An ANC school in Tanzania was named in his honour.[48]

MK enjoyed spectacular success in 1980 when it succeeded in blowing up SASOL's oil-from-coal refineries. These important symbols of apartheid-era self-sufficiency spewed fireballs and smoke that could be seen as far away as Soweto. The following year MK's Special Operations Unit mounted a rocket attack on the Voortrekkerhoogte military base in Pretoria, the army's headquarters. Another symbolic triumph was registered in 1982 when the Koeberg nuclear plant outside Cape Town was sabotaged by a unit that managed to infiltrate limpet mines into the as yet uncommissioned reactor core.[49] MK's code of conduct generally avoided attacks on civilians but there were notable exceptions, including the 1983 Church Street car bombing that exploded outside the Air Force headquarters in central Pretoria killing 19 (including two of the bombers) and wounding over 200. The ANC took responsibility but subsequently claimed that the device had not exploded as planned. Controversy also surrounded MK's use of landmines in 1985–7 along the borders of the northern and eastern Transvaal.

Although such attacks posed no serious threat to the state, they were incendiary as armed propaganda. At gatherings in the townships, often under the guise of political funerals which were attended by many thousands, the colours of the ANC and the symbols of military struggle—AK-47 guns and RPG 'bazookas'—were celebrated in songs and dance. The dramatic pageantry of raucous revolt suited the government insofar as it proved to its own satisfaction that 'terrorism' and 'intimidation' were ubiquitous. Yet the government also had to prove that its control over security and 'law and order' was absolute.

The state's military response was swift. In January 1981 the South African Defence Force mounted a commando raid on Matola, near Maputo, killing more than a dozen ANC members.[50] Eyewitness accounts spoke of blacked-up soldiers or mercenaries cutting off the ears of the dead. The following year there was a raid on Maseru, capital of Lesotho, which killed forty persons (only half of whom were associated with the ANC). There were also targeted assassinations. These included the ANC's much admired representative in newly independent Zimbabwe, Joe Gqabi, and the ANC-aligned socialist intellectual Ruth First, blown up by a parcel bomb in Maputo. The brutal message was that no one with ANC or MK/Communist Party sympathies was safe.[51]

The South African state's equivalent to the ANC's armed propaganda was armed diplomacy. Keen to reassert its regional dominance and to reimpose the *cordon sanitaire* which the Portuguese revolution had severed, Pretoria lent support to two armed counter-revolutionary movements in Angola and Mozambique. The military's campaign of destabilization in Mozambique continued throughout the 1980s. It involved direct and indirect support for Renamo, an armed resistance movement, which wreaked devastation in the Mozambican countryside and grew to control as much as a quarter of that country by the end of the decade. In Angola, South Africa gave direct and indirect support to Jonas Savimbi's UNITA movement which fought a relentless campaign against the Marxist government in Luanda. South African destabilization, largely tolerated by the Reagan administration on the grounds that it was part of the war against Communism,[52] was coupled with offers of infrastructural help and aid. This was part of a deliberate strategy to assert South Africa's position as the regional hegemon. Economic pressure was another favoured tactic in the package of what one analyst termed 'cooptive domination'.[53]

If Botha's constellation of states could not be brought about willingly, it would have to be imposed. In March 1984 South Africa signed the Nkomati Accord with Mozambique. This non-aggression pact, which stunned parties on the left as well as the right, was supposedly struck between equal sovereign partners. Signed in public with full diplomatic protocol, it represented a humiliating defeat for Mozambique's president Samora Machel. It was also a major setback for the ANC whose leadership was plainly shocked.[54] A separate agreement, signed in Lusaka in February 1984, committed South Africa to withdraw its troops from Angola on condition that the Luanda government would not allow Cuban or SWAPO liberation fighters to enter the vacated areas.

The Lusaka and Nkomati agreements served as the prelude to Botha's triumphant eight-nation European mission in June. South African newspapers crowed about the country's new-found international acceptability while business leaders spoke enthusiastically about investment possibilities in Mozambique. From Pretoria's perspective, the crowning achievement of Nkomati was the fact that the ANC was now compelled to remove its military bases from Mozambican territory. This was the culminating success of the 'Botha Doctrine' in the region and of total strategy more widely.[55]

The perils and prospects of reform in South Africa caught the attention of the conservative Harvard political theorist Samuel Huntington, who visited the country and proclaimed the Machiavellian virtues of 'reform by stealth'. In 1982 Huntington argued that the most successful political reformers were able to combine a 'Fabian' strategy involving incremental moves towards a carefully concealed, but well-defined goal, with the use of *blitzkreig* tactics designed to confuse adversaries. He warned that Botha might have got the sequence wrong by advancing on too broad a front and also too slowly (a *blitzkreig* strategy with 'Fabian' tactics), thereby inflating the expectations of blacks as well the fears of whites. Timing was everything. It was crucial that governments introduce reforms 'from a position of strength'.[56]

In August 1984, Botha boasted that South Africa was at a 'watershed': positive regional developments, new-found diplomatic respectability, and domestic reforms, were all grounds for optimism. A month later the townships exploded, demonstrating that he had got his calculations desperately wrong. South Africa was revealed to have violated the terms of the Lusaka Accord when the Angolan government announced in May

1985 that it had killed two South African commandos involved in a raid in the oil-rich region of Cabinda, and captured another, Wynand du Toit, who was forced to give a media interview. In June, South African Defence Force commandos launched a pre-dawn attack on ANC targets in Gaborone, the capital of Botswana, killing eighteen, including civilians and a child. The incursion was condemned by Botswanan president Masire as 'bloodcurdling'. It also caused a serious diplomatic rift with the United States, whose policy of 'constructive engagement' appeared less credible than ever. Most worrying from the government's perspective was the deterioration in the country's internal stability. The massacre of mourners at Langa, Uitenhage in March 1985 led many observers to conclude that violence in black townships was endemic: whilst the army and police could seal these areas off, they could not be effectively controlled.

Ethnicized Conflict

The imposition of the state of emergency in July 1985 was intended to give the government the opportunity to crush popular resistance. Instead, a new front opened up in August when dozens of people were killed in and around Durban in clashes between Zulu-speaking sup- porters of the Inkatha movement and Indian and African supporters of the UDF. The violence was touched off by the assassination of Victora Mxenge, a revered UDF leader widely known as 'mother of the nation'. Four years previously, her husband, civil rights lawyer Griffiths Mxenge, had also been murdered. There were well-founded suspicions that the police were involved in both deaths.[57]

Tensions had been simmering for some time in Natal between the UDF and Inkatha, the Zulu 'cultural' movement led by mercurial Chief Gatsha Buthelezi, leader of the KwaZulu homeland. Buthelezi toyed with supporting the UDF at the moment of its formation but he was rebuffed and humiliated by accusations that he was a divisive tribal leader who did more to perpetuate than to fight apartheid. In Natal, Buthelezi jealously guarded his power, viewing the UDF as a major threat. Obser- vers commonly ascribed tensions between these organizations to 'ethnic' differences, but this overlooked the fact that most UDF members in Natal were Zulu-speakers themselves.

Buthelezi embodied many of the contradictions of the late-apartheid state.[58] He professed peace and political pluralism yet adopted autocratic measures and sanctioned violence to preserve his political influence. He operated within the homeland system but refused to take independence for KwaZulu, always insisting that he was opposed to apartheid and would resist it from within. He was the political supremo of the Zulus who also nurtured ambitions to be a national leader. When Buthelezi formed Inkatha in 1975 as a cultural nationalist organization, he considered it to be a genuine legatee of the ANC tradition, used the colours and songs of the ANC, and spoke with pride of his personal connections with Mandela, Tambo, and Sobukwe.

At the height of Inkatha's popularity in the late 1970s, its appeal was regarded with a mixture of envy and suspicion by the ANC. Oliver Tambo actually encouraged the movement's formation and maintained occasional contact with Buthelezi, including in 1979 when the ANC met with a substantial Inkatha delegation for a 'consultative meeting' in London.[59] But the meeting did more to engender mistrust than understanding and, amidst mutual recrimination, relations between the two organizations continued to deteriorate through the 1980s.[60]

Buthelezi's predominantly traditionalist, rural-based, Zulu-speaking constituency was easily mobilized against 'progressive' non-Zulu African supporters of the UDF as well as Indians who occupied positions of prominence on the regional Natal executive. Rising tensions were evident in the township of Lamontville, south of Durban, where a UDF-affiliated civic organization, JORAC, began to campaign against rent increases. From 1983 an Inkatha vigilante group, known as the 'A-Team' (probably named after an action-adventure American television series), mounted attacks on JORAC supporters in Lamontville and Chesterville townships, resulting in the deaths of up to ten people, including JORAC founder Msizi Dube. Suspicion that the South African police were colluding in these attacks was later confirmed by the Truth and Reconciliation Commission.[61]

In August 1985 Mahatma Gandhi's eighty-year-old Phoenix settlement, including the house in which he developed his theory of passive resistance, was burnt down by spear-wielding Inkatha warriors. They made it clear that Indians had no place in Zululand. Shops owned by

Indian traders were destroyed and 500 Indian families in the neighbour-hood were forced to flee.[62] As well as being a powerful symbol of non-racism and peaceful coexistence, the Phoenix Settlement had been the venue of the first executive meeting of the UDF. The attack reminded many of clashes between Africans and Indians in 1949, and it raised the spectre of further communal violence. Above all, it was a political attack on the UDF and Charterists. Their support in urban areas of Natal was growing swiftly, underpinned by trade unions and COSAS (the Con-gress of South African Students). The latter was an ANC-aligned national students' organization and leading UDF affiliate which had emerged out of the remnants of the 1976–7 era to become the dominant students' organization in the country.[63]

Between 1985 and 1990 at least 3,500 people died in the escalating Natal conflict. As many as 50,000 people were displaced.[64] Political rivalry between Inkatha and the UDF/Cosatu played a major role. Endemic poverty, joblessness, and contestation for scarce resources facilitated the recruitment of foot-soldiers. Many journalists explained political conflict by reference to tribal atavism. Racial and ethnic stereo-types abounded. Government spokesmen alleged that political radicals were conspiring to sow division and render Natal ungovernable. There was plenty of circumstantial evidence suggesting that elements in the security forces were deliberately manipulating tensions in Natal so as to undermine the UDF. Notorious Inkatha warlord David Ntombela enjoyed effective immunity from prosecution for his involvement in the murder of members of the UDF. Suspicions that he was recruited as an informer by the Pietermaritzburg security police in the mid-1980s were eventually confirmed.[65]

Similar accusations of government complicity were levelled in Cape Town where clashes between squatters at the Crossroads 'emergency' camp resulted in deaths and hundreds of casualties. This was the start of a protracted series of battles in which Johnson Ngxobongwana, a local shacklord and strongman—who until 1985 posed as a progressive civic leader defying apartheid—marginalized the Crossroads Women's Com-mittee in 1979 and went on to mobilize vigilantes in defence of 'his' territory and against UDF-affiliated militants and squatters.

In 1986 around 70,000 people were driven from their dwellings in Crossroads and neighbouring areas by Ngxobongwana's thugs, supported by 'fathers' and 'witdoeke' (named after the white headbands they wore). They pursued a relentless war against young UDF 'comrades'.[66] At this point the police licensed their own vigilantes, the so-called 'kitskonstabels' (instant police) in the Cape Peninsula and elsewhere round the country. These ill-prepared and poorly equipped subalterns were given a few weeks' rudimentary training and then deployed to keep order in the townships where they encountered the full force of insurrectionary anger.[67]

The root causes of the vigilante-led violence in Durban, Cape Town, and many other areas was pent-up demand for housing and services, shortages of which had been greatly exacerbated by decades of apartheid-era influx control and ideologically motivated urban planning. According to one estimate, countrywide pass arrests for contravention of the influx control laws increased from 170,000 in 1981 to 250,000 in 1984. This placed more and more pressure on those living in illegal informal settlements and encouraged those with a foothold in the city to act against newcomers.[68] Elements in the security forces actively manipulated township-dwellers, inducing them to act as proxies in an attempt to drive out the UDF, destabilize communities, and sow confusion.

Vigilantism was in part a response by older, conservative groups (often comprising small-scale entrepreneurs, taxi-drivers, shopkeepers) who resented being dictated to by disrespectful and unruly young radicals.[69] A reassertion of masculine values was frequently added to the conservative, 'traditionalist', mix. This was starkly evident when hostel-dwelling migrant workers affiliated to Inkatha were enjoined to use their 'cultural weapons' (fighting sticks and stabbing spears) in attacks on UDF 'comrades'.[70]

The growing spectre of 'black on black' violence—a term that came increasingly into vogue during the mid-1980s to describe internecine conflict—played to stereotypes of tribal bloodlust and allowed the government to pose as the final guarantor of 'law and order'. This was a highly dangerous strategy since it amounted to a tacit admission that the government was not fully in control and that it merely held the balance in a state of growing terror. Destabilization, whether practised abroad or at home, also had the effect of corroding whatever moral legitimacy apartheid retained in the minds of its traditional supporters.

Faced with the choice of dismantling apartheid through further reforms (as Foreign Minister 'Pik' Botha was promising) or crushing revolutionary opposition (as many senior securocrats insisted), P. W. Botha decided on the latter course of action. The dilemma was captured in an extraordinary meeting of the State Security Council in July 1985. This noted the necessity for the government to retain the political initiative and to improve the quality of the life of the populace, but also included a chilling rider: 'A Government's goal should not only be to exterminate insurrectionists but also to eradicate their influence over the people.'[71]

The Rubicon, 1985

In August 1985, President Botha addressed party supporters in Durban in a widely trailed speech advertised as a 'Manifesto for a New South Africa'. Foreign governments had been alerted to the momentous significance of the impending announcements. The speech was watched live by millions overseas. Rather than beginning with what was reliably expected to have been the core message—'we are today crossing the Rubicon. *There can be no turning back*'—Botha started with an impetuous attack on those who had 'put words in my mouth in advance'. He insisted that South Africa was a 'a country of minorities' and rejected outright the principle of one-man-one-vote in a unitary system on the ground that this would only 'lead to chaos'. In a gruesome peroration, Botha declared that he would not lead 'White South Africans and other minority groups on a road to abdication and suicide'.

Botha's finger-wagging belligerence as he twice growled 'don't push us too far' had a profoundly disturbing effect on those who were hoping he might deliver substantial reforms. He also slapped down those who were pressing him to release Nelson Mandela, reminding his audience (at inordinate length) that Mandela and his associates were Communists and terrorists. Just why Botha decided to alter the text of his speech shortly before delivering it remains unclear: his stubborn determination to assert dominance over cabinet colleagues at home and critics abroad was undoubtedly a key factor. Botha was clearly irked by the way in which his Foreign Minister had oversold the speech in advance and he was, as ever, concerned to keep his party unified and avoid a right-wing backlash.[72] The result was an unmitigated public relations disaster. Despairing business leaders within the country publicly called for the state of emergency to be lifted, an end to all statutory racial discrimination, and negotiations with black leaders. Abroad, conservatives who had resisted calls from the international anti-apartheid movement to impose economic sanctions and disinvest from South Africa were forced to concede the need for action.

Immediately after the speech Chase Manhattan Bank made public its recent decision not to 'roll over' debts to South Africa on the grounds that the country was an unacceptable investment risk.[73] Other leading international finance institutions followed suit, triggering a liquidity crisis that compelled a humiliated South African government to declare a partial moratorium on repayments of its foreign debt. The South African rand plummeted, capital fled the country, and consumer demand was depressed, triggering protracted recessionary conditions. Interestingly, the option of debt default or unilateral rescheduling was not seriously considered, perhaps because this would be construed as something that 'third world' countries opted to do.

Sanctions and Disinvestment

Another direct consequence of Botha's intransigence was to shift the political balance in the debate over economic sanctions which, by the mid-1980s, had become a defining point of difference in American and British domestic politics. In the United States the call for sanctions was spearheaded by prominent Democratic politicians like Edward Kennedy and Howard Wolpe as well as the Congressional Black Caucus and the increasingly influential TransAfrica Forum led by civil rights activist Randall Robinson. The spread of anti-apartheid activism on United States campuses was on a larger scale than anything seen since the Vietnam War.

Up until 1985 the US administration resisted pressure for sanctions but the events of that year changed the political landscape decisively when the Reagan administration agreed a limited export ban in an effort to head off more severe measures. The momentum could not be halted and in 1986 the US Congress passed a landmark Comprehensive Anti-Apartheid Act (with substantial bipartisan support), thereby overcoming Ronald Reagan's veto. The Anti-Apartheid Act outlawed all new US investment and trade in South Africa, suspended direct flights, and restricted imports of key commodities from South Africa. It also specified a timetable for political change, including the release of Nelson Mandela. Many US companies withdrew from South Africa or severely reduced their operations as a result of the legislation, whose passage represented a rare political defeat for Reagan.

Members of the European Union and the Commonwealth also passed limited sanctions involving investment, the importation of iron, steel, and Kruger Rand gold coins. It was largely as a result of Margaret Thatcher's strenuous opposition to sanctions that the measures adopted by the Commonwealth and EU against South Africa were relatively mild. Thatcher claimed to oppose apartheid, yet maintained that ongoing trade and investment was the best way to promote political change. She had received Botha at her official residence, Chequers, in 1984 and quietly advised him to release Mandela. Yet Thatcher also regarded Mandela as a subversive and considered that anyone who thought the ANC could form a government was living in 'cloud-cuckoo land'. The British prime minister placed her real trust and hope in Inkatha's Buthelezi, seeing him as a moderate anti-sanctions black leader. At the 1985 Commonwealth Heads of Government Meeting in Nassau, whose proceedings were entirely dominated by the issue of South Africa, Thatcher gloated in front of television cameras that she had had to concede only 'a tiny little bit' on the matter of sanctions.[74]

By the middle of 1987 more than 120 companies and corporations including General Motors, IBM, Coca-Cola, Xerox, Exxon, General Electric, and Barclays disinvested from South Africa. The avalanche of bad publicity emanating from anti-apartheid campaigns on university campuses and in public legislatures was having an effect. Corporate decisions to divest were made for a mixture of political *and* commercial reasons: in the last analysis, these came down to a question of whether South Africa was an attractive and prudent place in which to do business (ironically, many of the companies which withdrew publicly gained advantage from doing so).[75]

While inconvenient and morale-sapping, the short-term effect of this withdrawal was not crippling to South Africa; in many cases local management and capital bought the shares at bargain prices and their products continued to be produced or imported under franchise or through intermediaries. Formal trade sanctions were invariably circumvented. The most costly and disruptive sanctions were the oil boycott imposed by OPEC in 1973 and the arms embargo brokered by the UN. In both cases, the South African government mitigated these effects through import substitution. It poured resources into large industrial parastatals dedicated to the production of oil from coal (SASOL) and a domestic arms industry (ARMSCOR) which included the barely concealed development of nuclear weapons. These prestige projects became lop-sided industrial engines of growth as well as important symbols of self-sufficiency, albeit at significant cost to economic efficiency.

Far more serious than trade boycotts, which may have cost South Africa half a percentage point of GDP in the mid-1980s, were financial sanctions. In this case the withdrawal of private financial credit facilities proved more damaging than publicly imposed measures, raising the question of the effectiveness of intergovernmental action.[76] Investment and capital flows into the country turned negative 1985–94, both because capital had to be exported in order to pay off debts and also as a consequence of covert capital flight. Exchange and interest rates were manipulated by the South African authorities in order to boost exports and reduce imports, vital from the point of view of the balance of payments, but with damaging results for industries requiring capital goods and advanced technology.[77] Business confidence, already low, was severely hit by the reality of operating in a siege economy. The net effect was to exacerbate structural economic problems in the South African economy and to compound the secular contraction in growth.

The clamour for sanctions in Britain and the United States reached fever pitch in 1985 and remained a live issue of contestation for the rest of the decade, effectively making European and American foreign policy a matter of intense domestic concern. Public demonstrations and activism, in particular on American university campuses, kept the issue to the fore throughout this period. In 1986, Denmark became the first western country to impose a total trade boycott on South Africa, breaking with the established Scandinavian policy of 'following' the UN.[78] For the overseas anti-apartheid movement, pro-sanctions activism and boycotts of South African goods was one of the few ways in which disapproval of apartheid could be registered, leading many to overstate their importance as a driver of change.

In South Africa the debate was not quite so polarized. True, the UDF and its trade union affiliates lent rhetorical support to sanctions, whereas Inkatha pronounced itself opposed. The anti-apartheid movement within South Africa appreciated that the effects of sanctions were complex and potentially damaging to ordinary people's livelihoods. Laurence Schlemmer, a respected pollster, concluded, on the basis of several surveys of black South Africans in 1985, that only a minority of blacks in urban areas supported total disinvestment and economic boycott. Conditional investment was the favoured position, indicating a more subtle appreciation of the issues.[79] The psychological and political impact of sanctions was probably more important than their direct economic effects (though it is difficult to disentangle these factors given the extent to which business decisions are affected by perceived risk).[80] Most importantly, sanctions de-legitimized the government, afforded political leverage to anti-apartheid leaders within the country, and gave succour to ordinary South Africans fighting apartheid by reminding them that world opinion was with them.

CHAPTER 8
A BALANCING OF FORCES

Notwithstanding the testimony by leaders, including Nelson Mandela and Desmond Tutu, of the importance of sanctions in maintaining pressure on the South African government, the most important dynamics of change in the 1980s were internally generated. The growing influence of the ANC in exile was also significantly conditioned by, and dependent upon, the 'new fronts of resistance' that were coalescing.[1]

In the second half of the 1980s, the government's legitimacy and authority weakened, though its capacity to enforce its will remained largely intact. The anti-apartheid movement within the country withstood the assault of the state and in many ways deepened its associational roots and democratic culture. The ANC became the primary beneficiary of these developments. Its rising standing within the country, and beyond, began to position it as the natural negotiating partner with, and the presumptive successor to, the white minority regime. The proliferation of competing forces in the 1980s, and the chaos and confusion that marked the states of emergency in the second half of the decade, explains the somewhat kaleidoscopic approach to events and processes adopted in this chapter and Chapter 7. The profusion of new struggle organizations, generating a vast alphabet soup of acronyms, further complicates the task.

The Power of Organized Labour

Perhaps the most important force for change in the 1980s was organized labour. The formation of the Congress of South African Trade Unions (COSATU) in 1985 gave new muscularity to industrial labour, surpassing by far the political and workplace strength of any existing or previous union federation. By the mid-1980s, the ANC in exile was gaining significant strength from a labour movement that it had done little to nurture—beyond rhetorical support for the toiling masses.

Most of the new 'emergent' unions that developed from the 1970s grew independently of the ANC. A decade after the Durban strikes, there existed a plethora of trade union bodies: some were craft-based, others operated industry-wide, still others were generalist. They all had their own distinctive traditions, organizational culture, and political orientation. This diversity makes generalization difficult, but for the purposes of analysis, they can be broadly configured as follows:[2]

1. Unions that developed out of Black Consciousness traditions and foregrounded the importance of black leadership were grouped within the Council of Unions of South Africa (CUSA). The National Union of Mineworkers (NUM), formed in 1982, outgrew CUSA to become the single largest and most influential union in the country. AZACTU (Azanian Confederation of Trade Unions) was even more firmly committed to Black Consciousness. It merged with CUSA to become NACTU (the National Council of Trade Unions) in 1987, with some 250,000 workers in its fold.

2. A second union formation, the Federation of South African Trade Unions (FOSATU) claimed to represent around 45,000 workers in twelve affiliates at its launch in 1979. It was committed to democratic workplace organization as the basis of a socialist future. The origins of key affiliates, like the Metal and Allied Workers' Union, lay in a conception of trade union organization developed by Marxist academics at the time of the 1973 Durban strikes. In this sense FOSATU was strongly political. However, its advocacy of worker control (for which FOSATU was sometimes labelled 'workerist'), and of the democratic accountability of leaders to union members, meant that it was disinclined to participate in 'populist' political organizations such as the UDF: FOSATU feared that working-class interests would be subverted in a larger political organization and that gains made at the workplace would suffer in a government crackdown (this was the fate of SACTU in the 1950s and 1960s).

227

Non-racialism was a fundamental tenet for FOSATU unions. It was this principle that most distinguished them from the CUSA unions.[3] Some smaller regionally based independent unions, like the General Workers' Union, shared FOSATU's 'workerist' orientation, while refusing the principle of industry-based unionization that would have threatened their composite nature.

3. A number of so-called 'community' or 'general' trade unions took the view that workers were invariably part of broader communal structures; these were disposed to affiliate with the United Democratic Front in pursuit of the ideals of the Freedom Charter. Their first loyalty was to the anti-apartheid struggle, and they preferred to lend industrial power to the UDF than to insist on the primacy of the working class. The South African Allied Workers' Union, which operated in the eastern Cape Border region and the Ciskei Bantustan, enjoyed rapid growth in the early 1980s. But its politically outspoken leadership became subject to brutal repression and union organization suffered as a result.

4. A fourth category were the 'parallel' unions that were set up as offshoots of the largely white Trade Union Council of South Africa (TUCSA) that represented around 500,000 members at its height in 1983. In the course of the 1980s, black and coloured workers in the vehicle and garment industries split away, prompting the disbandment of its white-dominated parent organization. This was a strong reminder of the demise of what had once been a powerful white trade union movement. Remnants of the tradition, such as the militant white mineworkers' union led by Arrie Paulus, gravitated to the Conservative Party. Other unions, like the Boilermakers' Society, continued as independents.

Unity talks between the different unions and their umbrella organizations were at first slow to achieve results, but this changed as broader political events intruded on complex negotiations and institutional loyalties. From 1982, FOSATU began to revisit its political caution. It joined CUSA in the two-day 1984 UDF-led stayaway which was supported by some 800,000 workers.

In 1985 a formidable new union grouping, the Congress of South African Trade Unions (COSATU), was created. Its emergence marked a melding together of independent trade union organization with the broad national liberation movement. This was a significant moment in the development of political radicalism underpinned by industrial strength. COSATU was immediately dubbed a 'super-union' on account of the fact it represented around half a million paid-up workers grouped in over thirty affiliates.[4]

COSATU was highly effective in the way it combined organizational strength with political muscle. Its first president, Elijah Barayi, came from the National Union of Mineworkers which had meanwhile slipped its connections to CUSA and adopted the Freedom Charter. Vice-president Chris Dlamini and general secretary Jay Naidoo came from FOSATU unions. Cosatu's political inclinations were made amply clear at its founding rally in Durban when Chris Dlamini pronounced that the 'time has run out for employers and their collaborators'. Barayi revealed his contempt for homeland leaders—provocatively in Buthelezi's back yard—and indicated support for the ANC.[5]

With the National Union of Mineworkers under the leadership of Cyril Ramaphosa and James Motlatsi as one of its most important affiliates, COSATU was unquestionably the most important union grouping in the country. COSATU initially kept a formal distance from political organizations but drew increasingly close to the UDF during the state of emergency. In 1986 COSATU brought out more than 1.5 million workers in a May Day stayaway, the largest strike in the country's history. During that year the total number of days lost to strikes exceeded one million. The mining industry was particularly affected. COSATU succeeded in forging a powerful link with the ANC (use of the word 'congress' was a hint of its affinities). The two organizations issued a joint statement in 1986 recognizing the ANC as the leading force in the liberation movement of which COSATU was an 'integral part'. It was further agreed that the political crisis of the country could only be resolved with the full participation of the ANC. This necessitated the release all political prisoners, including Nelson Mandela, as well as the removal of P. W. Botha.[6]

The emergence of COSATU as the country's dominant union federation, and its effective alliance with the UDF, had two major consequences. First, its considerable organizational and industrial power allowed the union movement to put pressure on the government through employers. This muscle was also exercised in defence of trade unionists detained by the state. The exigencies of survival meant that old tensions between 'workerists' and 'populists' (or Charterists) had of necessity to be overcome. COSATU endorsed the Freedom Charter in 1987 and participated in major stayaways in commemoration of 16 June and May Day as well as leading a campaign for living wages and taking a lead in issues concerning industrial health and safety. One sign of worker strength was that 16 June and May Day were becoming *de facto* public holidays.

COSATU unions, the National Union of Mineworkers in particular, proved adept in negotiating with employers such as the Chamber of Mines. In the process, a sophisticated national culture of industrial bargaining began to emerge which bound business and labour together in a developing quasi-corporatist relationship. The government was often confined to the sidelines. The political bargaining skills exemplified by NUM leader Cyril Ramaphosa propelled him to the forefront of politics. Notwithstanding attempts by the state to weaken COSATU, including the bombing of its offices in 1987, the labour federation showed great institutional resilience. Its deep roots at the workplace and its seasoned leadership together made it the single most powerful component of the anti-apartheid struggle.

A further consequence of COSATU's emergence was to draw it into direct conflict with Buthelezi. Inkatha responded by organizing its own affiliate union, the United Workers' Union of South Africa (UWUSA) in 1986. Outside of Natal, where the 'sweetheart' union was welcomed by many employers, UWUSA had little influence. However, tensions between the two unions became intense as they battled for supremacy in that province. Buthelezi immediately identified COSATU as a front for the ANC.

Youth Power

If the UDF is imagined as a chest-and-horns battle formation, one of its political flanks may be said to have comprised unions affiliated to COSATU. The centre was composed of hundreds of organizations

Figure 6. Picture of woman with hand aloft in front of armoured vehicles: Paul Weinberg, 'A lone woman protests as the soldiers occupying her township roll by in large armoured military vehicles called "hippos", Soweto, July 1985'.

which together gave the UDF many of the characteristics of a social movement rooted in civil society: these were the little platoons of churches, mosques, schools, sports-clubs, community organizations, universities, and paralegal aid groups. The other flank was comprised of students and youth affiliated to the Congress of South African Students (COSAS) and, later, the South African Youth Congress (SAYCO).

Formed in 1979, COSAS emerged out of the Soweto uprising. It was initially strongly influenced by Black Consciousness thinking but soon drew towards a Charterist position. As the dominant youth organization in the country COSAS claimed the support of as many as 3m students.[7] Ranged against it was the Azanian Students' Movement which remained true to Black Consciousness ideals. In an environment of growing popular insurrection and repression COSAS and its successor youth organizations provided the UDF with raw energy and a formidable street-fighting capacity. Faced with brutal repression, their courage and willingness to sacrifice all was remarkable. Journalist and commentator

Shaun Johnson identified youth as both 'the motor of the rebellion and its outriders'.[8] Sociologist Jonathan Hyslop argued that students and youth were 'the shock troops' of the 1984–7 revolt; they detonated 'an explosion of worker and community struggle' which confronted the governing class with its greatest challenge to date.[9]

In a wide-ranging and perceptive study, the historian Colin Bundy examined the importance of generational consciousness in the uprising of the mid-1980s. He argued that demographic and economic realities underpinned youth-led resistance: in the 1980s around 40 per cent of the African and coloured population were aged under 15. High levels of unemployment and frustration were channelled into intense political awareness. Ongoing confrontation with the police and army helped to shape an articulate 'grammar' of street sociology and pavement politics.[10]

COSAS took a lead in promoting the 'Free Mandela' campaign of 1980. It was also an early adopter of the Freedom Charter. At funerals, rallies, and demonstrations, COSAS played a key role in introducing the songs, banners, and iconography of the ANC, MK, and the Communist Party. COSAS also established regional youth congresses catering to unemployed youngsters who came to be known as the 'comrades' or 'young lions'. The 'toyi-toyi' dance, which combined high-step rhythmic marching with militant chanting, was an innovation of this period with the power to intimidate as well as impress. Hand-made replica AK-47 guns were often brandished as props in a theatre of rebellion which developed its own rules of public performance.

Such expressions of raw revolutionary energy were exhilarating for participants, and also for the 'struggle' photographers and TV reporters on the barricades who covered funerals, rallies, and other flashpoints for the benefit of a global audience.[11] A collective of local photographers, Afrapix, documented urban resistance from a socially engaged, politicized perspective. From the mid-1980s American television cameras brought images of state violence into the living rooms of a domestic American audience. The South African government was almost certainly panicking when it blamed foreign TV journalists for deliberately staging or fomenting incidents of unrest, but there was undoubtedly a relationship between the public performance of protest, its recording by television crews, and its ritual re-enactment.[12]

State-controlled media did all it could to portray protest and disorder as irrational mob violence. By contrast, the liberation movement drew simplistic distinctions between perpetrators and victims, popular masses and collaborators. Independent and overseas media, which were generally sympathetic towards the anti-apartheid cause, were apt to overlook strains of aggression and thuggishness that could be employed to enforce stayaways and boycotts.

Broad claims about township insurrection tend to fall short when disaggregated by region and place. Albeit broadly directed against apartheid, township resistance was local and parochial—both in respect to the specific grievances, and in regard to the individuals and institutions selected as targets of anger and aggression. Jacob Dlamini's finely worked memoir of growing up in Katlehong is an important reminder that no township was identical to another. To ignore this is to buy into the dangerous 'fiction that black South Africans lived, suffered and struggled the same way against apartheid'.[13]

Dlamini's suggestive account does not purport to be ethnographic in the sense that, say, Belinda Bozzoli's study of insurrection in Alexandra is conceived. In this highly congested urban space, which abutted the wealthiest white suburbs of the country, a revolt broke out at the start of 1986 that came to be known as the 'Six Day War'. For a brief moment Alexandra became a liberated zone combining what Bozzoli terms 'a callow Marxism, a naïve African nationalism and burning youth romanticism'. Bozzoli's sociological analysis centres on a 'theatre' of struggle where repertoires of resistance, at once generic yet also particular to the locality of Alexandra, were performed in public. One example concerns the precise manner in which street committees and 'people's courts' were created by the comrades in order to enforce discipline. In the staging of popular justice, high-minded morality could be combined with brutal, arbitrary punishment. The *carnivalesque* inversion of authority placed youth 'at the pinnacle of a reformed moral universe' in ways that many ordinary people, adults especially, deeply disapproved of.[14]

Ordinary township-dwellers in localities around South Africa were often reluctant participants in insurrection and did not relish the choice of supporting communal activism or being treated as enemies. Local jealousies, rivalries, and prejudices inevitably conditioned the selection of those targeted as enemies of the people. Demonstrations of power and aggression were often assertively masculine. Although young women were active participants in rebellion, the comrades were overwhelmingly male, and so was their leadership: 'violence and masculinity were closely intertwined in the macho culture of resistance' especially when corps of comrades were organized in youth militia known as *amabutho* who became a dominant presence in some townships.[15] Generational conflict and consciousness added a further dimension, not least in confrontations between the comrades and Inkatha, or in rural Sekhukuneland where comrades 'smelt-out' alleged 'witches' and burnt them to death in waves of village terror. The composition of 'The Youth' was a capacious formulation. It included activists well past their teens and did not always distinguish between students operating under organizational discipline and *tsotsi* hoodlums who saw politics as a cover for criminal activities such as looting and arson; hence the unflattering composite term 'comtsotsi' which began to appear in newspapers around 1986.[16]

As well as throwing stones and Molotov cocktails at the army and police, militant youths attacked township police and officials collaborating with 'the system', just as they had done a decade before. They also found themselves in the forefront of confrontations with the Inkatha youths and *impi* as well as vigilantes in townships round the country. Sometimes youngsters used the rough justice of neighbourhood 'people's courts' to settle disputes or impose sanctions. From 1985, a gruesome new method emerged to kill collaborators and those accused of being *impimpi* (informers). Tyres filled with petrol were put around such people and set alight, a practice known as 'necklacing'.

Winnie Mandela provoked intense anger when she lent legitimacy to summary executions by declaring at a political rally in 1986: 'with our boxes of matches and our necklaces we shall liberate this country.' In her apparent endorsement of extreme, nihilistic violence, Winnie Mandela (still in many people's eyes the epitome of struggle royalty) nurtured false expectations that white power was about to dissipate. Belief in the imminence of apartheid's collapse, which was not widely shared by the trade unions or the ANC, encouraged recklessness. From 1984 school boycotts became the rule rather than the exception, as slogans like 'liberation now, education later' gained in popularity. As a result boycotting became an end in itself rather than a mobilizing tactic with a clear strategic objective. There were calls to make 1986 a 'year of no schooling'.

Politically sympathetic parents, who were deeply concerned about the chaotic situation in schools, and also aware that the government was not about to collapse, formed the National Education Crisis Committee in 1986. This body sought to promote 'People's Education for People's Power' as an alternative to boycotting. A number of 'consultative conferences' were held to explain the idea of 'people's education' but the continuing state of repression was not conducive to a return to schools until 1987.[17] The clandestine launch of SAYCO that year, following COSAS' banning in 1985, represented an attempt to impose revolutionary self-discipline and to redefine the relationship of 'the youth' in the struggle, albeit without constraining its militancy. One consequence was SAYCO's acceptance of a more structured relationship with COSATU whose senior role in the vanguard of political change was explicitly recognized, if not always observed.[18]

The ANC's Consultative Conference, Kabwe 1985

In 1985 the ANC held a Consultative Conference at the small Zambian town of Kabwe, the first such general meeting since Morogoro in 1969. This gathering was held under far more propitious circumstances and an air of confidence was readily detectable. Whereas 1969 was a response to the conspicuous failures of guerrilla action, MK could now point to significant successes, not least to the rapturous way in which its colours and heroes were greeted at rallies and funerals within South Africa. Within the country whites as well as blacks were beginning to envision the ANC, with Nelson Mandela and Oliver Tambo at its head, as an alternative government. Kabwe was portrayed as a 'Council of War' preparatory to the seizure of power by the masses. There was much rhetorical support for the armed struggle. Yet it was equally remarkable as an example of democracy in practice. Debate was more open and vigorous than at any time in the organization's exile history. Papers and detailed submissions reveal much greater awareness of the political situation within the country than was the case just a few years previously.

In a departure from previous practice, non-Africans were allowed to stand for the National Executive Committee, elected by secret ballot for the first time in the organization's exile history.[19] A Code of Conduct was approved which, in recognizing the ANC as an 'embryonic state', adopted new rules about the administration of internal justice in respect of the treatment of detainees. Fiery rhetoric about the 'people's war' and the 'seizure of power' (including a statement that there would no longer be distinction between 'hard' and 'soft' targets) was offset by a far more realistic assessment of MK's military capacity as well as conditional acceptance of 'negotiations in principle'. By comparison with Botha's Rubicon display, the ANC was presenting itself as reasonable and confident; indeed, as a government-in-waiting. One enthusiastic young delegate referred to the gathering as 'a South African people's parliament'.[20]

The high morale at Kabwe could not disguise persistent problems. In the aftermath of the Nkomati Accord, the ANC's presence in Mozambique was depleted while Swaziland, an important entry-point to South Africa for MK guerrillas, cooperated with the South African government to restrict ANC activity. Relations with Zambia were also strained. One of the main reasons for holding the Kabwe conference was to deal with serious rifts in the organization arising out of mutinies in guerrilla camps in Angola. These were caused by a combination of frustration at MK leadership's inactivity and poor living conditions. Well-founded fears of South African government agents in MK camps engendered paranoia, leading to punitive treatment of cadres and in some cases torture. Sexual abuse of young women recruits was common. *Imbokodo*, the ANC's internal intelligence and security arm, was considered by some within the ANC to be out of control. Although not explicitly acknowledged, the Code of Conduct agreed at the Kabwe conference was a response to an internal investigation of the harsh discipline recently meted out at camps in Angola.[21]

The dual message sent out at Kabwe—readiness to consider negotiations coupled with intensified military activity—encapsulated the ANC's long-standing dilemma when it came to choosing between non-violence and insurrection. From 1960 onward the argument was made that violent resistance to apartheid was inescapable. Notwithstanding the generally mediocre performance of MK, sabotage and violence were justified in terms of the mutually reinforcing strategy of mass insurrection backed by military force. Yet, as Janet Cherry argues, the ANC was mired in 'strategic incoherence' in respect of the armed struggle. Ongoing commitment to the revolutionary seizure of power, either by MK, or by youth activists who acted in its name, was in many respects counter-productive. In particular, it could be detrimental to the emergence of proto-democratic popular institutions.[22]

Post hoc justifications of armed propaganda as a vital component of the political struggle are based on the knowledge that the ANC eventually prevailed. Yet it is possible that the ANC's victory was retarded by its poor military record which, at key moments, distracted the movement from engaging directly with mass action on the ground. It seems more likely that the ANC's dual strategy was a reflection of its own internal organizational weaknesses and composite ideology. In exile, and with only limited direct presence on home ground until the mid-1980s, the ANC was more often following events than leading them. Although Kabwe was in many ways a success, it was also, like Morogoro, something of a holding operation, albeit in circumstances that were far more advantageous.

The ANC's growing international stature in the 1980s represented a major advance. It was also beginning to attract inquisitive attention from opinion-formers within South Africa who despaired of the government's inability to address the country's problems. Shortly after Botha's Rubicon speech a delegation of South African industrialists, led by Gavin Relly of the vast Anglo-American mining conglomerate, met with senior members of the ANC (including Oliver Tambo and Thabo Mbeki) at Zambian president Kaunda's game lodge. It was agreed that the talks were not 'negotiations'. Rather, they were an occasion to gain mutual understanding in order to facilitate the 'complete removal of apartheid'. The record of the meeting noted that 'Big Business' was beginning to entertain the possibility that 'the Botha regime may not survive' and there was a need to find 'middle ground'.[23] Later in 1985, representatives of the opposition Progressive Federal Party, led by Frederik van Zyl Slabbert, travelled to Zambia for talks. A few months after this, Slabbert shocked the white political establishment by resigning from parliament on the grounds that the tricameral institution was fundamentally flawed and irrelevant to the country's future. In his view, the new constitution merely amounted to a shift from coercive to 'co-optive' domination.[24]

That such discussions between representatives of the liberal establishment and the ANC could take place at all was a remarkable indication of a political landscape whose topography was changing fast but had yet to be mapped. Even after meeting with the ANC, Gavin Relly did not think majority rule would be seen by his own generation. In November 1985, the editor of the *Cape Times* defied government proscriptions against quoting 'banned' people by publishing an interview with Oliver Tambo. Tambo indicated his willingness, under certain conditions, to negotiate with the government and gently assured white South Africans that the ANC was fighting against 'a system' not 'against people'.[25] This came as a welcome surprise to many whites. Up till now, the only occasions on which Tambo had been mentioned in South Africa was in connection with calls for armed struggle. It was the first time in two decades that the ANC had spoken, uncensored, in South Africa.

Just a few months before, in February, a well-connected South African journalist, Barry Streek, travelled to Lusaka to conduct a series of interviews with ANC leaders, including Tambo. He was informed that there was 'not the slightest chance' of direct talks between the ANC and the government. Even the unconditional release of Nelson Mandela would not be sufficient to persuade the ANC to enter into negotiations. Indeed, an intensification of the armed struggle was being considered.[26] But in April the *Washington Post* reported that Oliver Tambo was prepared to meet the South African government, perhaps without preconditions, and that the ANC was prepared to discuss and negotiate mechanisms 'to protect white rights'. Van Zyl Slabbert offered to act as an intermediary between Tambo and Botha. The South African government moved to end such speculation by announcing that the ANC offer of talks was unacceptable.[27]

These confusing claims and counter-claims were hesitant first steps. We now know that the ANC as well as the government were, at the time, tentatively beginning to explore the possibility of talks. Both parties were involved in delicate balancing acts designed to keep their own militants and moderates on side. Thus, contacts were pursued by intermediaries on the basis that the principals could deny that they were taking place.

Some of the earliest secret exploratory contacts with the ANC began in November 1985 when Justice Minister Kobie Coetsee visited Nelson Mandela as the ANC leader recovered in hospital from prostate surgery. Coetsee had earlier developed a line of communication with Winnie Mandela and it was as a result of a chance meeting with her that Coetsee decided to visit Mandela in hospital.[28]

A pattern of rumour, kite-flying, hints, and denials was all part of the phase of what in retrospect appear to be talks-about-talks-about-talks. There were certainly compelling reasons for the ANC and the government to establish some form of communication, but there was no necessity to do so and the process was fraught with dangers for both parties. Knowing as we now do the outcome of the negotiations a decade later, it would be mistaken to read any sense of inevitability into this process. We should bear in mind that neither side had a clear overview of what was going on, let alone a clear mandate upon which to proceed.

The precarious political climate was exemplified by the fate of the Commonwealth 'Eminent Persons' Group' led by two well-known former heads of state, Australian Malcolm Fraser and Nigerian Olusegun Obasanjo. Their task-force engaged in a frenetic bout of shuttle-diplomacy in southern Africa in order to establish an environment conducive to achieving a negotiated political settlement. Mandela's release was a key issue, with the ANC as well as the government insisting on preconditions that amounted to a mutual cessation of hostilities. For the ANC, a priority was the release of political prisoners in order to allow it to consult widely amongst its growing but fragmented support base. A significant breakthrough seemed possible when the EPG was permitted to meet Mandela in Pollsmoor Prison.[29]

Government tacticians were calculating that, by allowing the incarcerated Mandela into political play, they might induce a split between him, the ANC in exile, and the anti-apartheid movement within South Africa. This stratagem might have succeeded. But government hardliners with the ear of the president were disinclined to go down this route and determined instead to take matters into their own hands.[30] On the day that the EPG was scheduled to meet with members of the cabinet constitutional committee, 19 May 1986, the South African military launched a series of pre-dawn raids on targets purported to be ANC bases in Zambia, Zimbabwe, and Botswana (they turned out to be 'soft' targets and the victims were not South African). The EPG immediately terminated its mission and issued a statement calling for the imposition of comprehensive, mandatory sanctions on South Africa. Botha's obduracy, shown rhetorically in his Rubicon speech, was fully confirmed by his violation of national sovereignty under the full gaze of international opinion. The momentum in favour of US sanctions now became unstoppable.

Emergency Renewed

On 12 June 1986, State President Botha renewed the state of emergency on a national basis. This major escalation went significantly further than the September 1985 state of emergency (which had been lifted in March 1986). Around 8,000 people were detained over this period, more than 80 per cent associated with the UDF. Many others went into hiding, with leaders sheltered by sympathizers and popping up here and there for clandestine meetings. The renewed state of emergency was thoroughly planned and to a significant extent it succeeded in quelling revolt over the ensuing twelve months. During the second state of emergency, which remained in force until 1990, the state detained more than 25,000 people, perhaps more than all detentions combined since 1960 (estimates vary widely). The vast majority of those incarcerated were aged under 25, many of them under 18. Community workers and trade unionists made up the next highest categories. In a departure from established practice, the government did not make full disclosure of the names and numbers of detainees.[31] The Detainees Parents' Support Committee, a human rights organization formed by Max Coleman in 1981, did much of the groundwork in monitoring and analysing detentions until it was outlawed during a fresh crackdown in 1988.

There was some relaxation in government repression during the interlude between the first and second states of emergency. Civic and youth organizations began to rebuild as activists surfaced from hiding. Botha claimed at the time that he was lifting the regulations because levels of violence in black townships were declining, though it is more likely that he was seeking to assuage foreign pressure. Detentions continued under the Internal Security Act. Nevertheless, it was during this period of relative calm in 1986 that Botha's government moved to scrap the pass laws in favour of a new system of 'orderly urbanization'.

Had Botha announced the removal of this cornerstone of apartheid three years before, the single most hated dimension of white domination (and a key reason for the formation of the UDF and National Forum) would have been a much less important factor. But in the absence of comprehensive change on black political rights (citizenship was restored to some 2m qualifying Africans though several million in the four 'independent' homelands continued to be treated as foreigners) this significant departure from 'grand' apartheid proved underwhelming. A critical failure was the government's inability to explain clearly what its reforms were intended to achieve—rather than the grievances it hoped to relieve.

The period 1987–9 was aptly described by the academic and activist David Webster as a 'state of attrition' in which the prospect of a permanent state of emergency seemed a distinct possibility.[32] To a considerable extent, security forces succeeded in regaining effective control over urban townships by 1988. The UDF, along with sixteen other organizations, was effectively banned in February 1988, by which time it was already significantly weakened as a campaigning force, its access to overseas funds already cut off for over a year and several layers of leadership detained or in hiding. It survived in vestigial form through 1988 until it broke surface, freshly revitalized in alliance with COSATU, as the Mass Democratic Movement, in 1989. As well as reviving rallies and symbolic protests, the Mass Democratic Movement began to prepare the ground internally for negotiations and political transition.[33]

The second state of emergency was broad in scope but also more focused. The number of detentions decreased significantly from mid-1987 because the state was becoming more adept at targeting particular individuals and organizations. Other forms of repression were utilized in order to contain opposition. These included use of the Internal Security Act, press censorship, political trials, restrictions on organizations, intimidation, and targeted assassinations by shadowy right-wing forces. David Webster himself was killed in 1989 on the doorstep of his Johannesburg home, the victim of the Orwellian-named 'Civil Cooperation Bureau', a hit squad run out of the Defence Ministry.

Interregnum?

In 1982 the novelist Nadine Gordimer delivered a lecture in New York in which she developed an idea taken from the Italian Marxist theoretician Antonio Gramsci: 'The old is dying, and the new cannot be born; in this interregnum there arises a great diversity of morbid symptoms.' Gordimer's description of life 'in a society whirling, stamping, swaying with the force of revolutionary change', and yet unable to make that transition, was just as valid five years later.[34] A deadly stalemate existed as the forces of change, opposition, and reaction met in a state of violent, oscillating equilibrium. The government retained the capacity to impose its will by force but lacked the legitimacy to do so effectively; the anti-apartheid movement, increasingly coalescing around the UDF-ANC, demonstrably enjoyed majority support, but was in no position to overthrow the state.

The state of deadlock did not mean complete immobility. A gradual process of equalization had to take place between pro- and anti-apartheid forces before each recognized the other as insurmountable. The greatest problem facing the state was not so much the 'revolutionary onslaught' (a term connoting imminent danger which came to replace 'total onslaught') as a stagnant economy and increasing challenges to its authority and legitimacy.

The narrowing base of the government's authority was visible at multiple levels. In inner city Johannesburg, the cosmopolitan suburb of Hillbrow began to go 'grey' during the 1980s as Indian and coloured apartment-seekers, followed by Africans, ignored the strict provisions of the Group Areas Act (with the connivance of white landlords). The need to gain support for the tricameral parliament deterred the government from moving against Indian and coloured tenants. Far-right groups mounted protests but demographic pressure and immobility on the part of the authorities changed the facts on the ground. In the shifting geography of segregated space, the government was effectively relinquishing control of inner city Johannesburg in the knowledge that its real urban support-base was considerably suburbanized. A supreme court judgement in the case of *Govender* (1982) forbade evictions without alternative accommodation being found, and thereby gave legal basis to the process of *de facto*

Figure 7. Picture of woman at gunpoint: Paul Weinberg, 'Workers leaving a May Day meeting find riot police at the entrance blocking their way on the steps of Khotso House in Johannesburg, May 1985'.

deracialization. By 1987 'the Group' was effectively inoperable in central Johannesburg.[35]

The failure of the Conservative Party to prevent integration in Johannesburg was in part attributable to growing doubts within Afrikanerdom about the practical sustainability of strict separation. There was a moral dimension to this as well. In 1979, acclaimed Afrikaans writer Elsa Joubert published *The Long Journey of Poppie Nongena*. It was based on the distressing life story of a black woman who arrived on the novelist's doorstep having fled a conflict-ridden township. This narrative testimony of an ordinary black woman's epic struggle to survive the cruelties of apartheid South Africa proved sensational reading for middle-class Afrikaners.

Breast-beating within the Afrikaner elite was accompanied by a more iconoclastic and irreverent tearing down of cultural values on the part of its alienated youth, a phenomenon that far exceeded the anguished self-questioning of the *Sestiger* intellectuals. The emergence of *voëlvry* (free as a bird/outlaw) rock music in the 1980s, pioneered by Koos Kombuis, Barnoldus Niemand, and Johannes Kerkorrel (all ironic pseudonyms), proved deeply shocking to the Afrikaner establishment. This was Afrikaner youth's delayed counter-cultural 1960s. White youth, students in particular, flocked to live performances at which Afrikaner icons and apartheid nostrums were derided with gritty sarcasm and earthy wit.[36] An exception to the sardonic lyrics was the ballad to Hillbrow performed by the Gereformeerde Blues Band (a play on the dominant Afrikaner church) which enjoined listeners 'to give your heart' to the racially mixed suburb.

A process of breaking down barriers and the erosion of the government's political authority was discernible at many different levels through the 1980s. Senior British Foreign Office officials met with the ANC in Lusaka in 1986 in spite of Margaret Thatcher's visceral opposition to the ANC. Later that year, Oliver Tambo had meetings with British Foreign Secretary Geoffrey Howe and US Assistant Secretary of State for African Affairs Chester Crocker. Such meetings were an important indication of the ANC's new status as a potential government-in-waiting.

After Gavin Relly's business class trip to Lusaka, which was strenuously opposed by the South African government and also by Harry Oppenheimer, a number of further meetings were arranged to put the ANC in touch with official South African thinking. These discreet occasions typically took the form of African safaris or genteel get-togethers in the English countryside. Open discussions with the ANC remained taboo, but other forms of informal contact were proceeding apace.

Starting in 1987, Consolidated Goldfields' public affairs manager, Michael Young, convened a series of secret meetings at Mells Park, Somerset. These involved high-ranking members of the ANC, including Thabo Mbeki and Jacob Zuma, and prominent Stellenbosch academics Sampie Terreblanche and Willie Esterhuyse. A new twist to these proximity talks was added when Niël Barnard, Botha's influential intelligence chief, began to monitor the meetings. At the same time Barnard kept a line open to Mandela.[37]

One of the most high-profile meetings with the ANC was arranged by van Zyl Slabbert, of the Institute for Democratic Alternatives (IDASA), in Dakar in 1987. The delegation comprised sixty-one predominantly Afrikaans-speaking academics, artists, and professionals. Almost all found the trip revelatory. Some in this diverse group were as nervous of meeting the enemy as of incurring the label *verraiers* (traitors) or *oorbeligte* (over-enlightened). The government made its disapproval clear and tried to scupper the trip.

Novelist André Brink records that a common fear amongst the Dakar delegates was 'What will my mother say if she finds out?' Thabo Mbeki, the suave ANC princeling, made a huge impression when he introduced himself as 'an Afrikaner'. Preconceptions and prejudices dissolved in lengthy conversations smoothed by ample quantities of spirits, big hugs, and a mood of joking camaraderie. For both sides the occasion was a moment of emotional epiphany, 'an illustration of this almost fateful bond that, in spite of all, tied us together'. Frank Chikane, of the South African Council of Churches, stated that Dakar's major significance was 'its success in blowing the myth propagated by the South African government portraying the African National Congress as a group of terrorists who were incapable of reason'. A more cautious assessment by an ANC participant reflected that the meeting had helped to 'solidify the disaffection with the regime of an important group of intellectuals'.[38]

The Afrikaner *Broederbond* was also playing an important role as a political solvent. Having been split down the middle after the acrimonious departure of Treurnicht's right-wing followers, it was now chaired by Pieter de Lange, author of the 1979 education report. De Lange met Thabo Mbeki in New York at a Ford Foundation conference on education in 1986. Both were canny operators who could turn on the charm. After an extended conversation, whose cordial atmosphere was helped by pipe-smoking and a good lunch the following day, de Lange declared that his life's work was the cause of racial reconciliation.[39]

Beneath the fine words, hard-headed calculation was at work. In a secret *Broederbond* discussion document which circulated widely at this time, the organization accepted that the status quo was no longer viable. There were no guarantees for the future. 'The greatest risk that we are taking today is not taking any risks.' Power-sharing based on pre-defined 'groups' remained a key frame of reference but only insofar as it protected minorities and was not a means for one group to dominate another: in other words, 'there can no longer be a white government'. The document identified certain fundamental freedoms (language and cultural rights, private ownership, freedom of conscience, and freedom of speech) as 'prerequisites for survival'; these could also be termed 'basic human rights' and they ought to be given legally binding form.[40]

The Dutch Reformed Church was another key Afrikaner institution that moved decisively, if glacially, away from apartheid. At its 1986 general synod, the scriptural justification of apartheid was rejected and the church was declared open to all, prompting unreconstructed conservatives to split away and form the racially exclusive Afrikaans Protestant Church. It took another four years for the anguished DRC, under the leadership of its moderator, Johan Heyns, to condemn apartheid as a 'sin' and to confess the role of the church in apartheid's creation.[41]

Such developments have to be seen in the context of broader developments in the Christian churches, notably the 1985 *Kairos* document, a statement of liberation theology signed by 150 black theologians and clergy, which decried the use of religion by the state to bolster racist practices. It was read by some as coming close to endorsing violence in response to state oppression. Heyns disapproved of *Kairos* but was evidently affected by it. Black church leaders like Allan Boesak, Frank Chikane, and Desmond Tutu followed closely the deliberations in the Dutch Reformed Church and fully understood the dynamics and coded hermeneutics involved. Agreement or disagreement is not necessarily the issue if one accepts the de Gruchys' view that the church was both 'an agent and the site of the struggle'.[42] In other words, ecumenical and synodical debates were part of a larger moral conversation that helped to condition the institutional climate of political negotiations and reconciliation.

The process of familiarization between mutual enemies was also taking place in the flinty secular worlds of intelligence-gathering and policy formation. Two examples will have to suffice: an executive summary (in Afrikaans and marked 'secret') of the ANC's Kabwe conference exists in the P. W. Botha archive, while the *Broederbond* document 'Basic Political Values for the Survival of the Afrikaner' (in English and marked 'strictly confidential') made its way to the ANC in London.[43] A systematic study of how both sides assessed each other, the filtering mechanisms at work, and how public statements and personal knowledge correlated with private information-gathering has yet to be attempted. But in intelligence-gathering, as elsewhere, it is possible to detect a process of institutional mirroring whereby the ANC and the government replicated each other's agencies and approaches.

It has already been noted that the ANC and the government both relied on a strategy of political persuasion backed by force. The relative strength of force to persuasion was very different for the ANC and the government. Neither organization knew which strategy would prove decisive since both were feeling their way in the dark. Yet leaderships in both bureaucracies were careful to maintain this dual capacity, and they were ready to deploy their diplomatic and military assets as and when internal or external conditions required.

A New Symmetry

There is a striking symmetry in the manner by which groupings within the ANC and the government both started to think more seriously about the prospects of a negotiated settlement requiring a new constitution. In 1986, Justice Minister Kobie Coetsee instructed the government's statutory Law Commission to consider explicit protection for 'group' rights. It was anticipated that the Commission would pronounce against individual human rights. Some speculated that the initiative was a cynical manoeuvre motivated chiefly by the need to head off US sanctions. The Law Commission duly took extensive evidence but, to the surprise of insiders, it produced a draft bill of rights in 1989 that endorsed basic civic and political freedoms while firmly rejecting the principle of racially defined group rights.

In 1986, too, Oliver Tambo established an ANC Constitutional Committee, chaired by the respected struggle-intellectual Jack Simons, which began to explore the relevance and potential of a bill of rights. The following year the ANC National Executive endorsed the concept of a justiciable bill of rights based on fundamental freedoms and rights. This was given further credence by the publication in 1988 of the ANC's proposed 'Constitutional Guidelines', followed by the ANC's 1989 Harare Declaration which set out terms for negotiations with the government. It included the clause 'All shall enjoy universally recognised human rights, freedoms and civil liberties, protected under an entrenched Bill of Rights'. A draft bill of rights was meanwhile sketched out by Albie Sachs and Kader Asmal, both independent-minded lawyers and members of the ANC Constitutional Committee. These were much needed developments because the iconic Freedom Charter was as ambiguous about the constitutional details of a future democracy as it was about the extent to which the economy should be socialized. In style and in substance, the ANC's constitutional work marked a break with its programmatic approach to revolution while in exile, and began to reconnect the organization with its social democratic moment in the 1940s and 1950s.

Constitutionalists and rights-activists had to overcome a great deal of scepticism, not to say antagonism, within their own ranks. Within both the UDF and the ANC there were many who regarded a bill of rights as a sham form of bourgeois democracy. For its part, the government had long been ideologically opposed to the very concept of individual rights, viewing this as inimical to the tenets of Christian-Nationalism and the primacy of the *volk*. Individual rights were mistrusted since they might well be the route to majority rule in a unitary society, which would mean the effacement of white political power.[44]

Up to this point, advocates of constitutionally entrenched rights came from groupings to which the ANC and the government were entirely opposed: liberal lobbying organizations and the opposition Progressive Reform Party, as well as the KwaZulu-Natal 'Indaba' which, in 1986, recommended a federal form of consociational government featuring a comprehensive bill of rights. Samuel Huntington gave general support to the idea on a visit to Natal in 1986, and was reportedly highly impressed with Buthelezi as a leader.[45] Arend Lijphart had been part of the Buthelezi Commission which recommended a form of regional consociationalism in 1982. The ANC was implacably opposed to any initiative with which Buthelezi was associated and suspected that the Indaba or 'Natal Option' represented an attempt to 'privatize' apartheid; the government, while strongly interested in the principle of consociationalism, was likewise suspicious of a constitutional initiative driven by a homeland leader and self-appointed liberal experts in anglophone Natal.

The government and the ANC were also mutually wary of US foreign policy which, under the Reagan and especially the Carter administrations, increasingly pushed a human rights agenda. The ANC interpreted this as a form of imperialism, while the government resented external interference in its domestic affairs, often seeing human rights as a cover for Communism. Nevertheless, the growing global embrace of human rights was a palpable reality and opinion-formers on both sides saw this as an opportunity not to be squandered.

Constitutionalists within the ANC fully appreciated the advantages in seizing the moral high ground by endorsing individual rights and using this as a route to majority rule. Government advisers recognized that it would be prudent in a future political dispensation to secure constitutional guarantees on matters such as private property and free speech. In short, both the ANC and the government found compelling practical reasons to endorse constitutionalism and individual human rights. Over time, pragmatism became restated as principle such that the South African constitution, which finally emerged in the 1990s, floated on a groundswell of optimism that was fed by international approbation. Indeed, the final constitution and the Truth and Reconciliation Commission became global exemplars of how to move from authoritarianism to democracy. These mechanisms were important in underwriting the 'New South African miracle'.

An Expansion of Civic and Legal Space

It is doubtful whether the ANC or the government would have entertained constitutionalism so seriously in the absence of developments within South Africa favouring political pluralism and democracy. One of the paradoxes of the 1980s is that the repressive forces unleashed during the states of emergency had the effect of increasing awareness of the importance of civil society, democracy, and non-racism. South Africa was awash with new 'civil society' organizations in the 1980s. Their emergence was signalled by the proliferation of acronyms denoting their existence. The UDF, National Forum, community organizations, and the trade union movement spawned a huge number of groupings, large and small, the length of whose names were often disproportionate to the size of their followings. For almost every Charterist organization beginning with 'Congress' or 'League', there were comparable Black Consciousness organizations bearing a 'z' for Azania.

Although the emergency regulations imposed strict reporting restrictions on newspapers, most were able to circumvent these to get their messages across. The commercial press was most likely to comply with government regulations, but this did not mean that its journalism was uncritical. What really made a difference was the emergence of new independent newspapers that broke the commercial mould.

In 1980 *The Sowetan* was established as a daily paper, replacing the banned *World* and the closed *Transvaal Post*. Despite close surveillance by the state, which was responsible for the demise of its predecessors, *The Sowetan* managed to maintain substantial editorial independence. The commercial Argus group, owner of *The Sowetan*, adopted a hands-off approach and was generally content to allow the newspaper to serve as the 'voice' of black opinion. Editors Percy Qoboza, Joe Latakgomo, and Aggrey Klaaste skilfully positioned the newspaper as supportive of 'the struggle'. The task was a delicate one, not only because of the threat of government interference, but also because most of the journalists on the paper were inclined to Black Consciousness ideology, whereas its readership was gravitating towards COSATU and the ANC.

Even more forthright in its resistance to apartheid was *The New Nation*, formed in 1986 and edited by former *Sowetan* journalist Zwelakhe Sisulu. The paper and its editor were both subject to repression under the state of emergency. The *Weekly Mail*, which began publication in 1985, catered mainly for white professionals on the liberal-left end of the political spectrum. It provided a new outlet for investigative journalism and partially filled the vacuum left after the demise of the *Rand Daily Mail*. In 1988 the *Vrye Weekblad* was launched by resolutely anti-apartheid Afrikaner journalists who were overwhelmingly frustrated with the mainstream press. The approach of this Afrikaans newspaper amounted to a thorough break with the tradition of licensed 'loyale verset' (loyal opposition). These vigorous 'alternative' newspapers, forged in the heat of the state of emergency, distinguished themselves with their fearless investigative stories: major exposés included revelations about the notorious extra-judicial murders perpetrated by Eugene de Kok and his 'Askaris'

(ANC guerrillas who had been 'turned' to become government agents) at *Vlakplaas* farm, as well as secret government financial support given to Inkatha and RENAMO in Mozambique. *Die Suid-Afrikaan*, a periodical, catered for a more academically oriented Afrikaans readership.

A number of community-based and student-run newspapers also sprang up in the 1980s, such as *Grassroots* in the western Cape, the *New African* in Natal, and *SASPU National* on liberal university campuses. These additions to the commercially independent 'alternative press' lent support to political campaigning and covered stories that the mainstream press were apt to ignore. The government's monopoly of the airwaves was broken in 1979 by Capitol Radio, followed by Radio 702, which broadcast from the Transkei and Bophutatswana (nicely exploiting the nominal sovereignty of the Bantustans to do so). The professional presentation of independent news, along with uncensored music, on such commercial stations represented a cultural as much as a political challenge to apartheid. Turnstile news agency, which supplied copy to Capitol Radio and to news outlets overseas, owed its name to Rick Turner, whose original idea it had been.[46]

The operation of the law was severely deformed during the apartheid era as authoritarian rule by law replaced the rule of law. Yet a degree of respect for legality and the courts remained and this gave South Africa a deeper legal basis for the assertion of civic rights than in many other transitional societies, for example in eastern Europe and Latin America. Notwithstanding the state of emergency, there was a significant expansion of legal space in the mid-1980s. Left-wing lawyers Nicholas Haysom and Steven Kahanovitz noted with a mixture of delight and surprise:

One must go back 30 years to find a period in which human rights litigation enjoyed its current level of support and enthusiasm, when judges were regarded as potential allies in the struggle for democratic rights.[47]

Notable legal victories were registered against the government's revision of the pass laws and influx control with the *Komani* and *Rikhoto* supreme court judgements of 1980 and 1983.[48] These test cases brought by the Legal Resources Centre (a free legal clinic initiated by lawyer Felicia Kentridge and directed by future Constitutional Court judge Arthur

Chaskalson) showed how public interest law could help to frustrate the operation of apartheid.

Reforms in labour law opened up new possibilities for the emerging trade union movement to assert claims and rights. In 1986, the Metal and Allied Workers' Union lawyers secured a partial victory in the Durban supreme court when it challenged the validity of the state of emergency, a judgement that allowed detainees to access legal support. Human rights organizations and interest in public law developed rapidly from the mid-1970s; by the 1980s their reach was extending into the academic heartlands of conservative Afrikanerdom. One reason for the success enjoyed by human rights lawyers was a new willingness by judges to defend the institution of the law against a government patently lacking in legitimacy. Growing interest in a bill of rights within the wider legal fraternity was another important factor disposing judges to exercise greater judicial autonomy.[49]

A striking feature of the second state of emergency was the determination of the government to use the courts. There were no less than eight 'treason trials' and nearly 100 political trials in 1986. Remarkably, the conviction rate was low: three-quarters of cases that year concluding in acquittal or with cases withdrawn.[50] Political trials had long been used by the apartheid state as a strategy to discredit its opponents and remove leaders from circulation, just as anti-apartheid activists used such occasions as a platform to air their views. In 1985 the state arrested and charged with treason leading UDF figures at major show trials staged at Pietermaritzburg and Delmas. Amongst the defendants were 'Terror' Lekota, 'Popo' Molefe, and Moss Chikane.

The state's intention was to incapacitate the organization and delegitimize it by proving that the UDF behaved as the internal wing of the ANC and was responsible for fomenting violence. The Pietermaritzburg treason trial collapsed in 1986. In the long-running Delmas case, Lekota and Molefe were convicted and identified by the judge as part of the 'conspiratorial core inside the UDF apple'.[51] But the verdict was overturned (for technical reasons—an interesting twist in the context of a state of emergency) on appeal in 1989. From the perspective of the government the trial was a defeat. The legal processes were heavily criticized and, instead of being criminalized and destroyed, the UDF survived and succeeded in mobilizing political support nationally and internationally.[52]

In Splendid Isolation

The foregoing discussion has detailed a range of personal, collective, and institutional initiatives which together disposed moderate elements within the ANC and the government to enter into talks—or at least moderate their mutual antagonism. It suggests, too, that there was an expansion of civic and institutional space notwithstanding the state crackdown. But how to galvanize and capitalize upon these opportunities? Watching from 'splendid isolation' in his new cell in Pollsmoor Prison, Mandela understood as early as 1985 that a process of talks had to begin. The problem was that neither party felt sufficiently confident to make a decisive move in public and so risk being accused of weakness or betrayal. It was always tempting for the National Party to fall back on its public insistence that it would not talk to terrorists or Communists and for the ANC to brand the government as racist and fascist. Mandela decided that this was the moment when he should 'move out ahead of the flock'.[53]

The question of Mandela's release, mooted as early as 1976 by cabinet minister Jimmy Kruger, was a key indicator of the government's preparedness to break the political deadlock. In 1985 the prospect of Mandela being freed was raised by Botha, albeit under conditions that Mandela and the ANC could not accept. The ANC's willingness to endorse broad-based international campaigns for his release from 1978 helped to ensure that Mandela would once again come to personify the struggle, as he had done at the Rivonia trial and, before that, as chief volunteer in the Defiance Campaign.[54] The Release Mandela Campaign began to act in 1983. This political grouping, with Winnie Mandela as a prominent member, was a constituent (though not entirely cooperative) part of the evolving UDF.

In Britain, the Anti-Apartheid Movement was already playing an important role in projecting Mandela as the most inspirational leader of the South African liberation movement. Having for so long relied on small groups of politically engaged activists, the campaign was increasingly fronted by celebrities including musicians and actors. Support for Mandela's release became synonymous with opposition to apartheid. The spectacular success of this international campaign should not be taken for granted. In 1964 Amnesty International controversially decided that it could not adopt Mandela as a 'prisoner of conscience' because of his advocacy of violence.[55] A decade later he was remembered only dimly in South Africa and abroad. By the mid-1980s Mandela was the world's most famous prisoner and a global icon of freedom. Mandela's symbolic value was inestimable. Yet it was by no means clear exactly what his future role might be or whether he would be in a position to resume active political leadership.

Lines of communication between Mandela and Lusaka remained difficult, and although he reassured the movement that he was a loyal and disciplined member of the ANC, Mandela saw advantages in not having to consult at every stage of talks. Significantly, Mandela did not oppose being separated from close compatriots like Walter Sisulu and Ahmed Kathrada at Pollsmoor Prison. There was anxiety in some quarters of the ANC, and also within the UDF, that Mandela's African nationalism might emerge as being at odds with the movement's official commitment to socialism. There were particular fears that his isolation from daily politics—itself a contributor to Mandela's mystique—might induce him to strike a deal with the government without a mandate from the ANC. Even Mandela's oldest and most trusted associate, Oliver Tambo, had momentary concerns on this score.[56]

When Mandela was freed in 1990 and travelled to Lusaka to meet with the ANC in exile, he found his old comrade Oliver Tambo in a frail state, recovering from a stroke. Tambo suffered a further stroke in April. At this critical juncture there was a leadership vacuum in the ANC. Militants were by no means convinced that negotiations were the way forward and Mandela had to reassure followers that he had not compromised on revolutionary principles in his talks with the government. In 1990, Chris Hani continued to believe that power could be seized through insurrection, despite MK being in a state of operational and disciplinary chaos. Within the country, there were criticisms of Mandela's high-handed leadership style.[57] Mandela became deputy leader of the ANC and was only elected as its president in July 1991, more than a year after his release.

Mandela's greatest role was in the post-1990 era as international statesman and agent of national reconciliation, a leader who was as much above the struggle as of the struggle. In this elevated role Mandela proved to be indispensable. Mandela's singular importance did not mean that he had been leading the ANC from prison. Rather, he was feeling his way back. When prison guards took Mandela out on drives around Cape Town to familiarize him with change, he was not recognized by South Africans, white or black. Small wonder: the last published photographs of Mandela at this stage dated from 1962 and even these images had very limited public circulation.[58] On the eve of his release in 1990 a *Time Magazine* cover used speculative artwork to represent Mandela as it believed he might look.[59] The embodiment of black liberation and human freedom still remained intangible and invisible.

Tough Talk

Although the second state of emergency was a period in which civil society and institutional life within South Africa underwent expansion, its most striking feature was political immobility. Botha was firmly ensconced in his imperial presidency and showed every indication of being prepared to sit things out. After the Rubicon speech he was routinely spoken of in the press and by colleagues as the 'Groot Krokodil' (great crocodile).[60] This may not have been the bloodiest period in the country's long transition (that was between 1990 and 1994) but it was arguably the moment in which the militarized state was at its nastiest.

While some within the security establishment, National Intelligence for example, were probing the possibilities of talks with the ANC, other even more insidious agents were given full range to practise their 'dirty tricks'. At *Vlakplaas* farm near Pretoria death squads operated freely under the direction of Eugene 'Prime Evil' de Kok. The Defence Force's secret 'Project Coast' initiative involved a chemical and biological warfare unit run by P. W. Botha's personal physician, Wouter 'Dr Death' Basson, which experimented with ever more and more grisly devices to rid the government of its enemies.

Many hardliners were still persuaded that the townships could be contained and that the ANC could be displaced by striking deals with more congenial black leaders. At a briefing for foreign correspondents in 1986, Brigadier H. G. Stadler of the South African Police claimed that 'terrorism and guerrilla warfare' was a strategy of weakness. He insisted that there was little evidence to suggest the 'people's war' was succeeding. The ANC's military activities were being conducted by 'bomb-commuters, on a hit-and-run basis'.[61] Stadler was not altogether wrong. An internal ANC document in 1986 acknowledged that, in respect of its military accomplishments, 'we have not come anywhere near the achievement of the objectives we set ourselves'. MK was certainly a great deal more active than it had been a decade before. In 1988, for instance, there were around 300 armed attacks within South Africa. A new MK initiative, Operation Vula, sought to create a more permanent underground network within the country. Yet, as Lodge concludes, even at its peak Umkhonto 'scarcely represented a serious threat to South African security'.[62]

Brigadier Stadler's insistence that counter-terrorism measures were defeating the people's war overlooked the fact that 'MK wannabees' in the townships, using improvised weapons and techniques, continued to sustain a revolutionary climate.[63] At a meeting with the ANC at Henley in England in 1987 the Stellenbosch academic Willie Breytenbach offered a more subtle version of the ANC's military threat. The 'securocrats', he reported, were of the view that political stability required 20 per cent coercion and 80 per cent political solution. The political component involved co-optation through reforms, or recognition of the ANC as the principal actor in a negotiating process. Negotiations were possible precisely because of the government's success in curbing mass mobilization and 'alternative structures'. Indeed, the ANC would *have* to negotiate because it was 'deploying its weakest arm'—armed struggle—'against the regime at *its* strongest point'. Lacking the 'ideological emotionalism' of politicians, securocrats were far more amenable to negotiation than members of parliament.[64]

The government's greatest weakness was its lack of political legitimacy. At the 1987 general election the National Party, campaigning on the basis that it alone could preserve 'law and order', actually increased its majority and share of the vote. But the Conservative Party made gains and displaced the Progressive Federal Party as the official opposition. The position of the ultra-conservatives was bolstered by the *Afrikaner Volkswag*, created in 1984 as an umbrella 'cultural' organization, and led by Carel Boshoff, who chaired the *Broederbond* until the split of the previous year. On the far right, Eugene Terreblanche's neo-fascist paramilitary organization, the *Afrikaner Weerstandsbeweging*, held rallies threatening apocalypse. Terreblanche's influence was undoubtedly exaggerated by his outsize personality and his photogenic appeal to audiences who were at once fascinated and appalled by his bellicose Boer-on-commando performances. Boshoff and Treurnicht were experienced politicians with cooler heads. Although their hopes that Afrikanerdom could return to the days of Verwoerd were the stuff of fantasy, it was dangerous to write them off as irrelevant. By extension it was perilous to ignore the continuing salience of white politics—as many on the political left affected to do.[65]

At one level the spectre of right-wing emotionalism played into the hands of the government by allowing Botha to present the National Party as a voice of reason, though his obstinacy and tirades militated against this. The 1987 election also revealed that the National Party itself was in deep disarray. A small group of high-profile *verligte* reformists followed Wynand Malan out of the National Party and congregated in a new grouping, the Independent Movement. These defections weakened Botha's grip on his own base in the Cape, while the Conservative Party carved great holes in its Transvaal strongholds. The embattled leader of the Transvaal nationalists, F. W. de Klerk, was finding it hard to stem the drift to the right, and needed to burnish his credentials as a conservative. As a pragmatist, however, de Klerk was painfully aware that government policy was 'on the rocks'.[66] But this did not disclose which direction the ship of state should move in order to free itself. A 1988 opinion survey calculated that 93 per cent of Conservative and National Party supporters favoured intensified security action against the ANC while only 23 per cent of National Party voters thought negotiations with the ANC were 'important'.[67]

Political Violence

Ongoing political violence made the prospect of a negotiated political transition at once more urgent and less likely. To the question as to whether change would come through peaceful evolution or violent revolution, van Zyl Slabbert answered in 1986 that neither presented real possibilities: 'we are caught up in a process of violent evolution in which the only choice is more, or less, violence before—and if—we resolve our conflicts.'[68] A great deal hung on the 'if'.

Of the 5,000 or more people killed in political violence between 1984 and 1990 only around 10 per cent were members of the state security forces or the armed wings of the liberation movements.[69] This meant that the vast majority of fatalities occurred not directly in the war against apartheid, but rather as a result of internecine strife in black townships where responsibility for killing was often difficult to ascertain. A depressing daily drip-feed of newspaper reports detailed grisly incidents in which small groups or individuals died in clashes between *impis* and comrades, in feuding between opposition groups, as a result of bomb attacks, or at the hands of the security forces.

In the second half of the 1980s around 80 per cent of deaths attributable to political violence occurred in Natal. In 1989, the worst year for political fatalities to date, 90 per cent of the 1,400 recorded deaths took place in that province.[70] In Pietermaritzburg, the epicentre of killings in the Natal Midlands, violence was said to be beyond the control of political organizations with 'bands of armed killers rampaging in a vicious cycle of attacks and revenge and ignoring peace calls by their leaders'.[71] The government, and large sections of the media, routinely described such acts as 'black-on-black' conflict. This non-explanation had overtones of racialism: it suggested that the violence was somehow an expression of atavistic tribal instincts and that clashes between supporters of Inkatha and the ANC could be explained in terms of an ancient rivalry between Zulus and Xhosas. According to the same logic, only the government was capable of maintaining order and any future political dispensation that did not take account of ethnic constituencies would be plagued by conflict. By 1990 the situation was so serious that even the government was beginning to acknowledge that the conflict around Pietermaritzburg was no mere 'tribal infraction' but was taking on 'the dimensions of a regional civil war'.[72]

Opposition leaders blamed the government for stoking the violence through its shadowy 'third force'—which was indeed an important contributory factor. More fundamentally, apartheid was the cause because it was a system of 'structural violence' rooted in dispossession, social inequality, ethnic division, and minority power. In franchising out its monopoly of violence to surrogate groups, the state was hoping to weaken the ANC and demonstrate that other black leaders, especially those in homelands like Kwa-Zulu, deserved recognition in any future negotiations. For many years apartheid succeeded in constraining the violence that its strategy of ethnic division was helping to foment. As its repressive power waned, so the potential for ethnic violence grew. When this became a reality, the state tried to use the state of unrest and disorder to its own advantage. But the endemic climate of violence weakened the government's claim to be in control, undermined the economy, and exacerbated splits within its own ranks.

The conflict between Inkatha and the ANC was sustained by the fact that Buthelezi could make plausible claims to be a national leader. The fact that he was not nearly so pliable as some other homeland chief ministers lent him some credibility as an anti-apartheid figure: supporters argued that he could destroy apartheid from within, whereas antagonists charged him with being a stooge of Pretoria. Whatever one's view on this—and the arguments are complex—Buthelezi and Inkatha were visible reminders that apartheid's dissolution required more than the defeat or removal from power of a white minority regime. Inkatha's brinkmanship in respect to participation in the 1994 election became the single greatest threat to peaceful political transition. So serious was the threat that it impelled moderates in the ANC and the government, who shared a determination to forestall a blood-bath, to talk together as senior negotiating partners.

The 'system' continued to function because it managed to co-opt a very substantial degree of compliance from blacks whose own livelihoods depended on its patronage and survival. Notwithstanding violent attacks on government collaborators, the state was always able to recruit blacks to enforce its will throughout the apartheid period. Sociologist Michael Savage calculated that the South African political system, including the homelands, spawned no less than three houses of parliaments and ten legislative assemblies comprising 1,270 members, as well as 121 ministers and 151 government departments. Presiding over these were 11 presidents or prime/chief ministers. All of this was 'not cheap to run'. In Savage's estimation between 10 per cent and 21 per cent of South Africa's budget in 1985–6 was directed to maintaining and policing the apartheid system. Ending apartheid would liberate considerable economic resources and provide very substantial scope for redistribution.[73] Yet it was also the case that a lot of people had a direct stake in the status quo because each of the ten homelands had very substantial numbers of civil servants. As the future of these patronage networks became more uncertain, so violence and instability increased.

On the occasion of Transkeian 'independence' in 1975, journalist Donald Woods described the homeland policy as a 'girdle of political firebreaks to contain the bushfires of independence'.[74] This was no doubt the government's intention. Yet, as Tim Gibbs shows, rather than acting as 'a breakpoint that unmoored African nationalism from its rural roots', some ANC leaders maintained connections with Bantustan leaders through the 1970s. Mandela's willingness to maintain contact with Transkei's 'collaborationist' paramount chief Kaiser Matanzima, a kinsman and old student friend, is a case in point. When Bantu Holomisa mounted a coup in the Transkei in 1987, senior ANC and Communist Party leader Chris Hani was fully prepared to take advantage of the support offered by Holomisa. Thereafter, the Transkei became 'an important stepping stone for the ANC back into South Africa'.[75]

In KwaNdebele and in Sekhukuneland, too, the ANC maintained an ongoing underground presence. Enos Mabuza, Chief Minister of the tiny isiSwazi-speaking homeland of KaNgwane (population approximately 180,000), led a delegation to meet with Oliver Tambo in Lusaka in 1986, thus making clear his general support for the ANC and the UDF. This respect was reciprocated, in stark contrast to the Congress Movement's attitude to Buthelezi.[76] Unlike other tribal homelands, KaNgwane continued to fly the South African flag so as to reiterate its rejection of Bantustan independence.

As the likelihood of political transition became greater, so latent forces in Bantustan politics revived or took on new life. The emergence of the Congress of Traditional Leaders of South Africa as a national organization in 1989 provided an institutional forum for chiefs and indunas whose sympathies lay with the UDF and the ANC. Their espousal of progressive rural leadership was a reminder that Pretoria had never fully succeeded in capturing tribalism for its own purposes. Equally, it signalled that the politics of state patronage were shifting in anticipation of a change of government. Pretoria's hold on the levers of power at the margins weakened even further in the febrile post-1990 period. And with unpredictable results.

In 1992, an ANC-led march on the Ciskeian capital, Bisho, which had been designed to bounce the homeland back into South Africa (the so-called 'Leipzig option'), resulted in a massacre of ANC supporters by the Ciskei Defence Force. Conversely, in 1994, the Bophutatswanan government's invitation to the right-wing *Afrikaner Volksfront* to help in its defence against striking civil servants encouraged the intervention of a fascist rabble led by Eugene Terreblanche. TV cameras showed the summary execution of three of these deluded adventurers by a member of the Bophutatswana police force (later revealed to be an ANC supporter) who shouted: 'Who do you think you are? What are you doing in my country?' The dramatic act of routing fascist white extremists, engaged in an unlikely defence of a homeland leader, paved the way to the Bantustan's reincorporation into South Africa and helped to advance a negotiated settlement between the ANC and the government.

Tipping the Balance

Amongst academic observers and journalists there was a broad view in the 1980s that the crisis in South Africa was moving into a terminal phase but no clear view as to how it would end, or what would follow. Superficially at least, the government seemed to be more secure in the second state of emergency than it was during the preceding one. In 1987 the left-wing political analyst Mark Swilling concluded: 'the oppressed majority do not possess the organizational capacity, political power or coercive strength to overthrow the state. Nor does the state have the ideological or political resources required to re-establish its dominance without coercion.'[77] The journalist Roger Omond thought that 'Negotiation, from the perspective of early 1987, seems an unlikely possibility': the cost of civil unrest was not yet too high for the country's security budget, sanctions had not yet proven themselves, and there was a lowering of expectation that Nelson Mandela would be freed.[78]

Two years later, leading historians Shula Marks and Stanley Trapido concluded that 'South Africa has reached an oppressive stalemate' with the government unable to satisfy popular aspirations and the regime unlikely to be toppled by insurrection or through ungovernability.[79] Howard Barrell, an expert on the ANC, concurred. Although the possibility of a negotiated settlement could not be excluded, talks might stretch inconclusively over many years with much blood flowing in the meantime.[80] Van Zyl Slabbert was more optimistic. In August 1988 he analysed soberly the prospects for multi-party negotiations and what they might entail. A year later, with F. W. de Klerk installed as state president, Slabbert could not 'imagine an international, regional and domestic environment more conducive to successful negotiations than that which he has inherited'.[81]

Breakthrough

In his astute survey of the South African crisis of the 1980s, Robert Price maintained that the precondition for negotiations leading to fundamental change was an extended period of economic decline combined with political unrest.[82] This is precisely what occurred over the decade. But what would provide the catalyst for talks between two nationalist movements which both continued to proceed on parallel path-dependent trajectories? Two events, one domestic, the other international, finally broke the impasse and paved the way for political transition.

In January 1989 P. W. Botha suffered a second stroke. He was persuaded to step down as leader of the National Party, though he clung on to the state presidency, leaving doubt as to where real executive power lay. In elections for party leader F. W. de Klerk, leader of the Transvaal Nationalists, narrowly won after several rounds of voting by the parliamentary caucus. De Klerk, who did not quite fit into either the *verligte* or *verkrampte* camps, was a skilled political operator with a long record of supporting traditional apartheid measures but few deep ideological convictions other than his religious conservatism.[83] He moved decisively to establish his authority and eventually forced Botha to step down with the support of party leaders. In August de Klerk succeeded Botha as state president.[84] He called a general election in September. The National Party lost significant ground both to the Conservative Party and the liberal Democratic Party. It was the government's poorest electoral performance since coming to power in 1948 yet the government could still rely on its overall majority of twenty-one seats and claim a mandate for change—by aggregating its own support with that of the Democratic Party.

De Klerk now revealed himself, rather surprisingly, as a dynamic reformer. He drew on his political capital as a conservative in order to persuade reactionaries in his own cabinet to follow his lead or at least not to block him. Barely suppressed hostility against Botha in the parliamentary party gave de Klerk a window of opportunity to set a new tone.[85] One of his first acts as president was to prohibit the use of the *sjambok* whip, that potent symbol of rural disciplinary power and police brutality, for purposes of crowd control. Another portent of change was de Klerk's decision, under some pressure, to permit a Big March of over 20,000 people, led by Bishop Tutu and other church leaders, to proceed through central Cape Town. De Klerk said: 'The door to a new South Africa is open. It is not necessary to batter it down. ... I want to appeal to those involved to encourage their leaders to come to the negotiating table.'[86]

De Klerk moved swiftly to dismantle the National Security Management System and to restore cabinet government. That he was able to do so with only grumbling resignation from the securocrats demonstrated that the 'creeping coup' which allegedly took place under Botha was reversible. Here, de Klerk proved able to capitalize on resentment within the civil administration against the encroachment of the military, as well as Botha's autocratic style of government. Equally important, it was clear to many in government that the hardliners had run out of ideas. The army's inability to overcome the combined Cuban and Angolan forces at the battle of Cuito Cuanavale in 1988 led to a crisis of morale within the South African Defence Force and weakened the position of Pretoria's securocrats. The claim that Cuito Cuanavale was a military defeat for South Africa is an exaggeration, but it is certainly true that accounts of the battle helped to demystify white power. By so doing, it provided inspiration to the liberation movements.

In a speech delivered in Cuba in 1991, Nelson Mandela reflected that 'the decisive defeat of the aggressive apartheid forces [at Cuito Cuanavale] destroyed the myth of the invincibility of the white oppressor' and paved the way to Namibian independence.[87] The military reverse in Angola was certainly a decisive factor in persuading South Africa finally to accept Namibian independence, following the Angola–Namibia Accords signed in New York in 1988 and Sam Nujoma's installation as Namibian president in 1990. Namibia's new liberal democratic constitution showed South Africa's leaders what could be accomplished through negotiations.[88]

The single most transforming event was the fall of the Berlin Wall in November 1989 and the ensuing swift collapse of Communist rule in eastern Europe. At a stroke, a key factor underpinning National Party rule in South Africa—the threat of Soviet expansionism in southern Africa—was removed. Fear of Communism had been an obsessive preoccupation for P. W. Botha and his acolytes, as his personal archives show all too clearly. The political solution in Namibia, which involved the withdrawal of Cuban troops from Angola from January 1989, offered further proof that international Communism presented no credible threat (if ever it had).[89] Moreover, the end of Soviet Communism deprived MK of military aid from countries like East Germany, upon which it was reliant.

Soviet President Gorbachev's bold political moves may well have influenced de Klerk too. Like Gorbachev, de Klerk hoped that by seizing political opportunities and introducing rapid reforms it might be possible to outmanoeuvre opponents and preserve the core of the existing system. P. W. Botha had tried to do the same a decade earlier. De Klerk was alert to the possibilities as well as the pitfalls of this approach. He was reported to have told associates at an informal gathering in 1988 that he had 'jumped the gap'.[90] In his autobiography, de Klerk states that he was aware of the need to overcome his 'natural instinct' to move incrementally. He realized the importance of grasping the initiative 'right at the beginning' in order to 'convince the important players that we were not negotiating under pressure, but from the strength of our convictions. We had to convince them . . . that we were not trying to cling to elements of apartheid under a different guise.'[91]

The first part of this statement, that de Klerk moved far faster than political habit would have suggested, is more plausible than the second. In 1990, de Klerk had no intention of negotiating himself out of power. Rather, he gambled that there was now a unique opportunity to initiate a process which stood the best possible chance of preserving important aspects of white power and privilege. In this, he miscalculated, just as Gorbachev had done in respect of *perestroika* and *glasnost*. Processes of structural reforms could not easily be halted once they were initiated. The law of unintended consequences applied to South Africa as well as the Soviet Union.

De Klerk certainly put the anti-apartheid movement off balance on the occasion of the opening of parliament on 2 February 1990 speech. He dramatically announced the unbanning of all political organizations, including the ANC, PAC, and the Communist Party, as well as the release of political prisoners, including Nelson Mandela. He committed the government to the negotiation of a new constitutional order. And for good measure he announced a moratorium on the death penalty.

De Klerk's speech was calculated to stun the world and it succeeded in doing so, catching the ANC and the Mass Democratic Movement off guard as well. Mindful of Botha's Rubicon disaster, it was professionally news-managed so as to maximize coverage but minimize expectations. The outline was presented to the cabinet under strict conditions of secrecy and there were no leaks beforehand. Journalists were given prior sight of the speech though only under a strictly policed embargo. Allister Sparks, ex-editor of the *Rand Daily Mail*, was one of these. Flipping through the pages, he remarked to his *Washington Post* colleague David Ottoway, 'My God, he's done it all.' De Klerk personally teased interest by, for example, ringing up the British ambassador Robin Renwick on the eve of his address to assure him that Mrs Thatcher would not be disappointed.[92]

De Klerk's speech was certainly more surprising in its content and showmanship than the one that Mandela delivered on the Grand Parade in central Cape Town on 11 February, the day of his release. In this somewhat staid performance, reading passages that had been written in formulaic struggle-prose by committee, Mandela reassured supporters that he remained a loyal, disciplined member of the ANC. He reiterated its determination to intensify the struggle, including by force of arms. This important message was primarily directed to his domestic constituency. Only the next day, in the gardens of Bishop Tutu's official residence in Bishopscourt, did Mandela begin to reveal the humane, conciliatory, and charismatic personality for which he is justly famed.[93]

Mandela's halting performance on the day of his release was soon forgotten. What remain in public memory are the dramatic images of his leaving Victor Verster prison after twenty-seven years of incarceration, hand in hand with Winnie Mandela, flashing the ANC's clenched fist salute. The mass ranks of television cameras from around the world struggled for a moment to locate him, partly because he emerged later than expected but mostly because so few were familiar with what he looked like. Mandela's march to freedom proceeded in the brilliant sunshine and saturated colours of the high Cape summer. History, myth, and deliverance combined to make this theatrical moment one of the world's great global spectacles. No one could know what the immediate future held. But nor could anyone doubt that the epoch of white minority power in South Africa was very nearly over.

CHAPTER 9
CONCLUSION

Denouement

Or perhaps not. Six months after Mandela's release the highly regarded historian George Fredrickson surveyed the South African political landscape for the *New York Review of Books*. He described the difficult choices faced by Mandela and the ANC leadership as the following: if the liberation movement was to sacrifice long-standing objectives in pursuit of power, it risked estranging militants who remained committed to the idea that power could only come from the barrel of a gun; yet without moderation, the ANC would be unable to achieve the compromise with the government that was a precondition for a new constitution. Turning to the government's position, Fredrickson thought it unlikely that de Klerk would agree to move directly to 'one-person-one-vote'. To do so would be to lose the support of most whites, allow the Conservative Party to come to power on a platform of reinstating apartheid, and make 'civil war virtually inevitable'. Realizing a non-racial South Africa therefore amounted to a balancing act that depended enormously on Mandela's personal powers of persuasion and commanding presence: 'there is simply no one else who could conceivably do it.'[1]

These predictions were probably on the pessimistic side: Fredrickson overestimated the capacity of militants within the ANC alliance to seize power, and he surely underestimated the scale of the shift in white politics, including de Klerk's willingness to endorse a universal franchise (albeit still hedged about with veto rights for minority groups).[2] With Tambo incapacitated, and Mandela not yet confirmed as the undisputed

267

leader of the ANC, it was by no means a foregone conclusion that Mandela's commanding presence was sufficient to unify the ANC and the different elements of the Mass Democratic Movement. Overall, however, Fredrickson's assessment was not too far off the mark.

It took four years for the process of political transition to take place, culminating in South Africa's first non-racial democratic election and the victory of the ANC with Mandela as the country's president. The inauguration ceremony, on 10 May 1994, was witnessed by an audience of 100,000 assembled below the Union Buildings, together with all the world's great and good (and some not so good). It was a spectacle that could scarcely have been imagined in 1990. Not a few people wondered whether the low-flying fighter jets spewing out the colours of the New South Africa in ostentatious vapour trails might instead strafe the exultant crowds with bullets or worse. In a speech whose mixture of emotion and solemn dignity was fully equal to the majesty of the moment, Mandela proclaimed the birth of 'a rainbow nation at peace with itself and the world'.[3]

Hugo Young of the *Guardian* newspaper accurately predicted in 1990 that it would take up to four years for negotiations 'to reach agreement—or not. It will be one of the most protracted and intensive parlays of modern times.'[4] Consensus had to be sought not only between the principal parties contending for power, but within those groups too. The ANC, catapulted from liberation movement to government-in-waiting, had much to resolve within its own dispersed and disparate ranks. Would the ANC remain committed to nationalization and socialism, as Mandela appeared to promise on his release from prison? Who would sit at the negotiating table? Would those parties and groupings inclined to wreck the talks be able to prevail? Could the daily toll of politically related deaths be slowed down?

The period of transition was the most turbulent in the country's already deeply fractious history. This had everything to do with the prevailing climate of political uncertainty and the withdrawal of constraints that characterized forty years of authoritarian rule. In the six years leading up to 1990, around 5,000 people died as a result of political violence; between 1990 and 1994 three times more people were killed. These statistics were an accurate reflection of the government's fragmenting authority and the political vacuum that emerged in consequence.

Confrontation between Inkatha and the ANC accounted for the vast majority of these deaths. Having previously been largely contained in Natal, the scale of violence became deeper and more widespread as it spread to the migrant hostels on the Witwatersrand, where many Zulu-speakers were based. Contemporaneous accounts of these clashes tend to follow political affiliations, with commentators in the progressive movement apt to blame Inkatha and their sponsors in the 'third force' security units of the state. New research on the violence in Thokoza and Katlehong townships after 1990 reassesses the 'dominant narrative' of collusion between the government and Inkatha, indicating that the situation was far more fluid and often lacking in overall direction. ANC-aligned Self-Defence Units and Inkatha Self-Protection Units operated on a semi-autonomous basis. The police's Internal Stability Unit was biased towards Inkatha, but the army tended to be more even-handed.[5]

An absence of overall control helps to explain the levels of political violence, which was not always subject to political direction! A leadership deficit also helps to explain why opportunities to broker peace between the ANC and Inkatha after 1990 were squandered or not taken up. It was easier for political leaders to use the violence to consolidate their own political support and to delegitimize their opponents.

Right up the very eve of the 1994 election, it was touch-and-go as to whether Inkatha would participate. The prospect of a boycott threatened the legitimacy of the entire process. In March 1994, thousands of Inkatha supporters marched to the ANC headquarters in Johannesburg to protest against the election. ANC guards opened fire on the crowd, killing nineteen. Thirty more Inkatha supporters were killed in clashes around Johannesburg. At the very last moment ballot papers had to be physically extended with paste-on stickers to accommodate Inkatha's inclusion.

The elections took place on 27–9 April and proved largely peaceful. In the event, the ANC won a landslide with just under 63 per cent of the vote, de Klerk's National Party secured 20 per cent, and the Inkatha Freedom Party just over 10 per cent. The Pan Africanist Congress and the Democratic Party attained less than 2 per cent each. In all, nineteen parties competed for the nearly 20m ballots that were cast.

In general, political violence took two forms. The first concerned the ANC and the government. Such violence tended to be perpetrated by proxies because both parties recognized the other's indispensable role in the transition and realized that direct, authorized confrontation carried serious dangers. It was to the advantage of the two leading contenders (as well as factions within them) to weaken the other. But it would be mistaken to assume that either side was fully in control of those forces which acted on their behalf.

The government's 'third force' was active in using Inkatha to weaken the ANC as part of a strategy to weaken its principal opponent's position at the bargaining table. For its part, the ANC targeted the regime at its perceived weak points, notably, the homeland governments where the liberation movements (including the PAC) could count on local support. The ANC authorized a clandestine military initiative, Operation Vula, to strengthen its underground capacity within the country. Vula may have been the most sophisticated field operation in MK's history, yet its accomplishments could not belie the rapid decline in MK capacity and effectiveness since 1989. When Vula's existence was exposed in 1990 by the security services, the government castigated the ANC for its lack of commitment to a peaceful settlement and made the most of the fact that Vula was dominated by Communist Party members; the ANC countered that Vula was merely designed as an insurance policy and was not a substitute for talks.[6]

Another source of violence came from fringe parties on the left and the right who were anxious to improve their visibility and bargaining power and, failing this, sought to wreck the negotiations. With the lifting of restrictions on political organizations, the PAC re-emerged into the open. Its armed wing, the Azanian People's Liberation Army (APLA), mounted nearly 150 operations in 1993, the so-called 'Year of the Great Storm'. Many of APLA's victims were farmers and farm-workers. Civilians were also targeted in urban areas, including worshippers at a church service in Cape Town. APLA's slogan of 'one settler, one bullet' gained publicity for the internally divided PAC yet did little to improve its political standing or rebuild its political constituency—as the party's poor showing in the 1994 election made clear.

Such attacks provided ammunition for the far right which also resorted to random violence. In 1993, the ANC's popular military hero and head of the Communist Party, Chris Hani, was gunned down outside his house outside Johannesburg. Three right-wingers, one English-speaking, another Polish, were arrested. The assassination raised political tensions to dangerous levels amidst fears that black anger would explode into violence. In an act of consummate statesmanship Mandela intervened publicly to call for calm. Hani's burial, which was covered in full by South African television, amounted to an unofficial state funeral. The shock of the killing prompted the leading negotiating participants to press harder to resolve the country's future.

As many as a dozen, mostly very small, paramilitary groups emerged after 1990 to defend Afrikanerdom.[7] Bellicose predictions of a 'third Boer war' were accompanied by acts of violence and intimidation, including indiscriminate shootings of black civilians in rural towns. The largest of the fascist paramilitary groups was the AWB, led by demagogue Eugene Terreblanche. In 1991, 2,000 AWB members tried to prevent President de Klerk from addressing a crowd in the organization's stronghold of Ventersdorp. To the shock and indignation of the AWB, three of its members were killed and many were injured in clashes with the police.[8]

Even more dramatic was the AWB's storming of the World Trade Centre in 1993 where the constitutional negotiations were taking place. An armoured car was used to smash through glass doors and delegates were forced to flee. The stunt ended in farce and failed to ignite broader right-wing support. General Constand Viljoen, ex-chief of the armed forces and now leader of the right-wing *Afrikaner Volksfront*, declined to support Terreblanche's rabble. Viljoen also drew back from supporting the AWB in March 1994 during the debacle of the 'defence' of Bophu-tatswana, when there was a distinct possibility of counter-revolution against de Klerk. The public execution of three AWB supporters in the full glare of television cameras finally punctured fantasies of far-right power and a return to the apartheid era.

Constand Viljoen has since claimed that in 1993 he could call upon as many as 60,000 trained and armed Afrikaners to go to battle with the ANC but he did not do so for fear of precipitating an all-out war.[9] Whatever his motivation, Viljoen drew the sting of the far right and acted as a moderating influence. In the end, the appeal of extreme ethno-nationalism—either in the form of unilateral independence for an Afrikaner *volkstaat*, or in the guise of virtual autonomy for Kwa-Zulu Natal—proved to be limited.

In a perverse alliance of convenience, Inkatha and the white right were joined together with two other Bantustan leaders. Their only real point of unity was common opposition to the ongoing negotiating process, a position that strengthened those parties who remained committed to peaceful resolution of the country's problems. When, at the very last moment, the right-wing Freedom Front and Buthelezi's Inkatha Freedom Party agreed to participate in the 1994 election, the way for a constitutional solution was made clear.

The political centre-ground, incongruously held by the ANC and the government, managed at crucial moments to hold together. There were severe tests, which included public fall-outs between de Klerk and Mandela and the suspension of constitutional talks. Yet it was evident that both parties increasingly depended on each other's cooperation. By entering into public negotiations after 1990, the ANC and the government crossed a political threshold that made retreat impossible. To do so would be to lose all credibility amongst their core supporters. Both had to rein in their own militants or rogue elements, but this was not always possible to accomplish.

Negotiations

The initial negotiations process began with the Convention for a Democratic South Africa (CODESA) at the end of 1991. This involved nineteen parties ranged along the ideological spectrum. It marked the beginning of a process of winnowing out more peripheral parties which left two principal participants, the ANC and the government, seeking to establish common ground on the principle of 'sufficient consensus'. Even when the government and the ANC were traducing each other in public, the skilled negotiating skills of Cyril Ramphosa for the ANC and Roelf Meyer representing the government brought them back from the brink. Journalists spoke of the 'Cyril and Roelf show'.

In effect, the ANC and the government had developed an unspoken 'pact'. This narrowly based agreement was intended to avert national disaster and implied their proceeding 'on their terms alone'.[10] The

CODESA process broke down in July 1992 after nearly fifty people were stabbed and hacked to death at Boipatong, a squatter camp south of Johannesburg. Many more were injured. The perpetrators were local Inkatha hostel-dwellers, the victims were said to be ANC supporters. There were reports, never proven, of police involvement, including by men with blacked-up faces. Either way, de Klerk said nothing and did nothing. Mandela blamed the government for the massacre and withdrew from the negotiations.

'The abyss was glimpsed at Boipatong, but its depths had yet to be plumbed.'[11] So writes Patti Waldmeier, whose account of the transition process after 1990 remains one of the best. With the negotiations in abeyance, Mandela needed to demonstrate the ANC's capacity to mobilize support. He led 50,000 supporters in a march to the Union buildings. A two-day national stoppage brought out millions of workers in sympathy. ANC radicals, led by Ronnie Kasrils, decided on a more insurrectionary path. In what was called the 'Leipzig option' (a reference to the mass demonstrations that helped to bring down the Berlin Wall) 70,000 or more ANC supporters converged on the capital of the Ciskei homeland, Bisho. Soldiers of the Ciskei Defence force opened fire. Around 30 marchers were killed and some 200 wounded. De Klerk was censured by the ANC, but it was apparent that Kasrils's impetuousness was also to blame.

In a highly flammable situation, Ramaphosa and Meyer steered the ANC and the government back from the brink. A 'Record of Understanding' was signed between the two parties in September 1992 which opened the way to the resumption of talks. The government and the ANC were in effect acknowledging that there was no alternative to striking a deal with one another: the risks of an extended impasse were demonstrably too great. 'They concluded that if they did not move forward quickly to agree on rule after apartheid, there might be little over which to rule.'[12]

Marginalized and enraged, Buthelezi sought to form an alliance with intransigent parties like Treurnicht's Conservatives. When, in July 1993, the government and the ANC finally agreed that national elections would be held the following year, Inkatha and the Conservative Party left the negotiations. Agreement on an interim constitution was reached in November 1993 and a multi-party interim government began to operate at the end of the year.

The story of the negotiations is enthralling, with plenty of sub-plots and dramatic twists. Although not inevitable, some form of negotiated settlement was always likely after 1990—if only because the survival of the ANC and the government increasingly depended on it. In 1990 de Klerk did not intend to negotiate himself out of power, and in the ensuing years he did all he could to manage the process so that he could weaken the ANC and preserve key elements of 'power-sharing'. One favoured tactic on the government's part was to stall for time, in the hope that the ANC would fragment, though this option narrowed as the 1994 deadline for an election drew closer. For its part, the ANC sought to compress the negotiations timetable, hoping that key decisions could be deferred until after an election, which it would undoubtedly win. There was no longer any realistic sense in which the ANC could seize power, as it had so often promised to do. MK was in disarray and its chief sponsor, the Soviet Union, was no more.

The terms of the talks changed over time, as did bargaining positions. Many of the ANC's more radical social demands were compromised or dropped altogether. The realities of operating in a global world, where neo-liberalism rippled forth from Washington, dampened calls for nationalization and socialist transformation. The apartheid government came into being in 1948 at a moment in world history when national states bore enormous prestige; in 1994, by contrast, nation states were declining in importance relative to the power of global markets and finance. Major South African corporations, their images burnished by glossy advertising agencies, were active in reaching out to the new elite, offering reassurances and promises. With remarkable speed, ANC leaders positioned themselves to accept the fruits of office. The white establishment was persuaded that their own fundamental economic interests would not be threatened by political transition. In the end a negotiated solution, well short of a revolution, was achieved.

Apartheid

In 1985, when interviewed by Ted Koppel for the American television programme *Nightline*, president P. W. Botha replied to a question about the future of apartheid by saying that it 'all depends on what you mean'.

'If you mean by apartheid the deprivement [*sic*] of fundamental rights to people, I say I'm all against it.'[13] These remarks came from the man who embodied the system. In the warm glow of the New South Africa, few admitted to ever having been in favour of apartheid. Its adherents slowly slipped away, gathering in the rueful recesses of the Conservative Party where they cried betrayal and sought to defend racial segregation on a local level.

Strikingly, when parliament agreed to the abolition of all remaining apartheid legislation in 1991, there was remarkably little political reaction; it was greeted as yesterday's news. Many key legislative acts, like the pass laws, had already been revoked. Some of apartheid's most hated proscriptions, like the Group Areas Act, were no longer being rigidly enforced. Job reservation had fallen into abeyance. A new, confident generation of South Africans was happy to honour the struggle against apartheid, yet often disinclined to remember the daily humiliations their parents had endured. The nation was enjoined to 'move on' and, if not to forget the past, to commemorate and memorialize it in ways that were politically unthreatening.

To be sure, there were some public apologies for apartheid on the part of senior members of the government and the churches. However, most simply spoke of regret in ways that avoided responsibility. The Truth and Reconciliation Commission was an important means of recording gross violations of human rights. It drew a great deal of attention while it went about its work in public, yet by the time it reported in 1998, the public seemed to have lost interest. Controversial on account of its preference for achieving emotional reconciliation over justice and economic restitution, the most important contribution of the TRC was probably its role in promoting the process of political transition and 'nation-building'.

For practical reasons the TRC decided to limit its purview to the period 1960–94. This did not make good historical sense. Nor was the TRC effective, if this was its purpose, in explaining or examining the underlying structural reasons for apartheid. Needless to say, the suspension and withdrawal of apartheid legislation did not mean that its legacy was terminated. As a consequence of generations, if not centuries, of conquest, inequality, and racism, apartheid remained imprinted on the landscape and in the mind. Left-wing critics denounced the deals struck by the ANC and the government which, in the view of critics like Patrick Bond, amounted to an 'elite transition' or pact.[14] The veteran left-wing Australian journalist John Pilger produced a film in 1998 entitled 'Apartheid did not Die'. Its underlying argument was that apartheid continued through economic means, notwithstanding deracialization.

There is no space to pursue this line of argument here. Suffice to say that the long shadow of apartheid remained a live issue in the centenary year of the ANC's foundation, as the shootings by police of platinum miners at Marikana in 2012 so graphically illustrates. It makes little sense to argue that, because the transition to a post-apartheid society has been incomplete, and the high hopes for liberation seldom realized, something very fundamental did not shift after 1990. As Mandela pointed out in reply to Pilger's sceptical questioning: the reason 'why South Africa was regarded as enforcing an evil system is the fact that racism was entrenched in the constitution of the country and in its laws'.[15] At the heart of that system of white supremacy, as Pilger was at pains to point out, was a capitalist economy which was reinvigorated by the end of apartheid. But for all that it profited from racial discrimination, capitalism did not create racism. To lose sight of apartheid's distinctiveness as a racially based regime of power is to overlook its singular importance in world history.

The policy of apartheid was born in fear, nurtured in hubris, and sustained through obfuscation. Its combination of perverse idealism and banal pragmatism helped it to endure for the greater part of the second half of the twentieth century. American journalist Jim Hoagland shrewdly observed that the defining difference between white supremacy as practised in South Africa, and in his native state of South Carolina, was that apartheid was projected as a 'mission'. At the height of apartheid, in the early 1970s, whites were 'always "giving" blacks freedom, or material rewards, or whatever'.[16]

In practice, apartheid was a highly exploitative system of racial domination which was underwritten by force and abetted by internalized rules of conduct. South Africa may not have been the most exploitative capitalist society in the world (though it was surely one of these). Nor was it the only society in the world founded on racial and ethnic division. But its statutory entrenchment of racial categories, coupled with the enormous disparity in wealth existing between rich and poor, was unparalleled in the second half of the twentieth century.

The extent to which South African racism and capitalism were mutually dependent remains subject to contestation. Wherever the emphasis is laid, the fact that the overwhelming bulk of the poor were black, and that most, if not all, rich people were white, is inescapable. In a world recoiling from the consequences of race supremacy and colonial domination, apartheid South Africa became the object of global—if not universal—condemnation. This qualification is important: although almost no one outside of South Africa expressed support for apartheid as such, there was no lack of international sympathizers for a white minority regime that claimed to stand as a bastion of Christian civilization, anti-communism, and the free market. This, too, is why apartheid had global ramifications: anti-apartheid activists in countries like the United States and Britain were, by opposing apartheid, engaged in fighting domestic political battles against the political right as well.

In a Word

The conspicuous use of 'apartheid' in the 1948 election brought South Africa to international attention. Although it was a neologism coined in a foreign language, 'apartheid' scarcely needed translation.[17] This single word, with its faintly Germanic taint and suggestion of hatred (apartheid-hate), crystallized the meaning of an entire system and helped to set the country on its way to pariah status. Had Malan merely insisted in 1948 on an intensification of segregation it is quite possible that South Africa's discriminatory policies would not have been singled out as a special case meriting international condemnation in the way that it was. By the same token, if Malan had not approved 'apartheid' as the National Party's unifying slogan, it is unlikely that he would have taken power in 1948.

The word 'apartheid' drew attention to policies that the post-war world increasingly found obnoxious. In an image borrowed from a poem by van Wyk Louw, veteran Afrikaans journalist Piet Cillié likened the word 'apartheid' to a small honed chisel (*'n klein, klein beiteltjie*) with the magical capacity to split first a pebble and then the entire world. In other words, 'apartheid' was a symbol, a lightning-rod, even a scapegoat that took away the sins of the world (*qui tollis peccata mundi*).[18]

Allowing for a measure of self-exculpation, Cillié had a point. For its detractors, apartheid was an affront to the principle of racial justice and a paradigm case of the denial of human rights. The same strictures were not applied to other societies where injustice was ingrained. It was accidental that modern concepts of human rights and of universal racial equality were being worked out at just the moment that Malan came to power: 1948 was the year in which the UN Declaration of Human Rights came into existence; in 1950 UNESCO published its first 'Statement on Race'.[19] Not only was the immediate post-war world a moment of revived internationalism, it was also one in which new states exchanged the yoke of colonial rule to bear the hopes of a better world to come.

Within a relatively short space of time, South Africa became a test case of the United Nations' capacity to act as a moral agent on behalf of humanity. This was particularly evident in the emerging field of international human rights, whose legal instruments were sharpened on the South African case. Defined as a 'crime against humanity' by the Apartheid Convention adopted by the United Nations General Assembly in 1973, 'apartheid' was designated as a 'grave breach' of the Geneva Convention (Additional Protocol 1 of 1977) and as a crime against humanity by the Rome Statute of the International Criminal Court in 1998. In this manner, its meaning and applicability was universalized so as to encompass ethnic or racially based state policies without geographical specificity—though this definition has never been successfully applied elsewhere. Nor has any South African ever been prosecuted for perpetrating apartheid which in reality (and for all practical legal purposes) remains *sui generis*.

Just as racism spawned its negation (anti-racism) so apartheid invited the term 'anti-apartheid'. This label was adopted by the boycott activists in Britain in 1960 and thereafter came to define a growing social movement. A year later, as South Africa's future in the Commonwealth was being debated, the South African Broadcasting Corporation announced that it would use the term 'apartheid' only in direct quotation marks—the euphemism 'self-development' was preferred.[20] Attempts by Verwoerd to describe apartheid as a synonym for 'good neighbourliness', or as a mechanism for 'separate development', were the first of many exercises at rebranding. Yet, for all that the system of apartheid evolved over the second half of the twentieth century, the word could not be expunged. It continues to exist as a free-floating linguistic grab-handle to characterize systematized racism and inequality.

Another reason why apartheid came to occupy a unique place in the world's attention was its prominent place in bi-polar international politics. Apartheid's rise as well as its fall broadly tracked the history of the Cold War. From first to last, apartheid was defended by its supporters in terms of anti-communism. Conversely, it was condemned by countries on both sides of the iron curtain, as well as by new states emerging from colonialism. Apartheid aroused horror and indignation on the part of democrats and anti-racists everywhere. There was, however, no unanimity about how to act against it.

In the West, sympathizers with the South African government weighed disapproval of racism against the greater evil of Soviet expansionism. This meant that powerful countries, notably members of the UN Security Council, were inclined to appease the South African government. Socialist and non-aligned countries identified in South Africa a unique confluence of racism and imperialism. They, or their leaders, were more prepared to countenance armed struggle to overthrow apartheid.

The region of southern Africa became a major theatre of the 'hot' Cold War from 1975. Liberation struggles in Mozambique, Angola, Zimbabwe, and Namibia were all deeply inflected by Cold War calculations, as testified by the involvement of the United States, Soviet Union, and China in sponsoring rival nationalist movements. In this geopolitical struggle, South Africa, the regional hegemon, was the single most important element. The arrival of the Cold War on South Africa's 'doorstep' created 'the spectre of the country being surrounded by hostile states directed by Moscow'.[21] This provided opportunities for South Africa's reformers to downplay apartheid as a system of racial rule by emphasizing the country's commitment to the defence of western interests. It also had the effect of broadening the base of anti-apartheid resistance by strengthening the idea that apartheid was not capable of reform without an end to the system of capitalist exploitation that underwrote racial rule.

The intensification of the anti-apartheid struggle and of the Cold War in the mid-1980s kept South Africa constantly in the international news, placing further pressure on the country's leadership. The issue was to the fore in editorial columns. Conservative British philosopher Roger Scruton spoke for many on the right when he alleged in the London *Times* that the ANC was 'the spearhead of Soviet domination'. Were it to 'accomplish its purpose, not only will the people of South Africa be deprived of their little freedom, but the West as a whole will receive a political, economic and strategic blow from which it will never recover.'[22] In a mirror image of such thinking, liberation in South Africa offered socialists and new left internationalists a rare prospect of socialist victory, crucial at a time when Reaganite and Thatcherite economic policies were making deep inroads. In a special 1986 issue of the socialist *Monthly Review*, devoted solely to South Africa, the editors emphasized the profound implications of the struggle against apartheid for 'world-wide revolutionary struggle' and the global future of capitalism: 'there is no other country in the world that has anything like the material and symbolic significance of South Africa *for both sides* in the conflict that rends the world today.'[23]

Anti-apartheid movements within the country were also deeply affected by the politics and ideology of the Cold War. The very meaning of the struggle against apartheid depended on whether apartheid was seen as separable from capitalism, and whether the nationalist struggle was viewed as a stage towards revolutionary socialism or principally in terms of the fight against racial oppression. In exile, it was the ANC's visible capacity to gain humanitarian, logistical, and humanitarian assistance across the ideo-logical divide that proved decisive in its survival. The ANC's capacity to combine nationalist and socialist constituencies as elements in a broad-based alliance assisted it to gain pre-eminence over its main rival, the PAC, whose fortunes were more closely tied to the political prospects and declining moral claims of post-colonial African states.

The politics of the Cold War were of key significance, too, in the timing of political transition, and in the character of the new democracy. Post-apartheid South Africa emerged at a moment of remarkable ideological hiatus in twentieth-century world history. Nelson Mandela's emergence as an icon of transcendent humanity and human rights was inextricably linked to this Cold War catharsis. The brief vogue for neo-liberalism helped to usher the ANC into power by creating a sudden vacuum which the oldest liberation movement on the African continent was best placed to fill. Neo-liberalism also helped to dissolve the ANC's commitment to socialism and fundamental economic redistribution (though this persisted at the level of rhetoric). Instead, redistribution became the means to satisfy the expectations of a relatively small group of politically connected individuals. The code word for this was 'black empowerment'. In effect, corporate resources were redistributed at the top in order to purchase political protection for those with wealth and influence but no direct power.

Global or Local?

Colin Bundy has pointed out that the anti-apartheid struggle was one of three great international causes to have galvanized transnational political solidarity in the twentieth century—the Spanish Civil War and Vietnam War being the others.[24] But, whereas the latter two were predominantly fought out on the battlefield, military conflict was only one aspect of apartheid, and by no means the most important. The struggle against apartheid endured much longer than either the wars in Spain or Vietnam. Whereas affiliations in Spain and Vietnam hinged on relatively clear choices, there were multiple claimants to justice and freedom in South Africa. Uniquely, the international fight against apartheid was not confined to Africa. It involved publics and governments in the socialist, capitalist, and non-aligned spheres too.

One of the first major international theorists to address South Africa in global terms was Hannah Arendt. In *The Origins of Totalitarianism* (1951) Arendt singles out South Africa as a paradigm example of racism and imperialism, maintaining that the country's modern history is defined by the confluence of (British) imperialism and (Boer) racism. 'South Africa's race society', she explains, teaches 'that through sheer violence an underprivileged group could create a class lower than itself, that for this purpose it did not even need a revolution but could band together with groups of the ruling classes, and that foreign or backward peoples offered the best opportunities for such tactics'. Arendt goes on to distinguish between the discovery of 'race as a principle of the body politic' in southern Africa, and of 'bureaucracy in Algeria, Egypt and India'. Had *Origins* been written a decade later she might have had occasion to revisit this judgement, because under Verwoerd bureaucratic control became a key dimension of racial rule.[25]

Arendt's historical analysis of South Africa does not bear close scrutiny (which is perhaps the reason why it is barely noted by scholars of that country). Yet the prominence that she ascribes to southern Africa in her account of the rise of totalitarianism is striking. Arendt did not explicitly mention apartheid (her manuscript was completed in 1950) but many others were quick to cast the new Nationalist regime as totalitarian or fascist.

In *The Rise of the South African Reich* (1964) the Communist journalist and activist Brian Bunting drew attention to the demonstrable affinities between leading Afrikaner nationalists of the 1930s and 1940s and national-socialism.[26] This line of argument was in keeping with the Communist Party's official position that the apartheid state was moving 'increasingly towards the pattern of fascism: an open, terrorist dictatorship of the most reactionary and racialist section of capitalists'.[27] Sociologist Pierre van den Berghe considered white supremacy in South Africa a form of *herrenvolk* democracy, although he thought the racism practised in southern states of the United States approximated more closely to apartheid than did Nazi Germany.[28]

That fascism and national-socialism were formative influences on substantial sections of the radical Afrikaner nationalist right is undeniable. But the influence was not overwhelming or enduring. There were equally strong Afrikaner nationalist traditions that were suspicious of Nazism as a 'foreign' ideology. Key Christian-Nationalists were concerned that national-socialism was a form of idolatry which, by idealizing individuals and the state, posed a challenge to the supremacy of God and the hallowed principle of *volk*-based nationalism.

In common with national-socialism, apartheid was racist, authoritarian, despotic, and bureaucratic. Another historical parallel lies in the strains of anti-Semitism that were especially evident in the 1930s and

1940s (though deliberately de-emphasized as overall white unity became a priority). For all that it was a totalizing ideology, apartheid was never totalitarian; a measure of dissent was always permitted and, notwithstanding censorship, a rich anti-apartheid culture of literature and music developed. Nor was apartheid exterminationist, though it is undeniable that countless people died as a direct and indirect result of its policies.[29]

In 1984 the celebrated French theorist Jacques Derrida pronounced apartheid to be 'Racism's Last Word'. He called it 'the unique appellation for the ultimate racism in the world, the last of many'.[30] Derrida's loose remarks were picked up by two South African literary scholars, Anne McClintock and Rob Nixon, who criticized him for blurring historical differences by 'conferring on the single term *apartheid* a spurious autonomy and agency'. They argued that in separating out the word from its history, changes in meaning and in the system risked being overlooked. Derrida shot back with a blistering, condescending, attack: 'Historical reality, dear comrades, is that in spite of all the lexicological contortions you point out, those in power in South Africa have not managed to convince the world, and first of all because, still today, they have refused to change the real, effective, fundamental meaning of their watchword: *apartheid*.'[31]

Grand-standing aside, Derrida had a point: the word apartheid had by now acquired a life of its own; its referents were no longer specific to South Africa, nor limited to the particular context in which it operated and evolved. Apartheid became a universal metaphor. For example, it became widely used to describe Algeria under French colonial rule or Israeli practices in occupied Palestine. The term 'global apartheid' began to circulate in the 1990s. This phrase denotes a world in which resources and wealth are unfairly distributed and controlled by a minority of rich (predominantly white) countries in the industrial 'North'.[32]

Closer to home, Mahmood Mamdani took issue with South African 'exceptionalism' in his widely discussed book *Citizen and Subject* (1996). Rather than focusing on the uniqueness of apartheid, Mamdani insisted that it should be situated in a comparative African context and seen as part of a common history of European colonialism. Apartheid, Mamdani argues, is 'the generic form of the colonial state in Africa'. It exemplifies a 'bifurcated' form of governance that combines aspects of 'decentralised despotism' (indirect rule) in the rural areas, with direct 'centralised despotism' (direct rule) in the cities. Thus, instead of understanding apartheid as 'institutionalized racial domination', it should be viewed as 'an attempt to soften racial antagonism by mediating and thereby refracting the impact of racial domination through a range of Native Authorities'.[33]

Mamdani's concern with indirect/direct rule is in some respects congruent with Harold Wolpe's earlier interpretation, from a Marxist perspective, of the key role of the migrant labour system in sustaining South African capitalism. Whereas Mamdani is mostly concerned with forms of governance and legitimization, Wolpe's focus is on political economy. Nevertheless, both view the relationship between rural and industrial areas as critical. Neither is concerned with racial ideology in the apartheid era. Both see apartheid as an extension of segregation and for this reason they tend to elide key differences between the two.

According to Wolpe, the key difference between apartheid and segregation lies in the changing needs of capitalism. In the segregationist era, he explains, capitalism relied on cheap labour provided by the migrant labour system. Under apartheid, levels of rural impoverishment meant that migrant labour, based on the exploitation of women's reproductive and productive capacities, was beginning to collapse. Apartheid thus marks 'the attempt of the capitalist class to meet the expanding demand for cheap African labour in the era of industrial manufacturing capital'. The retribalization of the reserves by means of the homeland policy has to be explained in terms of the 'control and supply of a cheap labour force, *but in a new form*'.[34]

Arendt, Derrida, Mamdani, and Wolpe all share a political present-mindedness that downplays historical specificity in favour of theoretical generalization: South Africa is thus seen as a paradigm example of racial rule (Arendt and Derrida); as the archetypal form of African colonial governance (Mamdani); or as the exemplification of a society based on maintaining a high rate of capitalist exploitation (Wolpe).

Historians, by contrast, are generally disposed to work from the particular to the general, to highlight differences as well as complementarities, and to be sceptical of overarching claims. In this book we approach apartheid from several perspectives: ideological, temporal, spatial, and experiential. Running through the analysis is a strong disinclination to flatten differences, or to confuse means with ends.

The Radical Critique

Liberal analysts like Michael O'Dowd were ultimately proved correct in their prediction that apartheid would prove economically unsustainable, at least in the long run.[35] Yet, at its height, in the 1950s and 1960s, apartheid delivered rapid economic growth and unprecedented levels of prosperity for whites. In these years it was demonstrably functional to capitalist growth. While highly exploitative, apartheid was economically inefficient, particularly for manufacturing industries that required increasing skills and investment. An economy based on the exploitation of cheap labour and the perpetuation of gross economic inequities had the effect of depressing domestic demand by restricting most consumers to satisfying the most basic of human needs. Continued economic growth required external investment, but this vital ingredient was increasingly constrained by political instability or, in other words, by sustained resistance to white minority rule.

These structural problems were not generally apparent in the early 1970s when the economy was still in a growth phase. The rise of the radical critique of apartheid at that time drew on broader post-colonial and Marxisant ideas, including the widely prevalent economic 'dependency thesis' associated with writers like Andre Gunder Frank, Samir Amin, and Walter Rodney. This critique of post-war modernization denied that the wealth of the capitalist industrial nations had been acquired as a result of the singular genius of the West; on the contrary, it was proposed that wealth was accumulated by actively impoverishing the rest of the world (the slave trade was an important part of this process). South Africa offered a striking twist to this conception because it exemplified rapid economic growth *notwithstanding* a long colonial history, with white prosperity existing alongside black poverty and manifestly benefiting from it.

How was this achieved? The theory of 'internal colonialism' or 'colonialism of a special type' was utilized by Communist Party intellectuals to explain how the extraordinary wealth enjoyed by the white minority (as a result of imperialism and monopoly capitalism) was acquired by systematically exploiting the black majority. Sociologist Harold Wolpe was one of the more sophisticated of these theorists. His conceptualization of segregation and apartheid was, in effect, an 'internal form of dependency theory'.[36] There were many variants of Marxisant analysis and lively, sometimes acrimonious, debates between them. For all these differences in approach there was a broad consensus on the left that liberal economists were fundamentally wrong (as well as self-serving) in presuming that racial strictures were inimical to economic growth and modernization.

These ideas were worked out at a sophisticated level both within South Africa and elsewhere. From the early 1970s a number of influential academic networks developed at centres in Britain, the United States, and South Africa, which subjected liberal assumptions about South African history and society to intense scrutiny. The 'revisionist' or 'radical' approach was energized by a political commitment to fundamental social transformation in South Africa. Politically engaged scholarship flourished. The liberal/radical or race/class debate, as it soon became known, centred on two key problems: the relationship of apartheid to capitalism, and the relative importance of ideology and political economy as a means of understanding race, ethnicity, and nationalism. These debates no longer command the attention and passions that they once did, but it is impossible to understand modern South African historiography without understanding their key points of difference and reference.

Most liberal scholars took for granted that apartheid was an Afrikaner creation and sought to explain apartheid in terms of ethnic power and racial ideology. Liberal economists took the view that the free market was rational and colour-blind; left alone, it would tend to dissolve racism. By contrast, radicals maintained that capitalism was integral to apartheid and that racial ideology could be explained in terms of the 'needs' of capitalism. The strong version of this thesis held that apartheid directly served the interests of capitalism or particular sections of the capitalist class. Weaker variants maintained that capitalism benefited from apartheid, though without insisting that race was entirely directly reducible to class. Common to both was the assumption that the struggle against apartheid was inseparable from the struggle to overcome capitalism.

Marxist analysts tended to divide between (a) 'structuralists' who theorized about the precise relationship between capitalism, race, and the state, and (b) social historians who eschewed deterministic forms of analysis and cavilled at functionalist or instrumentalist efforts to explain apartheid policies and the workings of the state in terms of the require-ments of the dominant class (or class fraction). Social historians were increasingly concerned with the texture of class domination as well as with manifestations of popular resistance by workers and peasants to segregation and apartheid. For a decade or more from the early 1970s, the debates between the Marxist structuralists and social historians were conducted with an intensity matching that of their arguments with liberals.

Marxist radicals or 'revisionists' attacked liberal scholars for failing to understand the salience of class, as well as for complacency in holding Afrikaners responsible for apartheid. In staking out new territory, the 'liberal school' was apt to be caricatured. As a result, there was greater accentuation of differences than was strictly justified. By the mid-1980s, when theoretically oriented 'structuralist' Marxism was in decline, the lines of division between radical and liberal historians were becoming blurred. Almost everyone agreed that class was an important dimension of apartheid and, reciprocally, that race and ethnicity could not be mechanically reduced to class.

In retrospect, the liberal/radical debate was not quite as polarized or novel as many presumed at the time. Prior to the emergence of the revisionist school, there was already a considerable tradition of Marxist historical analysis of resistance that emanated from outside the academy.[37] Class was a key concept for revisionists, but there were other non-Marxist attempts to understand key issues such as labour migration and social stratification in fields such as economics, sociology, and anthropology. Here, the influence of Weber and Durkheim, rather than Marx, was clear.[38] Even as the radical critique was gathering force, Weber remained an underlying influence. In the case of apartheid's origins, for example, Dunbar Moodie's Weberian *The Rise of Afrikanerdom* (1975) was com-monly read alongside, rather than against, Dan O'Meara's Marxist *Volks-kapitalisme* (1983). Heribert Adam's important study *Modernizing Racial Domination* (1971) was terminologically, rather than analytically, at variance with contemporaneous Marxist theories of nationalism and the state.[39]

Liberals and Marxists were also in broad agreement about the defi-ciencies of Afrikaner nationalist historiography, though they differed about the salience of 'ideology' and 'ethnicity' as explanatory variables. Afrikaner nationalist historiography dominated the South African school curriculum from the 1960s, placing particular emphasis on the Afrikaners' dual struggle to (i) secure Christian civilization against the forces of African barbarism and (ii) overcome British imperialism. Liberals and radicals both attacked the central foundation myths of Afrikaner nationalism. These included the demonstrably fallacious claim that white settlement was largely based in areas where blacks were not present, as well as Afrikaner nationalism's veneration of the Boers' 'Great Trek' into the interior and their unquenchable desire to achieve republican status. From the 1970s, dissident Afrikaner historians, philosophers, and theologians deepened this critique from within. In the process they helped to open up political fissures within the Afrikaner nationalist movement.

Ideas and ideology seemed to matter more in the 1970s and 1980s than at any stage of modern South African history. Norman Etherington rightly spoke of history as the 'master tool of intellectual resistance to apartheid'.[40] History fed into political debates, awakened consciousness, and conditioned understandings of the present. It would be difficult, for example, to understand the emergence of the independent union movement at this time without an appreciation of the contribution of Marxist theories of the labour process. Support for economic sanctions, particularly on campuses in the United States and Britain, was explained and debated in terms of theories of exploitation and western imperialism that were widely taught in classrooms and seminars. Support for non-racism in the ANC and the UDF was significantly influenced by discussions about the relationship between race, class, and nationalism. At the other end of the political spectrum, conservative thinking about consociationalism and federalism were influential in neo-apartheid government reforms. Theories about counter-revolutionary action were taught in military academies, with demonstrable practical consequences.

Forty years after the explosion of the historical and sociological debates of the early 1970s, it is time to stand back and see the intellectual expansion of this period in broader terms. This requires less concentration on the scholastic divisions of that era, and more attention to broader currents of thought which elude compartmentalization. The spread of new left thinking had echoes in white radicalism as well as in Black

Consciousness circles. It is palpable, for example, in the Spro-cas commission, whose reports served as an intellectual clearing house for new ideas—so crucial at a time of severe repression and political quiescence within South Africa.

The relative neglect of Spro-cas may have to do with the fact that it was intellectually diverse, reformist, and Christian-inspired, drawing as it did on liberal, Marxist, and Black Consciousness ideas. This eclecticism was remarkable in a society that was so divided. The intellectual activists of the Black Consciousness movement were in many ways far more radical than either the left or the right realized at the time. Black Consciousness articulated a view of liberation that had to begin with a transformation in the black self-image. It had no set view on capitalism or socialism, nor any clear political programme.

Radicals and Marxists, schooled alike in secular rationalism (and disinclined to subject the tenets of non-racism to deep scrutiny), often found Black Consciousness unpalatable and discomfiting. It was tempting to treat its political emotionalism with condescension, or to see it as merely a transitory phenomenon. Political radicals were inclined to explain Black Consciousness away by deploying class analysis, that is, by seeing it as the ideology of urban middle-class student intellectuals who were alienated from the real agents of change, the (black) working class.

The contemporaneous feminist movement in Europe and North America faced similar critiques when it argued that true liberation could be achieved only by focusing on 'the personal' as well as 'the political'. Historical materialists took comfort in the idea that their analyses were scientifically based and validated by the laws of history, rather than affected by subjective feelings. Yet there were important, mostly unacknowledged, emotional and political issues at stake for white radicals too.

It should not be overlooked that Marxist analysis permitted white intellectuals and activists to project themselves as equals in the struggle. This was so because it appealed to universal principles (class, internationalism) in much the same way that liberals appealed to transcendent ideas (democracy, humanity). Radical white intellectuals also thought it their duty to educate the black working class about the nature of their oppression. They were not so quick to appreciate how their ideas reflected their own experience and place in society. The discussions between Steve Biko and Rick Turner alert us to some of these dynamics.

Ideas feature more strongly in this book than in many other accounts of apartheid, not least because they have the power to animate action and therefore have real consequences. Indeed, one of the arguments in this book is that apartheid was itself an idea as well as a reality. This helps to explain why it caught the conscience of the world and also why so much intellectual effort was put in to redefine and reformulate it from the 1970s. All South African leaders 1948–94 were drawn into tortuous definitions and redefinitions of apartheid—probably to a greater extent than, say, Israeli leaders have felt it necessary to formulate 'Zionism', or Irish leaders have had to explain 'Unionism' or 'republicanism' to outside audiences.[41] Notably, apartheid acquired overwhelmingly negative connotations for all but its adherents almost as soon as it was coined. It was this point that Jacques Derrida was seeking to make when he called apartheid 'the ultimate racism'.

A Protean Ideology and Set of Practices

As Derrida's interlocutors were quick and correct to point out, apartheid's meaning was pliable and unstable, rather like the system it denoted. For those who sought to attack it from a distance, it was tempting to overlook the complexities and contradictions that made up the system of apartheid, lent it its dynamism, and allowed it to adapt in form and content. Apartheid was never one thing. Its meaning changed over time, it was experienced differently from region to region, its effect on people varied by class, age, and gender. The world condemned apartheid as though it was a unitary phenomenon. But most South Africans would probably have condemned specific policies of 'the government' or the practices of its functionaries. We should not therefore presume that ordinary South Africans thought of themselves constantly as living 'under' apartheid. Oppression was experienced at the hands of the police, the employer, the farmer, the official. Apartheid was a more abstract political conception, signalling an awareness that there was a 'system' responsible for oppression.

No general statement about what apartheid *was* is likely to be convincing. In 1948 South Africa was only one of several settler states in Africa characterized by minority racial rule. It was still a respected member of the British Commonwealth. In some respects, 'apartheid' made South Africa appear more exceptional than it actually was by comparison to other colonial societies at the time. Two decades later it was a truly exceptional pariah state.

Over the course of forty years the system of apartheid was elaborated, refined, and remixed. By 1990 the ideology of apartheid was so discredited that even the government was apt to deny that it supported the system of governance and exploitation it had built up over forty years. Ultimately, the end of apartheid signalled not so much the eradication of a system—key structural components of which remained intact—as the removal from power of the last regime in Africa where a white minority remained in power. It was far easier to define the abolition of the apartheid *state*—its constitution, its leaders, its legislation, its capacity to repress—than it was to efface the underlying system of inequality that it underwrote.

The argument presented here is that apartheid was, in the first instance, the specific means by which radical Afrikaner nationalists realized their ambitions to achieve political mastery over South Africa. Apartheid was not in these very early years a radical innovation. It was, as Malan claimed, an intensification of the segregationist system of racial rule which emerged together with the South African nation state in the early years of the twentieth century. The origins of segregation can in turn be traced back to forms of colonial rule in the mid-nineteenth-century British colonies of Natal and the Cape. Apartheid's distinctiveness lay (i) in the fact that it was an ethno-nationalist project; (ii) that it amounted to a very significant intensification of a corroding segregationist regime; and (iii) that this intensification occurred just as the climate of international opinion was becoming increasingly antagonistic to imperialism and racism.

Neither of the first two prime ministers responsible for introducing apartheid was much concerned with its ideological aspects. For Malan, apartheid was the means to unify the *volk* and achieve Afrikaner political supremacy. For Strijdom, apartheid was quite simply about domination or *baaskap*: it was as simple as ensuring that blacks and whites did not compete for jobs or sit on the same buses. Under Verwoerd, apartheid became not just a means to an end, but increasingly an end in itself. Crude racial domination or *baaskap* was always central to the lived experience of apartheid. Verwoerdian ideology took this further and consummated apartheid as the highest stage of white supremacy. The level of social and spatial engineering undertaken by Verwoerd and his successors created stubborn 'facts on the ground' that have proved very difficult to undo in the post-apartheid era.

Crucially, apartheid provided Verwoerd with the opportunity to seal the two political objectives with which he began his political career: Afrikaner ethno-nationalism and the cause of republicanism. Verwoerd understood that protecting poor whites required racially based job reservation but it was only later that he came to focus on the broader ideological aspects of apartheid. The issue of apartheid proved to be the point of rupture with the Commonwealth and so ushered in a republican state; the breach with the Commonwealth and the experience of Sharpeville also shifted the government's emphasis from Afrikaner exclusivity to white supremacy more generally.

As Minister of Native Affairs Verwoerd came to realize that maintaining administrative control over the vast majority of the population offered him a hitherto untapped source of political power. As prime minister, Verwoerd persuaded himself that the ideal of total racial separation might be achievable if the homelands could be configured as quasi-independent, ethnically bounded, sovereign states. In this way apartheid would not only guarantee white supremacy and prosperity, but might also provide a permanent solution to African political aspirations—so long as these were expressed within the context of ethnic separation.

This enhanced vision of apartheid had already been adumbrated by Afrikaner intellectuals and theologians who viewed apartheid as a logical extension of nationalist destiny and also as a morally sound solution to the intractable problem of colour. Considerable national pride was invested in the idea that apartheid was an indigenous Afrikaner creation grounded in the long experience of the *volk* and therefore consistent with its unique, divinely ordained mission in Africa. Verwoerd's talent for social engineering, coupled with his ideological dogmatism, offered the possibility of translating a utopian vision into reality. There was no necessary reason why the system of apartheid that emerged under Malan and Strijdom should acquire the ideological intensity and rigorous self-deluding logic that Verwoerd invested it with. This was distinctive. Nowhere else in the post-war world was racial rule justified and entrenched with such systematic thoroughness. To lose sight of this doctrinaire quality is to misunderstand apartheid.

Verwoerd could also be pragmatic (most politically successful ideologists are also realists). He was not prepared to dispense with the system of cheap African labour upon which the South African industrial economy and white supremacy depended. Only a handful of idealists were ever prepared to sacrifice white prosperity for the apartheid utopia. Apartheid was therefore not ultimately driven by ideology. It did not, for example, represent the imposition, on a modern industrial society, of a racially based system grounded in the experience and theology of stubborn, isolated Boer frontiersmen. At least until the early 1970s, apartheid proved compatible with rapid economic growth. It was far more adaptable and less monolithic than critics allowed. It was fully geared towards modernization in areas like agriculture, industry, and technology. In short, apartheid was one of many extra-European instances of the post-war developmentalist state.

Apartheid was a multi-dimensional set of practices. It was an economic system that turned people into closely controlled labour units; it was an expression of Afrikaner nationalism; it was an elaborate form of racial and ethnic division; it was social engineering on the grand scale; it was a method of governance combining outright repression with internalized habits of deference and paternalism born of centuries of master–servant relations. As a system, it went through several different phases. In the first decade after 1948, key foundational apartheid legislation was laid down, most of which amounted to a strengthening of existing legislation and the application of *baaskap*. From 1959, the Verwoerdian idea of 'separate development' was unveiled and the principle of ethno-nationalism was extended to Africans by way of ethnic homelands. Opposition was crushed after Sharpeville, 1960, and driven underground. This was the period of 'high' apartheid.

From the late 1960s, the beginnings of a more flexible form of apartheid, involving very limited reforms, were introduced. Structural reform began in the 1970s, principally in response to the revival of domestic black opposition and relative economic decline. The 1976–7 Soweto uprising was a key inflection point. After this moment, old-style apartheid ideology was in retreat, and there were ambitious, if ad hoc, attempts to remodel thoroughly the foundations of white supremacy. This was the ambiguous moment of neo-apartheid. By the mid-1980s, government-led reforms stalled and a violent stalemate was reached between the forces of liberation and those of reaction. From the end of the 1980s, it was apparent that political negotiations, without preconditions, were the only possible way of averting civil war.

Fragmented Experience

A black person living in a resettlement camp in the 1970s would have experienced the effects of apartheid very differently from a family member with rights to live in an urban area. A 'coloured' labourer on a wine farm or a fishing community in the south-west Cape might not automatically feel kinship with an Indian sugar-cane worker in Natal. The lives of both were significantly different from that of an itinerant African sheep-shearer in the Karoo. The world of a middle-class Indian family in Chatsworth, Durban, did not necessarily coincide with a prosperous coloured family in Bellville, Cape Town, or an African family in one of the wealthier neighbourhoods in Soweto. Political constraints on these communities varied, as did their schooling and access to jobs. Apartheid ideology relied on a vision of separate development for communities imagined in terms of officially coded categories. In many respects, social engineering gave these categories a reality on the ground. The fight against apartheid made it incumbent upon diverse communities to reimagine themselves as united in oppression.

This process of reimagining was not easy to achieve. South Africa's existence as a unitary state only goes back to its (unlikely) unification in 1910. Regional differences, based on the existence in the nineteenth century of multiple African kingdoms, two Afrikaner republics, and two British colonies, continued to affect South Africa's historical development. Hence, the characterization of pre-1948 South Africa as a 'state without a nation'.[42] Social and political geography was almost as divisive as racial or ethnic diversity. Apartheid's grand planners were more than alert to the fact that control of space, both in urban and in rural areas, was key to the maintenance of power. This underlay the conspicuous determination to enforce the Group Areas Act in urban areas and to remove untidy 'black spots' in the countryside.

Afrikaner and African nationalism shared an ambition to control a centralized state. Yet both nationalisms remained regionally based in profound ways, which is why the National Party, the African National Congress, and the UDF were all constituted on a provincial basis. These organizations had to work hard to overcome regional differences and power-bases that were in turn correlated with distinct political traditions. There was widespread recognition that, in order to be effective at a national level, regionalism had to be contained. This was an essential part of nation-building.

In the case of the National Party, power meant white unity under Afrikaner leadership, as opposed to divided nationality for everyone else—in other words, divide and rule. The fiction by which the white demographic *minority* came to be conceived as a political *majority* involved sleight of hand; it persuaded most whites even though it convinced no one else. Multiple layers of ideology and readings of history worked to remind whites of their inalienable rights to South Africa. The strategy of ethnic division failed to achieve legitimacy. Yet it worked well enough to persuade a substantial minority of Africans that they had real material interests in upholding the Bantustan system—which represented the apogee of ethnic division. Apartheid's high ideologists insisted that blacks had no permanent place in the cities and purported to treat all urban Africans more or less the same, regardless of class or status. This attitude was exemplified by the levelling effects of Bantu Education. Even so, counter-measures were introduced to maintain social gradations through co-optation, above all by differentiating between urban 'insiders' and 'outsiders' via the influx control and labour bureaux system.

Similar countervailing forces can be seen in the case of the removal of coloureds from the common voters' roll in the mid-1950s, which was often understood as an effort to reduce all 'non-whites' to a common state of rightlessness. No homeland was created for coloureds, yet the introduction of the so-called 'Eiselen line' in the western Cape was

effective for some considerable time in insulating working-class coloureds from competition with African labour. This, too, was a means
of distinguishing between 'insiders' and 'outsiders', configured according
to conceptions of racial difference. The enforcement of separate residential areas for coloureds, Indians, and Africans in metropolitan areas was
another instance where ethnic and racial distinctions, often overlaid by
the faultlines of class, were utilized to fragment the possibility of united
opposition to apartheid.

As white power began to weaken from the mid-1970s, so the state's
tendency to flatten social and class differences rendered it increasingly
vulnerable. This was the lesson of 1976–7: there were insufficient internally policed social constraints amongst urban blacks to stem revolt. The
government reforms introduced after the Soweto uprising marked a
revived attempt to reconstitute social and ethnic buffers, in particular
by removing some of the arbitrary constraints on social mobility. A key
aspect of this strategy was the attempt to foster the development of an
African middle class with a more permanent foothold in the cities. This
amounted to a sharp break from Verwoerd's ruthless attack on the
established African middle class.

In order further to divide political opposition, which increasingly
identified itself as 'black', constitutional changes were introduced featuring new parliamentary houses for coloureds and Indians. The government's strategy of co-optive domination did not succeed, partly because
the reforms were introduced too late, but mostly because a key legacy of
1976 was that 'the system' itself was now the object of attack. Reforms
were never able to restore the legitimacy of the state and compliance
became more and more difficult to achieve. Nevertheless, it remained
true that compliance could be secured without active consent. As conservative political theorists have long taught, it is possible for deeply
unpopular regimes to maintain power with only minority support so
long as sufficient compliance can be secured from the majority. Conservatives and cynics are not the only commentators to make this point.
James Scott, whose sympathies lie firmly with the poor and the dispos-
sessed, has equally observed:

No matter how conscious members of a subordinate class may be of having gotten a raw deal, the daily pressure of making a living and the risks of open defiance are usually enough to skew the ethnographical record systematically in the direction of compliance, if not acceptance, of the inevitable. . . . A certain tone of resignation is entirely likely in the face of a situation that cannot, in the short run, be materially altered.[43]

The questions that no one could reliable answer were (a) at what cost would this compliance be procured? and (b) for how long?

Historical Inevitability

All blacks did not resist all of the time: they 'did not live by politics alone'.[44] This is amply borne out by Jacob Dlamini who eloquently evokes the sensory aspects of township life. In doing so, Dlamini warns against the tendency, evident on both sides of the apartheid divide, to homogenize Africans and to neglect people as individuals. This was evident both in respect to apartheid ideology that often treated black people as 'one undifferentiated mass', as well as 'a liberation movement that almost always depicted blacks as indistinguishable heroic "masses of our people"'. Both views obscured 'the differences that made black life interesting and complex'.[45]

Although academic historians have been alert to the differences that make people and situations 'interesting and complex', many politically engaged narratives of 'the struggle' have been disinclined to ask probing questions about what motivates people, whether as individuals or as groups. Endless liberation movement narratives have spoken of victories and defeats along the certain—if long and bumpy—road to freedom. Such teleological accounts pay considerably less attention to defeats or periods of hiatus than to victories and active phases of resistance. This is in the nature of patriotic or propagandist history.

In order better to understand the longevity of apartheid, and the scale of the task involved in overthrowing it, historians have surely to account for evidence of accommodation or coexistence. Dlamini does just this in the case of Katlehong, a large township east of Johannesburg that became synonymous with fratricidal war and violence in the 1990s—but which was far more settled in the decades before, when the distinction between resistance and collaboration was rather less clear. Another historian who takes this approach, Tshepo Moloi, considers why Maokeng township in Kroonstad was relatively slow to join in the rebellion of the mid-1980s. Part of the reason for restraint in Maokeng, Moloi explains, has to do with the influence of 'respectables' on the local council chaired by mayor Caswell Koekoe, who was seen to act effectively on behalf of local residents by improving infrastructure while holding down rents. This helped to forestall UDF activism against 'sell-outs'.[46]

These local studies bear out Jeremy Seekings's observation that there was a general absence of confrontationary protests in the major urban conurbations of the Gauteng region (including Soweto and Mamelodi) between 1977 and 1984. Revolt was not always the norm; states of relative 'quiescence' also have to be accounted for.[47] It is generally more difficult to account for events that did not occur than for those that did. But even the latter forms of explanation are elusive. Compelling reasons why outbreaks of violence or defiance occurred at a particular moment and in a particular place are difficult to provide: neither Sharpeville (1960), Durban (1973) Soweto (1976), nor even the Vaal Uprising (1984) has been definitively 'explained' in this sense. Levels of political alienation can be gauged, relative deprivation can be measured, employment rates and the cost of living can be tracked. All these, and more, are key factors that condition revolt. But the precise grievances and triggers for political tumult can only ever be identified in retrospect; the ramifications take even longer to explore and understand.

From the 1950s onwards, observers and activists argued that the end of apartheid was inevitable. After Sharpeville, many forecast that the apartheid regime would soon collapse. The PAC claimed victory would be won by 1963. Within ANC circles, it was often said that apartheid would end 'within five years', but no one could say with confidence when to start counting. In 1976 the ANC adopted the slogan 'The Struggle Continues! Victory is Certain!' This rallying cry (which is best read as an expression of faith) was adopted from the slogan 'a luta continua—a victoria é certa', in common use in Mozambique and Angola. Yet, as the two-part expression implies, it is one thing to declare ongoing struggle, quite another to forecast victory, and something else again to specify exactly what victory comprises.[48]

In a very general sense the end of apartheid *was* inevitable. But this does not mean the manner of its ending was predictable. One major constraint to the continuation of minority rule was South Africa's changing demographic reality. William Beinart observes that population growth and African urbanization were realities that apartheid could modify, but not control. He is undoubtedly correct to argue that apartheid's failure to change fundamental demographic facts 'played a central role in the demise of the policy'.[49] Demographic shifts saw the white proportion of the total population almost halve from 19.5 per cent in 1948, to 11.3 per cent in 1994.[50]

The other major constraint was the secular decline in economic performance. Charles Feinstein's analysis of South Africa's performance against a sample of thirty comparable market economies offers some striking insights. From 1913 to 1950 South Africa topped his sample in respect of annual GDP growth per capita (1.3 per cent); in the period 1950–73, its annual growth rate (2.2 per cent) exceeded only the African countries in the sample; in the period 1973–94, South Africa was the only country to experience negative growth (–0.6 per cent) as compared to a sample average of 2 per cent. This dismal overall performance has also to be seen in terms of relative economic deprivation. Per capita income in South Africa for whites was around 13 times higher than for Africans in the 1960s era of 'high' apartheid. By 1994 the differential had narrowed to 8.6. The gap was still so large that, when measured on the Gini coefficient of inequality, only one country in Feinstein's sample, Brazil, had a more unequal distribution of pre-tax income.[51]

South Africa's changing demographics and deteriorating economic conditions undoubtedly had major effects on apartheid. But these facts do not of themselves explain the erosion of apartheid. A generation after the defeat of white minority rule, it may therefore be appropriate not only to ask why apartheid was defeated, but also to pose the question as to why it survived so long. Inverting the expectation of rebellion does not do disservice to revolutionary movements or the individuals that comprised such movements. On the contrary it highlights all the more clearly those who made enormous sacrifices to secure a better future, as against others, often the majority, who opted to work within, or accommodate themselves to, the iniquities of the present.

This point also reminds us that, although apartheid was at its core a system of racial rule, it was never just a simple struggle waged between blacks and whites, let alone between African and Afrikaner nationalism. The system of apartheid was always dependent on a degree of black support. The Bantustans were designed to give at least some Africans some considerable stake in the system by providing them with civil service jobs and affording them powers of patronage. As apartheid reformed from the late 1970s, there were concerted, if belated, efforts to create a buffer African middle class in the urban areas. Clumsy attempts were also made to give Indians and coloureds a stake in the system through the tricameral parliament. The vast majority of whites supported apartheid. But a significant minority opposed the system. Their contribution to opposition groups, ranging from liberal organizations to the liberation movements, was considerable and often disproportionate, not least (but not only) because of the resources and contacts they had access to. No liberation struggle in Africa was more committed to the principles of non-racialism than the fight against apartheid. This feature of resistance is apt to be overlooked.

A number of books presume the fall of apartheid with titles bearing versions of 'rise and fall'. This book resists such teleological readings, pointing out that neither apartheid's emergence nor its dissipation was ordained. A few examples must suffice: almost no one expected the National Party to win the 1948 election; having done so, it was not clear how apartheid would be implemented; apartheid's trajectory from the late 1950s took it into a higher ideological orbit than anyone other than its most starry-eyed supporters could have imagined; had Verwoerd died at the hands of David Pratt in 1960 it is unlikely that apartheid would have been pursued with comparable ideological vigour; the ANC's decision to embrace the armed struggle may have extended, rather than reduced, the longevity of white minority rule; the vicissitudes of the ANC in exile were such that its survival as the leading element of the liberation movement could not be assured; outlasting the PAC was always likely, but internal political mobilization on the part of Inkatha, Black Consciousness, and the trade union movement in the course of the 1970s posed serious challenges to the ANC's position; the support given by the international community to the anti-apartheid struggle periodically waxed and waned, particularly in the case of the United States; only from the beginning of the 1980s did the ANC begin to look like a credible government-in-waiting.

The approach taken in this book is sensitive to historical contingency and to the need to break down prevailing assumptions and categories. Yet it is alert to the danger of disaggregating apartheid to the point that it becomes meaningless or incomprehensible. Case studies and history 'from below' have on occasion to be balanced by the view from above, in particular, by a close understanding of political power in all its variant forms. We need to bear in mind not only the liberation that the people were fighting for but also the totality of the forces they were fighting against.

In the case of the Nazi holocaust, historian Saul Friedländer (who is also a survivor of those times) argues for an 'integrated history'. This makes it possible to combine a discussion of policy, power, the voices of victims, and a sense of wider European context together—in short, 'a totality defined by this very convergence of distinct elements'.[52] It is perhaps too soon to attempt this in South Africa, which is only a generation removed from apartheid, and where the temporal period concerned is so much more extended than in Nazi Germany. Nevertheless, it is time we began to interweave accounts of state power, ideology, resistance, religion, international politics, and transnational solidarity, within a common frame of analysis. This book represents the start of an attempt to do so.

ENDNOTES

Chapter 1

1. A. Paton, *Hofmeyr* (Cape Town, 1964), 487. One of the few who did forecast the success of the Nationalists, historian Arthur Keppel-Jones, speculated that this would happen in 1952. See A. Keppel-Jones, *When Smuts Goes* (Cape Town, 1947). Ray Alexander, the veteran trade union organizer and Communist stalwart, claims in her autobiography that she foresaw the result and subsequently told Smuts herself that 'the people did not have enough wages, nor proper housing, and that the cost of living was too high, so it was clear to me that they would not vote for him'. Ray Alexander Simons, *All my Life and All my Strength* (Johannesburg, 2004), 187.
2. A. Luthuli, *Let my People Go* (London, 1962), 106, 107.
3. Luli Callinicos, *Oliver Tambo: Beyond the Engeli Mountains* (Cape Town, 2004), 157–8.
4. K. A. Heard, *General Elections in South Africa 1943–1970* (London, 1974), 41–2. When account is taken of the 12 uncontested seats, all but one of which returned United Party members, the opposition vote was probably closer to 53.3 per cent.
5. S. Patterson, *The Last Trek: A Study of the Boer People and the Afrikaner Nation* (London, 1957), 104. This quote from Patterson is widely repeated. But Lindie Koorts, the foremost expert on Malan, has found nothing in his papers, including his written radio acceptance speech, to bear out Patterson's unsourced quote.
6. Heard, *General Elections*, 50.
7. L. Koorts, 'An Ageing Anachronism: D. F. Malan as Prime Minister, 1948–1954', *Kronos*, 36, 1 (2010), 108–35. See also L. Korf, 'D. F. Malan: A Political Biography', D.Phil. thesis, University of Stellenbosch, 2010.

8. C. H. Feinstein, *An Economic History of South Africa* (Cambridge, 2005), tables 6.2 and 6.4, 122, 129.

9. H. Giliomee, *The Afrikaners: Biography of a People* (London, 2003), 405–6; W. P. Visser, 'Urbanization and Afrikaner Class Formation: The Mine Workers' Union and the Search for a Cultural Identity', paper presented to African Urban Spaces Conference, University of Texas, Austin, March 2003, 2.

10. A detailed contemporary demographic study calculated that in 1946 the relative proportion of the population (total 11.25m) broken down by racial categories was whites (20.7 per cent), Africans (68.7 per cent), coloured (8 per cent), and Asians (2.6 per cent). H. Sonnabend, 'Population', in E. Hellman (ed.), *Handbook on Race Relations in South Africa* (Cape Town, 1949). A. Mager and M. Mulaudzi, 'Popular Responses to Apartheid: 1948–c.1975', in R. Ross et al. (eds), *Cambridge History of South Africa*, vol. ii (New York, 2011), 370.

11. P. Bonner, 'Eluding Capture: African Grass-Roots Struggles in 1940s Benoni', in S. Dubow and A. Jeeves (eds), *South Africa's 1940s: Worlds of Possibilities* (Cape Town, 2005), 170–1.

12. C. Bloomberg, *Christian-Nationalism and the Rise of the Afrikaner Broederbond in South Africa 1918–48*, ed. S. Dubow (London, 1990), 178; P. J. Furlong, *Between Crown and Swastika: The Impact of the Radical Right on the Afrikaner Nationalist Movement in the Fascist Era* (Middletown, Conn., 1991), 186–8.

13. Paton, *Hofmeyr*, 490.

14. Paton, *Hofmeyr*, 482, 487, 490.

15. W. K. Hancock, *Smuts*, i: *The Fields of Force* (Cambridge, 1968), 500.

16. N. Mandela, *Long Walk to Freedom* (London, 1994), 104.

17. See J. Krikler, 'Re-thinking Race and Class in South Africa: Some Ways Forward', in Wulf D. Hund, Jeremy Krikler, and David Roediger (eds) *Wages of Whiteness & Racist Symbolic Capital* (Berlin, 2010).

18. Visser, 'Urbanization and Afrikaner Class Formation', 12–13; D. O'Meara, 'The 1946 African Mineworkers' Strike and the Political Economy of South Africa', *Journal of Commonwealth and Comparative Politics*, 13, 2 (1975), 153, 165.

19. N. M. Stultz, *Afrikaner Politics in South Africa, 1934–1948* (Berkeley, 1974), 136.

20. Giliomee, *The Afrikaners*, 480–1.

21. Cited in H. Giliomee, 'The Making of the Apartheid Plan, 1929–1948', *Journal of Southern African Studies*, 29, 2 (2003), 374.

22. *Cape Argus*, 'Divide and Ruin', 23 March 1948.
23. E. A. Tiryakian, 'Apartheid and Politics in South Africa', *Journal of Politics*, 22, 4 (1960), 686.
24. A. Keppel-Jones, *Friends or Foes?* (Pietermaritzburg, [1950]), 48.
25. C. Walker, *Landmarked* (Auckland Park, 2008), 36, 43; see also 'Land Reform in SA must Consider Changes over 100 Years', *Weekend Argus*, 30 March 2013.
26. A. N. Pelzer (ed.), *Verwoerd Speaks: Speeches 1948–1966* (Johannesburg, 1966), 'The Policy of Apartheid, September 3, 1948', 2–3 and *passim*.
27. D. F. Malan to Reverend John Piersma, Grand Rapids, Mich., 12 February 1954, copy to editor, *The Argus*, 4 March 1954 with a release date of 1 April.
28. Feinstein, *Economic History of South Africa*, 127.
29. J. P. Brits, 'The Voice of the "People"? Memoranda presented in 1947 to the Sauer Commission by "Knowledgeable" Afrikaners', *Kleio*, 32 (2000).
30. Giliomee, *The Afrikaners*, 477; D. Posel, 'The Meaning of Apartheid before 1948: Conflicting Interests and Forces within the Afrikaner Nationalist Alliance', *JSAS*, 14, 1 (1987), 137–8.
31. For context, see S. Dubow, *Racial Segregation and the Origins of Apartheid in South Africa, 1919–36* (London, 1989).
32. E. G. Jansen papers, PV94 1/3/1/2, Institute of Contemporary History, University of the Free State.
33. J. G. Strydom, 'Die Enigste Praktiese Apartheidsbeleid vir Suid-Afrika', 30 July 1948; W. M. M. Eiselen, 'The Meaning of Apartheid', 5 July 1948; N. J. Van Warmelo, 'Memorandum on Extension of Self-Government Amongst the Native People', 19 October 1948, in E. G. Jansen papers, PV94 1/3/1/1, Institute of Contemporary History, University of the Free State. Eiselen used Gerard Sekoto's recent painting 'Song of the Pick', which shows a gang of muscular black labourers with pickaxes raised above their heads in the foreground, and the slouching figure of a white overseer, pipe in mouth, in the background, as a 'fine work of art turned into a poignant shame-provoking illustration of the workings of domination'. We may safely assume that the memorandum from the Johannesburg Joint Council of Europeans and Natives (14 September 1948) opposing proposed apartheid policies was ignored.
34. 'Hoofpunte I/S Apartheidsbeleid soos Uiteengesit deur Dr D. F. Malan op 2 September 1948', in Van Warmelo, 'Memorandum on Extension of Self-Government Amongst the Native People'.
35. M. Du Toit, 'The Domesticity of Afrikaner Nationalism: *Volksmoeders* and the ACVV, 1904–1929', *JSAS*, 29, 1 (2003).

36. T. Kuperus, *State, Civil Society and Apartheid in South Africa: An Examination of Dutch Reformed Church–State Relations* (London, 1999), 43–5.

37. Giliomee, 'The Making of the Apartheid Plan', 381–2.

38. J. Kinghorn (ed.), *Die NG Kerk en Apartheid* (Johannesburg, 1986), 87–90. According to Richard Elphick, 'Missions and Afrikaner Nationalism: Soundings in the Prehistory of Apartheid', in B. Stanley (ed.), *Missions, Nationalism, and the End of Empire* (Grand Rapids, Mich., 2003), 66, the Orange Free State missionary J. C. du Plessis characterized Dutch Reformed Church policy as 'apartheid' in 1929, but the word does not seem to have been picked up immediately. The term 'apartheid' began to circulate political circles in 1936 when it was adopted as a slogan by the newly formed *Suid-Afrikaanse Bond vir Rassestudie*.

39. L. van der Watt, 'Savagery and Civilisation: Race as a Signifier of Difference in Afrikaner Nationalist Art', *De arte*, 55 (April 1997).

40. J. A. Loubser, *The Apartheid Bible* (Cape Town, 1987), 61.

41. Furlong, *Between Crown and Swastika*, 92.

42. For a Freudian reading of Cronjé's racial obsessions, see J. M. Coetzee, 'The Mind of Apartheid: Geoffrey Cronjé (1907–)', *Social Dynamics*, 17, 1 (1991).

43. See e.g. M. Shain, *The Roots of Antisemitism in South Africa* (Charlottesville, Va., 1994); Furlong, *Between Crown and Swastika*.

44. G. Eloff, *Rasse en Rassevermenging: Die Boerevolk Gesien van die Standpunt van die Rasseleer* (Bloemfontein, 1942), foreword and 104.

45. Ivan Evans, *Cultures of Violence: Racial Violence and the Origins of Segregation in South Africa and the American South* (Manchester, 2009).

46. Kinghorn, *NG Kerk en Apartheid*, 91; S. Dubow, 'Afrikaner Nationalism, Apartheid and the Conceptualization of "Race"', *Journal of African History*, 33 (1992), 211.

47. D. O'Meara, *Volkskapitalisme: Class, Capital and Ideology in the Development of Afrikaner Nationalism, 1934–1948* (Cambridge, 1983), ch. 12.

48. M. Roberts and A. E. G. Trollip, *The South African Opposition 1939–1945: An Essay in Contemporary History* (London, 1947).

49. Cited in B. Bunting, *The Rise of the South African Reich* (London, 1986), 194.

50. Giliomee, *The Afrikaners*, 470.

Chapter 2

1. House of Assembly Debates, 16 August 1948, reproduced in D. W. Krüger (ed.), *South African Parties and Policies 1910–1960* (Cape Town, 1960), 410–17.

2. House of Assembly Debates, 21 September 1948, in Krüger (ed.), *South African Parties and Policies*, 422–7.

3. Cited in Paton, *Hofmeyr*, 471.

4. J. Barber and J. Barratt, *South Africa's Foreign Policy: The Search for Status and Security 1945–1988* (Cambridge, 1990), 2.

5. The terms 'European and non-European' were commonly used in the 1950s and 1960s as a synonym for white and black, notwithstanding the manifest inconsistencies involved.

6. M. Ballinger, *From Union to Apartheid* (Folkestone, 1969), 229–31; Paton, *Hofmeyr*, 506–7, 510, 519.

7. Koorts, 'An Ageing Anachronism', 116.

8. Barber and Barratt, *South Africa's Foreign Policy*, 36.

9. D. Posel, 'Whiteness and Power in the South African Civil Service: Paradoxes of the Apartheid State', *JSAS*, 25, 1 (1999), 105.

10. D. O'Meara, *Forty Lost Years: The Apartheid State and the Politics of the National Party 1948–1994* (Randburg, 1996), 76.

11. Mandela, *Long Walk to Freedom*, 105.

12. Leslie Witz, *Apartheid's Festival: Contesting South Africa's National Pasts* (Bloomington, Ind., 2003).

13. B. Hirson, *A History of the Left in South Africa: Writings of Baruch Hirson* (London, 2005), 154.

14. Letter from W. M. Sisulu to Prime Minister D. F. Malan on behalf of the African National Congress, 21 Jan. 1952 and reply from M. Aucamp, 29 Jan. 1952; <www.anc.org.za/show.php?id=4576>.

15. Julian Brown, 'Public Protest and Violence in South Africa, 1948–1976', D.Phil. thesis, Oxford University, 2009, ch. 1.

16. O. M. Murphy, 'Race, Violence and Nation: African Nationalism and Popular Politics in South Africa's Eastern Cape, 1948–1970', D.Phil. thesis, Oxford, 2013, ch. 1.

17. N. Roos, *Ordinary Springboks: White Servicemen and Social Justice in South Africa, 1939–1961* (Aldershot, 2005), 134–7, 154–5.

18. Colin Eglin, *Crossing the Borders of Power* (Johannesburg, 2007), 48.

19. Eglin, *Crossing the Borders of Power*, 157.

20. Mark Mazower, *Governing the World: The History of an Idea* (London, 2012), 319.

21. M. Lake and H. Reynolds, *Drawing the Global Colour Line* (Cambridge, 2008), 344–5; S. Dubow, 'Smuts, the United Nations and the Rhetoric of Race and Rights', *Journal of Contemporary History*, 43, 1 (2008). India, which

imposed full economic sanctions on South Africa in 1946 (at the cost of 5.5 per cent of its export earnings), was the first country to do so.

22. Xuma travelled to New York in 1946 to lobby General Assembly members. When he ran into Smuts, who questioned Xuma as to why he was in New York, Xuma is said to have replied: 'I have had to fly 10,000 miles to meet my Prime Minister. He talks about us but he won't talk to us.'

23. 'Report of the United Nations Commission on the Racial Situation in the Union of South Africa', A/2505 and Add. 1, 1953, 901 (ix).

24. R. Hyam and P. Henshaw, *The Lion and Springbok: Britain and South Africa since the Boer War* (Cambridge, 2003), 161, 165. The so-called 'famous five' countries who opposed or abstained on resolutions criticizing the South African government (on the grounds that these were not a matter of legitimate UN concern) were Britain, France, Portugal, Belgium, and Australia—all of whom, with the exception of Australia, a leading member of the 'old' Commonwealth, were African colonial powers.

25. J. E. Spence, *Republic under Pressure: A Study of South African Foreign Policy* (London, 1965), 65, 106.

26. In January 1953 Malan stated that he would prefer South African membership of NATO to membership of the United Nations. *New York Times*, 18 January 1953.

27. W. Minter and S. Hill, 'Anti-apartheid Solidarity in United States–South Africa Relations: From the Margins to the Mainstream', in SADET, *The Road to Democracy in South Africa*, iii: *International Solidarity Part 2* (Cape Town, 2004), 750.

28. Hyam and Henshaw, *The Lion and Springbok*, 156–7.

29. *The Times* (editorial), 2 April 1951.

30. *The Times*, 'South African Government's Defeat', 29 May 1948.

31. Kitty Hauser, 'Bowling Along', *London Review of Books*, 17 March 2005, 28–9.

32. Barber and Barrett, *South Africa's Foreign Policy*, 157.

33. C. Gurney, '"A Great Cause": The Origins of the Anti-Apartheid Movement, June 1959–March 1960', *JSAS*, 26, 1 (2000), 123–44.

34. R. Skinner, 'The Moral Foundations of British Anti-Apartheid Activism, 1946–1960', *JSAS*, 35, 2 (2009).

35. <http://www.liberationafrica.se/intervstories/interviews/wastberg/>.

36. T. Sellström, *Sweden and National Liberation in Southern Africa*, vol. i (Uppsala, 1999), 18–19, 140.

37. Edwin S. Munger, *Afrikaner and African Nationalism: South African Parallels and Parameters* (Oxford, 1967), 45.

38. Helen Joseph, *Side by Side* (London, 1986), 1–2.
39. P. Christie and C. Collins, 'Bantu Education: Apartheid Ideology and Labour Reproduction', in P. Kallaway (ed.), *Apartheid and Education* (Johannesburg, 1984), 173.
40. I. B. Tabata, *Education for Barbarism in South Africa* (London, 1960).
41. Duma Nokwe, 'Verwoerd's Camps and Colleges', *Fighting Talk* (September 1955), 12.
42. J. Hyslop, '"A Destruction Coming in": Bantu Education as Response to Social Crisis', in P. Bonner et al., *Apartheid's Genesis 1935–1962* (Johannesburg, 2001).
43. Isabella Kentridge, '"And so they moved one by one": Forced Removals in a Free State Town (1956–1977)', *Journal of Southern African Studies*, 39, 1 (2013), 140–1, and *passim*.
44. For example, the Public Safety Act (1953); Criminal Law Amendment Act (1953) which provided for the declaration of a State of Emergency; and the Riotous Assemblies and Suppression of Communism Amendment Act (1954).
45. I. Evans, *Bureaucracy and Race: Native Administration in South Africa* (Berkeley, 1997), 100.
46. C. de Wet, 'Betterment Planning in South Africa: Some Thoughts on its History, Feasibility and Wider Policy Implications', *Journal of Contemporary African Studies*, 6, 1–2 (1987), 85–122; W. Beinart, *The Rise of Conservation in South Africa* (Oxford, 2003), ch. 10.
47. Evans, *Bureaucracy and Race*, 205, 206.
48. D. Posel, 'The Apartheid Project, 1948–1970', in Ross et al. (eds), *Cambridge History of South Africa*, ii. 340.
49. K. Breckenridge, 'Verwoerd's Bureau of Proof: Total Information in the Making of Apartheid', *History Workshop Journal*, 59, 1 (2005).
50. Breckenridge, 'Verwoerd's Bureau of Proof', 104.
51. 'The Policy of Apartheid', speech to the Senate, 2 September 1948, reproduced in Pelzer (ed.), *Verwoerd Speaks*, 1–19.
52. Ballinger, *From Union to Apartheid*, 212.
53. Evans, *Bureaucracy and Race*, 241–2.
54. S. Dubow, 'Macmillan, Verwoerd, and the 1960 "Wind of Change" Speech', *Historical Journal*, 54, 4 (2011), 1087–114.
55. Lionel Bernstein, *Memory Against Forgetting* (London, 1999).
56. G. Bizos, *Odyssey to Freedom* (Houghton, 2007), 173.
57. A. Luthuli, *Let my People Go* (London, 1962), 170. On the drafting of the Freedom Charter, see J. Lazerson, *Against the Tide: Whites in the Struggle Against Apartheid* (Boulder, Colo., 1994), ch. 8.

58. There was a vogue for 'multi-racial' initiatives in the mid-1950s. One notable example was the 1957 Multi-Racial Conference at Wits University, which brought together prominent churchmen, liberals, the ANC, and other interested parties.

59. Elinor Sisulu, *Walter and Albertina Sisulu: In our Lifetime* (Cape Town, 2002), 141.

60. Bizos, *Odyssey*, 176.

61. L. J. Blom-Cooper, 'The South African Treason Trial: R. *v.* Adams and Others', *International and Comparative Law Quarterly*, 8, 1 (1959), 59.

62. Erwin N. Griswold, 'Treason Trial in South Africa', *The Times*, 25 September 1958.

63. E. Hellman (ed.), *Handbook on Race Relations in South Africa* (Cape Town, 1949), 511.

64. Thomas G. Karis, 'The South African Treason Trial', *Political Science Quarterly*, 76, 2 (1961), 235.

Chapter 3

1. Benjamin Pogrund, *War of Words: Memoirs of a South African Journalist* (New York, 2000), 80; *Time*, 1 February 1960. The Coalbrook disaster was largely treated as a technical failure—it prompted large investments in scientific research into coal pillar strength—but the inquest revealed that it was also the result of lax management which placed productivity above safety: the catastrophic collapse had been preceded by collapses on 28 December 1959—and also hours before the disaster—which the mine management took little account of.

2. 'Speech of thanks addressed to Mr Harold Macmillan', 3 February 1960, in Pelzer (ed.), *Verwoerd Speaks*, 336–8.

3. Dubow, 'Macmillan, Verwoerd, and the 1960 "Wind of Change" Speech', 1087–114.

4. This analysis is drawn from P. Frankel, *An Ordinary Atrocity: Sharpeville and its Massacre* (New Haven, 2001); also K. Shear, 'Tested Loyalties: Police and Politics in South Africa, 1939–63', *Journal of African* History, 53, 2 (2012), 192.

5. Murphy, 'Race, Violence, and Nation', 193–6.

6. H. Suzman, *In No Uncertain Terms* (Johannesburg, 1993), 52.

7. SADET, *The Road to Democracy: South Africans Telling their Stories*, vol. i (Johannesburg, 2008), testimony of Phillip Kgosana, 156.

8. P. Delius, 'Sebatakgomo and the Zoutpansberg Balemi Association: The ANC, the Communist Party and Rural Organisation, 1939–1955', *Journal of African History*, 34, 2 (1993), 293–313.

9. Anne Mager and Maanda Mulaudzi, 'Popular Responses to Apartheid: 1948–*c*.1975', in *The Cambridge History of South Africa*, vol. ii (New York, 2011), 388–9.

10. Anthony Delius, 'Travels in Tribalism', *Africa South*, 50, 4.2 (January–March 1960).

11. S. Matote and L. Ntsebeza, 'Rural Resistance in Mpondoland and Thembuland, 1960–1963', in SADET, *The Road to Democracy in South Africa*, vol. i (Cape Town, 2004).

12. Govan Mbeki, *South Africa: The Peasants' Revolt* (Harmondsworth, 1964), 130, 131.

13. Murphy, 'Race, Violence, and Nation', 178, 183.

14. Delius, 'Sebatakgomo and the Zoutpansberg Balemi Association', 302; James Fairbairn (Ralph Halpern), 'Mass Trials', *Africa South* (April/June 195); Charles Hooper, *Brief Authority* (London, 1960).

15. O'Meara, *Forty Lost Years*, 103–4; Giliomee, *The Afrikaners*, 522–3.

16. SAIRR, *A Survey of Race Relations in South Africa: 1961* (Johannesburg, 1962), 10, 63 and ff.

17. *The Times*, 23 March 1960.

18. *The Times*, 23 March 1960; 26 March 1960.

19. Ballinger, *From Union to Apartheid*, 427.

20. Peter Brown, 'Fear, not Tradition, Inspired Nat Handshake Order', *Contact*, 3, 7 (1960), 7.

21. *Time*, 'South Africa: The Assassin of Milner Park', 18 April 1960; J. Botha, *Verwoerd is Dead* (Cape Town, 1967), 66.

22. O'Meara, *Forty Lost Years*, 104.

23. *Star*, 1 December 1960.

24. N. M. Stultz and J. Butler, 'The South African General Election of 1961', *Political Science Quarterly*, 78, 1 (1963), 107.

25. From 1962 to 1970 white immigration to South Africa amounted to around 30,000–40,000 per year, whereas annual emigration was less than 10,000. No less than 40 per cent of the more than 400,000 immigrants to South Africa in the period 1964–73 were British.

26. In October the National Party increased its majority at the polls, winning more than twice the number of seats of the official opposition. Verwoerd interpreted this as proof that the party's base was extending amongst all whites.

27. Nadine Gordimer, writing in 1959, called Luthuli 'the one man in black politics in South Africa whose personality is a symbol of human dignity which Africans as a whole, no matter what their individual or political affiliations are and no matter what state of enlightenment or ignorance they may be in, recognise as *their* dignity'. Reprinted in S. Clingman (ed.), *Nadine Gordimer. The Essential Gesture: Writing, Politics and Places* (London, 1988), 38.

28. S. Ellis, 'The Genesis of the ANC's Armed Struggle in South Africa 1948–1961', *JSAS*, 37, 4 (2011), 668–9; SADET, *The Road to Democracy: South Africans Telling their Stories*, vol. i (Johannesburg, 2008), evidence of Fred Dube, 105. Mandela, *Long Walk to Freedom*, 259.

29. Interview with Joe Matthews in *Road to Democracy: South Africans Telling their Stories*, i. 19–21.

30. Tom Lodge, *Sharpeville and its Consequences* (Oxford, 2011), 214.

31. R. Suttner, 'The African National Congress (ANC) Underground: From the M-Plan to Rivonia', *South African Historical Journal*, 49 (2003), 129. Gail Gerhart has pointed out to me the Africanist claim that the 'M-Plan' was so-called because its real originator was A. P. Mda, *éminence grise* of the Pan-Africanists.

32. Ellis, 'The Genesis of the ANC's Armed Struggle', 657–76. See also Bernard Magubane et al., 'The Turn to Armed Struggle', in SADET, *The Road to Democracy in South Africa*, i. 82–3.

33. Ellis, 'The Genesis of the ANC's Armed Struggle', 667.

34. P. S. Landau, 'The ANC, MK, and the "Turn to Violence" (1960–1962)', *South African Historical Journal*, 64, 3 (2012), 548, 553.

35. J. Lewin, 'No Revolution Around the Corner', *Africa South* (October/December 1958).

36. H. J. Simons, 'An Addendum', *Africa South* (October/December 1958), 58; M. Harmel, 'Revolutions are not Abnormal', *Africa South* (January/March 1959).

37. Edward Roux, 'Revolution in South Africa', *Africa South* (January/March 1959). See also the contribution by the British historian G. D. H. Cole, 'The Anatomy of Revolution', *Africa South* (April/June 1959), and the leading ANC and Communist Party intellectual Joe Matthews, 'Revolution: Further Reflections', *Africa South* (July/September 1959).

38. R. W. Johnson, *How Long Will South Africa Survive?* (London, 1977), 18–20.

39. Mandela, *Long Walk to Freedom*, 273–4.

40. M. Gunther, 'The National Committee of Liberation (NCL) African Resistance Movement (ARM)', in *The Road to Democracy in South Africa*, vol. i.

41. Another small revolutionary grouping whose activities were disrupted at this time was the Yu Chi Chan Club, which later became known as the National Liberation Front; its leader, Neville Alexander, a maverick intellectual figure on the left with close links to the Unity Movement, was sentenced to ten years' imprisonment on Robben Island in 1964.

42. Brown Bavusile Maaba, 'The PAC's War against the State, 1960–1963', in *The Road to Democracy*, i. 264.

43. Lodge, *Black Politics*, 243, 247, and ff.

44. G. Frankel, *Rivonia's Children: Three Families and the Price of Freedom in South Africa* (London, 1999).

45. John D'Oliveira, *Vorster—The Man* (Johannesburg, 1977), 125.

46. Frankel, *Rivonia's Children*, 227–30; Lodge, *Mandela*, 112–14.

47. *The Times*, 12 June 1964.

48. K. S. Broun, *Saving Nelson Mandela* (Oxford, 2012), 101.

49. Luthuli wrote to Strydom in 1957 calling for a multi-racial convention to address the 'growing deterioration in race relations' but received no response.

50. On the day that the Group of Experts reported, 20 April 1964, *The Times* carried a number of business news reports indicating that trade and investment in South Africa was buoyant.

Chapter 4

1. D. Hobart Houghton and J. Dagut, *Source Material on the South African Economy*, iii: *1920–70* (Cape Town, 1973), 174–5.

2. H. Adam, *Modernising Racial Domination* (Berkeley, 1971), 7; M. Leibbrandt et al., 'Trends in South African Income Distribution and Poverty since the Fall of Apartheid', *OECD Social, Employment and Migration Working Papers*, No. 101 (2010), doi:10.1787/5kmmsot7pims-en, 14.

3. P. Rouillard, 'Paths of Plenty', University of Natal BA (Hons.) thesis, 1997, cited in Albert Grundlingh, '"Are We Afrikaners Getting too Rich?" Cornucopia and Change in Afrikanerdom in the 1960s', *Journal of Historical Sociology*, 21, 2/3 (2008), 146.

4. J. Hoagland, *South Africa: Civilizations in Conflict* (London, 1973), 6.

5. W. Beinart, *Twentieth Century South Africa* (Oxford, 1994), 174; Grundlingh, 'Are We Afrikaners Getting too Rich?", 150.

6. D. Hobart Houghton, *The South African Economy* (4th edn, Cape Town, 1976), 212; Hoagland, *South Africa*, 338.

7. C. W. de Kiewiet, *History of South Africa* (London, 1941), 9.

8. Feinstein, *Economic History of South Africa*, 167–73.

9. N. Nattrass, 'Economic Aspects of the Construction of Apartheid', in P. Bonner et al. (eds), *Apartheid's Genesis 1935–1962* (Johannesburg, 2001), 49, 50, 61.

10. J. Seekings and N. Nattrass, *Class, Race and Inequality in South Africa* (New Haven, 2005), 137.

11. Francis Wilson, 'Farming', in M. Wilson and L. Thompson (eds), *Oxford History of South Africa*, vol. ii (London, 1971), 165.

12. W. Beinart, *Twentieth-Century South Africa* (Oxford, 1994), ch. 8; Ross et al. (eds), *Cambridge History of South Africa*, vol. ii, statistical appendix, table 9, 650.

13. C. van Onselen, *The Seed is Mine: The Life of a South African Sharecropper, 1894–1985* (Oxford, 1996), 305–6, 531.

14. E. Dommisse, *Anton Rupert: A Biography* (Cape Town, 1985), 58.

15. Albert Wessels, *Farmboy and Industrialist* (Cape Town, 1987), ch. 6.

16. Grundlingh, 'Are We Afrikaners Getting too Rich?'

17. Dommisse, *Anton Rupert*, 161.

18. Adam, *Modernising Racial Domination*, 29. In 1977 leading Afrikaner businessman A. D. Wassenaar warned that state corporatism rather than Communism threatened South Africa's future.

19. S. Dubow, *A Commonwealth of Knowledge: Science, Sensibility, and White South Africa* (Oxford, 2006), 258.

20. D. Bunn, 'White Sepulchres: On the Reluctance of Monuments' and Melinda Silverman, 'Nationalism, Architecture and Volkskas Bank', in H. Judin and I. Vladislavić (eds), *Blank: Architecture, Apartheid and After* (Rotterdam, 1998).

21. W. W. M. Eiselen, 'Harmonious Multi-Community Development', *Optima*, 9, 1 (1959).

22. S. P. Lekgoathi, ' "You are Listening to Radio Lebowa of the South African Broadcasting Corporation": Vernacular Radio, Bantustan Identity and Listenership, 1960–1994', *JSAS*, 35, 3 (2009); L. Gunner, 'Supping with the Devil: Zulu Radio Drama under Apartheid—The Case of Alexius Buthelezi', *Social Identities*, 11, 2 (2005); J. Dlamini, *Native Nostalgia* (Johannesburg, 2009), ch. 1; H. Adam, *Modernizing Racial Domination* (Berkeley, 1971), 106.

23. For a good overview, see Robert Gordon, 'Apartheid's Anthropologists: The Genealogy of Afrikaner Anthropology', *American Ethnologist*, 15, 3 (1988), 535–53.
24. David Goldblatt, *The Transported of Kwandebele* (New York, 1989).
25. W. Beinart, 'Beyond "Homelands": Some Ideas about the History of African Rural Areas in South Africa', *South African Historical Journal*, 64, 1 (2012), 6, 13.
26. B. Bozzoli, *Theatres of Struggle and the End of Apartheid* (Edinburgh, 2004), 62.
27. The material on housing is drawn from Evans, *Bureaucracy and Race*, ch. 4; C. M. Chipkin, *Johannesburg Style: Architecture and Society 1880s–1960s* (Cape Town, 1993), ch. 8; D. Japha, 'The Social Programme of the South African Modern Movement', in Judin and Vladislavić, *Blank*.
28. Evans, *Bureaucracy and Race*, ch. 3.
29. M. Savage, 'The Imposition of Pass Laws on the African Population in South Africa 1916–1984', *African Affairs*, 85, 339 (1986), table 3, 190–1.
30. Surplus People Project, *Forced Removals in South Africa*, vol. i (Cape Town, 1983), 1; L. Platzky and C. Walker, *The Surplus People: Forced Removals in South Africa* (Johannesburg, 1985), 9. This figure excludes certain categories, for example, people removed as a result of influx control and those moved within the Bantustans as part of 'Betterment' planning.
31. C. Simkins, 'The Evolution of the South African Population in the Twentieth Century', in *Cambridge History of South Africa*, vol. ii, and statistical appendix table 9, 650.
32. C. Murray, 'Displaced Urbanisation: South Africa's Rural Slums', *African Affairs*, 86, 344 (1987), 311–29.
33. M. Mazower, *Governing the World: The History of an Idea* (London, 2012), 156.
34. E. D. Weitz, 'From the Vienna to the Paris System: International Politics and the Entangled Histories of Human Rights, Forced Deportations, and Civilizing Missions', *American Historical Review*, 113, 5 (2008), 1313–43.
35. Maano Ramutsindela, 'Resilient Geographies: Land, Boundaries and the Consolidation of the Former Bantustans in Post-1994 South Africa', *Geographical Journal*, 173, 1 (2007), 46.
36. A. Baldwin, 'Mass Removals and Separate Development', *JSAS*, 1, 2 (1975); L. Platzky and C. Walker, *The Surplus People: Forced Removals in South Africa* (Johannesburg, 1985).
37. Foreword to Platzky and Walker, *The Surplus People*, p. xviii.

38. For an illuminating discussion of these issues, see H. Bradford, 'Reformulating Resettlement: A Review of the Surplus People', *Social Dynamics*, 14, 1 (1988), 67–74, and the ensuing exchange between Bradford and Cheryl Walker in *Social Dynamics*, 14, 2 (1988), 107–12.

39. L. Evans, 'Gender, Generation and the Experiences of Farm Dwellers Resettled in the Ciskei Bantustan, South Africa *ca* 1960–1976', *Journal of Agrarian Change*, online version 20 September 2012.

40. R. Slater, 'Differentiation and Diversification: Changing Livelihoods in Qwa-Qwa, South Africa, 1970–2000', *Journal of Southern African Studies*, 28, 3 (2002), 601.

41. Patrick O'Meara, 'Black Man Alive. Last Grave at Dimbaza. Land of Promise. Films on South Africa', *Jump Cut*, 18 (1978), 7–8; *New York Times*, 27 October 1975, articles by John J. O'Connor and C. Geraldine Fraser; Jean Sinclair, 'The Black Sash President's Address to the National Conference', Historical Papers, AE862 D19, National Conference, 1972.

42. D. Posel, 'The Apartheid Project, 1948–1970', in *Cambridge History of South Africa*, ii. 348.

43. Historical Papers, Wits University, Black Sash AE862 G23.4, 'Interview with Mr De Wet Nel—Minister for Bantu Administration and Development', at Pretoria on 4 November 1963.

44. Cited in Gordon, 'Apartheid's Anthropologists', 540.

45. M. A. Beale, 'Apartheid and University Education, 1948–1970', Ph.D. thesis, Wits University, 1998, 5, calculates that by 1970 the former 'open' universities and Rhodes were 96 per cent white.

46. Black university enrolment rose from 2,172 in 1948 to 9,933 in 1970. The respective figures for whites were 20,046 and 83,137. See Beale, 'Apartheid and University Education, 1948–1970', 6.

47. 'The Man with the Apartheid Brain', *Contact*, 1, 17 (1958).

48. M. Nkomo, D. Swartz, and B. Maja (eds), *Within the Realm of Possibility: From Disadvantage to Development at the University of Fort Hare and the University of the North* (Cape Town, 2006).

49. Giliomee, *The Afrikaners*, 531.

50. Giliomee, *The Afrikaners*, 548–50; A. Mouton, *Voorlooper: Die Lewe van Schalk Pienaar* (Cape Town, 2002), 41–3. Pienaar was posthumously awarded the South African government's 'Order of Ikhamanga in Silver' for 'raising consciousness in the Afrikaner community, particularly among journalists, about the immorality of apartheid and making them open to change through his daring questioning of the status quo'.

51. A. Brink, *A Fork in the Road* (London, 2009), 224. See 207 and ff. for an excellent discussion of the *Sestigers*; also Michael Chapman, *South African Literatures* (London, 1996), 250; P. D. McDonald, *The Literature Police* (Oxford, 2009), 54–7.

52. L. Viljoen, *Ingrid Jonker* (Johannesburg, 2012), 81–2.

53. A. Brink, personal communication, 18 May 2012; Chapman, *Southern African Literatures*, 250.

54. S. Lewis, 'Tradurre e Tradire: The Treason and Translation of Breyten Breytenbach', *Poetics Today*, 22, 2 (2001), 435–52.

55. Mark Sanders, *Complicities: The Intellectual and Apartheid* (Durham, NC, 2002). I have drawn on Sanders's analysis of van Wyk Louw and Breytenbach.

56. A. Mason, *What's So Funny? Under the Skin of South African Cartooning* (Cape Town, 2010), 57; and P. Vale's excellent *Keeping a Sharp Eye: A Century of Cartoons on South Africa's International Relations 1910–2010* (Johannesburg, 2011).

57. H. Lunn, '"Hippies, Radicals, and the Sounds of Silence": Cultural Dialectics at Two South African Universities 1966–1976', Ph.D. thesis, University of KwaZulu-Natal, 2009, ch. 5.

58. The remarkable story of Rodriguez's life and iconic status in South Africa is brilliantly told in the film *Searching for Sugarman* (2012).

59. An interesting reappraisal of *Cry the Beloved Country* is offered by Andrew van der Vlies in his *South African Textual Cultures: White, Black, Read all Over* (Manchester, 2007). For a general overview, see also Van der Vlies, 'The Novel and Apartheid', in Simon Gikandi (ed.), *The Oxford History of the Novel in English* (forthcoming, 2014).

60. James Stern, 'The Lying Days', *New York Times*, 4 October 1953.

61. *The Times*, 9 April 1969.

62. Per Wästberg, 'On Nadine Gordimer', in Andries Oliphant (ed.), *A Writing Life: Celebrating Nadine Gordimer* (London, 1998), 87.

63. This discussion draws on a reading of Denis Walder, *Athol Fugard* (London, 2003) and A. Wertheim, *The Dramatic Art of Athol Fugard: From South Africa to the World* (Bloomington, Ind., 2000).

64. Fugard's work also served as a reference point—and a point of critical departure—for collaborative workshopped theatre (Barney Simon, Junction Avenue) as well as Black Consciousness playwrights like Zakes Mda, Matsemala Manaka, and Maishe Maponya in the 1970s and 1980s.

65. Walder, *Athol Fugard*, 4.

66. Ursula A. Barnett, *A Vision of Order: A Study of Black South African Literature in English (1914–1980)*, 20.
67. Allan Boesak, *Running With Horses: Reflections of an Accidental Politician* (Cape Town, 2009), 46.
68. There were pockets of important dissident thinking even in Afrikaner universities loyal to government, such as Stellenbosch and Potchefstroom.
69. Fred Hendricks, 'The Mafeje Affair: The University of Cape Town and Apartheid', *African Studies*, 67, 3 (2008), 441; M. Plaut, 'South African Student Protest, 1968: Remembering the Mafeje Sit-in', *History Workshop Journal*, 69 (2010).
70. John Daniel and Peter Vale, 'South Africa: Where Were we Looking in 1968', in P. Gassert and M. Klimke (eds), *1968: Memories and Legacies of a Global Revolt* (Washington, 2009), remark that Kennedy's visit to Soweto and to Albert Luthuli in Groutville was seen as an important validation of the ANC and of black South Africans more generally (141).
71. Cited in M. Legassick and C. Saunders, 'Aboveground Activity in the 1960s', *Road to Democracy*, i. 681.
72. Lunn, 'Hippies, Radicals and the Sounds of Silence', 96, 97.

Chapter 5

1. SADET, *The Road to Democracy: South Africans Telling their Stories*, vol. i (Johannesburg, 2008), testimony of Andrew Masondo, 256–7; Barber and Barratt, *South Africa's Foreign Policy*, 81.
2. Oswald Joseph Mtshali, *Sounds of a Cowhide Drum* (Johannesburg, 1971), 24.
3. F. Meli, *South Africa Belongs to Us: A History of the ANC* (Harare, 1988), 160–1.
4. Steven Ellis and Tsepo Sechaba, *Comrades Against Apartheid: The ANC and the South African Communist Party in Exile* (London, 1992), 40.
5. J. Slovo, *Slovo: The Unfinished Autobiography* (Johannesburg, 1995), 152; Ben Turok, *Nothing But the Truth: Behind the ANC's Struggle Politics* (Johannesburg, 2003), 198 and ff.
6. A. Lissoni, 'The South African Liberation Movements in Exile, c.1945–1970', Ph.D. thesis, University of London, 2008, 24.
7. A. Sampson, *Mandela: The Authorised Biography* (London, 2000), 164.
8. A. Lissoni, 'Transformations in the ANC External Mission and Umkhonto we Sizwe, c.1960–1969', *JSAS*, 35, 2 (2009).
9. Lissoni, 'The South African Liberation Movements in Exile', 146 and ff.

10. Leballo was deposed from his leadership position in 1979. Robert Sobukwe remained the official leader while on Robben Island, from which he was released in 1969 and confined to house arrest in Kimberley. He died in 1978.

11. 'Azania' probably derives from the Arabic word 'Zanj' or 'Zenj' and refers to the black nation or nations. It is reflected in the name 'Zanzibar'. Evelyn Waugh used the term Azania to designate an eastern coast island off Africa in his satirical novel *Black Mischief* (1932).

12. Lissoni, 'Transformations in the ANC External Mission', 300.

13. <http://www.sahistory.org.za/pages/library-resources/official%20docs/1966_dissolution-barneydesai.htm>.

14. Lissoni, 'Transformations in the ANC External Mission', 295–6.

15. Callinicos, *Oliver Tambo*, 326; Turok, *Nothing but the Truth*, 216–17.

16. N. Ndebele and N. Nieftagodien, 'The Morogoro Conference: A Moment of Self-Reflection', in *The Road to Democracy*, i. 584; *The Road to Democracy: South Africans Telling their Stories*, i, evidence of Wilton Mkwayi, 273.

17. Turok, *Nothing but the Truth*, 218.

18. T. Lodge, *Black Politics Since 1945* (Johannesburg, 1983), 295; Callinicos, *Oliver Tambo*.

19. Lodge, *Sharpeville*, 235, 242.

20. Turok, *Nothing but the Truth*, 49.

21. Gurney, '"A Great Cause": The Origins of the Anti-Apartheid Movement, June 1959–March 1960', 137–8; Lissoni, 'The South African Liberation Movements in Exile', 845.

22. In 1986, Black Action for the Liberation of South Africa was formed by British activists critical of the AAM's racially integrated constituency.

23. Loskop translates as 'loose head'.

24. R. Archer and A. Bouillon, *The South African Game: Sport and Racism* (London, 1982), 74, 206.

25. Quotes are from Joseph Leyveld's introduction to Ernest Cole's *House of Bondage* (Toronto, 1967). A retrospective exhibition of Cole's photographs, the negatives of which were found by the South African photographer David Goldblatt in Sweden, was mounted in Johannesburg and Cape Town in 2010.

26. Lissoni, 'The South African Liberation Movements in Exile', 56, 57.

27. Amongst those ANC leaders said to have received training in China were Wilton Mkwayi, Raymond Mhlaba, Patrick Mthembu, Andrew Mlangeni, and Joe Gqabi. See *The Road to Democracy: South Africans Telling their Stories*, i, evidence of Wilton Mkwayi, 268–9.

28. V. Shubin, *ANC: A View from Moscow* (Cape Town, 1999), 62, 66, 68. Shubin calculates that the grant of $560,000 in 1965 ranked 7th in the subventions of the International Fund.

29. Shubin, *ANC: A View from Moscow*, 63–4.

30. P. O'Malley, *Shades of Difference: Mac Maharaj and the Struggle for South Africa* (London, 2007), 89.

31. Ellis, *External Mission*, 152 and ff.

32. *The Road to Democracy: South Africans Telling their Stories*, i, testimony of Isaac Lesibe Maphoto, 239.

33. Indres Naidoo, *Island in Chains* (Harmondsworth, 1982), 86–7.

34. Naidoo, *Island in Chains*, testimony of Andrew Masondo, 261–3.

35. P. Lane, '"Heroes as Ordinary People": A Social and Cultural History of Political Imprisonment in South Africa, 1960–1992', Ph.D. thesis, Essex University, 2010, 92.

36. A. Kathrada, *Letters from Robben Island* (Cape Town, 1999), 45.

37. *Road to Democracy*, i, ch. 12.

38. Cited in *Road to Democracy*, i. 502.

39. *Road to Democracy*, i. 524. See also the account by Shubin, *ANC: A View from Moscow*, 77–83.

40. General Laws Amendment Act No. 83 of 1967.

41. Meli, *South Africa Belongs to Us*, 162.

42. H. Macmillan, 'The Hani Memorandum', *Transformation*, 69 (2009), 106–29; O'Malley, *Shades of Difference*, 186–7.

43. 'Agenda. African National Congress Consultative Conference. Morogoro', MCH 02-1 ANC-London, Mayibuye Archives, University of the Western Cape.

44. Callinicos, *Oliver Tambo*, 333–4.

45. See the account by Ellis and Sechaba, *Comrades Against Apartheid*, 56.

46. 'Strategy and Tactics', whose principal author was Joe Slovo, also supplanted the Communist Party's programme, 'The Road to South African Freedom', adopted in 1962. See e.g. R. P. Ngcobo, 'Twenty Years of the Freedom Charter', *African Communist*, 63 (1975), 22–57; *Road to Democracy: South Africans Telling their Stories*, i, testimony of Joe Matthews, 30–1.

47. SADET, *Road to Democracy: South Africans Telling their Stories*, i, testimony of Joe Matthews, 31. Also important in this regard was Joe Matthews's paper on the Freedom Charter, 'The Revolutionary Programme'.

48. T. G. Karis and G. M. Gerhart, *From Protest to Challenge: A Documentary History of African Politics in South Africa, 1882–1990*, v: *Nadir and Resurgence, 1964–1979* (Berkeley, 1997), 36 and doc. 14.

49. S. Ellis, *External Mission: The ANC in Exile, 1960–1990* (London, 2012), 76.
50. Ellis and Sechaba, *Comrades Against Apartheid*, has a chapter titled 'The Party Triumphant: 1969–75'. See also P. Trewelha, *Inside Quatro: Uncovering the Exile History of the ANC and Swapo* (Johannesburg, 2009).
51. Larry Bowman, 'South Africa's Southern Strategy and its Implications for the United States', *International Affairs*, 47, 1 (1971), 27.
52. Shubin, *ANC: A View from Moscow*, 99.
53. Writer and activist Paul Trewelha suggests that the hounding and assassination had the support of the SACP. <http://www.politicsweb.co.za/politicsweb/view/politicsweb/en/page71619?oid=104857&sn=Detail>. For the Communist angle on Makiwane and the 'Gang of 8', see South African Communist Party, *South African Communists Speak* (London, 1981), doc. 131.
54. B. M. Schoeman, cited in Giliomee, *The Afrikaners*, 530; O'Meara, *Forty Lost Years*, 154–5.
55. Opening Address by Jean Sinclair, National President to The Black Sash, national conference, 1967, Historical Papers, Wits, AE862 D14 Black Sash National Conference 1967.
56. Address by P. Cillié to South Africa Club, 29 October 1968, B. J. Vorster papers, PV132 2/6/1/16, Institute of Contemporary History, University of the Free State.
57. *Time Magazine*, 1 November 1971.
58. D. Geldenhuys, *The Diplomacy of Isolation* (London, 1984), 34.
59. *Cambridge History of South Africa*, ii, statistical appendix, table 1a, 627. Compound population growth between 1960 and 1970 at 2.64 per cent was the highest in recorded history.
60. A. Lewis, 'The Relentless Arithmetic of the Future', *New York Times*, 21 September 1975; J. L. Sadie, *Projections of the South African Population* (Johannesburg, 1974).
61. Lewis, 'The Relentless Arithmetic of the Future'; Sadie, *Projections of the South African Population*. Typical of the newspaper stories pointing to a plummeting white birth rate and growing African population was 'White Out!', *Sunday Tribune*, 9 April 1978. Calls for birth control programmes evoked fears on the part of blacks that this was politically motivated.
62. See entries on 'verlig' and 'verkramp' in *A Dictionary of South African English on Historical Principles* (Oxford, 1996).
63. *New York Times*, 29 January 1970. Leading South African tennis players like Cliff Drysdale and Abe Segal said the decision was 'the end of the road' for the country's participation in international tennis.
64. Adam, *Modernizing Racial Domination*, 16.

Chapter 6

1. J. Hoagland, *South Africa: Civilizations in Conflict* (London, 1973), xiv, 392–4.
2. O'Meara, *Forty Lost Years*, 170.
3. In 1968–9, Moore was twice refused a lectureship at Rhodes by the politically conservative University Council.
4. J. W. De Gruchy, *The Church Struggle in South Africa* (2nd edn, London, 1990), 154.
5. On the composite origins of BC, see I. Macqueen, 'Reimagining Reality: Black Consciousness, Radical Christianity and the New Left in South Africa, 1967–76', University of Sussex, Ph.D. thesis, 2012.
6. De Gruchy, *The Church Struggle in South Africa*, 60–1. Representations from the Dutch Reformed Church were one reason for Verwoerd's failure to impose his will.
7. It was only in the 'independent' black churches that racialization was complete.
8. F. Denis, 'Seminary Networks and Black Consciousness in South Africa in the 1970s', *South African Historical Journal*, 62, 1 (2010), 162–82.
9. Steve Biko, *I Write What I Like* (London, 1987), 28.
10. D. R. Magaziner, *The Law and the Prophets: Black Consciousness in South Africa, 1968–1977* (Athens, Oh., 2010).
11. Karis and Gerhart, *From Protest to Challenge*, v. 100, 124–5; 'Notes and Documents—United Nations Centre Against Apartheid Special Issue, October 1977', <http://www.aluka.org/action/showMetadata?doi=10. 5555/AL.SFF.DOCUMENT.nuun1977_33>, 8; A. J. Norval, *Deconstructing Apartheid Discourse* (London, 1996), 197.
12. Magaziner, *The Law and the Prophets*, 50.
13. The term was borrowed from the Brazilian Paulo Freire. By the late 1970s it approximated more closely to ideological action than self-awareness.
14. M. Legassick and C. Saunders, 'Aboveground Activity in the 1960s', in *Road to Democracy*, i. 684–5.
15. Biko, *I Write What I Like*, 5.
16. Biko, *I Write What I Like*, 23.
17. Informal links between SASO and the NUSAS leadership continued despite SASO's withdrawal.
18. G. M. Gerhart, *Black Power in South Africa: The Evolution of an Ideology* (London, 1978), 268–9. A senior security policeman, Lieut. Rein Botha, noted ruefully in evidence to the Cillie Commission in 1977: 'Black

Consciousness applied to each tribe would be wonderful, but "Black Power" organisations tried to combine all race groups.' *Star*, 7 March 1977.

19. For good overviews, see e.g. Bhekizizwe Peterson, 'Culture, Resistance and Representation', in *The Road to Democracy in South Africa*, vol. ii; M. Chapman, *Southern African Literatures* (London, 1996); *Soweto Poetry* (Pietermaritzburg, 2007). For a representative collection of black South African poetry, see T. Couzens and E. Patel (eds), *The Return of the Amasi Bird* (Johannesburg, 1982).

20. There were of course intense arguments about the relative importance of aesthetic formalism and political 'relevance'.

21. Lindy Wilson, 'Bantu Stephen Biko: A Life', in B. Pityana et al., *Bounds of Possibility: The Legacy of Steve Biko and Black Consciousness* (Cape Town, 1991), 29. A source in the United States Consulate and a Lutheran bookshop were repositories of 'banned' books.

22. See e.g. Macqueen, 'Reimagining Reality', ch. 2.

23. Her husband, William Kgware, was Turfloop's first black rector in 1977 and was then somewhat unfairly denounced as a stooge.

24. Mbulelo Vizikhungo Mzamane, Bavusile Maaba, and Nkosinathi Biko, 'The Black Consciousness Movement', in SADET, *The Road to Democracy in South Africa*, ii. 132–9.

25. Leslie Hadfield, 'Christian Action and Black Consciousness Community Programmes in South Africa', *Journal for the Study of Religion*, 23, 1 & 2 (2010), 105–30.

26. Document 47 in Karis and Gerhart, *From Protest to Challenge*, v. 498–9.

27. J. Brown, 'Public Protest and Violence in South Africa, 1948–1976', D. Phil. thesis, Oxford University, 2009, 200. See also Daniel and Vale, 'South Africa: Where were we Looking in 1968?', in Gassert and Klimke (eds), *1968: Memories and Legacies of a Global Revolt*, 144; M. Legassick, 'NUSAS in the 1970s', in SADET, *The Road to Democracy in South Africa*, vol. ii; Karis and Gerhart, *From Protest to Challenge*, v. 127.

28. Brown, 'Public Protest and Violence', 173, 175–6.

29. Colleen Ryan, *Beyers Naudé: Pilgrimage of Faith* (Cape Town, 1990), ch. 13; International Commission of Jurists (eds), *The Trial of Beyers Naudé: Christian Witness and the Rule of Law* (London, 1975).

30. N. Curtis and C. Keegan, 'The Aspiration to a Just Society', in H. W. van der Merwe and D. Welsh (eds), *Student Perspectives on South Africa* (Cape Town, 1972), 120.

31. Ryan, *Beyers Naudé*, 130–3. Spro-cas's budget for the period 1969–73 was over R200,000 (roughly 1.5m US dollars in today's money). Spro-cas had precursors in the Carnegie Corporation's Poor White Commission (1930–2) which was externally funded and had a more limited remit, and the South African Bureau of Racial Affairs, est. 1948, which sought to advise government on the best means of implementing apartheid.

32. *The Star*, 11 July 1969, in Wits Historical Mansucripts, SACC AC623 38.1/11. Notable books include Rick Turner's *Eye of the Needle*; F. Wilson's *Migrant Labour in South Africa*; N. C. Manganyi's *Being-Black-In-The-World*; an abbreviated version of Peter Walshe's *Black Nationalism in South Africa*; and *Towards an Open Society* by P. Laurence and F. van Zyl Slabbert.

33. Amongst the older generation of liberals were Edgar Brookes, Leo Marquard, and Alan Paton. The newer generation included Rick Turner, Francis Wilson, Laurie Schlemmer, Desmond Tutu, F. van Zyl Slabbert, John Dugard, and André du Toit. Amongst the black and Afrikaner representatives were M. T. Moerane, W. M. Kgware, W. F. Nkomo, S. B. Ngcobo, W. A. de Klerk, N. J. Olivier, and C. C. Oosthuizen.

34. 'Spro-cas 2: Special Project for Christian Action in Society', Wits Historical Manuscripts, SACC papers, AC623 38.1 CS/61A.

35. P. Randall, *A Taste of Power* (Johannesburg, 1973), 6.

36. Biko, *I Write What I Like*, 90.

37. Ryan, *Beyers Naudé*, 132–3; Wits Historical Manuscripts, SACC AC623 38.1 CS/59A, 'Spro-cas: All Commissions. Some Reactions to the Social Report', 20 June 1972.

38. For an evaluation of the Spro-cas reports, see Macqueen, 'Re-imagining South Africa', ch. 5. Here, and in the following discussion of the 'Durban Moment', I am grateful for Macqueen's guidance.

39. Turner also served, somewhat controversially, on the Spro-cas economics and politics commissions.

40. Richard Turner, 'Black Consciousness and White Liberals', July 1972, document 27 in Karis and Gerhart, *From Protest to Challenge*, v. 431.

41. Biko, *I Write What I Like*, 89; M. Ramphele, *Across the Boundaries* (New York, 1996), 63. For an extended discussion of the 'Durban Moment' and the discussions between Biko and Turner, see Macqueen, 'Re-imagining South Africa', ch. 6.

42. Mamphele Ramphele, 'Empowerment and Symbols of Hope: Black Consciousness and Community Development', in Pityana et al. (eds), *Bounds of Possibility*, 158.

43. Fatton, *Black Consciousness in South Africa*, 77; Biko, 'Black Consciousness and the Quest for a True Humanity', in *I Write What I Like*, 90.

44. Karis and Gerhart, *From Protest to Challenge*, v. 139. Other speakers at the Athlone rally were Gatsha Buthelezi, Adam Small, and Sonny Leon.

45. Magaziner, *The Law and the Prophets*, 179.

46. S. Friedman, *Building Tomorrow Today: African Workers in Trade Unions, 1970–1984* (Johannesburg, 1987), 37–8.

47. G. Davie, 'Strength in Numbers: The Durban Student Wages Commission, Dockworkers and the Poverty Datum Line, 1971–73', *JSAS*, 33, 2 (2007).

48. Brown, 'Public Protest and Violence', ch. 5.

49. 'The Trial of SASO/BPC detainees', 1975, <http://www.aluka.org/action/showMetadata?doi=10.5555/AL.SFF.DOCUMENT.mem19750000.032.009.757>.

50. Given the real prospect of the death penalty, their sentences (which ranged between 5 and 6 years) were relatively lenient.

51. Biko, *I Write What I Like*, 104.

52. E. Lockwood, 'National Security Study Memorandum 39 and the Future of United States Policy Toward Southern Africa', *Issue: A Quarterly Journal of Africanist Opinion*, 4, 3 (1974); L. Thompson and A. Prior, *South African Politics* (Cape Town, 1982), 226; *The Dispatch*, 3 (October 1972). Hurd, a right-wing Harvard-educated Texas oilman with strong Republican party links, embarrassed the US embassy in Cape Town when news of his 1972 hunting expedition emerged. He also defied liberal opinion by attending the opening of the controversial whites-only Nico Malan Opera House in 1971.

53. *South Africa: Time Running Out. The Report of the Study Commission on U.S. Policy Toward Southern Africa* (California, 1981), 234.

54. This was Schalk Pienaar's 'ligte mistykie'. See O'Meara, *Forty Lost Years*, 180.

55. G. Bender, 'Kissinger in Angola: Anatomy of Failure', in R. Lemarchand (ed.), *American Policy in Southern Africa* (Washington, 1978). See also O'Meara, *Forty Lost Years*, 219–22, and Odd Arne Westad, *The Global Cold War* (Cambridge, 2007), 245–6.

56. H. F. De Wet and C. E. Coetzee, 'South African Defence Expenditure in the 20th Century', 2002 <http://129.3.20.41/eps/othr/papers/0205/0205003.pdf>; P. H. Frankel, *Pretoria's Praetorians* (Cambridge, 1984), 73. By contrast, in 1960/1 defence expenditure constituted less than 1 per cent of state expenditure. It is difficult to present precise figures because a lot of defence expenditure was routed through secret accounts and other budgets.

57. Feinstein, *Economic History of South Africa*, 200–3; Nattrass and Seekings, 'The Economy and Poverty in the Twentieth Century', in *Cambridge History*, ii. 541–2; A. D. Lowenberg. 'Why South Africa's Apartheid Economy Failed', *Contemporary Economic Policy*, 15, 3 (2007), 65.

58. F. Wilson, *Migrant Labour in South Africa* (Johannesburg, 1972), preface.

59. F. Wilson, *Labour in the South African Gold Mines 1911–1969* (Cambridge, 1972), 141.

60. J. Nattrass, *The South African Economy* (Cape Town, 1981), 139–40; Feinstein, *Economic History of South Africa*, 231–2.

61. In 1993, when formal apartheid came to an end, the per capita personal incomes relative to whites were 10.9 per cent for Africans, 42 per cent for Asians, and 19.3 per cent for coloureds. See Leibbrandt et al., 'Trends in South African Income Distribution and Poverty since the Fall of Apartheid', table 1.1, OECD working paper no. 101 (2010), <http://dx.doi.org/10.1787/5kmmsot7p-en>.

62. Sanders, *South Africa and the International Media*, ch. 5.

63. Ruth First, Jonathan Steele, and Christabel Gurney, *The South African Connection: Western Investment in Apartheid* (Harmondsworth, 1973), 15, 29–30.

64. 'The Milton Friedman View', <http://0055d26.netsolhost.com/friedman/pdfs/other_commentary/SundayTimes.1976.2.pdf>.

65. Giliomee, *The Afrikaners*, 599.

66. Hastings Ndlovu, not Hector Pieterson, was the first child to be killed.

67. Evidence of Mangaliso Alf Khumalo to (Cillé) *Commission of Inquiry into the riots at Soweto and other places in South Africa held on 13 and 14 October 1976*, vol. 27, p. 1221, <http://www.aluka.org/action/showMetadata?doi=10.5555/AL.SFF.DOCUMENT.tra19761013.026.019b>.

68. *Rand Daily Mail*, 26 June 1976; 28 June 1976.

69. C. Glaser, '"We must infiltrate the tsotsis": School Politics and Youth Gangs in Soweto, 1968–1976', *JSAS*, 24, 2 (1998).

70. In addition to the deaths, more than 2,000 people were shot by police.

71. Dr Melville Edelstein, who was beaten to death on the first day of the uprising, had undertaken a survey of 'attitudes' for his master's dissertation which drew attention to a sense of black pride among Soweto's high school children and concluded that influx control, inadequate educational facilities, and the absence of political rights were among their foremost grievances.

72. See e.g. *Star*, 24 June 1976, 26 June 1976; *Cape Times*, 7 July 1976.

73. *Sunday Express*, 27 June 1976. As a member of the Soweto Urban Bantu Council, Mosala admitted that many blacks regarded him as a 'collaborator'.

74. J. Allen, *Rabble-Rouser for Peace: The Authorised Biography of Desmond Tutu* (New York, 2006), 154; *The Times*, 15 June 1976.

75. Jerome Caminada, *The Times*, 14 June 1976.

76. N. Diseko, 'The Origins and Development of the South African Student's Movement (SASM): 1968–1976', *JSAS*, 18, 1 (1991).

77. O'Malley, *Shades of Difference*, 218, 220–1.

78. *Sechaba* was slow to react, devoting substantial coverage to the revolt only in 1977 (first quarter, vol. 11). In the following issue (second quarter, 1977) the ANC reaffirmed its role in the vanguard of the struggle. This issue featured an interview with Nkosazana Dlamini, vice-president of SASO, entitled 'The ANC is the Answer'. On the ANC's ambivalence towards the BCM, see also Sanders, *South Africa and the International Media*, 95.

79. R. S. Nyameko and G. Singh, 'The Role of Black Consciousness in the South African Revolution', *African Communist*, 68 (1977), 46. In *African Communist*, 60 (1975), 110, a review of Basil Moore's edited collection *Black Theology* was headed 'Black Consciousness—A Blind Alley'. See also Joe Slovo's contribution, 'No Middle Road', in B. Davidson et al., *Southern Africa: The New Politics of Southern Africa* (Harmondsworth, 1976), which dismisses Black Consciousness as a term which 'does not in itself express a coherent programme, still less an ideology', 177. This widely cited text was for many years seen as an authoritative statement of Communist Party and ANC thought.

80. Minutes of 'Consultative Meeting' 29–30 October 1979, London, 9, in H. J. Coetsee papers, Institute of Contemporary Research, Free State University, PV357 1/A1/5.

81. Sifiso Mxolisi Ndlovu, 'The Soweto Uprising', in *The Road to Democracy in South Africa*, ii. 337–8.

82. *Rand Daily Mail*, 18 January 1977; *Sunday Times*, 30 January 1977.

83. Shortly after the revolt's explosion, the government rescinded Treurnicht's injunction, but this concession had no effect in quelling the violence.

84. From 1955 to 1976 the overall proportion of high school enrolment amongst African teenagers rose from 3.5 per cent to 12.8 per cent (it was closer to 20 per cent in Soweto). Most of that increase took place after 1971. In 1975 there were nearly 320,000 Africans in secondary school by which time per capita spending on white to black school children was of the order of 15:1. High student/teacher ratios (around 50:1 in 1977), poorly trained teachers, and classroom shortages were a source of enormous frustration. See e.g. John Kane-Berman, *South Africa: The Method in the Madness* (London,

1979), 185–7; Lodge, 'Resistance and Reform', in Ross et al. (eds), *Cambridge History of South Africa*, ii. 419; C. Bundy, 'Street Sociology and Pavement Politics: Aspects of Youth and Student Resistance in Cape Town, 1985', *JSAS*, 13, 3 (1987), 311–12.

85. According to World Bank Indicators, 42 per cent of Africans were under the age of 15 in 1976. The figure in 2010 was 30 per cent.
86. Kane-Berman, *South Africa: The Method in the Madness*, 19–20.
87. Cited in Kane-Berman, *South Africa: The Method in the Madness*, 110.
88. Buntman, 'How Best to Resist?', 151.
89. A. Brooks and J. Brickhill, *Whirlwind Before the Storm* (London, 1980), 104 and ff.
90. B. Hirson, *Year of Fire, Year of Ash. The Soweto Revolt: Roots of a Revolution?* (London, 1979), 9.
91. Robert Fatton Jr, *Black Consciousness in South Africa* (Albany, NY, 1986), 82–3.
92. *Cape Times*, 31 August 1976 (editorial).
93. Biko, *I Write What I Like*, 145–50.
94. *New York Times*, 14 November 1977.
95. Lane, '"Heroes as Ordinary People"', 53. Deaths in this period represented a major upward spike. In the period up to 1976 some 22 people died in police detention.
96. B. Pityana, 'Reflections on 30 Years Since the Death of Steve Biko: A Legacy Revisited', 2007 Steve Biko Lecture, Senate Hall, Unisa, 12 September 2007.
97. *The Times*, 26 September 1977.
98. 'Notes and Documents—United Nations Centre Against Apartheid Special Issue, October 1977', <http://www.aluka.org/action/showMetadata?doi=10.5555/AL.SFF.DOCUMENT.nuun1977_33>, 12–17.
99. Sanders, *South Africa and the International Media*, ch. 7. The quote is from an article by journalist Jim Hoagland, cited by Sanders on 181.
100. 'Statement by Oliver Tambo at the plenary meeting of the United Nations General Assembly', 26 October 1976, <http://www.anc.org.za/show.php?id=4331>.
101. *The Times*, 21 September 1976.
102. Kissinger also spoke of the need to bring about 'peaceful change, equality of opportunity and basic rights in South Africa'. *New York Times*, 2 September 1976; *Observer-Reporter*, 1 September 1976. For analysis, see R. W. Johnson, *How Long will South Africa Survive?* (London, 1977), 246; also C. Legum, *Southern Africa: The Year of the Whirlwind* (London, 1977).

103. 'Statement by Oliver Tambo at the plenary meeting of the United Nations General Assembly', 26 October 1976.

104. *New York Times*, 29 May 1977; 23 May 1977.

105. *New York Times*, 4 May 1977; 17 May 1977.

106. United Nations Security Council Resolution 418, 4 November 1977. The United States, Britain, and France nevertheless vetoed proposals by African countries for mandatory economic sanctions.

107. M. Rees and C. Day, *Muldergate* (Johannesburg, 1980), 186.

108. The phrase 'war of representation' appears in J. Sanders, *South Africa and the International Media 1972–1979* (London, 2000), 3.

109. J. Sanders, *Apartheid's Friends: The Rise and Fall of South Africa's Secret Service* (London, 2006), ch. 5, O'Meara, *Forty Lost Years*, ch. 12.

110. Welile Bottoman, cited in J. Cherry, *Umkhonto we Sizwe* (Auckland Park, 2012), 63.

111. Shubin, *ANC: A View from Moscow*, 180–1, 194; Callinicos, *Oliver Tambo*, 383.

112. Mandela, *Long Walk to Freedom*, 472.

113. F. Buntman, *Robben Island and Prisoner Resistance to Apartheid* (Cambridge, 2003), 131–6; Lane, '"Heroes as Ordinary People"', 104.

114. E. Boehmer, *Nelson Mandela: A Very Short Introduction* (Oxford, 2008), 54; Colin Bundy, *Govan Mbeki* (Johannesburg, 2012), 131–2.

115. F. Buntman, 'How to Resist? Robben Island after 1976', in H. Deacon (ed.), *The Island* (Cape Town, 1996), 140, 143, 149; A. Kathrada, *Memoirs* (Cape Town, 2004), 277.

Chapter 7

1. C. McCarthy, 'Productivity Performance in Developing Countries. Country Case Studies: South Africa', (UNIDO, 2005), 7 <http://www.unido.org/fileadmin/user_media/Publications/Pub_free/Productivity_performance_in_DCs_South_Africa.pdf>.

2. *The Star*, 31 December 1981.

3. L. Thompson and A. Prior, *South African Politics* (Cape Town, 1982), 232, calculate that in 1980 total 'western' investments exceeded $25bn and produced an excellent rate of return; in aggregate, they exported more than $5bn goods to South Africa and imported even more.

4. O. Crankshaw, 'Changes in the Racial Division of Labour During the Apartheid Era', *JSAS*, 22, 4 (1996), 644 fig. 1, 655–6.

5. Leibbrandt et al., 'Trends in South African Income Distribution', 14.
6. H. Giliomee and L. Schlemmer, *From Apartheid to Nation-Building* (Cape Town, 1989), table 3.5, p. 106. Spending on coloured and Indian education doubled in real terms between 1977 and 1987.
7. L. Chisholm, 'Continuity and Change in Education Policy Research and Borrowing in South Africa', in P. Kallaway (ed.), *The History of Education Under Apartheid 1948–1994* (Cape Town, 2002), 98–9; K. Harshorne, *Crisis and Challenge: Black Education 1910–1990* (Cape Town, 1992), ch. 6 and 42–3.
8. W. Cobbett et al., 'A Critical Analysis of the South African State's Reform Strategies in the 1980s', in P. Frankel et al. (eds), *State, Resistance and Change in South Africa* (London, 1988); R. M. Price, *The Apartheid State in Crisis* (New York, 1991), 83.
9. André Beaufre, *An Introduction to Strategy* (New York, 1965), 30. See also *Strategy of Action* (London, 1967), ch. 1.
10. Frankel, *Pretoria's Praetorians*, 46, 53.
11. A. D. Wassenaar, *Assault on Private Enterprise: The Freeway to Communism* (Cape Town, 1977), 13.
12. O'Meara, *Forty Lost Years*, 195, 258, 294, 301. An equally well-publicized conference in 1981 revealed that business leaders were not convinced that the government was moving fast enough with reform.
13. A. Seegers, *The Military in the Making of Modern South Africa* (London, 1996), 163.
14. Seegers, *The Military in the Making of Modern South Africa*, 165.
15. P. Vale, 'Cold War in Southern Africa: White Power, Black Liberation', *Safundi*, 12, 2 (2011), 320, traces the first use of this term to Stellenbosch academic Willie Breytenbach in 1987. It was used in the United States as early as 1949.
16. D. Posel, 'The Language of Domination, 1978–1983', in S. Marks and S. Trapido (eds), *The Politics of Race, Class and Nationalism in Twentieth Century South Africa* (Harlow, 1987), 419 and ff.
17. F. W. de Klerk, *The Last Trek: A New Beginning* (Basingstoke, 1998), 89.
18. Norval, *Deconstructing Apartheid Discourse*, ch. 4.
19. A. Lijphart, *Power-Sharing in South Africa* (Berkeley, 1985). For a critical account, see R. Taylor, 'South Africa: A Consociational Path to Peace?', *Transformation*, 17 (1992), 1–11.
20. 'Address by Dr the Honorable PGJ Koornhof, Minister of Cooperation and Development, at a lunch meeting of the National Press Club, Washington DC', 15 June 1979. Leon Wessels papers, PV883 4/1/1 Institute of

Contemporary History, University of the Free State. The quote is often rendered as 'apartheid is dead', which is not quite what Koornhof was claiming. See also *New York Times*, 4 August 1979, 'South Africa's Reforms' by P. G. Koornhof. Late in life Koornhof (who became known as 'Piet Promises') divorced his wife and moved in with Marcelle Adams, a much younger coloured woman, pronouncing that his relationship was 'the answer to apartheid, an answer by deed'.

21. Cited in *A Dictionary of South African English on Historical Principles*.

22. Cited in S. Dubow, 'Ethnic Euphemisms and Racial Echoes', *JSAS*, 20, 3 (1994), 355.

23. *New York Times*, 1 November 1980.

24. 'The Orderly Movement and Settlement of Black Persons Bill. Comment addressed to the Churches', by Sheena Duncan, 1982, Black Sash archives, AE862 G23.5, Cullen Library, Wits University.

25. Fewer than one in five of eligible Indians and coloureds voted for their respective parliamentary assemblies.

26. A. de Tocqueville, *The Old Regime and the Revolution*, trans. John Bonner (New York, 1856), 214.

27. The National Forum emerged directly out of Azapo (the Azanian People's Organization), which was formed in 1978 to provide a political home for the Black Consciousness Movement.

28. *Rand Daily Mail* (editorial), 15 June 1983.

29. The term 'Azania' in preference to South Africa was used occasionally in circles associated with the Pan-Africanist Movement. The derivation of the term is not clear but there is some irony in its use by Evelyn Waugh in his satirical novel *Black Mischief* (1932) and also in the claim that its origins are Persian or Arabic and that it was used by Arabic-speakers to denote dark-skinned Africans in eastern Africa.

30. 'A "Socialist" SA is in the Air', *Rand Daily Mail*, 13 June 1983; *The Sowetan*, 16 June 1983.

31. A. W. Marx, *Lessons of Struggle* (New York, 1992), 239.

32. Cited in H. Barrell, 'The United Democratic Front and National Forum: Their Emergence, Composition and Trends', in SARS (ed.), *South African Review II* (Johannesburg, 1984), 10.

33. Mandela, *Long Walk to Freedom*, 473. Lekota was assaulted by prisoners affiliated to the BCM for doing so.

34. Document 35 in Gerhart and Glaser, *From Protest to Challenge*, vi. 314.

35. Boesak, *Running With Horses*, 10–11.

36. S. W. Martin, 'Faithful Treason: The Theology and Politics of Allan A. Boesak', *Journal of Theology for Southern Africa*, 118 (March 2004), 80–99. Boesak was always a controversial figure and he was never deeply involved in day-to-day UDF politics. His rapid ascent was shortlived as reports of his infidelity, egotism, and allegations of corruption overwhelmed him.

37. Gerhart and Glaser, *From Protest to Challenge*, vi, doc. 86.

38. Jo-Anne Collinge, 'Can Security Laws Really Check the UDF Hydra?', *Star*, 30 April 1985.

39. Interview with Trevor Manuel, *Financial Mail*, 19 October 1984.

40. R. M. Price, *The Apartheid State in Crisis* (New York, 1991), 191–2 and ff.

41. M. Swilling, 'Stayaways, Urban Protest and the State', in SARS, *South African Review 3* (Johannesburg, 1986), 23–7; Price, *The Apartheid State*, 196.

42. Callinicos, *Oliver Tambo*, 548.

43. 'The First 100 Days', *Weekly Mail*, 1 November 1985.

44. Christopher Nicholson, *Permanent Removal: Who Killed the Cradock Four* (Johannesburg, 2004).

45. M. Murray, *South Africa: Time of Agony, Time of Destiny* (London, 1987), 254–5.

46. L. Nathan, '"Marching to a Different Beat": The History of the End Conscription Campaign', in J. Cock and L. Nathan (eds), *War and Society: The Militarisation of South Africa* (Cape Town, 1989).

47. T. Lodge and Bill Nasson, *All Here and Now: Black Politics in South Africa in the 1980s* (London, 1992), table 4, 178.

48. Cherry, *Umkhonto We Sizwe*, 50–1; H. Barrell, *MK: The ANC's Armed Struggle* (London, 1990), 34–6.

49. The individual responsible for the Koeberg bombing was Rodney Wilkinson, an ANC sympathizer and former national sword-fighting champion who had lived on a commune near Koeberg and was at the time working on the nuclear construction site.

50. Nadja Manghezi, *The Maputo Connection: The ANC in the World of Frelimo* (Johannesburg, 2009), 128.

51. Gqabi was gunned down in 1981, Ruth First was killed by a parcel bomb in 1982. They had worked together on the radical newspaper *New Age* in Johannesburg in the 1950s.

52. J. Hanlon, *Beggar your Neighbours: Apartheid Power in Southern Africa* (London, 1991).

53. Price, *The Apartheid State in Crisis*, 95.

54. G. M. Gerhart and C. L. Glaser, *From Protest to Challenge*, vol. vi (Bloomington, Ind., 2010), doc. 114.

55. P. Vale, 'The Botha Doctrine: Pretoria's Response to the West and to its Neighbours', *South African Review II*, 189 and ff.

56. Samuel Huntington, 'Reform and Stability in South Africa', *Politikon*, 6, 4 (1982), 16–17. See also Hermann Giliomee's discussion in *Rand Daily Mail*, 1 February 1982.

57. In 1997 Dirk Coetzee, Almond Nofemela, and David Tshikalanga admitted to the murder of the Mxenges and received amnesty from the Truth and Reconciliation Commission.

58. See e.g. G. Maré and G. Hamilton, *An Appetite for Power: Buthelezi's Inkatha and South Africa* (Johannesburg, 1987); S. Marks, *The Ambiguities of Dependence in South Africa: Class, Nationalism, and the State in Twentieth-Century Natal* (Baltimore, 1986).

59. Minutes of 'Consultative Meeting' 29–30 October 1979, London, in H. J. Coetsee papers, Institute of Contemporary Research, Free State University, PV357 1/A1/5.

60. Mimeo of 'Consultative Meeting 29/10/79 to 30/10/79 London' between Inkatha and the ANC in H. J. Coetsee papers, Institute of Contemporary History, University of the Free State; Callinicos, *Oliver Tambo*, 394–7.

61. *Truth and Reconciliation Commission of South Africa Final Report*, vol. iii (1998), ch. 3, paras. 139–45.

62. *Truth and Reconciliation Commission of South Africa Final Report*, vol. iii, paras. 203–6.

63. Black Consciousness students who did not make the 'transition' to Charterism were grouped together in AZASM (the Azanian Students' Movement, est. 1983), which was affiliated to the National Forum but much smaller than COSAS.

64. J. Aitcheson, 'Interpreting Violence: The Struggle to Understand the Natal Conflict', paper presented to Institute of Commonwealth Studies, London University, 1990, 1–2.

65. M. Kentridge, *An Unofficial War: Inside the Conflict in Pietermaritzburg* (Cape Town, 1990), 198 and ff., *Mail and Guardian*, 19 February 1992.

66. J. Cole, *Crossroads: The Politics of Reform and Repression 1976–1986* (Johannesburg, 1987).

67. The term 'kitskonstabel' was derisory: like instant coffee, it denoted police who were not the real thing.

68. M. Savage, 'The Imposition of Pass Laws on the African Population in South Africa 1916–1984', *African Affairs*, 85, 339 (1986), 183, 201. It is worth noting that these figures are still significantly lower than the high-point of 694,000 prosecutions in 1967.

69. Jeremy Seekings, 'The Savage World of the Vigilantes', *Weekly Mail*, 4 April 1986.

70. Jo Beall et al., 'African Women in the Durban Struggle, 1985–6: Towards a Transformation of Roles?', in G. Moss and J. Obery, *South African Review 4* (Johannesburg, 1987); Cole, *Crossroads*.

71. Cited in H. Giliomee, 'Great Expectations: Pres. Botha's Rubicon Speech of 1985', *New Contree*, 5 (May, 2008), 6.

72. A full analysis is provided by Giliomee in 'Great Expectations', 1–41. Giliomee suggests that Botha suffered a stroke shortly before the speech and that this had the effect of disinhibiting his emotions. For informed contemporary political comment, see e.g. David Braun in *The Star*, 17 August 1985.

73. It has been claimed that Chase made its decision before the Rubicon speech and that this was made on grounds of perceived risk rather than in order to facilitate political change in South Africa. Either way, this was a significant turn-around. In 1967 Chase Manhattan's head, David Rockefeller, had argued that the Bank could 'exert a constructive influence on racial conditions in South Africa'.

74. Hugo Young, *One of Us* (London, 1989), 483; Sampson, *Mandela*, 352.

75. J. F. Posnikoff, 'Disinvestment from South Africa: They did Well by Doing Good', *Contemporary Economic Policy*, 15 (January 1997), 76–86.

76. P. I. Levy, 'Sanctions on South Africa: What did they Do?', Yale University Economic Growth Center, Discussion Paper No. 796 (1999), 6, 9.

77. Feinstein, *Economic History of South Africa*, table 10.2, 227, 230.

78. C. M. Morgenstierne, *Denmark and National Liberation in South Africa* (Stockholm, 2003), 13. Denmark and other Nordic countries coupled sanctions with very substantial contributions to organizations and individuals involved in the freedom struggle. Sweden imposed an investment ban in 1979.

79. L. Schlemmer, 'Were we Really Polls Apart?', *Sunday Times*, 15 September 1985. Schlemmer's analysis pointed out that oversimplified and over-generalized questions were generating poor-quality results.

80. Levy, 'Sanctions on South Africa', 10, 12.

Chapter 8

1. This phrase is used by G. M. Gerhart and C. L. Glaser in *From Protest to Challenge*, vi: *Challenge and Victory* (Bloomington, Ind., 2010), 46.
2. The following discussion draws on Gerhart and Glaser's discussion in *From Protest to Challenge*, vi. 61 and ff., as well as P. Van Niekerk, 'The Trade Union Movement in the Politics of Resistance in South Africa', in S. Johnson (ed.), *South Africa: No Turning Back* (London, 1989), 153–71.
3. 'FOSATU—Its Policies and Objectives', FOSATU archives, AH1999 C1.1, Wits University. At the end of 1982 FOSATU was comprised of nine affiliates and claimed in excess of 100,000 signed-up members.
4. By 1987 COSATU claimed a paid-up membership of 750,000. Total unionization in South Africa at this time was about 2m, perhaps 15–20 per cent of the active working population.
5. *Weekly Mail*, 6 December 1985; 14 February 1986.
6. Communiqué of the meeting between COSATU, SACTU, and the ANC 5–6 March 1986, <http://www.anc.org.za/show.php?id=3818>. This was the basis of the 'tripartite alliance'—the ANC, COSATU, and the South African Communist Party—which ushered South Africa into the democratic era post-1994.
7. COSAS was banned in the first emergency of 1985 but continued to operate until it was reconstituted in 1989–90. In the intervening period it supported the South African Youth Congress (SAYCO), which was formed in 1987. AZASM was affiliated to the National Forum.
8. S. Johnson, ' "The Soldiers of Luthuli" ': Youth in the Politics of Resistance in South Africa', in S. Johnson (ed.), *South Africa: No Turning Back* (London, 1989), 94.
9. Johnson, 'The Soldiers of Luthuli', 94; J. Hyslop, 'School Student Movements and State Education Policy: 972–87', in W. Cobbett et al. (eds), *Popular Struggles in South Africa* (London, 1988), 183.
10. C. Bundy, 'Street Sociology and Pavement Politics: Aspects of Youth and Student Resistance in Cape Town, 1985', *JSAS*, 13, 3 (1987), 303–30.
11. Much, though not all, of its work documented urban resistance. In the early 1990s a group of photojournalists known as the 'bang-bang club' covered the urban insurrection with an emphasis on fearless reportage. One of their number, Ken Oosterbroek, was shot and killed in Thokoza township in 1994. See e.g. D. L. Krantz, 'Politics and Photography in Apartheid South Africa', *History of Photography*, 32, 4 (Winter 2008), 290–300.

12. R. Nixon, *Homelands, Harlem and Hollywood: South African Culture and World Beyond* (New York, 1994), 82.

13. Jacob Dlamini, *Native Nostalgia* (Johannesburg, 2009), 21. For a finely realized local sociology of insurrection, see e.g. Bozzoli, *Theatres of Struggle and the End of Apartheid*. For an important discussion of the treatment of township insurrection in the 1980s, see Hilary Sapire's 'Township Histories, Insurrection and Liberation Late Apartheid South Africa', *South African Historical Journal*, 65, 2 (2013).

14. Bozzoli, *Theatres of Struggle and the End of Apartheid*, 143, 175.

15. C. Campbell, 'Learning to Kill? Masculinity, the Family and Violence in Natal', *Journal of Southern African Studies*, 18, 3 (1992), 624; Gerhart and Glaser, *From Protest to Challenge*, vi. 100.

16. The historiography of the 1980s insurrection is treated in J. Seekings, 'Whose Voices? Politics and Methodology in the Study of Political Organisation and Protest in the Final Phase of the "Struggle" in South Africa', *South African Historical Journal*, 62, 1 (2010), 7–28; also Sapire, 'Township Histories'.

17. J. Muller, 'People's Education and the National Education Crisis Committee', in G. Moss and I. Obery (eds), *South African Review 4* (Johannesburg, 1987).

18. Johnson, 'The Soldiers of Luthuli', 137–9.

19. Non-African entrants to the NEC were Joe Slovo, Mac Maharaj, Hermanus Loots (James Stuart), Aziz Pahad, and Reg September.

20. Callinicos, *Oliver Tambo*, 552–4; Gerhart and Glaser, *From Protest to Challenge*, vi, docs. 124, 125.

21. Stuart Commission Report, 'Commission of inquiry into recent developments in the People's Republic of Angola', <http://www.anc.org.za/show.php?id=87>.

22. J. Cherry, 'The Intersection of Violent and Non-Violent Strategies in the South African Liberation Struggle', in H. Sapire and C. C. Saunders (eds), *Southern African Liberation Struggles: New Local, Regional and Global Perspectives* (Cape Town, 2012), 144, 157–8.

23. Gerhart and Glaser, *From Protest to Challenge*, vi, doc. 126, 'Summary of Discussions between Certain Representatives of Big Business and Opinion-Makers in South Africa and the ANC', ANC memorandum, 14 September 1985.

24. *Star*, 8 February 1986; F. van Zyl Slabbert, *The Last White Parliament* (London, 1985), 106.

25. *New York Times*, 9 December 1990. The government dropped charges against Heard—who faced a three-year prison sentence—but the newspaper editor was fired by his company.

26. Barry Streek's report of his interview with Oliver Tambo and other ANC leaders, see *Rand Daily Mail*, 8 February 1985.

27. *Star*, 24 April 1985; 26 April 1985.

28. P. Waldmeier, *Anatomy of a Miracle* (London, 1997), 91–2; A. Sparks, *Tomorrow is Another Country: The Inside Story of South Africa's Negotiated Revolution* (Cape Town, 1994), 21–2, 24–5.

29. Mandela was alive to the risk and sent back a message to Lusaka with the EPG that he saw himself as just an ordinary member of the ANC.

30. Sparks, *Tomorrow is Another Country*, 34–5.

31. D. Webster, 'Repression and the State of Emergency', in Moss and Obery (eds), *South African Review 4*, 142–3, 152–6.

32. D. Webster and M. Friedman, 'Repression and the State of Emergency: June 1987–March 1989', in G. Moss and I. Obery (eds), *South African Review 5* (Johannesburg, 1989), 18–19.

33. Seekings, *The UDF*, 228–9; I. Van Kessel, *'Beyond our Wildest Dreams': The United Democratic Front and the Transformation of South Africa* (Charlottesville, Va., 2000), 44.

34. N. Gordimer, 'Living in the Interregnum', *New York Review of Books*, 20 January 1983. Cf. 'Living in the Interregnum', *Rand Daily Mail*, 2 September 1983.

35. A. Morris, 'When All Tenants were No Longer "Shiny White and Legal": The Increasing Integration of the Johannesburg Inner City and the Response of the White Right, 1977–1991', History Workshop, Wits, 1994.

36. A. Grundlingh, '"Rocking the Boat" in South Africa? Voëlvry Music and Afrikaans Anti-Apartheid Social Protest in the 1980s', *International Journal of African Historical Studies*, 37, 3 (2004), 483–514.

37. Sparks, *Tomorrow is Another Country*, 78–86.

38. Brink, *A Fork in the Road*, 365–8; Gevisser, *Thabo Mbeki*, 510–13; Revd F. Chikane 'Statement on the Dakar Summit', 15 July 1987, SACC papers AC623/34.17 (IDASA file), Wits University; Gerhart and Glaser, *Protest to Challenge*, vol. vi, doc. 138 'Evaluation of Dakar conference by ANC participant, July 1987'.

39. Gevisser, *Thabo Mbeki*, 506–7.

40. Giliomee, *The Afrikaners*, 621–2. The document reached the ANC as 'Basic Political Values for the Survival of the Afrikaner', ANC Archives, London MCH02-57, Mayibuye Centre, University of the Western Cape.

41. J. M. van der Merwe, 'Cottesloe 50 Years Later: Did the Dutch Reformed Church Answer to the Call?', *Nederduitse Gereformeerde Teologiese Tydskrif*, 51, 3 & 4 (2010), 160–2. Johan Heyns also challenged the church's hostility to homosexuality. In 1994 Heyns was shot and killed at his home by right-wing extremists.

42. J. and S. De Gruchy, *The Church Struggle in South Africa* (London, 2005), 185; *The Kairos Document: A Theological Comment on the Political Crisis in South Africa* (2nd edn, Johannesburg, 1986). For a strong attack on historians' failure to acknowledge 'God in the struggle', see Boesak, *Running With Horses*, 342 and ff.

43. 'ANC: Voorlopige Evaluering van Nastionale Konferensie', P. W. Botha papers, PV203 PS4/3/6; 'Broederbond Document: Basic Political Values for the Survival of the Afrikaner', MCH02-57, ANC-London, Mayibuye archive, University of the Western Cape.

44. S. Dubow, *The Struggle for Human Rights in South Africa* (Johannesburg, 2012), 79–80, 91, 104, 111.

45. G. Maré, '"Mixed, Capitalist and Free": The Aims of the "Natal Option"', in Moss and Obery (eds), *South African Review 4*, 511.

46. My thanks to Beatrice Hollyer for this point.

47. N. Haysom and S. Kahanovitz, 'Courts and the State of Emergency', in Moss and Obery (eds), *South African Review 4*, 188.

48. *Acta Juridica* (1984).

49. Haysom and Kahanovitz, 'Courts and the State of Emergency', 198.

50. Webster, 'Repression and the State of Emergency', 159–60.

51. *New York Times*, 19 November 1988.

52. Seekings, *The UDF*, 290, 300–1.

53. Mandela, *Long Walk to Freedom*, 513–14.

54. Lodge, *Mandela*, 155.

55. But in 2006 Amnesty gave Mandela its most prestigious honour: the Ambassador of Conscience Award.

56. Callinicos, *Oliver Tambo*, 590–1; Lodge, *Mandela*, 160; Seekings, *The UDF*, 242.

57. Lodge, *Mandela*, 171, 173; Sampson, *Mandela*, 428–30; T. Simpson, 'Toyi-Toyi-ing to Freedom: The Endgame in the ANC's Armed Struggle, 1989–1990', *JSAS*, 35, 2 (2009), 508.

58. Mandela, *Long Walk to Freedom*, 521.

59. The contorted image made it look as though he was trying to smile while in physical pain.

60. Sometimes Ou Krokodil (old crocodile). It is widely believed that Botha suffered a stroke in 1985. Analysts like Hermann Giliomee suggest, on medical evidence, that this may have affected his mental balance.

61. 'Press Briefing for Accredited Foreign Correspondents on the ANC, and Security Aspects Concerning South Africa', 2 April 1986, H. J. Coetsee papers, PV357 1/A1/6 1986, Institute for Contemporary History, University of the Free State.

62. Lodge, 'Resistance and Reform', 463.

63. Cherry, *Umkhonto we Sizwe*, 91–3.

64. Gerhart and Glaser, *From Protest to Challenge*, vol. vi, doc. 146 'ANC Report on a meeting in Henley-on-Thames, England, with three Stellenbosch academics', 31 October–1 November 1987.

65. J. Hyslop, 'The Impact of the Ultra-Right on South African Politics', in Moss and Obery (eds), *South African Review 4*.

66. O'Meara, *Forty Lost Years*, 373.

67. Giliomee and Schlemmer, *From Apartheid to Nation*-Building, table 6.2, 196. By comparison, 16 per cent of Conservative Party supporters and 75 per cent of PFP supporters rated negotiations with the ANC 'important'.

68. F. van Zyl Slabbert, *The System and the Struggle* (Johannesburg, 1989), 84.

69. Slabbert, *The System and the Struggle*, 155.

70. *Race Relations Survey 1989/90*, 235.

71. *Cape Argus*, 27 October 1987.

72. M. Kentridge, *An Unofficial War: Inside the Conflict in Pietermaritzburg* (Cape Town, 1990), 2.

73. M. Savage, *The Cost of Apartheid* (Cape Town, 1986), 8; 'The Cost of Apartheid', *Third World Quarterly*, 9, 2 (1987), 620.

74. D. Woods, 'Transkei Independence: South Africa's Calculated Risk', *Optima*, 25, 4 (1975).

75. T. Gibbs, 'Chris Hani's "Country Bumpkins": Regional Networks in the African National Congress Underground, 1974–1994', *JSAS*, 37, 4 (2011), 678, 687; Mandela, *Long Walk to Freedom*, 86. Mandela's willingness to engage with Matanzima was bitterly criticized on Robben Island, but he argued that the ANC could be strengthened by participating in government-sponsored organizations.

76. Welsh, *The Rise and Fall of Apartheid*, 328–9.

77. M. Swilling, 'Living in the Interregnum: Crisis, Reform and the Socialist Alternative in South Africa', *Third World Quarterly*, 9, 2 (1987), 421.

78. R. Omond, 'South Africa's Post-Apartheid Constitution', *Third World Quarterly*, 9, 2 (1987), 622–3.

79. S. Marks and S. Trapido, 'South Africa Since 1976: An Historical Perspective', in Johnson (ed.), *South Africa: No Turning Back*, 46.

80. H. Barrell, 'The Outlawed South African Liberation Movements', in Johnson (ed.), *South Africa: No Turning Back*, 86.

81. F. van Zyl Slabbert, *The System and the Struggle* (Johannesburg, 1989), 181–94, 220.

82. R. M. Price, *The Apartheid State in Crisis: Political Transformation of South Africa, 1975–1990* (New York, 1991), 12.

83. For a discussion of de Klerk's voting record, see e.g. T. Leon, *On the Contrary* (Johannesburg, 2008), 167–8.

84. Sparks, *Tomorrow is Another Country*, 88–90.

85. Waldmeier, *Anatomy of a Miracle*, 112.

86. *New York Times*, 15 September 1989; R. Renwick, *Unconventional Diplomacy in Southern Africa* (Basingstoke, 1997), 138.

87. Cited in Odd Arne Westad, *The Global Cold War* (Cambridge, 2007), 393.

88. Sparks, *Tomorrow is Another Country*, 98.

89. As many as 450,000 Cuban troops and civilian workers had served in Angola by the time of their final withdrawal in 1991.

90. *New York Times*, 19 November 1989.

91. F. W. de Klerk, *The Last Trek: A New Beginning* (Basingstoke, 1998) 162–3.

92. Sparks, *Tomorrow is Another Country*, 107; Renwick, *Unconventional Diplomacy*, 142.

93. Sampson, *Mandela*, 408–10.

Chapter 9

1. G. M. Fredrickson, 'The Making of Mandela', *New York Review of Books*, 27 September 1990.

2. H. Adam and K. Moodley, *The Opening of the Apartheid Mind* (London, 1993), 59.

3. The term 'rainbow nation' was coined by Bishop Desmond Tutu.

4. Hugo Young, 'Frontiers of a New Land', in *Altered State: South Africa 1990* (London, 1990), 17.

5. G. Kynoch, 'Reassessing Transition Violence: Voices from South Africa's Township Wars, 1990–1994', *African Affairs*, 112, 447 (2013), 283–303.

6. T. Simpson, 'Toyi-Toyi-ing to Freedom: The Endgame in the ANC's Armed Struggle, 1989–1990', *JSAS*, 35, 2 (2009), 512–14; R. De'A. Henderson, 'Operation Vula against Apartheid', *International Journal of Intelligence and CounterIntelligence*, 10, 4 (1997), 418–55.

7. D. Welsh, 'Right-Wing Terrorism in South Africa', *Terrorism and Political Violence*, 7, 1 (1995).

8. A more obvious parallel would be the state's response to *Ossewabrandwag* and *Stormjaer* public violence in 1941–2. On this occasion, however, Smuts exercised caution and relied instead on internment and other measures.

9. 'Viljoen reveals just how close South Africa came to War', by Max du Preez, *IOL News*, 24 March 2001, <http://www.iol.co.za/news/politics/viljoen-reveals-just-how-close-sa-came-to-war-1.62836>. Right-wingers never forgave Viljoen for holding back, and there were many (unsubstantiated) rumours that he was deliberately acting as a lightning-rod for disgruntled Afrikaners while secretly acting in concert with de Klerk.

10. S. Friedman and D. Atkinson (eds), *The Small Miracle: South Africa's Negotiated Settlement* (Johannesburg, 1994), xii.

11. Waldmeier, *Anatomy of a Miracle*, 207.

12. D. Atkinson, 'Brokering a Miracle', in Friedman and Atkinson (eds), *The Small Miracle*, 13.

13. Transcript of *Nightline* interview with Ted Koppel, March 1985, P. W. Botha papers, PV203 PS4/1/51, Institute of Contemporary History, University of Free State.

14. P. Bond, *Elite Transition: From Apartheid to Neoliberalism in South Africa* (London, 2000).

15. <http://johnpilger.com/videos/apartheid-did-not-die>.

16. J. Hoagland, *South Africa: Civilizations in Conflict* (London, 1973), 44.

17. Perhaps the only other Afrikaans word which had the same power was 'trek'.

18. P. Cillié, 'Bestek van Apartheid', *Die Suid-Afrikaan*, 5 (1985), 19.

19. On the UNESCO statements on the scientific validity of the concept of race, see e.g. E. Barkan, *The Retreat of Scientific Racism* (Cambridge, 1992). On human rights and South Africa, see S. Dubow, *South Africa's Struggle for Human Rights* (Johannesburg, 2012).

20. *The Times*, 15 March 1961.

21. C. C. Saunders and S. Onslow, 'The Cold War and Southern Africa, 1976–1990', in M. P. Leffler and O. A. Westad (eds), *The Cambridge History of the Cold War*, iii (Cambridge, 2010), 225.

22. *The Times*, 'Mandela the Manipulated', 17 December 1985.

23. 'The Stakes in South Africa', *Monthly Review*, 37, 11 (1986), 4, 5.

24. C. Bundy, 'National Liberation and International Solidarity: Anatomy of a Special Relationship', in H. Sapire and C. Saunders (eds), *Southern African Liberation Struggles: New Local, Regional and Global Perspectives* (Cape Town, 2012), 212.

25. Hannah Arendt, *The Origins of Totalitarianism* (Cleveland, 1958), 206–7, 185. Although she must have been aware of the Nationalist victory in 1948, Arendt does not mention the word 'apartheid'. See C. Lee, 'Race and Bureacracy Revisited: Hannah Arendt's Recent Emergence in African Studies', in R. H. King and D. Stone (eds), *Hannah Arendt and the Uses of History* (New York, 2007).

26. B. Bunting, *The Rise of the South African Reich* (Harmondsworth, 1964). See also C. Bloomberg, *Christian-Nationalism and the Rise of the Afrikaner Broederbond in South Africa 1918–48* (Basingstoke, 1990). For a much more sophisticated treatment of the links between the Afrikaner nationalist movement and National Socialism, see Furlong, *Between Crown and Swastika*.

27. *Programme of the South African Communist Party: The Road to South African Freedom* (London, [1962]).

28. P. van den Berghe, *South Africa: A Study in Conflict* (Berkeley, 1967), 80, 86.

29. An analogy with Franco's Spain may be more pertinent, not only in respect of the longevity of the regime, but also in respect of clerico-fascism, regionalism, the existence of a powerful trade union movement alongside an established bourgeoisie, and experiments in economic autarky, including state-sponsored oil-from-coal ventures.

30. J. Derrida, 'Racism's Last Word', *Critical Enquiry*, 12 (Autumn 1985), 291. Also: 'APARTHEID: by itself the word occupies the terrain like a concentration camp. Systems of partition, barbed wire, crowds of mapped out solitudes. Within the limits of this untranslateable idiom, a violent arrest of the mark, the glaring harshness of abstract essence (*heid*) seems to speculate in another regime of abstraction, that of confined separation.' 292.

31. Anne McClintock and R. Nixon, 'Critical Response I', *Critical Enquiry*, 13 (Autumn 1986), 140; J. Derrida, 'Critical Response II', *Critical Enquiry*, 13 (Autumn 1986), 155–70.

32. There are a number of books featuring titles with the phrase 'global apartheid'. For discussion, see e.g. G. Köhler, 'The Three Meanings of Global Apartheid: Empirical, Normative, Existential', *Alternatives*, 20, 3 (1995), 403–13.

33. M. Mamdani, *Citizen and Subject: Contemporary Africa and the Legacy of Late Colonialism* (Princeton, 1996), 8, 27.

34. H. Wolpe, 'Capitalism and Cheap Labour Power in South Africa: From Segregation to Apartheid', in W. Beinart and S. Dubow (eds), *Segregation and Apartheid in Twentieth-Century South Africa* (London, 1995), 62, 82.

35. M. O'Dowd, 'South Africa in the Light of the Stages of Economic Growth', in A. Leftwich (ed.), *Economic Growth and Political Change* (New York, 1974).

36. P. Bond, *Cities of Gold, Townships of Coal* (Trenton, NJ, 2000), 238.
37. Important works in this category include the Simons' *Class & Colour in South Africa, 1850–1950* (1969), Govan Mbeki's *The Peasants' Revolt* (1964), and Eddie Roux's *Time Longer than Rope* (1948).
38. J. Seekings, 'The Rise and Fall of the Weberian Analysis of Class in South Africa between 1949 and the Early 1970s', *JSAS*, 35, 4 (2009).
39. Adam, *Modernizing Racial Domination*, 16.
40. N. Etherington, 'Edward Palmer Thompson (1924–1993)', *Southern African Review of Books* (November–December 1993).
41. Zionists and Irish Unionists, like Afrikaner nationalists, justify their existence in terms of a reading of history that assigns them particular rights. Apartheid went further by claiming that it was not only good for its advocates but it conferred benefits on everyone else affected by its policies. Interestingly, attempts to equate Zionism with racism at the United Nations has by and large not been a success.
42. Beinart, *Twentieth-Century South Africa*, 4, and Part One.
43. James C. Scott, *Weapons of the Weak* (New Haven, 1985), 324.
44. Beinart, *Twentieth Century South Africa*, 181.
45. Dlamini, *Native Nostalgia*, 122, also 158–9.
46. T. C. Moloi, 'Black Politics in Kroonstad: Political Mobilisation, Protests, Local Government, and Generational Struggles, 1976–1995', Wits University Ph.D. thesis, 2012, 27, 186–7, 238.
47. J. Seekings, 'Powerlessness and Politics: "Quiescence" and Protest in Pretoria—Witwatersrand-Waal Townships c.1973–1985', *Collected Seminar Papers*, vol. 16 (1990), Institute of Commonwealth Studies, University of London.
48. <http://h-net.msu.edu/cgi-bin/logbrowse.pl?trx=vx&list=h-luso-africa&month=1011&week=a&msg=4gqsPAZv5kToHEXhdtwfmA&user=&pw=>.
49. Beinart, *Twentieth Century South Africa*, 138.
50. Ross et al., *Cambridge History of South Africa*, vol. ii, statistical appendix, tables 1A and B.
51. Feinstein, *Economic History of South Africa*, 3–11.
52. S. Friedländer, 'An Integrated History of the Holocaust: Possibilities and Challenges', in C. Wiese and P. Betts, *Years of Persecution, Years of Extermination: Saul Friedländer and the Future of Holocaust Studies* (London, 2010); also 'Introduction' in this volume, 8.

A GUIDE TO FURTHER READING

Readers who wish to pursue particular topics may profit from the following books, not all of which appear in the endnotes. These are listed by date of publication.

Amongst the best large-scale studies of apartheid as a system are H. Adam, *Modernizing Racial Domination* (Berkeley, 1971); H. Wolpe, *Race, Class and the Apartheid State* (London, 1988); Deborah Posel, *The Making of Apartheid, 1948–1961: Conflict and Compromise* (Oxford, 1991); I. Evans, *Bureaucracy and Race: Native Administration in South Africa* (Berkeley, 1997); D. O'Meara, *Forty Lost Years: The Apartheid State and the Politics of the National Party 1948–1994* (Randburg, 1996); H. Giliomee, *The Afrikaners: Biography of a People* (London, 2003); and David Welsh, *The Rise and Fall of Apartheid* (Johannesburg, 2009). Shorter overviews include N. L. Clark and W. H. Worger, *South Africa: The Rise and Fall of Apartheid* (New York, 2004); and A. Guelke, *Rethinking the Rise and Fall of Apartheid* (London, 2005).

On the history of racial segregation, the precursor to apartheid, see C. M. Tatz, *'Shadow and Substance in South Africa': A Study in Land and Franchise Policies Affecting Africans, 1910–1960* (Pietermaritzburg, 1962); M. Lacey, *Working for Boroko: The Origins of a Coercive Labour System in South Africa* (Johannesburg, 1981); D. Yudelman, *The Emergence of Modern South Africa* (Westport, Conn., 1983); P. Rich, *White Power and the Liberal Conscience: Racial Segregation in South Africa and South African Liberalism 1921–1960* (Johannesburg, 1984); S. Dubow, *Racial Segregation and the Origins of Apartheid in South Africa 1919–36* (London, 1989).

Useful edited collections dealing with apartheid include: S. Marks and S. Trapido (eds), *The Politics of Class, Race and Nationalism in Twentieth-Century South Africa* (Harlow, 1987); S. Johnson (ed.), *South Africa: No Turning Back* (Basingstoke, 1988); R. Cohen, Y. Muthien, and A. Zegeye (eds), *Repression and Resistance: Insider Accounts of Apartheid* (Sevenoaks,

1990); N. Etherington (ed.), *Peace, Politics and Violence in the New South Africa* (London, 1992); W. Beinart and S. Dubow (eds), *Segregation and Apartheid in Twentieth-Century South Africa* (London, 1995); P. Bonner et al. (eds), *Apartheid's Genesis 1935–1962* (Johannesburg, 2001); S. Dubow and A. Jeeves (eds), *South Africa's 1940s: Worlds of Possibilities* (Cape Town, 2005); R. Ross et al. (eds), *Cambridge History of South Africa*, Vol. ii (New York, 2011). The series edited by Glenn Moss and Ingrid Obery in Johannesburg and known as *South African Review* produced five excellent volumes between 1983 and 1989 drawing on the direct experience of activists.

Texts dealing with the history of African nationalist resistance to apartheid include P. Walshe, *The Rise of African Nationalism in South Africa* (London, 1970); G. Gerhart, *Black Power in South Africa* (Berkeley, 1978); T. Lodge, *Black Politics in South Africa since 1945* (Johannesburg, 1983); Robert Fatton Jr., *Black Consciousness in South Africa* (Albany, NY, 1986); F. Meli, *South Africa Belongs to Us* (Harare, 1988); B. Pityana et al., *Bounds of Possibility: The Legacy of Steve Biko and Black Consciousness* (Cape Town, 1991); A. W. Marx, *Lessons of Struggle: South African Internal Opposition, 1960–1990* (New York, 1992); T. Lodge and B. Nasson, *All Here and Now: Black Politics in South Africa in the 1980s* (London, 1992); S. Dubow, *The African National Congress* (Johannesburg, 2000); R. Suttner, *The ANC Underground in South Africa* (Johannesburg, 2008); C. Glaser, *The ANC Youth League* (Auckland Park, 2012).

Influential monographs dealing with the history of Afrikaner nationalism and apartheid include S. Patterson, *The Last Trek: A Study of the Boer People and the Afrikaner Nation* (London, 1957); D. Moodie, *The Rise of Afrikanerdom: Power, Apartheid, and the Afrikaner Civil Religion* (Berkeley, 1975); D. O'Meara, *Volkskapitalisme: Class, Capital, and Ideology in the Development of Afrikaner Nationalism, 1934–1948* (Cambridge, 1983); L. Thompson, *The Political Mythology of Apartheid* (New Haven, 1985); H. Giliomee, *The Afrikaners: Biography of a People* (London, 2003).

A (highly selective) range of biographies and autobiographies of key figures in the apartheid era include: A. Luthuli, *Let my People Go* (London, 1962); John D'Oliveira, *Vorster—The Man* (Johannesburg, 1977); H. Kenney, *Architect of Apartheid: H. F. Verwoerd. An Appraisal* (Johannesburg, 1980); Ellen Kuzwayo, *Call Me Woman* (London, 1985); Helen Joseph, *Side by Side* (London, 1986); Steve Biko, *I Write What I Like* (London, 1987); S. Clingman, *Bram Fischer: Afrikaner Revolutionary* (Cape Town, 1988); F. Chikane, *No Life of my Own: An Autobiography* (Johannesburg, 1988); B. Pogrund, *How Can Man Die Better... Sobukwe and Apartheid* (London, 1990); G. Buthelezi, *South Africa:*

My Vision of the Future (London, 1990); E. Gilbey, *The Lady: The Life and Times of Winnie Mandela* (Cape Town, 1993); N. Mandela, *Long Walk to Freedom* (London, 1994); M. Ramphele, *Across the Boundaries* (New York, 1996); F. W. de Klerk, *The Last Trek: A New Beginning* (Basingstoke, 1998); Lionel Bernstein, *Memory Against Forgetting* (London, 1999); A. Sampson, *Mandela: The Authorised Biography* (London, 2000); Elinor Sisulu, *Walter and Albertina Sisulu: In our Lifetime* (Cape Town, 2002); I. Meer, *A Fortunate Man* (Cape Town, 2002); A. Kathrada, *Memoirs* (Cape Town, 2004); Harold Strachan, *Maak 'n Skyf Man* (Johannesburg, 2004); Luli Callinicos, *Oliver Tambo: Beyond the Engeli Mountains* (Cape Town, 2004); J. Allen, *Rabble-Rouser for Peace: The Authorised Biography of Desmond Tutu* (New York, 2006); P. O'Malley, *Shades of Difference: Mac Maharaj and the Struggle for South Africa* (New York, 2007); Allan Boesak, *Running With Horses: Reflections of an Accidental Politician* (Cape Town, 2009).

In addition to the books mentioned above on Afrikaner nationalism, the rise and consolidation of apartheid ideology is addressed by M. Ballinger, *From Union to Apartheid* (Folkestone, 1969); N. M. Stultz, *Afrikaner Politics in South Africa, 1934–1948* (Berkeley, 1974); J. Kinghorn (ed.), *Die NG Kerk en Apartheid* (Johannesburg, 1986); C. Bloomberg, *Christian-Nationalism and the Rise of the Afrikaner Broederbond in South Africa 1918–48*, ed. S. Dubow (London, 1990); P. J. Furlong, *Between Crown and Swastika: The Impact of the Radical Right on the Afrikaner Nationalist Movement in the Fascist Era* (Middletown, Conn., 1991); S. Dubow, *Scientific Racism in Modern South Africa* (Cambridge, 1995); A. J. Norval, *Deconstructing Apartheid Discourse* (London, 1996); T. Kuperus, *State, Civil Society and Apartheid in South Africa: An Examination of Dutch Reformed Church–State Relations* (London, 1999); Christof Marx, *Oxwagon Sentinel: Radical Afrikaner Nationalism and the History of the Ossewabrandwag* (Pretoria, 2008).

The international and regional dimensions of apartheid are covered by S. C. Nolutshungu, *South Africa in Africa: A Study of Ideology and Foreign Policy* (Manchester, 1975); S. M. Davis, *Apartheid's Rebels: Inside South Africa's Hidden War* (New Haven, 1987); J. Barber and J. Barratt, *South Africa's Foreign Policy: The Search for Status and Security 1945–1988* (Cambridge, 1990); J. Hanlon, *Beggar your Neighbours: Apartheid Power in Southern Africa* (London, 1991); R. Nixon, *Homelands, Harlem and Hollywood: South African Culture and World Beyond* (New York, 1994); J. Slovo, *Slovo: The Unfinished Autobiography* (Johannesburg, 1995); V. Shubin, *ANC: A View from Moscow* (Cape Town, 1999); R. Hyam and P. Henshaw, *The Lion and Springbok: Britain and South Africa since the Boer War* (Cambridge, 2003); V. Shubin, *ANC: A View from Moscow* (Cape Town, 1999); P. Vale, *Security and Politics in South Africa: The Regional Dimension* (Boulder, Colo., 2003); D. Herbstein, *White Lies: Canon Collins and the Secret War against Apartheid* (London, 2005); R. Fieldhouse, *Anti-Apartheid: A History of the Movement in Britain* (London, 2005); H. Thörn, *Anti-Apartheid and the Emergence of a Global Civil Society* (Basingstoke, 2006); J. Sanders, *Apartheid's Friends: The Rise and Fall of South Africa's Secret Service* (London, 2006); R. M. Irwin, *Gordian Knot: Apartheid and the Unmaking of the Liberal World Order* (Oxford, 2012).

For the economic dimensions of apartheid, see F. Wilson, *Migrant Labour in South Africa* (Johannesburg, 1972); J. Nattrass, *The South African Economy* (Cape Town, 1981); M. Lipton, *Capitalism and Apartheid: South Africa, 1910–84* (Aldershot, 1985); O. Crankshaw, *Race, Class and the Changing Division of Labour Under Apartheid* (London, 1997); S. Terreblanche, *A History of Inequality in South Africa: 1652–2002* (Pietermaritzburg, 2002); C. H. Feinstein, *An Economic History of South Africa* (Cambridge, 2005); J. Seekings and N. Nattrass, *Class, Race and Inequality in South Africa* (New Haven, 2005).

Education is the subject of I. B. Tabata, *Education for Barbarism in South Africa* (London, 1960); K. Hartshorne, *Crisis and Challenge: Black Education 1910–1990* (Cape Town, 1992); J. Hyslop, *The Classroom Struggle: Policy and Resistance in South Africa, 1940–1990* (Pietermaritzburg, 1999); P. Kallaway (ed.), *The History of Education Under Apartheid 1948–1994* (Cape Town, 2002).

On apartheid land policy, see Cosmas Desmond, *The Discarded People* (Harmondsworth, 1971); L. Platzky and C. Walker, *The Surplus People: Forced Removals in South Africa* (Johannesburg, 1985); C. Murray, *Black Mountain: Land, Class and Power in the Eastern Orange Free State, 1880s–1980s* (Edinburgh, 1992); C. Walker, *Landmarked* (Auckland Park, 2008).

On apartheid health, see S. Marks and N. Andersson, *Apartheid and Health* (Geneva, 1983); R. M. Packard, *White Plague, Black Labour* (Berkeley, 1989); S. Marks, *Divided Sisterhood: Race, Class and Gender in the South African Nursing Profession* (Johannesburg, 1994).

For the churches see C. Villa-Vicenzio, *A Theology of Reconstruction: Nation-Building and Human Rights* (Cambridge, 1992); R. Elphick and R. Davenport (eds), *Christianity in South Africa: A Political, Social and Cultural History* (Cape Town, 1997); J. and S. De Gruchy, *The Church Struggle in South Africa* (London, 2005).

On conditions in the countryside and the Bantustans see R. Southall, *South Africa's Transkei: The Political Economy of an Independent Bantustan* (London,

1982); F. Wilson and M. Ramphele, *Uprooting Poverty: The South African Challenge* (Cape Town, 1989); C. van Onselen, *The Seed is Mine: The Life of a South African Sharecropper, 1894–1985* (Oxford, 1996); Peter Delius, *A Lion amongst the Cattle: Reconstruction and Resistance in the Northern Transvaal* (Johannesburg, 1996); Anne Mager, *Gender and the Making of a South African Bantustan: A Social History of the Ciskei, 1945–1959* (Oxford, 1999).

Urban township-based resistance is the subject of J. Cole, *Crossroads: The Politics of Reform and Repression 1976–1986* (Johannesburg, 1987); M. Swilling et al. (eds), *Apartheid City in Transition* (Cape Town, 1991); B. Bozzoli, *Theatres of Struggle and the End of Apartheid* (Edinburgh, 2004); P. Bonner and N. Nieftagodien, *Alexandra: A History* (Johannesburg, 2008); J. Dlamini, *Native Nostalgia* (Johannesburg, 2009).

The period of the Treason Trial, Sharpeville massacre, and Rivonia Trial is covered by G. Frankel, *Rivonia's Children: Three Families and the Price of Freedom in South Africa* (London, 1999); Benjamin Pogrund, *War of Words: Memoirs of a South African Journalist* (New York, 2000); P. Frankel, *An Ordinary Atrocity: Sharpeville and its Massacre* (New Haven, 2001); G. Bizos, *Odyssey to Freedom* (Houghton, 2007); Tom Lodge, *Sharpeville and its Consequences* (Oxford, 2011); K. S. Broun, *Saving Nelson Mandela: The Rivonia Trial and the Fate of South Africa* (Oxford, 2012).

Accounts of Black Consciousness and the Soweto uprising of 1976 include John Kane-Berman, *South Africa: The Method in the Madness* (London, 1979); B. Hirson, *Year of Fire, Year of Ash. The Soweto Revolt: Roots of a Revolution?* (London, 1979); A. Brooks and J. Brickhill, *Whirlwind Before the Storm* (London, 1980); B. Pityana et al., *Bounds of Possibility: The Legacy of Steve Biko and Black Consciousness* (Cape Town, 1991); C. Glaser, *Bo-tsotsi: The Youth Gangs of Soweto, 1935–1976* (Portsmouth, NH, 2000); D. R. Magaziner, *The Law and the Prophets: Black Consciousness in South Africa, 1968–1977* (Athens, Oh., 2010).

On the ANC in exile see H. Barrell, *MK: The ANC's Armed Struggle* (London, 1990); S. Ellis and T. Sechaba, *Comrades Against Apartheid* (London, 1992); H. Bernstein, *The Rift: The Exile Experience of South Africans* (London, 1994); D. McKinley, *The ANC and the Liberation Struggle* (London, 1997); Ben Turok, *Nothing But the Truth: Behind the ANC's Struggle Politics* (Johannesburg, 2003); M. Gevisser, *Thabo Mbeki. The Dream Deferred* (Johannesburg, 2007); S. Ellis, *External Mission: The ANC in Exile, 1960–1990* (London, 2012); J. Cherry, *Umkhonto we Sizwe* (Auckland Park, 2012).

Imprisonment on Robben Island is discussed by Indres Naidoo, *Island in Chains* (Harmondsworth, 1982); H. Deacon, *The Island: A History of Robben Island, 1488–1990* (Cape Town, 1996); Eddie Daniels, *There and Back: Robben Island 1964–1979* (Cape Town, 1998); A. Kathrada, *Letters from Robben Island* (Cape Town, 1999); F. Buntman, *Robben Island and Prisoner Resistance to Apartheid* (Cambridge, 2003); N. Mandela, *A Prisoner in the Garden* (Houghton, 2005); Colin Bundy, *Govan Mbeki* (Johannesburg, 2012).

Accounts of the modern South African trade union movement include S. Friedman, *Building Tomorrow Today: African Workers in Trade Unions, 1970–1984* (Johannesburg, 1987); J. Maree (ed.), *The Independent Trade Unions, 1974–1984* (Johannesburg, 1987); J. Baskin, *Striking Back: A History of COSATU* (Johannesburg, 1991).

The era of political reform and mass internal resistance from the late 1970s to the 1980s is represented from a range of perspectives by L. Thompson and A. Prior (eds), *South African Politics* (Cape Town, 1982); P. Frankel, *Pretoria's Praetorians* (Cambridge, 1984); M. Murray, *South Africa: Time of Agony, Time of Destiny* (London, 1987); G. Maré and G. Hamilton, *An Appetite for Power: Buthelezi's Inkatha and South Africa* (Johannesburg, 1987); J. Butler et al. (eds), *Democratic Liberalism in South Africa* (Cape Town, 1987); S. Greenberg, *Legitimating the Illegitimate: State, Markets, and Resistance in South Africa* (Berkeley, 1987); W. Cobbett and R. Cohen (eds), *Popular Struggles in South Africa* (London, 1988); F. van Zyl Slabbert, *The System and the Struggle* (Johannesburg, 1989); H. Giliomee and L. Schlemmer, *From Apartheid to Nation-Building* (Cape Town, 1989); J. Cock and L. Nathan (eds), *War and Society: The Militarisation of South Africa* (Cape Town, 1989); M. Kentridge, *An Unofficial War: Inside the Conflict in Pietermaritzburg* (Cape Town, 1990); R. M. Price, *The Apartheid State in Crisis* (New York, 1991); R. Schrire, *Adapt or Die: The End of White Politics in South Africa* (New York, 1991); A. Seegers, *The Military in the Making of Modern South Africa* (London, 1996); I. Van Kessel, *'Beyond our Wildest Dreams': The United Democratic Front and the Transformation of South Africa* (Charlottesville, Va., 2000); J. Seekings, *The UDF: A History of the United Democratic Front in South Africa 1983–1991* (Cape Town, 2000); W. Beinart and M. C. Dawson, *Popular Politics and Resistance Movements in South Africa* (Johannesburg, 2010); H. Sapire and C. Saunders (eds), *Southern African Liberation Struggles: New Local, Regional and Global Perspectives* (Cape Town, 2012).

On the period of negotiations and political transformation from 1990 to 1994 see H. Adam and K. Moodley, *The Opening of the Apartheid Mind* (London, 1993);

A. Sparks, *Tomorrow is Another Country: The Inside Story of South Africa's Negotiated Revolution* (Cape Town, 1994); S. Friedman and D. Atkinson (eds), *The Small Miracle: South Africa's Negotiated Settlement* (Johannesburg, 1994); P. Waldmeier, *Anatomy of a Miracle* (London, 1997); S. Nuttall and C. Coetzee (eds), *Negotiating the Past: The Making of Memory in South Africa* (Cape Town, 1998); A. Krog, *Country of my Skull* (Johannesburg, 1998); P. Bond, *Elite Transition: From Apartheid to Neoliberalism in South Africa* (London, 2000); H. Klug, *Constituting Democracy* (Cambridge, 2000); R. Wilson, *The Politics of Truth and Reconciliation in South Africa: Legitimizing the Post-Apartheid State* (Cambridge, 2001); D. Posel and G. Simpson (eds), *Commissioning the Past: Understanding South Africa's Truth and Reconciliation Commission* (Johannesburg, 2002); P. Harris, *In a Different Time: The Inside Story of the Delmas Four* (Cape Town, 2008).

Two multi-volume series are indispensable for the study of apartheid. These are the collections produced by the South African Democracy Education Trust, *The Road to Democracy in South Africa* (4 vols, 2004–10) which cover the period 1960–94 and the authoritative six volume series, edited by T. Karis, G. Carter, G. Gerhart, Sheridan Johns, and C. L. Glaser, *From Protest to Challenge: A Documentary History of African Politics in South Africa, 1882–1990* (6 vols, 1972–2010), which combines rich documentary evidence with astute commentary.

INDEX

Printed and bound by CPI Group (UK) Ltd, Croydon, CR0 4YY